ROCKY

VOL. 1: THE BIG PAYBACK

BY MARTIN KELLERMAN

FANTAGRAPHICS BOOKS

EDITORS: There are over 1200 daily *Rocky* strips and 200 Sunday-format strips available for syndication. If you are interested in running *Rocky* in your paper of magazine contact Håkon Strand at haastra@online.no.

Edited and translated by Kim Thompson
Designed by Adam Grano
Production Assistance by Paul Baresh
Promotion by Eric Reynolds
Special thanks to Hakon Strand, Lasse Espe, Kristy Valenti, and Martin Kellerman.

Published by Gary Groth and Kim Thompson

Distributed in the U.S. by W.W. Norton and Company, Inc. (212-354-5500)
Distributed Canada by Raincoast Books (800-663-5714)
Distributed in the United Kingdom by Turnaround Distribution (208-829-3009)

To receive a free catalog of cool comics, call 1-800-657-1100 or write us at Fantagraphics Books, 7563 Lake City Way NE, Seattle, WA 98115; you can also visit the Fantagraphics website at www.fantagraphics.com!

First printing: November 2005

ISBN: 0-56097-679-9
Printed in the Goddamn USA, Motherfucker!

FOREWORD

On 1998, I started drawing a comic strip about me and my friends and our daily life on the south side of Stockholm, Sweden. I had just been fired from my job as a cartoonist for a porn magazine, my girlfriend had just dumped me and I was living with my brother in my family's house in the suburbs. I needed a new job, but I was in no mood to be funny, so I just started drawing this comic strip about me and the mess I was in. It was a really nice feeling getting it all down on paper.

All my friends became characters in it, and in the beginning I thought of it mostly as a joke, something funny for my friends to read and something for me to do while I figured out what to do with my life. I was twenty-four and hadn't achieved any of my goals yet, and I was thinking of giving up comics and going to filmschool or something. But the Swedish free newspaper "Metro" picked up the strip and started running it, and pretty soon people were reading it on the subway and talking about it. Even people I knew talked to me about it, not knowing I was the one drawing it and that they were actually in it! They just thought it was weird that they could relate to the stuff that went on in there... Well, it turned out our lives were very unoriginal, because a lot of people that I didn't think I had anything in common with reacted the same way. Punk rockers thought Rocky was a punk rocker, techno heads and heavy metal freaks and skaters and just ordinary beer-drinking soccer-watching idiots all projected themselves and their lifestyles on my cartoon character, which really irritated me, 'cause I hate all that crap and thought it was obvious that Rocky was into hiphop and nothing else.

BUT BASICALLY I WAS THRILLED THAT PEOPLE LIKED MY COMIC, BECAUSE NOBODY HAD EVER REACTED IN ANY WAY TO ANYTHING I HAD DONE BEFORE. MY FRIENDS HELPED ME PRINT A WALL CALENDAR FOR 1999 WITH SOME ROCKY STRIPS IN IT, AND IT SOLD 6000 COPIES FROM JUST ONE STORE! WHEN WE RELEASED IT I WENT TO THIS BIG MALL TO SIGN THE CALENDARS, AND THERE WAS A LINE OF PEOPLE STRAIGHT THROUGH THE WHOLE MALL AND OUT INTO THE STREET! I WAS COMPLETELY SHOCKED. AFTER THAT I WENT AND BOUGHT THIS RIDICULOUS GUCCI COAT FOR A THOUSAND DOLLARS AND GOT ON TRAIN BACK TO THE SUBURBS, HA HA! I STILL DIDN'T HAVE ANY PLACE TO STAY, BUT THEN I SIGNED A CONTRACT WITH A PUBLISHING COMPANY, AFTER FORCING THEM TO GET ME AN APARTMENT. IN STOCKHOLM IT'S IMPOSSIBLE TO GET AN APARTMENT UNLESS YOU'RE A MILLIONAIRE. SO AFTER DRAWING THE COMIC STRIP FOR SIX MONTHS, ROCKY HAD COMPLETELY CHANGED MY LIFE AROUND. NOW ALL I HAD TO DO WAS GET MY GIRL BACK... BUT OF COURSE I MANAGED TO FUCK THAT UP.

IN 2001 I TOOK A BREAK FROM DRAWING AFTER SELLING 60000 BOOKS AND WRITING AND DIRECTING A PLAY BASED ON ROCKY, AND I TRIED TO DEVELOP IT INTO A TV SERIES BUT FAILED. THEN I TRIED TO WRITE A MOVIE BUT FAILED, THEN ANOTHER MOVIE BUT FAILED AGAIN! SO THEN I GOT DEPRESSED AND STARTED DRAWING THE COMIC AGAIN. IT SEEMS TO WORK BEST WHEN I'M AT MY LOWEST, WHENEVER I FEEL GOOD AND THINGS ARE GOING RIGHT PEOPLE START COMPLAINING. IT'S A GIFT AND A CURSE, SORT OF LIKE BEING SPIDER-MAN...

I THINK I'LL DRAW THIS COMIC ON AND OFF FOR MY WHOLE LIFE. I GUESS I'LL TAKE A BREAK WHEN I GET KIDS, BECAUSE PEOPLE WITH KIDS TEND TO GET ALL HAPPY AND MUSHY. BUT THEN EVENTUALLY YOU GET DIVORCED AND YOUR KIDS START TO HATE YOU AND THEN THE COMIC STRIP GETS INTERESTING AGAIN! I'M GONNA DRAW MY LAST STRIP WHEN I'M 112 YEARS OLD, SITTING IN A RETIREMENT HOME YELLING AT THE NURSES. IT'S JUST GONNA END WITH THE LINE GOING

SO ANYWAY, NOW I'VE SOLD 300000 BOOKS, AND THE NINTH VOLUME HAS JUST BEEN RELEASED IN SWEDEN, SO IT FEELS A LITTLE WEIRD TO READ THE FIRST ROCKY BOOK IN ENGLISH! IT'S LIKE READING A SEVEN YEAR OLD DIARY. I WAS SUCH A STUPID LITTLE IDIOT BACK THEN. I DON'T KNOW IF I'M ALL THAT MUCH SMARTER NOW, BUT NOW I HAVE A BOOK OUT IN THE UNITED STATES OF AMERICA SO WHO GIVES A SHIT!

I HOPE YOU LIKE IT!
MARTIN KELLERMAN
STOCKHOLM 2005

DUMPED AND EVICTED

ROCKY THE ROOMMATE...

YOU LIKE EMMA, DON'TCHA?

SURE! SHE'S ALL RIGHT!

WELL, HER MOM JUST KICKED HER OUT. SO SHE'S GONNA BE MOVING IN HERE WITH ME NOW.

THAT'S FINE BY ME. YOU TWO MAKE A CUTE COUPLE.

THE THING IS... SHE'S NOT REAL KEEN ON YOU LIVING HERE WITH US.

...IF YOU CATCH MY DRIFT.

OKAY. FINE. BUT MARK MY WORDS: GIRLS-WHO'VE-FUCKED-ALL-YOUR-BUDDIES-AND-HAVE-CHLAMYDIA-MAY COME AND GO... BUT REAL FRIENDS ARE FOREVER...!

HOW THE HELL COULD MANNY THROW ME OVER FOR A SKANK WHO'S TAKEN IT UP THE ASS FROM EVERY LAST GODDAMN MEMBER OF OUR CIRCLE OF ACQUAINTANCES!?

THE ONLY GOOD THING ABOUT THOSE TWO GETTING TOGETHER IS, I WON'T HAVE TO WASTE ANY TIME WONDERING WHAT IT'S LIKE TO PORK MY BEST FRIEND'S GIRLFRIEND!

SHIT, IF ONLY I HADN'T BEEN SUCH A DUD IN THE SACK THAT NIGHT. I'D MUCH RATHER BE REMEMBERED AS "ROCKY THE TURBOCHARGED SEX MACHINE" THAN "MISTER WILT 'N' SNOOZE"...

OH MANNY! YOU REALLY ROCKED MY WORLD!

ALL IN A DAY'S WORK, BABE.

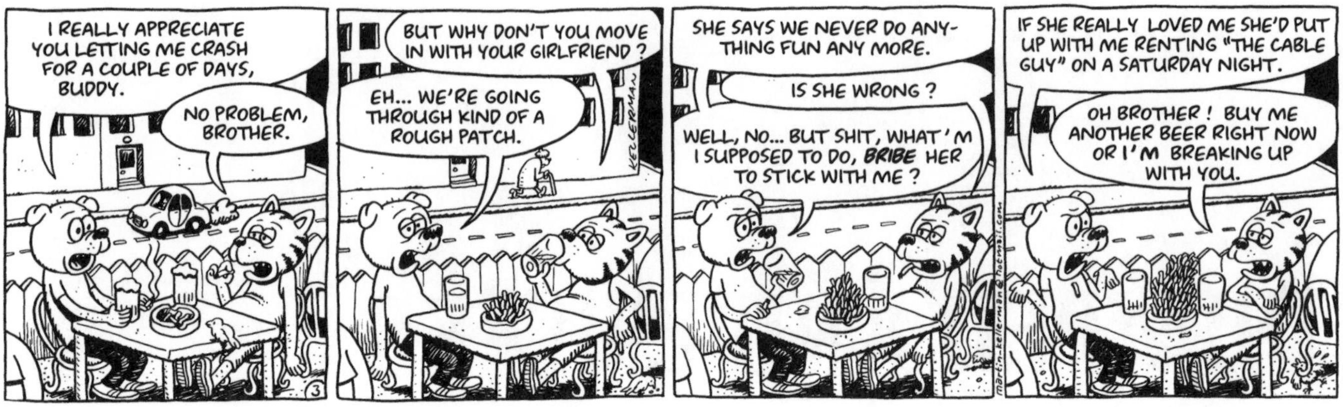
I REALLY APPRECIATE YOU LETTING ME CRASH FOR A COUPLE OF DAYS, BUDDY.
NO PROBLEM, BROTHER.
BUT WHY DON'T YOU MOVE IN WITH YOUR GIRLFRIEND ?
EH... WE'RE GOING THROUGH KIND OF A ROUGH PATCH.
KELLERMAN
SHE SAYS WE NEVER DO ANYTHING FUN ANY MORE.
IS SHE WRONG ?
WELL, NO... BUT SHIT, WHAT'M I SUPPOSED TO DO, BRIBE HER TO STICK WITH ME ?
martin.kellerman@hotmail.com
IF SHE REALLY LOVED ME SHE'D PUT UP WITH ME RENTING "THE CABLE GUY" ON A SATURDAY NIGHT.
OH BROTHER ! BUY ME ANOTHER BEER RIGHT NOW OR I'M BREAKING UP WITH YOU.
3

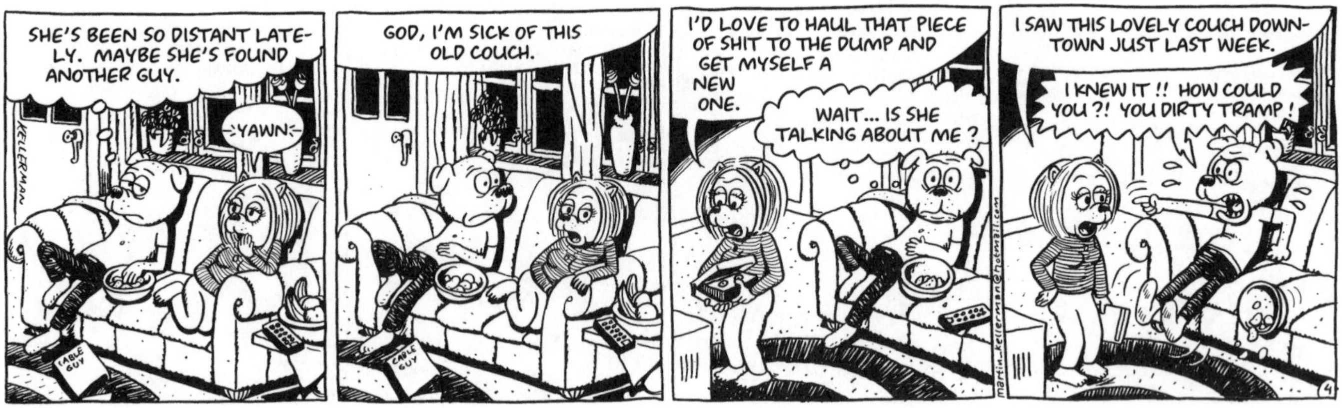
SHE'S BEEN SO DISTANT LATELY. MAYBE SHE'S FOUND ANOTHER GUY.
YAWN
KELLERMAN
TABLE GUY
GOD, I'M SICK OF THIS OLD COUCH.
CABLE GUY
I'D LOVE TO HAUL THAT PIECE OF SHIT TO THE DUMP AND GET MYSELF A NEW ONE.
WAIT... IS SHE TALKING ABOUT ME ?
martin.kellerman@hotmail.com
I SAW THIS LOVELY COUCH DOWNTOWN JUST LAST WEEK.
I KNEW IT !! HOW COULD YOU ?! YOU DIRTY TRAMP !
4

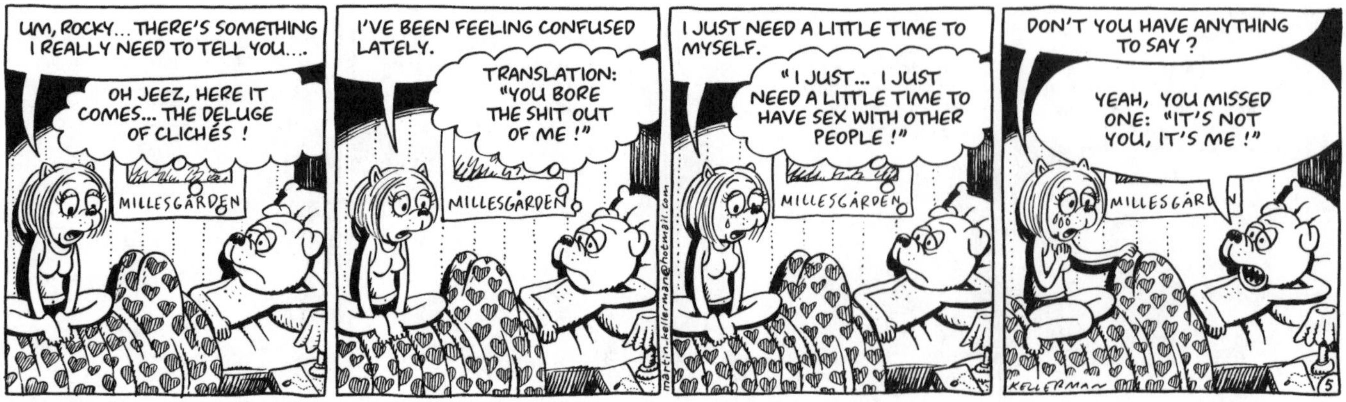
UM, ROCKY... THERE'S SOMETHING I REALLY NEED TO TELL YOU....
OH JEEZ, HERE IT COMES... THE DELUGE OF CLICHÉS !
MILLESGÅRDEN
I'VE BEEN FEELING CONFUSED LATELY.
TRANSLATION: "YOU BORE THE SHIT OUT OF ME !"
MILLESGÅRDEN
martin.kellerman@hotmail.com
I JUST NEED A LITTLE TIME TO MYSELF.
"I JUST... I JUST NEED A LITTLE TIME TO HAVE SEX WITH OTHER PEOPLE !"
MILLESGÅRDEN
DON'T YOU HAVE ANYTHING TO SAY ?
YEAH, YOU MISSED ONE: "IT'S NOT YOU, IT'S ME !"
KELLERMAN
5

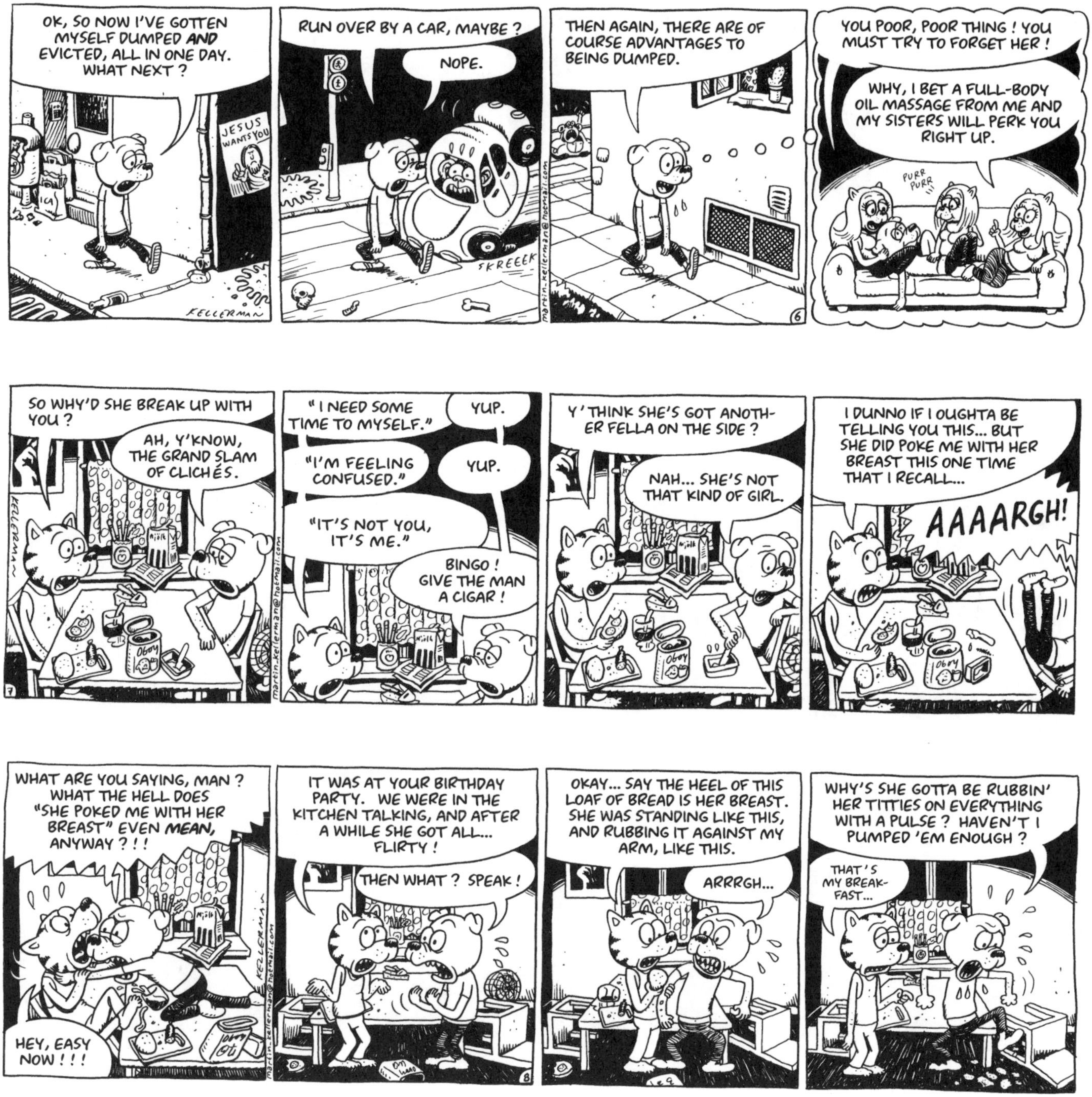
OK, SO NOW I'VE GOTTEN MYSELF DUMPED AND EVICTED, ALL IN ONE DAY. WHAT NEXT ?
JESUS WANTS YOU
KELLERMAN
RUN OVER BY A CAR, MAYBE ?
NOPE.
SKREEEK
martin.kellerman@hotmail.com
THEN AGAIN, THERE ARE OF COURSE ADVANTAGES TO BEING DUMPED.
6
YOU POOR, POOR THING ! YOU MUST TRY TO FORGET HER !
WHY, I BET A FULL-BODY OIL MASSAGE FROM ME AND MY SISTERS WILL PERK YOU RIGHT UP.
PURR PURR
SO WHY'D SHE BREAK UP WITH YOU ?
AH, Y'KNOW, THE GRAND SLAM OF CLICHÉS.
KELLERMAN
7
"I NEED SOME TIME TO MYSELF."
YUP.
"I'M FEELING CONFUSED."
YUP.
"IT'S NOT YOU, IT'S ME."
BINGO ! GIVE THE MAN A CIGAR !
martin.kellerman@hotmail.com
Y'THINK SHE'S GOT ANOTH-ER FELLA ON THE SIDE ?
NAH... SHE'S NOT THAT KIND OF GIRL.
I DUNNO IF I OUGHTA BE TELLING YOU THIS... BUT SHE DID POKE ME WITH HER BREAST THIS ONE TIME THAT I RECALL...
AAAARGH!
WHAT ARE YOU SAYING, MAN ? WHAT THE HELL DOES "SHE POKED ME WITH HER BREAST" EVEN MEAN, ANYWAY ? ! !
HEY, EASY NOW ! ! !
KELLERMAN
martin.kellerman@hotmail.com
IT WAS AT YOUR BIRTHDAY PARTY. WE WERE IN THE KITCHEN TALKING, AND AFTER A WHILE SHE GOT ALL... FLIRTY !
THEN WHAT ? SPEAK !
8
OKAY... SAY THE HEEL OF THIS LOAF OF BREAD IS HER BREAST. SHE WAS STANDING LIKE THIS, AND RUBBING IT AGAINST MY ARM, LIKE THIS.
ARRRGH...
WHY'S SHE GOTTA BE RUBBIN' HER TITTIES ON EVERYTHING WITH A PULSE ? HAVEN'T I PUMPED 'EM ENOUGH ?
THAT'S MY BREAK-FAST...

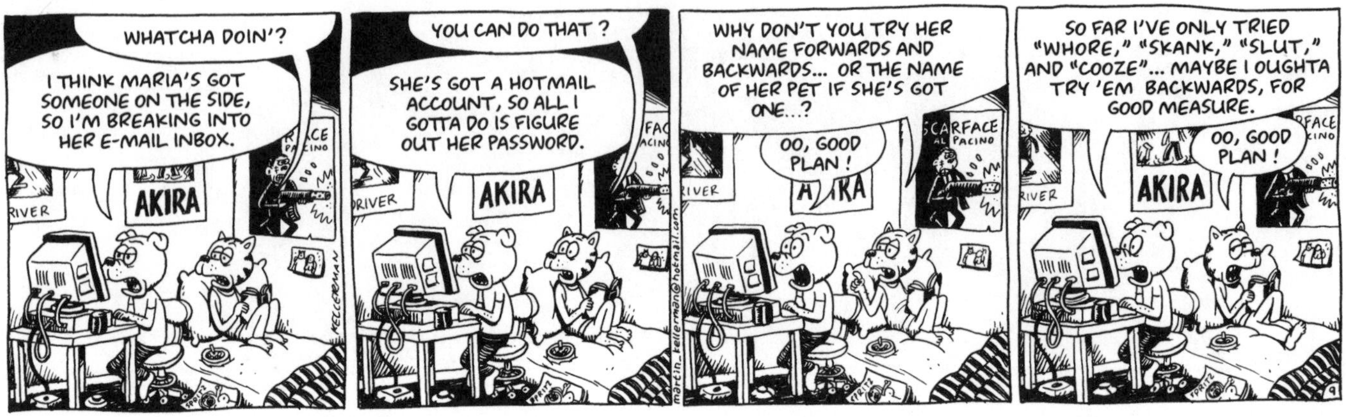
WHATCHA DOIN'?
I THINK MARIA'S GOT SOMEONE ON THE SIDE, SO I'M BREAKING INTO HER E-MAIL INBOX.
AKIRA
RIVER
KELLERMAN
YOU CAN DO THAT ?
SHE'S GOT A HOTMAIL ACCOUNT, SO ALL I GOTTA DO IS FIGURE OUT HER PASSWORD.
AKIRA
RIVER
martin_kellerman@hotmail.com
WHY DON'T YOU TRY HER NAME FORWARDS AND BACKWARDS... OR THE NAME OF HER PET IF SHE'S GOT ONE...?
OO, GOOD PLAN !
SCARFACE AL PACINO
RIVER
SO FAR I'VE ONLY TRIED "WHORE," "SKANK," "SLUT," AND "COOZE"... MAYBE I OUGHTA TRY 'EM BACKWARDS, FOR GOOD MEASURE.
OO, GOOD PLAN !
AKIRA
RIVER
9

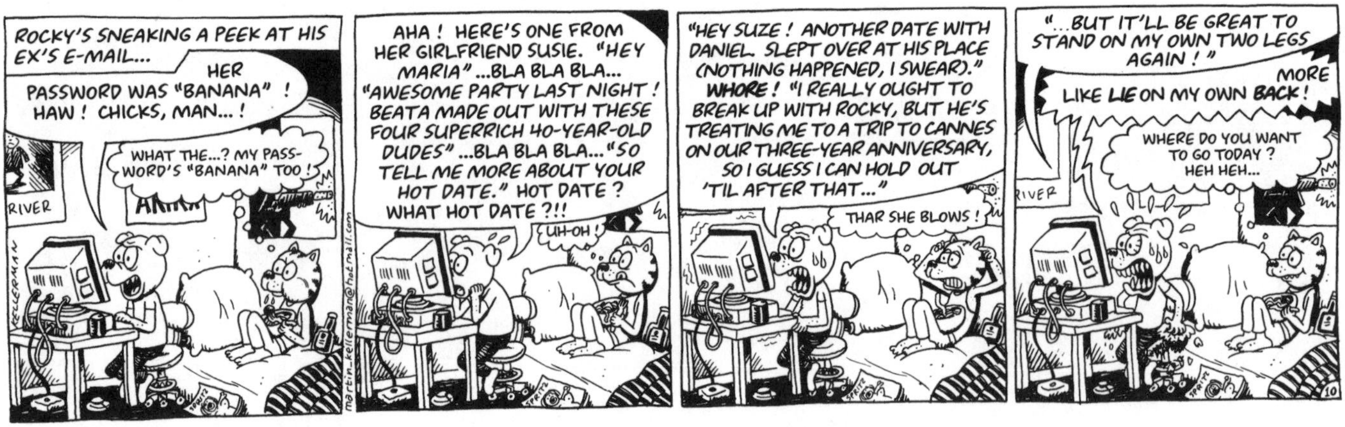
ROCKY'S SNEAKING A PEEK AT HIS EX'S E-MAIL...
HER PASSWORD WAS "BANANA" ! HAW ! CHICKS, MAN... !
WHAT THE...? MY PASSWORD'S "BANANA" TOO !
RIVER
KELLERMAN
AHA ! HERE'S ONE FROM HER GIRLFRIEND SUSIE. "HEY MARIA" ...BLA BLA BLA... "AWESOME PARTY LAST NIGHT ! BEATA MADE OUT WITH THESE FOUR SUPERRICH 40-YEAR-OLD DUDES" ...BLA BLA BLA... "SO TELL ME MORE ABOUT YOUR HOT DATE." HOT DATE ? WHAT HOT DATE ?!!
UH-OH !
martin_kellerman@hotmail.com
"HEY SUZE ! ANOTHER DATE WITH DANIEL. SLEPT OVER AT HIS PLACE (NOTHING HAPPENED, I SWEAR)." WHORE ! "I REALLY OUGHT TO BREAK UP WITH ROCKY, BUT HE'S TREATING ME TO A TRIP TO CANNES ON OUR THREE-YEAR ANNIVERSARY, SO I GUESS I CAN HOLD OUT 'TIL AFTER THAT..."
THAR SHE BLOWS !
"...BUT IT'LL BE GREAT TO STAND ON MY OWN TWO LEGS AGAIN !"
MORE LIKE LIE ON MY OWN BACK !
WHERE DO YOU WANT TO GO TODAY ? HEH HEH...
RIVER
10

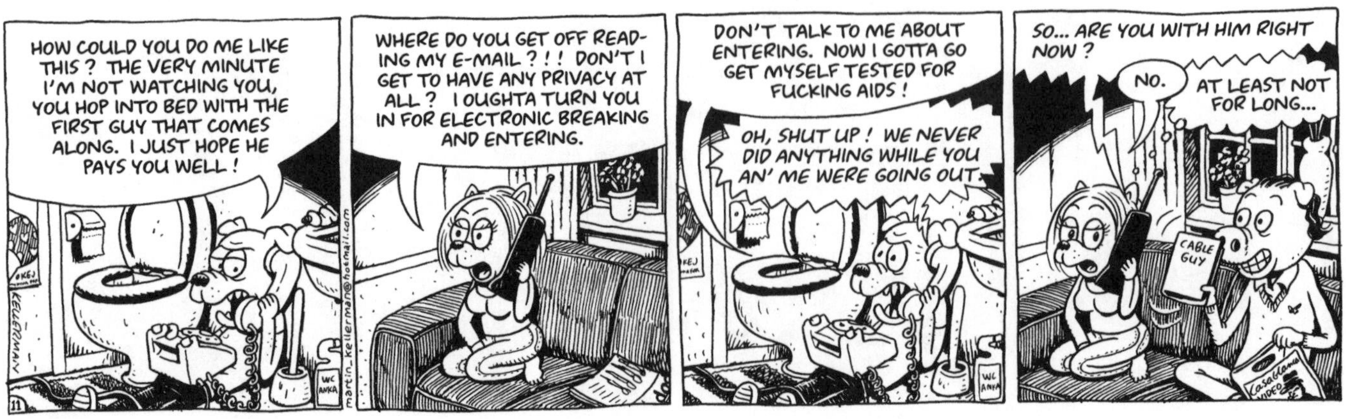
HOW COULD YOU DO ME LIKE THIS ? THE VERY MINUTE I'M NOT WATCHING YOU, YOU HOP INTO BED WITH THE FIRST GUY THAT COMES ALONG. I JUST HOPE HE PAYS YOU WELL !
KELLERMAN
11
WC ANKA
WHERE DO YOU GET OFF READING MY E-MAIL ? ! ! DON'T I GET TO HAVE ANY PRIVACY AT ALL ? I OUGHTA TURN YOU IN FOR ELECTRONIC BREAKING AND ENTERING.
martin_kellerman@hotmail.com
DON'T TALK TO ME ABOUT ENTERING. NOW I GOTTA GO GET MYSELF TESTED FOR FUCKING AIDS !
OH, SHUT UP ! WE NEVER DID ANYTHING WHILE YOU AN' ME WERE GOING OUT.
WC ANKA
SO... ARE YOU WITH HIM RIGHT NOW ?
NO.
AT LEAST NOT FOR LONG...
CABLE GUY

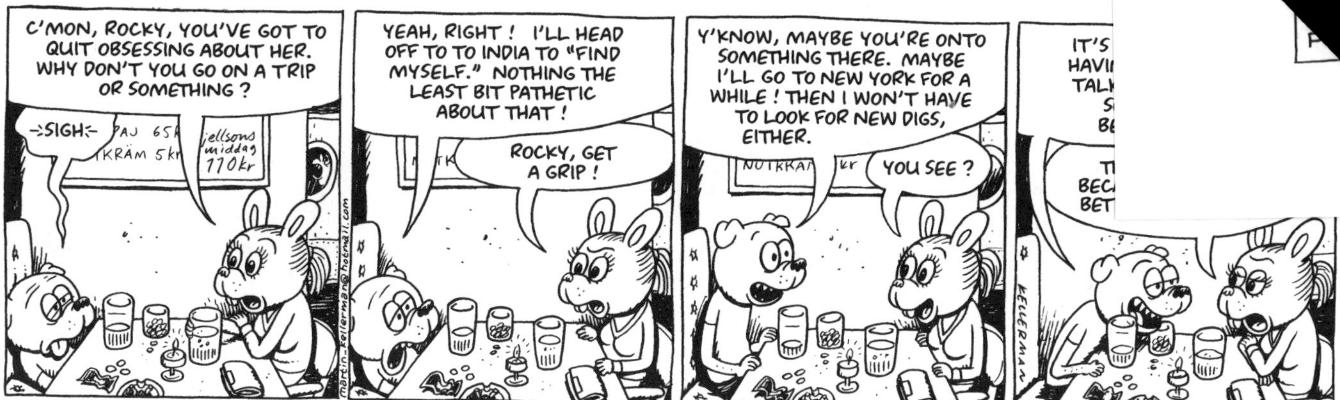
C'MON, ROCKY, YOU'VE GOT TO QUIT OBSESSING ABOUT HER. WHY DON'T YOU GO ON A TRIP OR SOMETHING ?
→SIGH←
martin_kellerman@hotmail.com
YEAH, RIGHT ! I'LL HEAD OFF TO TO INDIA TO "FIND MYSELF." NOTHING THE LEAST BIT PATHETIC ABOUT THAT !
ROCKY, GET A GRIP !
Y'KNOW, MAYBE YOU'RE ONTO SOMETHING THERE. MAYBE I'LL GO TO NEW YORK FOR A WHILE ! THEN I WON'T HAVE TO LOOK FOR NEW DIGS, EITHER.
YOU SEE ?
KELLERMAN
IT'S
12

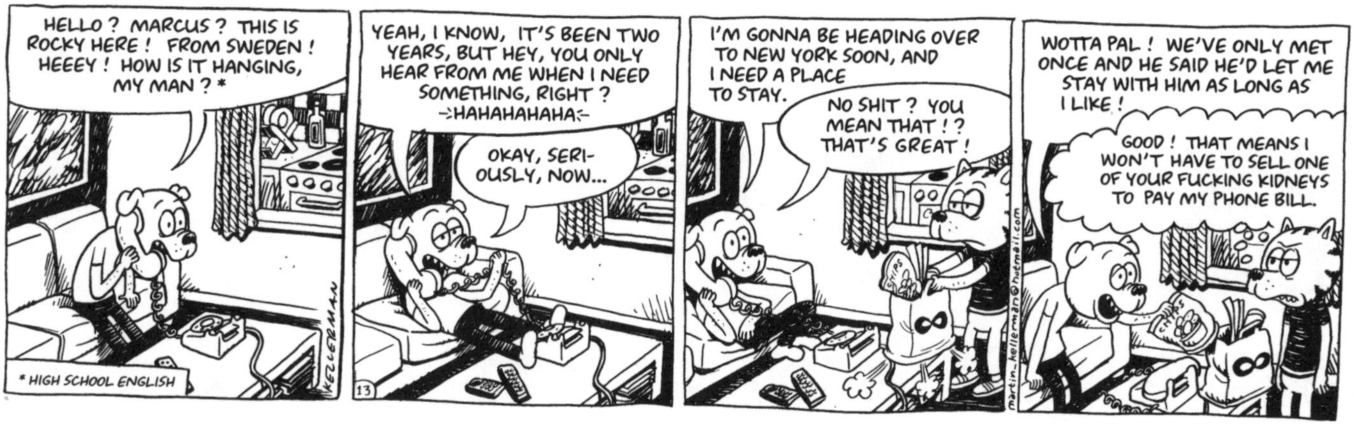
HELLO ? MARCUS ? THIS IS ROCKY HERE ! FROM SWEDEN ! HEEEY ! HOW IS IT HANGING, MY MAN ? *
* HIGH SCHOOL ENGLISH
KELLERMAN
YEAH, I KNOW, IT'S BEEN TWO YEARS, BUT HEY, YOU ONLY HEAR FROM ME WHEN I NEED SOMETHING, RIGHT ? →HAHAHAHAHA←
OKAY, SERIOUSLY, NOW...
13
I'M GONNA BE HEADING OVER TO NEW YORK SOON, AND I NEED A PLACE TO STAY.
NO SHIT ? YOU MEAN THAT ! ? THAT'S GREAT !
martin_kellerman@hotmail.com
WOTTA PAL ! WE'VE ONLY MET ONCE AND HE SAID HE'D LET ME STAY WITH HIM AS LONG AS I LIKE !
GOOD ! THAT MEANS I WON'T HAVE TO SELL ONE OF YOUR FUCKING KIDNEYS TO PAY MY PHONE BILL.

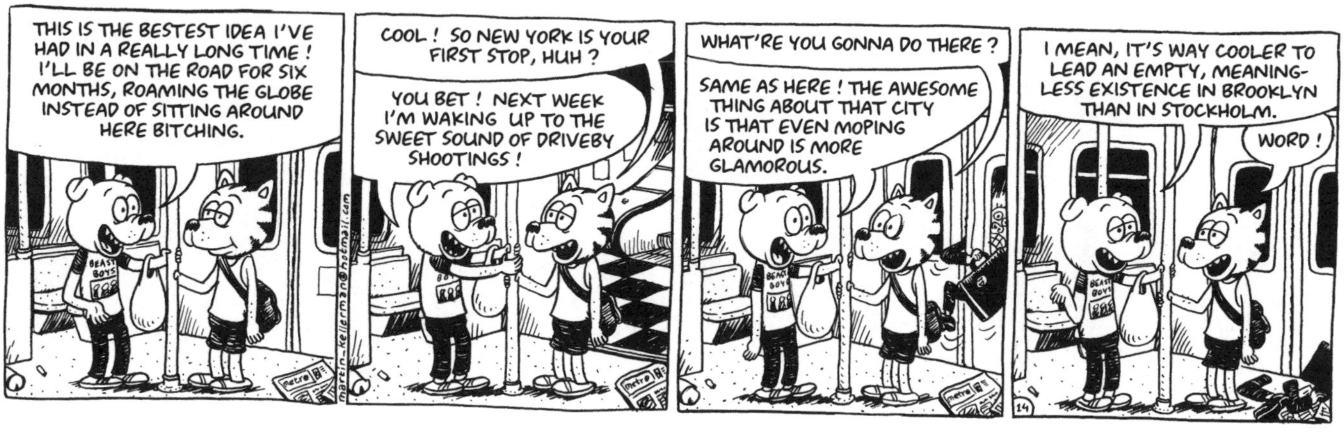
THIS IS THE BESTEST IDEA I'VE HAD IN A REALLY LONG TIME ! I'LL BE ON THE ROAD FOR SIX MONTHS, ROAMING THE GLOBE INSTEAD OF SITTING AROUND HERE BITCHING.
martin_kellerman@hotmail.com
COOL ! SO NEW YORK IS YOUR FIRST STOP, HUH ?
YOU BET ! NEXT WEEK I'M WAKING UP TO THE SWEET SOUND OF DRIVEBY SHOOTINGS !
WHAT'RE YOU GONNA DO THERE ?
SAME AS HERE ! THE AWESOME THING ABOUT THAT CITY IS THAT EVEN MOPING AROUND IS MORE GLAMOROUS.
14
I MEAN, IT'S WAY COOLER TO LEAD AN EMPTY, MEANINGLESS EXISTENCE IN BROOKLYN THAN IN STOCKHOLM.
WORD !

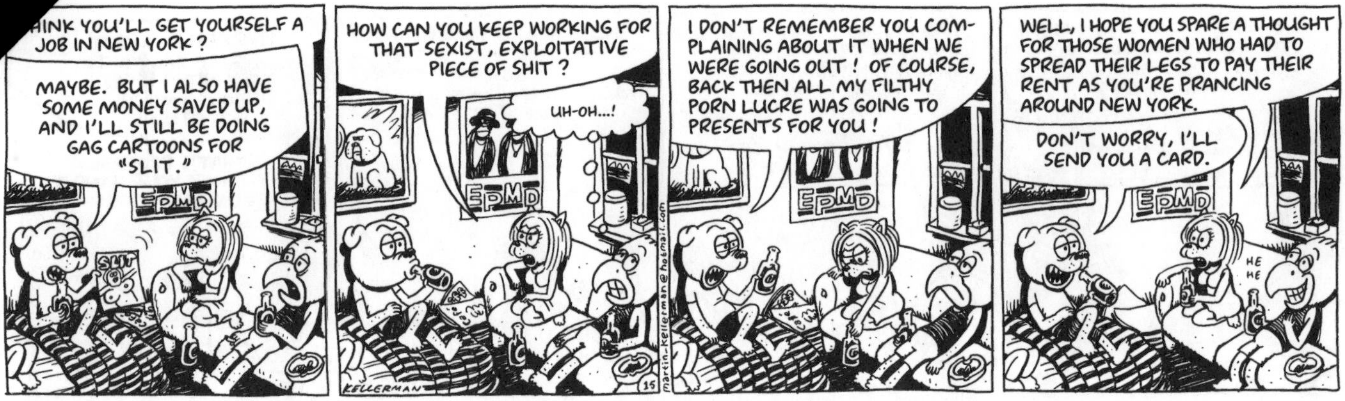
HINK YOU'LL GET YOURSELF A JOB IN NEW YORK ?
MAYBE. BUT I ALSO HAVE SOME MONEY SAVED UP, AND I'LL STILL BE DOING GAG CARTOONS FOR "SLIT."
SLIT
EPMD
HOW CAN YOU KEEP WORKING FOR THAT SEXIST, EXPLOITATIVE PIECE OF SHIT ?
UH-OH...!
KELLERMAN
15
martin-kellerman@hotmail.com
I DON'T REMEMBER YOU COMPLAINING ABOUT IT WHEN WE WERE GOING OUT ! OF COURSE, BACK THEN ALL MY FILTHY PORN LUCRE WAS GOING TO PRESENTS FOR YOU !
WELL, I HOPE YOU SPARE A THOUGHT FOR THOSE WOMEN WHO HAD TO SPREAD THEIR LEGS TO PAY THEIR RENT AS YOU'RE PRANCING AROUND NEW YORK.
DON'T WORRY, I'LL SEND YOU A CARD.
HE HE

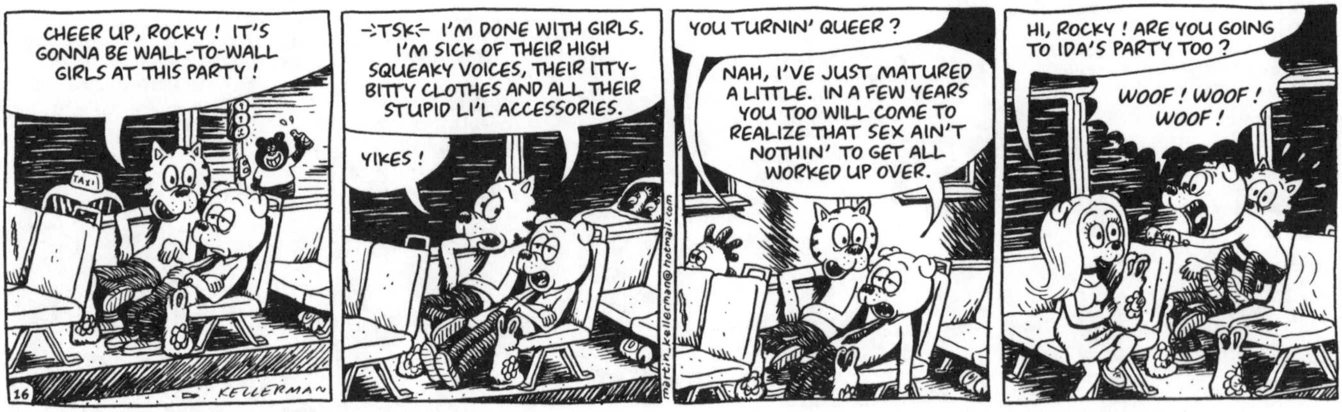
CHEER UP, ROCKY ! IT'S GONNA BE WALL-TO-WALL GIRLS AT THIS PARTY !
TAXI
16
KELLERMAN
-TSK- I'M DONE WITH GIRLS. I'M SICK OF THEIR HIGH SQUEAKY VOICES, THEIR ITTY-BITTY CLOTHES AND ALL THEIR STUPID LI'L ACCESSORIES.
YIKES !
martin_kellerman@hotmail.com
YOU TURNIN' QUEER ?
NAH, I'VE JUST MATURED A LITTLE. IN A FEW YEARS YOU TOO WILL COME TO REALIZE THAT SEX AIN'T NOTHIN' TO GET ALL WORKED UP OVER.
HI, ROCKY ! ARE YOU GOING TO IDA'S PARTY TOO ?
WOOF ! WOOF ! WOOF !

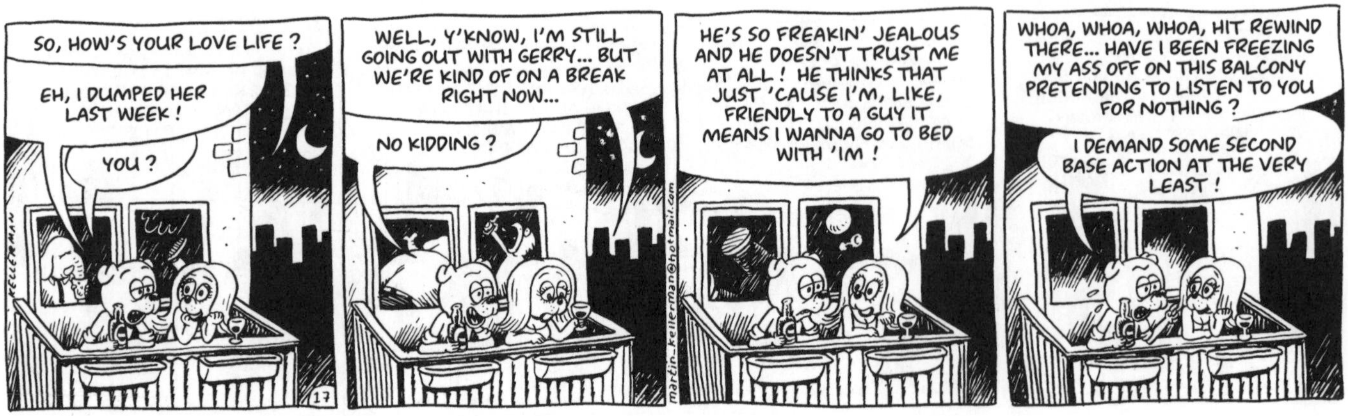
SO, HOW'S YOUR LOVE LIFE ?
EH, I DUMPED HER LAST WEEK !
YOU ?
KELLERMAN
17
WELL, Y'KNOW, I'M STILL GOING OUT WITH GERRY... BUT WE'RE KIND OF ON A BREAK RIGHT NOW...
NO KIDDING ?
martin_kellerman@hotmail.com
HE'S SO FREAKIN' JEALOUS AND HE DOESN'T TRUST ME AT ALL ! HE THINKS THAT JUST 'CAUSE I'M, LIKE, FRIENDLY TO A GUY IT MEANS I WANNA GO TO BED WITH 'IM !
WHOA, WHOA, WHOA, HIT REWIND THERE... HAVE I BEEN FREEZING MY ASS OFF ON THIS BALCONY PRETENDING TO LISTEN TO YOU FOR NOTHING ?
I DEMAND SOME SECOND BASE ACTION AT THE VERY LEAST !

HOLY SHIT ! I THINK SHE WANTS TO GO AT IT RIGHT HERE IN THE FUCKIN' KITCHEN !
18
martin_kellerman@hotmail.com
ANY MOMENT NOW SHE'S GONNA HAUL OFF AND SLAP ME AND THAT'LL BE THAT.
E-E-E-ASY NOW... WORK THAT PANTYHOSE OFF...
KELLERMAN
WAIT, ROCKY. DO YOU HAVE ANY... PROTECTION ?
I'LL CHECK THE BATHROOM.
HE SHOOTS...
HE SCORES !
KABRAK !
THAT WAS THE WORST PARTY EVER. I'M TOO FUCKIN' OLD TO BE DIDDLING AROUND WITH A SEVENTEEN-YEAR-OLD IN THE KITCHEN !
MY TONGUE'S GRAY, AND MY ARMS AND LEGS ARE ASLEEP. I'D ALMOST FORGOTTEN HOW MUCH GODDAMN WORK THOSE TEENAGE MAKE-OUT SESSIONS ARE.
BUT THE WORST THING ABOUT BEING A TEENAGER WAS THE FRUSTRATION OF NEVER GOING ALL THE WAY ! YOU'D MAKE OUT FOR SIX HOURS AND THEN YOU'D HOP ON YOUR SCOOTER AND HEAD HOME TO THE PORN COLLECTION.
19
martin_kellerman@hotmail.com
SO IN SIX YEARS I'VE MOVED UP FROM A MOPED TO THE LATE-NIGHT BUS. NOW THAT'S WHAT I CALL PROGRESS.
WHERE AM I ?
KELLERMAN
REMIND ME AGAIN WHY WE'RE WORKING OUT WITH GODDAMNED HANGOVERS ?
BECAUSE YOU'RE HOOKING UP WITH THAT CHICK FROM LAST NIGHT AND YOU NEED TO BE FRESH AND CLEAN.
ME, I'M HERE TO AVOID HAVING LUNCH WITH THE GIRL I DRAGGED HOME YESTERDAY.
YIKES ! HOW BAD WAS IT ?
KELLERMAN
PRETTY DAMN BAD ! LAST THING I REMEMBER WAS TRYING TO PICK UP A GIRL IN THIS MARDI GRAS GET-UP... NEXT THING I KNOW, I WAKE UP AT HOME WITH A MOUTHFUL OF GLITTER.
STOP ! I'M GONNA HURL !
20
martin_kellerman@hotmail.com
HOW LONG D'YOU PLAN TO "WORK OUT" ? YOU'VE BEEN SITTING ON THOSE MACHINES FOR AN HOUR !
I NEED A BUCKET AND I NEED IT NOW.

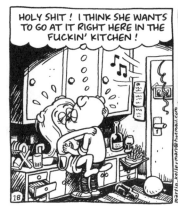

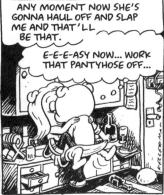

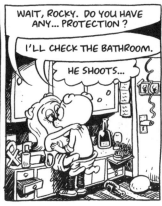

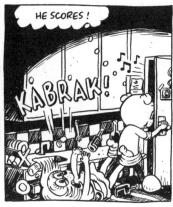

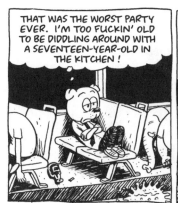

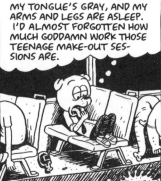

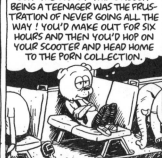

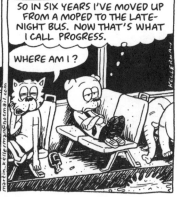

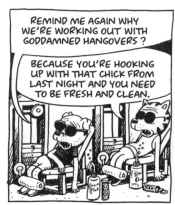

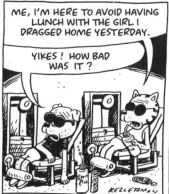

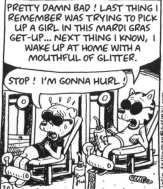

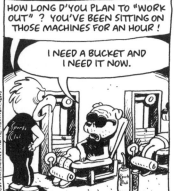

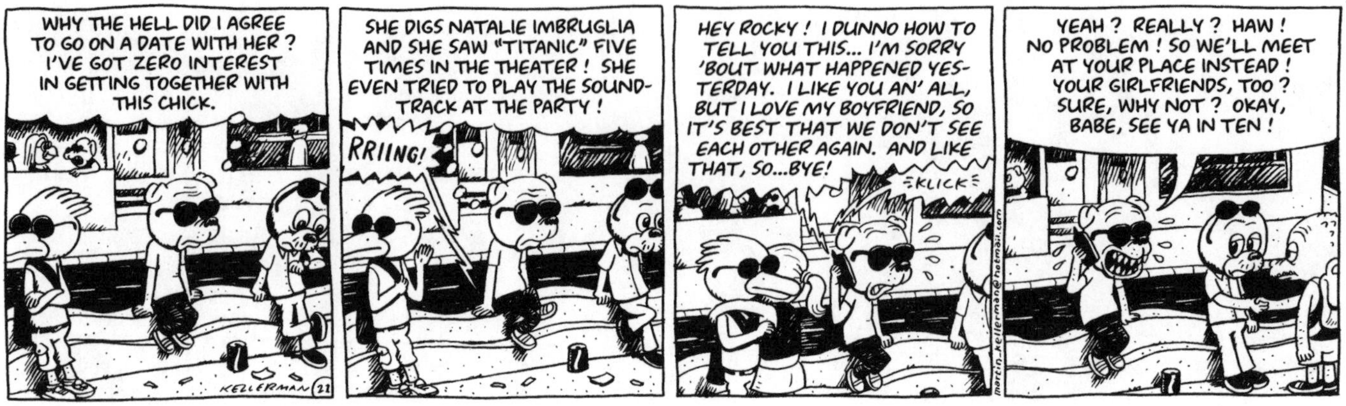
WHY THE HELL DID I AGREE TO GO ON A DATE WITH HER ? I'VE GOT ZERO INTEREST IN GETTING TOGETHER WITH THIS CHICK.
KELLERMAN 21
SHE DIGS NATALIE IMBRUGLIA AND SHE SAW "TITANIC" FIVE TIMES IN THE THEATER ! SHE EVEN TRIED TO PLAY THE SOUND-TRACK AT THE PARTY !
RRIING!
HEY ROCKY ! I DUNNO HOW TO TELL YOU THIS... I'M SORRY 'BOUT WHAT HAPPENED YES-TERDAY. I LIKE YOU AN' ALL, BUT I LOVE MY BOYFRIEND, SO IT'S BEST THAT WE DON'T SEE EACH OTHER AGAIN. AND LIKE THAT, SO...BYE!
KLICK
martin_kellerman@hotmail.com
YEAH ? REALLY ? HAW ! NO PROBLEM ! SO WE'LL MEET AT YOUR PLACE INSTEAD ! YOUR GIRLFRIENDS, TOO ? SURE, WHY NOT ? OKAY, BABE, SEE YA IN TEN !

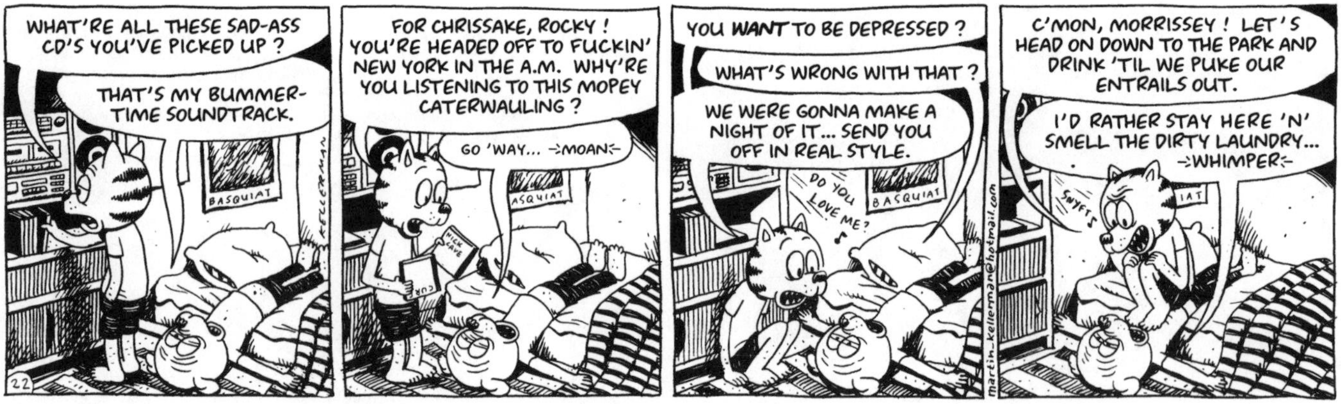
WHAT'RE ALL THESE SAD-ASS CD'S YOU'VE PICKED UP ?
THAT'S MY BUMMER-TIME SOUNDTRACK.
BASQUIAT
KELLERMAN
22
FOR CHRISSAKE, ROCKY ! YOU'RE HEADED OFF TO FUCKIN' NEW YORK IN THE A.M. WHY'RE YOU LISTENING TO THIS MOPEY CATERWAULING ?
GO 'WAY... MOAN
YOU WANT TO BE DEPRESSED ?
WHAT'S WRONG WITH THAT ?
WE WERE GONNA MAKE A NIGHT OF IT... SEND YOU OFF IN REAL STYLE.
DO YOU LOVE ME?
BASQUIAT
martin_kellerman@hotmail.com
C'MON, MORRISSEY ! LET'S HEAD ON DOWN TO THE PARK AND DRINK 'TIL WE PUKE OUR ENTRAILS OUT.
I'D RATHER STAY HERE 'N' SMELL THE DIRTY LAUNDRY... WHIMPER

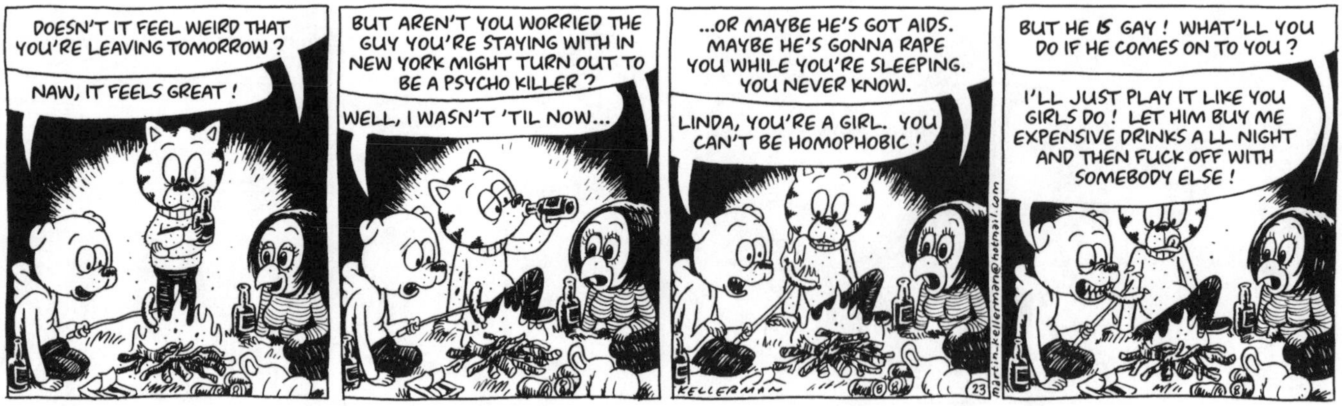
DOESN'T IT FEEL WEIRD THAT YOU'RE LEAVING TOMORROW ?
NAW, IT FEELS GREAT !
BUT AREN'T YOU WORRIED THE GUY YOU'RE STAYING WITH IN NEW YORK MIGHT TURN OUT TO BE A PSYCHO KILLER ?
WELL, I WASN'T 'TIL NOW...
...OR MAYBE HE'S GOT AIDS. MAYBE HE'S GONNA RAPE YOU WHILE YOU'RE SLEEPING. YOU NEVER KNOW.
LINDA, YOU'RE A GIRL. YOU CAN'T BE HOMOPHOBIC !
KELLERMAN
23
martin_kellerman@hotmail.com
BUT HE IS GAY ! WHAT'LL YOU DO IF HE COMES ON TO YOU ?
I'LL JUST PLAY IT LIKE YOU GIRLS DO ! LET HIM BUY ME EXPENSIVE DRINKS A LL NIGHT AND THEN FUCK OFF WITH SOMEBODY ELSE !

NEW YORK

THIS IS YOUR CAPTAIN SPEAKING. OUR ESTIMATED TIME OF ARRIVAL IS EIGHT HOURS FROM NOW, AND WE HOPE YOU HAVE A PLEASANT FLIGHT.
YOU LOOK LIKE SHIT, EBBE! ROUGH NIGHT?
HAW HAW! CHECK IT OUT! HE FORGOT TO SWITCH OFF THE MIKE! LISSEN!
martin_kellerman@hotmail.com
24
NAH, NOTHIN' A HOT PUSSY AND A COLD BEER COULDN'T CURE!
DON'T SAY IT! DON'T SAY IT!
HAHAHA!
KELLERMAN
HEY! HEY! YA FORGOT THE BEER!

HEYA, MARCUS! I JUST GOT OFF THE PLANE, SO IF YOU GIVE ME THE ADDRESS I'LL GRAB A CAB.
KELLERMAN
martin_kellerman@hotmail.com
25
ALL RIGHT! I AM GOING TO 214 WEST 112TH STREET, PLEASE.
UH, YOU SURE THAT'S THE RIGHT ADDRESS, MISTER?
6A92
TOTALLY! A FRIEND OF MINE LIVES THERE. WHY, IS THAT NOT A GOOD ADDRESS OR SOMETHING?
NO, NO! IT'S A FINE NEIGHBORHOOD! LOVELY!
BUT I WANT THE FARE UPFRONT... AND GET YOURSELF READY, 'CAUSE I'M GONNA SLOW DOWN SO'S YOU CAN JUMP OUT, OKAY?

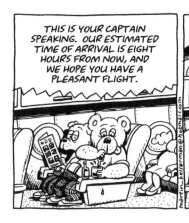

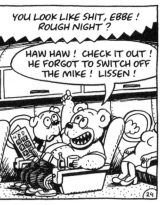

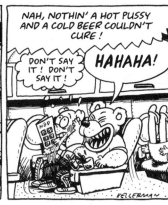

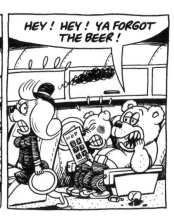

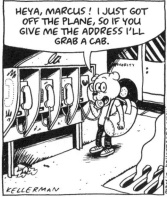

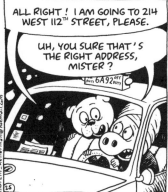

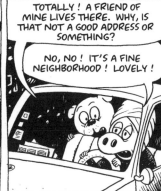

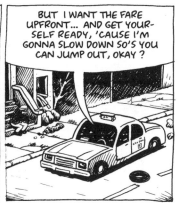

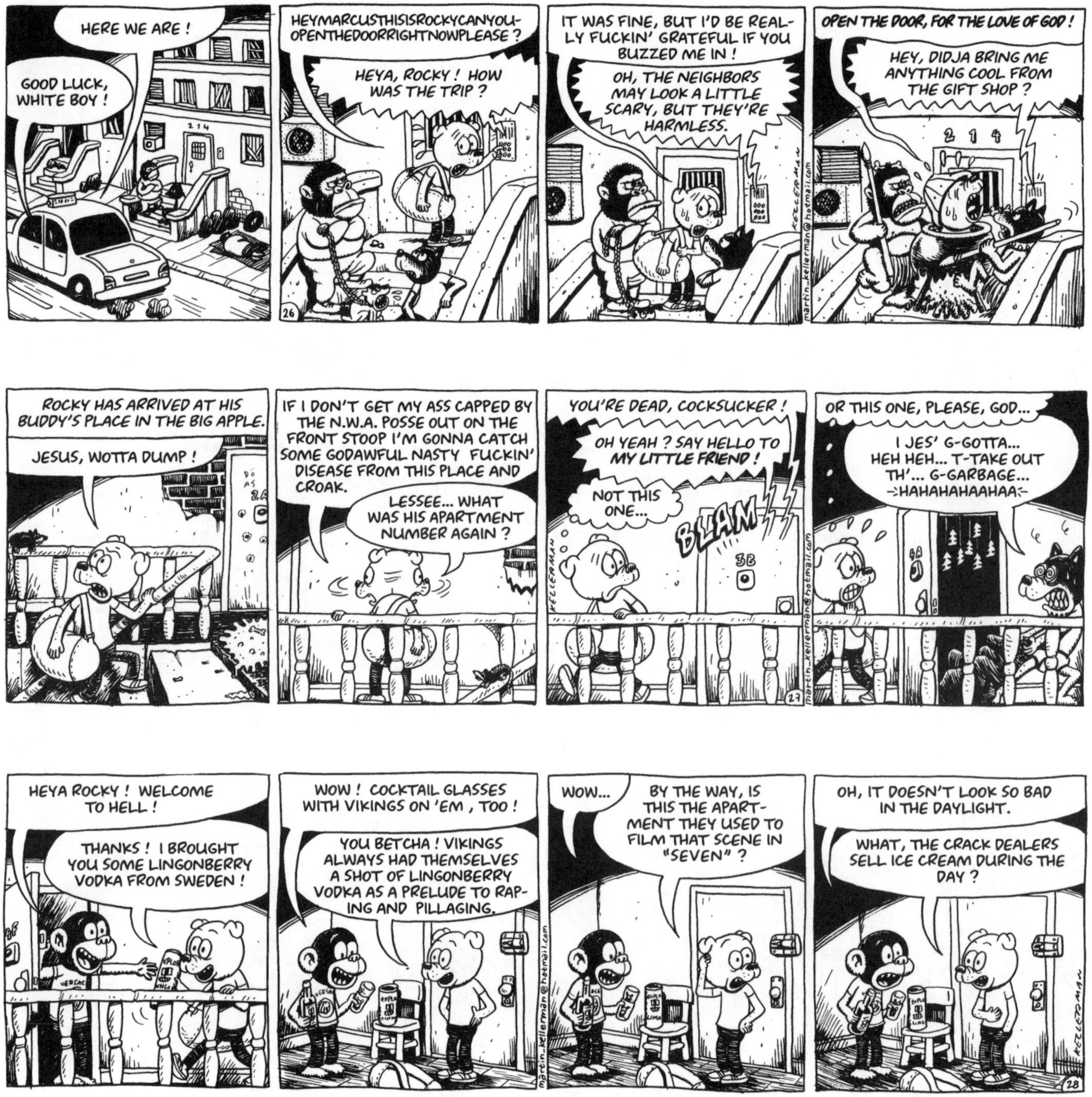
HERE WE ARE !
GOOD LUCK, WHITE BOY !
HEYMARCUSTHISISROCKYCANYOU-OPENTHEDOORRIGHTNOWPLEASE ?
HEYA, ROCKY ! HOW WAS THE TRIP ?
26
IT WAS FINE, BUT I'D BE REAL-LY FUCKIN' GRATEFUL IF YOU BUZZED ME IN !
OH, THE NEIGHBORS MAY LOOK A LITTLE SCARY, BUT THEY'RE HARMLESS.
KELLERMAN
martin_kellerman@hotmail.com
OPEN THE DOOR, FOR THE LOVE OF GOD !
HEY, DIDJA BRING ME ANYTHING COOL FROM THE GIFT SHOP ?
2 1 4
ROCKY HAS ARRIVED AT HIS BUDDY'S PLACE IN THE BIG APPLE.
JESUS, WOTTA DUMP !
IF I DON'T GET MY ASS CAPPED BY THE N.W.A. POSSE OUT ON THE FRONT STOOP I'M GONNA CATCH SOME GODAWFUL NASTY FUCKIN' DISEASE FROM THIS PLACE AND CROAK.
LESSEE... WHAT WAS HIS APARTMENT NUMBER AGAIN ?
YOU'RE DEAD, COCKSUCKER !
OH YEAH ? SAY HELLO TO MY LITTLE FRIEND !
NOT THIS ONE...
BLAM
3B
KELLERMAN
27
martin_kellerman@hotmail.com
OR THIS ONE, PLEASE, GOD...
I JES' G-GOTTA... HEH HEH... T-TAKE OUT TH'... G-GARBAGE... HAHAHAHAHAAHAA
HEYA ROCKY ! WELCOME TO HELL !
THANKS ! I BROUGHT YOU SOME LINGONBERRY VODKA FROM SWEDEN !
WOW ! COCKTAIL GLASSES WITH VIKINGS ON 'EM , TOO !
YOU BETCHA ! VIKINGS ALWAYS HAD THEMSELVES A SHOT OF LINGONBERRY VODKA AS A PRELUDE TO RAP-ING AND PILLAGING.
martin_kellerman@hotmail.com
WOW...
BY THE WAY, IS THIS THE APART-MENT THEY USED TO FILM THAT SCENE IN "SEVEN" ?
OH, IT DOESN'T LOOK SO BAD IN THE DAYLIGHT.
WHAT, THE CRACK DEALERS SELL ICE CREAM DURING THE DAY ?
KELLERMAN
28

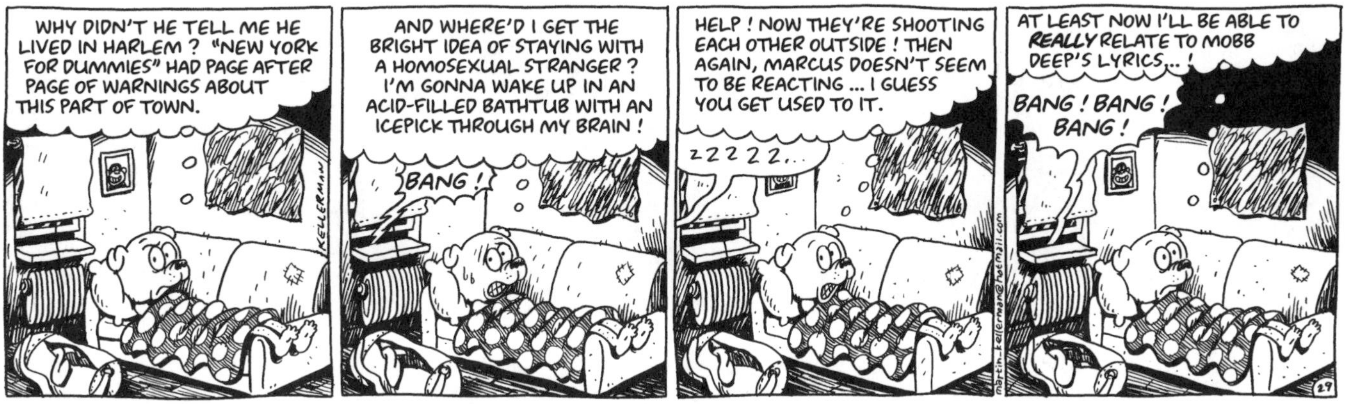
WHY DIDN'T HE TELL ME HE LIVED IN HARLEM ? "NEW YORK FOR DUMMIES" HAD PAGE AFTER PAGE OF WARNINGS ABOUT THIS PART OF TOWN.
KELLERMAN
AND WHERE'D I GET THE BRIGHT IDEA OF STAYING WITH A HOMOSEXUAL STRANGER ? I'M GONNA WAKE UP IN AN ACID-FILLED BATHTUB WITH AN ICEPICK THROUGH MY BRAIN !
BANG !
HELP ! NOW THEY'RE SHOOTING EACH OTHER OUTSIDE ! THEN AGAIN, MARCUS DOESN'T SEEM TO BE REACTING ... I GUESS YOU GET USED TO IT.
ZZZZZ...
martin-kellerman@hotmail.com
AT LEAST NOW I'LL BE ABLE TO REALLY RELATE TO MOBB DEEP'S LYRICS... !
BANG ! BANG ! BANG !
29

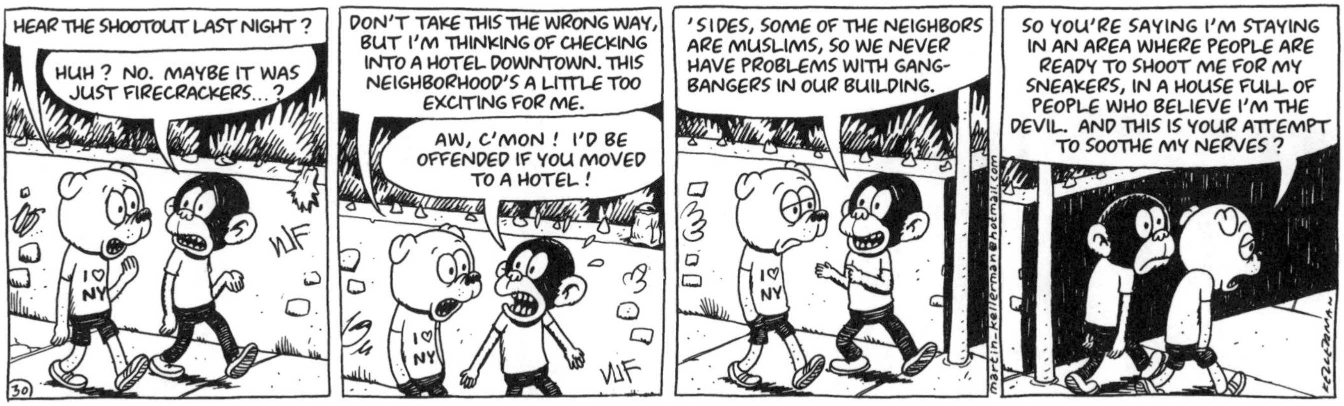
HEAR THE SHOOTOUT LAST NIGHT ?
HUH ? NO. MAYBE IT WAS JUST FIRECRACKERS... ?
I ♥ NY
WF
30
DON'T TAKE THIS THE WRONG WAY, BUT I'M THINKING OF CHECKING INTO A HOTEL DOWNTOWN. THIS NEIGHBORHOOD'S A LITTLE TOO EXCITING FOR ME.
AW, C'MON ! I'D BE OFFENDED IF YOU MOVED TO A HOTEL !
I ♥ NY
WF
'SIDES, SOME OF THE NEIGHBORS ARE MUSLIMS, SO WE NEVER HAVE PROBLEMS WITH GANG-BANGERS IN OUR BUILDING.
I ♥ NY
martin-kellerman@hotmail.com
SO YOU'RE SAYING I'M STAYING IN AN AREA WHERE PEOPLE ARE READY TO SHOOT ME FOR MY SNEAKERS, IN A HOUSE FULL OF PEOPLE WHO BELIEVE I'M THE DEVIL. AND THIS IS YOUR ATTEMPT TO SOOTHE MY NERVES ?
KELLERMAN

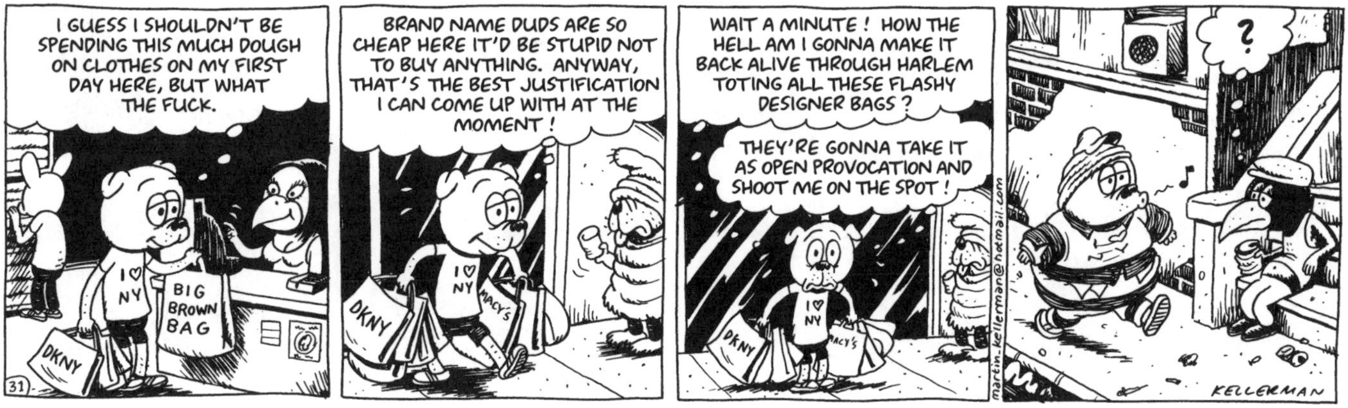
I GUESS I SHOULDN'T BE SPENDING THIS MUCH DOUGH ON CLOTHES ON MY FIRST DAY HERE, BUT WHAT THE FUCK.
I ♥ NY
BIG BROWN BAG
DKNY
31
BRAND NAME DUDS ARE SO CHEAP HERE IT'D BE STUPID NOT TO BUY ANYTHING. ANYWAY, THAT'S THE BEST JUSTIFICATION I CAN COME UP WITH AT THE MOMENT !
I ♥ NY
DKNY
MACY'S
WAIT A MINUTE ! HOW THE HELL AM I GONNA MAKE IT BACK ALIVE THROUGH HARLEM TOTING ALL THESE FLASHY DESIGNER BAGS ?
THEY'RE GONNA TAKE IT AS OPEN PROVOCATION AND SHOOT ME ON THE SPOT !
I ♥ NY
DKNY
MACY'S
martin-kellerman@hotmail.com
?
KELLERMAN

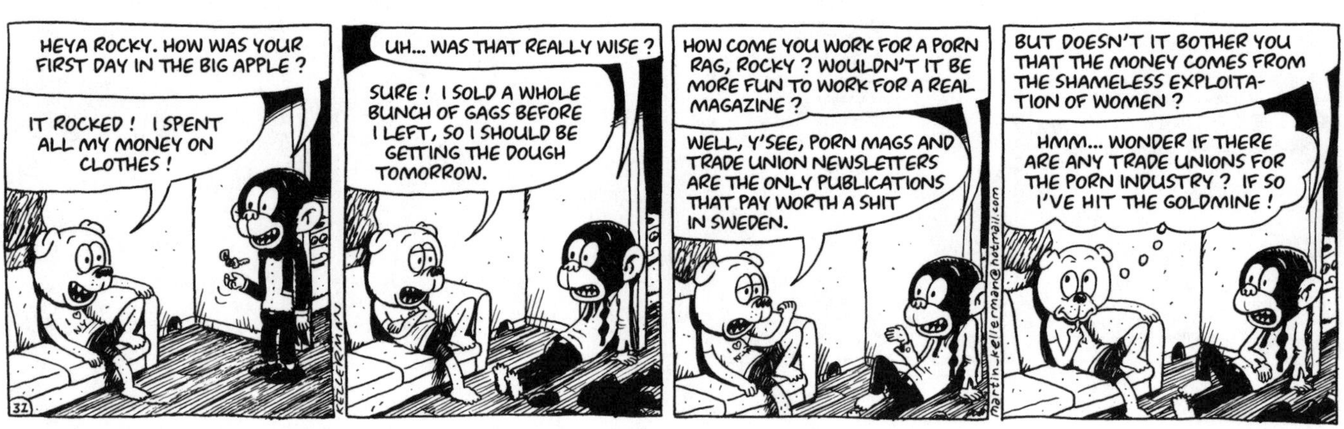
HEYA ROCKY. HOW WAS YOUR FIRST DAY IN THE BIG APPLE ?
IT ROCKED ! I SPENT ALL MY MONEY ON CLOTHES !
UH... WAS THAT REALLY WISE ?
SURE ! I SOLD A WHOLE BUNCH OF GAGS BEFORE I LEFT, SO I SHOULD BE GETTING THE DOUGH TOMORROW.
HOW COME YOU WORK FOR A PORN RAG, ROCKY ? WOULDN'T IT BE MORE FUN TO WORK FOR A REAL MAGAZINE ?
WELL, Y'SEE, PORN MAGS AND TRADE UNION NEWSLETTERS ARE THE ONLY PUBLICATIONS THAT PAY WORTH A SHIT IN SWEDEN.
BUT DOESN'T IT BOTHER YOU THAT THE MONEY COMES FROM THE SHAMELESS EXPLOITATION OF WOMEN ?
HMM... WONDER IF THERE ARE ANY TRADE UNIONS FOR THE PORN INDUSTRY ? IF SO I'VE HIT THE GOLDMINE !
32
KELLERMAN
martin_kellerman@hotmail.com

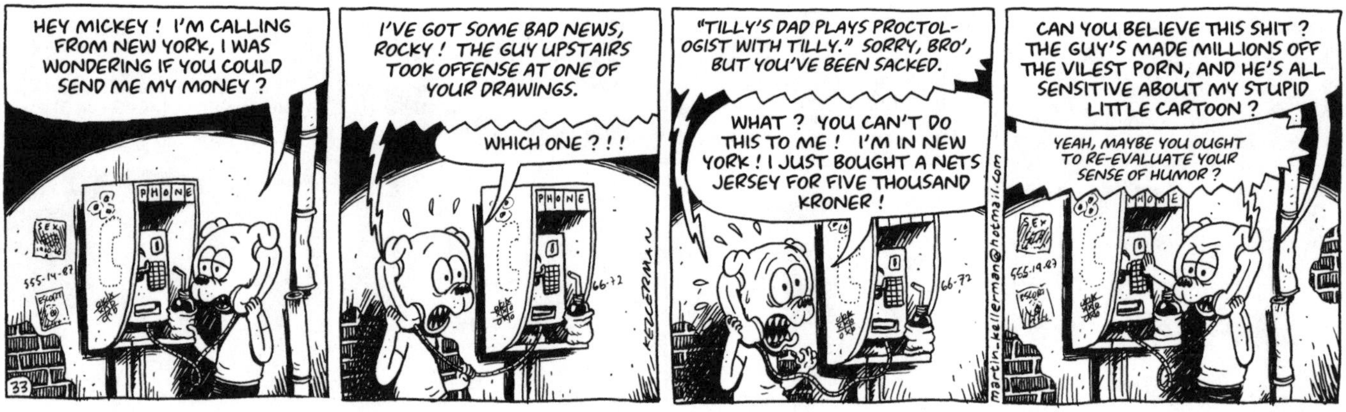
HEY MICKEY ! I'M CALLING FROM NEW YORK, I WAS WONDERING IF YOU COULD SEND ME MY MONEY ?
I'VE GOT SOME BAD NEWS, ROCKY ! THE GUY UPSTAIRS TOOK OFFENSE AT ONE OF YOUR DRAWINGS.
WHICH ONE ? ! !
"TILLY'S DAD PLAYS PROCTOLOGIST WITH TILLY." SORRY, BRO', BUT YOU'VE BEEN SACKED.
WHAT ? YOU CAN'T DO THIS TO ME ! I'M IN NEW YORK ! I JUST BOUGHT A NETS JERSEY FOR FIVE THOUSAND KRONER !
CAN YOU BELIEVE THIS SHIT ? THE GUY'S MADE MILLIONS OFF THE VILEST PORN, AND HE'S ALL SENSITIVE ABOUT MY STUPID LITTLE CARTOON ?
YEAH, MAYBE YOU OUGHT TO RE-EVALUATE YOUR SENSE OF HUMOR ?
PHONE
33
KELLERMAN
martin_kellerman@hotmail.com

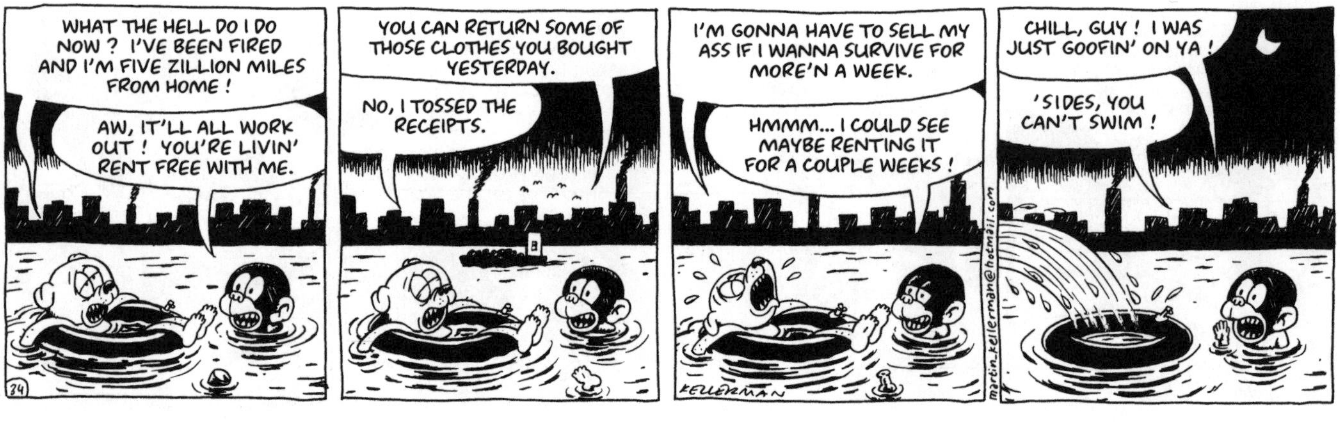
WHAT THE HELL DO I DO NOW ? I'VE BEEN FIRED AND I'M FIVE ZILLION MILES FROM HOME !
AW, IT'LL ALL WORK OUT ! YOU'RE LIVIN' RENT FREE WITH ME.
YOU CAN RETURN SOME OF THOSE CLOTHES YOU BOUGHT YESTERDAY.
NO, I TOSSED THE RECEIPTS.
I'M GONNA HAVE TO SELL MY ASS IF I WANNA SURVIVE FOR MORE'N A WEEK.
HMMM... I COULD SEE MAYBE RENTING IT FOR A COUPLE WEEKS !
CHILL, GUY ! I WAS JUST GOOFIN' ON YA !
'SIDES, YOU CAN'T SWIM !
34
KELLERMAN
martin_kellerman@hotmail.com

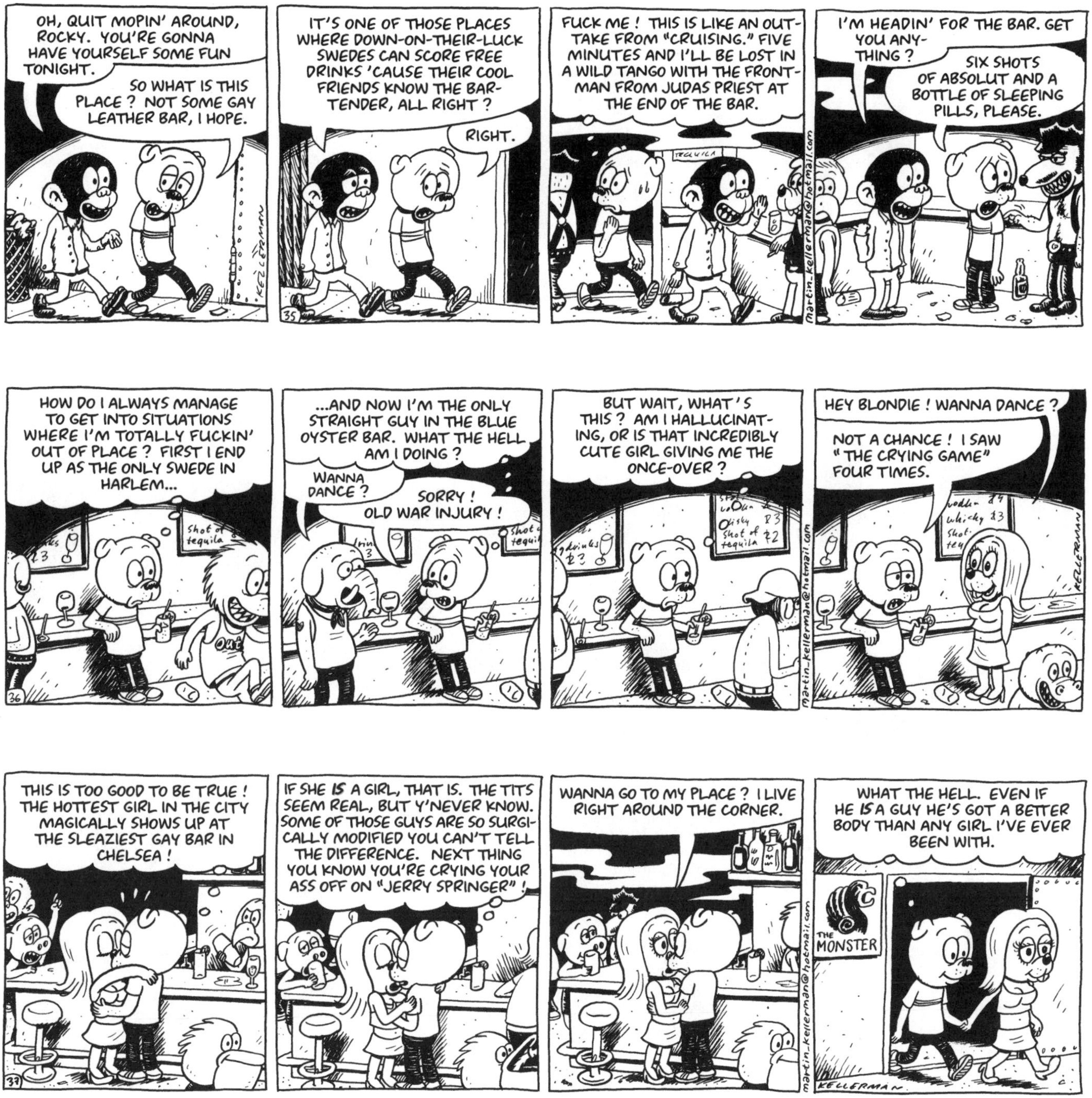
OH, QUIT MOPIN' AROUND, ROCKY. YOU'RE GONNA HAVE YOURSELF SOME FUN TONIGHT.
SO WHAT IS THIS PLACE? NOT SOME GAY LEATHER BAR, I HOPE.
KELLERMAN
IT'S ONE OF THOSE PLACES WHERE DOWN-ON-THEIR-LUCK SWEDES CAN SCORE FREE DRINKS 'CAUSE THEIR COOL FRIENDS KNOW THE BARTENDER, ALL RIGHT?
RIGHT.
35
FUCK ME! THIS IS LIKE AN OUTTAKE FROM "CRUISING." FIVE MINUTES AND I'LL BE LOST IN A WILD TANGO WITH THE FRONTMAN FROM JUDAS PRIEST AT THE END OF THE BAR.
martin_kellerman@hotmail.com
I'M HEADIN' FOR THE BAR. GET YOU ANYTHING?
SIX SHOTS OF ABSOLUT AND A BOTTLE OF SLEEPING PILLS, PLEASE.
HOW DO I ALWAYS MANAGE TO GET INTO SITUATIONS WHERE I'M TOTALLY FUCKIN' OUT OF PLACE? FIRST I END UP AS THE ONLY SWEDE IN HARLEM...
Shot of tequila
36
...AND NOW I'M THE ONLY STRAIGHT GUY IN THE BLUE OYSTER BAR. WHAT THE HELL AM I DOING?
WANNA DANCE?
SORRY! OLD WAR INJURY!
BUT WAIT, WHAT'S THIS? AM I HALLUCINATING, OR IS THAT INCREDIBLY CUTE GIRL GIVING ME THE ONCE-OVER?
martin_kellerman@hotmail.com
HEY BLONDIE! WANNA DANCE?
NOT A CHANCE! I SAW "THE CRYING GAME" FOUR TIMES.
KELLERMAN
THIS IS TOO GOOD TO BE TRUE! THE HOTTEST GIRL IN THE CITY MAGICALLY SHOWS UP AT THE SLEAZIEST GAY BAR IN CHELSEA!
37
IF SHE IS A GIRL, THAT IS. THE TITS SEEM REAL, BUT Y'NEVER KNOW. SOME OF THOSE GUYS ARE SO SURGICALLY MODIFIED YOU CAN'T TELL THE DIFFERENCE. NEXT THING YOU KNOW YOU'RE CRYING YOUR ASS OFF ON "JERRY SPRINGER"!
WANNA GO TO MY PLACE? I LIVE RIGHT AROUND THE CORNER.
martin_kellerman@hotmail.com
WHAT THE HELL. EVEN IF HE IS A GUY HE'S GOT A BETTER BODY THAN ANY GIRL I'VE EVER BEEN WITH.
THE MONSTER
KELLERMAN

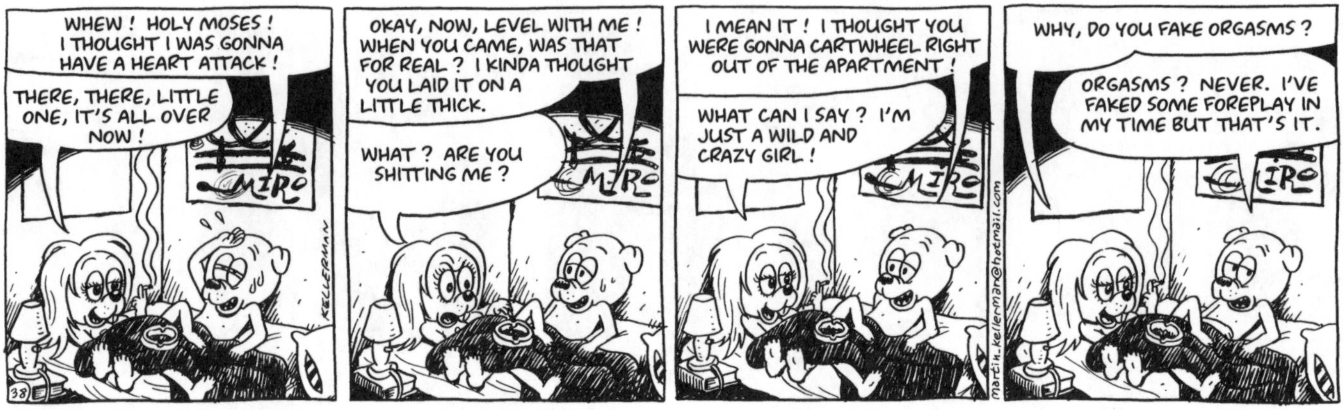
WHEW ! HOLY MOSES ! I THOUGHT I WAS GONNA HAVE A HEART ATTACK !
THERE, THERE, LITTLE ONE, IT'S ALL OVER NOW !
KELLERMAN
38
OKAY, NOW, LEVEL WITH ME ! WHEN YOU CAME, WAS THAT FOR REAL ? I KINDA THOUGHT YOU LAID IT ON A LITTLE THICK.
WHAT ? ARE YOU SHITTING ME ?
I MEAN IT ! I THOUGHT YOU WERE GONNA CARTWHEEL RIGHT OUT OF THE APARTMENT !
WHAT CAN I SAY ? I'M JUST A WILD AND CRAZY GIRL !
martin_kellerman@hotmail.com
WHY, DO YOU FAKE ORGASMS ?
ORGASMS ? NEVER. I'VE FAKED SOME FOREPLAY IN MY TIME BUT THAT'S IT.

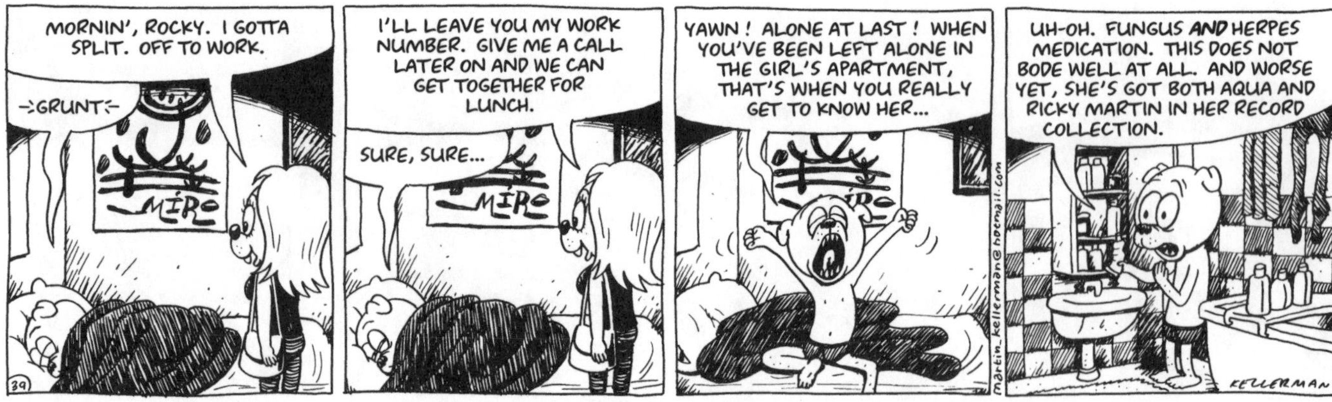
MORNIN', ROCKY. I GOTTA SPLIT. OFF TO WORK.
-GRUNT-
39
I'LL LEAVE YOU MY WORK NUMBER. GIVE ME A CALL LATER ON AND WE CAN GET TOGETHER FOR LUNCH.
SURE, SURE...
YAWN ! ALONE AT LAST ! WHEN YOU'VE BEEN LEFT ALONE IN THE GIRL'S APARTMENT, THAT'S WHEN YOU REALLY GET TO KNOW HER...
martin_kellerman@hotmail.com
UH-OH. FUNGUS **AND** HERPES MEDICATION. THIS DOES NOT BODE WELL AT ALL. AND WORSE YET, SHE'S GOT BOTH AQUA AND RICKY MARTIN IN HER RECORD COLLECTION.
KELLERMAN

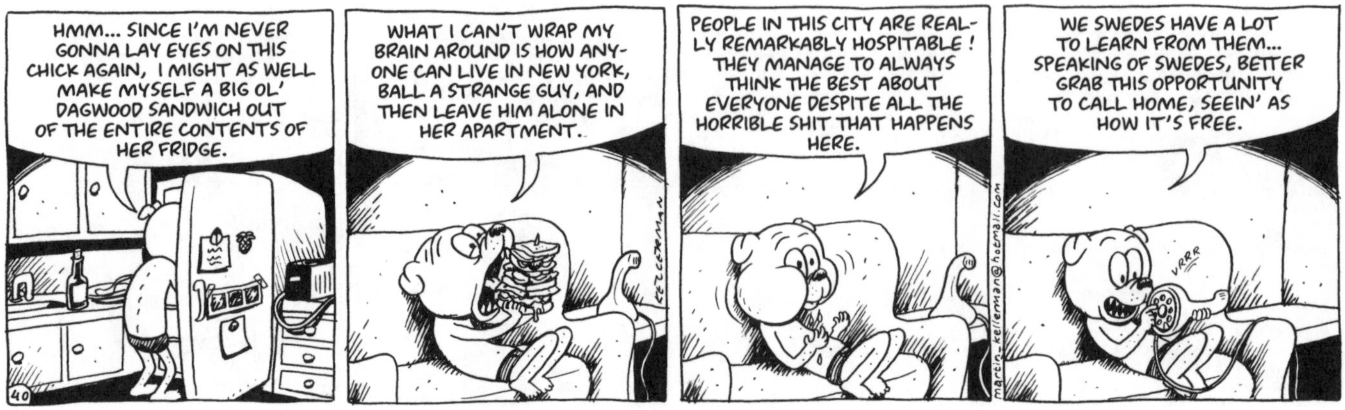
HMM... SINCE I'M NEVER GONNA LAY EYES ON THIS CHICK AGAIN, I MIGHT AS WELL MAKE MYSELF A BIG OL' DAGWOOD SANDWICH OUT OF THE ENTIRE CONTENTS OF HER FRIDGE.
40
WHAT I CAN'T WRAP MY BRAIN AROUND IS HOW ANY-ONE CAN LIVE IN NEW YORK, BALL A STRANGE GUY, AND THEN LEAVE HIM ALONE IN HER APARTMENT.
KELLERMAN
PEOPLE IN THIS CITY ARE REAL-LY REMARKABLY HOSPITABLE ! THEY MANAGE TO ALWAYS THINK THE BEST ABOUT EVERYONE DESPITE ALL THE HORRIBLE SHIT THAT HAPPENS HERE.
martin_kellerman@hotmail.com
WE SWEDES HAVE A LOT TO LEARN FROM THEM... SPEAKING OF SWEDES, BETTER GRAB THIS OPPORTUNITY TO CALL HOME, SEEIN' AS HOW IT'S FREE.
VRRR

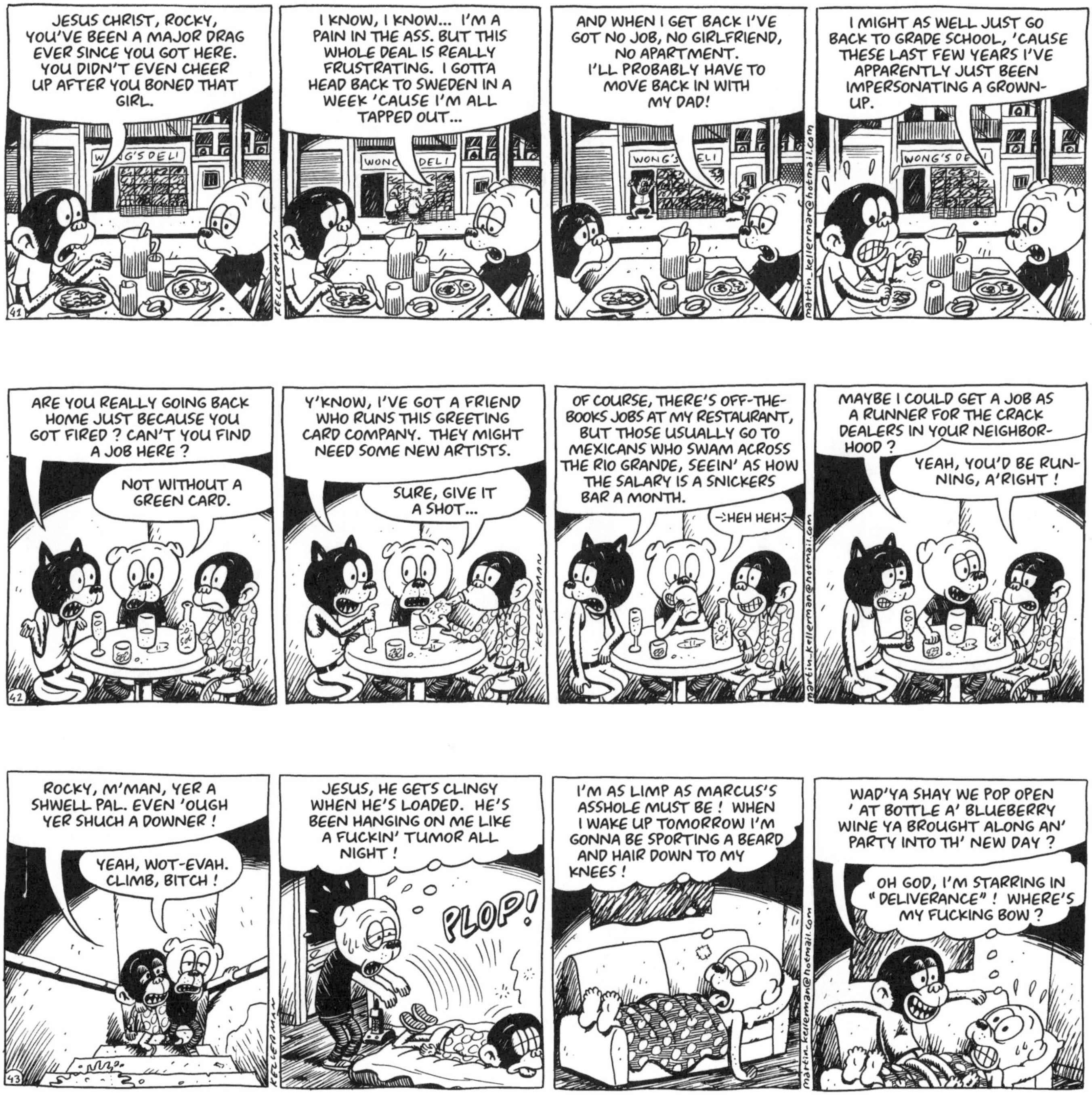
JESUS CHRIST, ROCKY, YOU'VE BEEN A MAJOR DRAG EVER SINCE YOU GOT HERE. YOU DIDN'T EVEN CHEER UP AFTER YOU BONED THAT GIRL.
WONG'S DELI
I KNOW, I KNOW... I'M A PAIN IN THE ASS. BUT THIS WHOLE DEAL IS REALLY FRUSTRATING. I GOTTA HEAD BACK TO SWEDEN IN A WEEK 'CAUSE I'M ALL TAPPED OUT...
AND WHEN I GET BACK I'VE GOT NO JOB, NO GIRLFRIEND, NO APARTMENT. I'LL PROBABLY HAVE TO MOVE BACK IN WITH MY DAD!
I MIGHT AS WELL JUST GO BACK TO GRADE SCHOOL, 'CAUSE THESE LAST FEW YEARS I'VE APPARENTLY JUST BEEN IMPERSONATING A GROWN-UP.
ARE YOU REALLY GOING BACK HOME JUST BECAUSE YOU GOT FIRED? CAN'T YOU FIND A JOB HERE?
NOT WITHOUT A GREEN CARD.
Y'KNOW, I'VE GOT A FRIEND WHO RUNS THIS GREETING CARD COMPANY. THEY MIGHT NEED SOME NEW ARTISTS.
SURE, GIVE IT A SHOT...
OF COURSE, THERE'S OFF-THE-BOOKS JOBS AT MY RESTAURANT, BUT THOSE USUALLY GO TO MEXICANS WHO SWAM ACROSS THE RIO GRANDE, SEEIN' AS HOW THE SALARY IS A SNICKERS BAR A MONTH.
HEH HEH
MAYBE I COULD GET A JOB AS A RUNNER FOR THE CRACK DEALERS IN YOUR NEIGHBOR-HOOD?
YEAH, YOU'D BE RUN-NING, A'RIGHT!
ROCKY, M'MAN, YER A SHWELL PAL. EVEN 'OUGH YER SHUCH A DOWNER!
YEAH, WOT-EVAH. CLIMB, BITCH!
JESUS, HE GETS CLINGY WHEN HE'S LOADED. HE'S BEEN HANGING ON ME LIKE A FUCKIN' TUMOR ALL NIGHT!
PLOP!
I'M AS LIMP AS MARCUS'S ASSHOLE MUST BE! WHEN I WAKE UP TOMORROW I'M GONNA BE SPORTING A BEARD AND HAIR DOWN TO MY KNEES!
WAD'YA SHAY WE POP OPEN 'AT BOTTLE A' BLUEBERRY WINE YA BROUGHT ALONG AN' PARTY INTO TH' NEW DAY?
OH GOD, I'M STARRING IN "DELIVERANCE"! WHERE'S MY FUCKING BOW?
KELLERMAN
martin_kellerman@hotmail.com

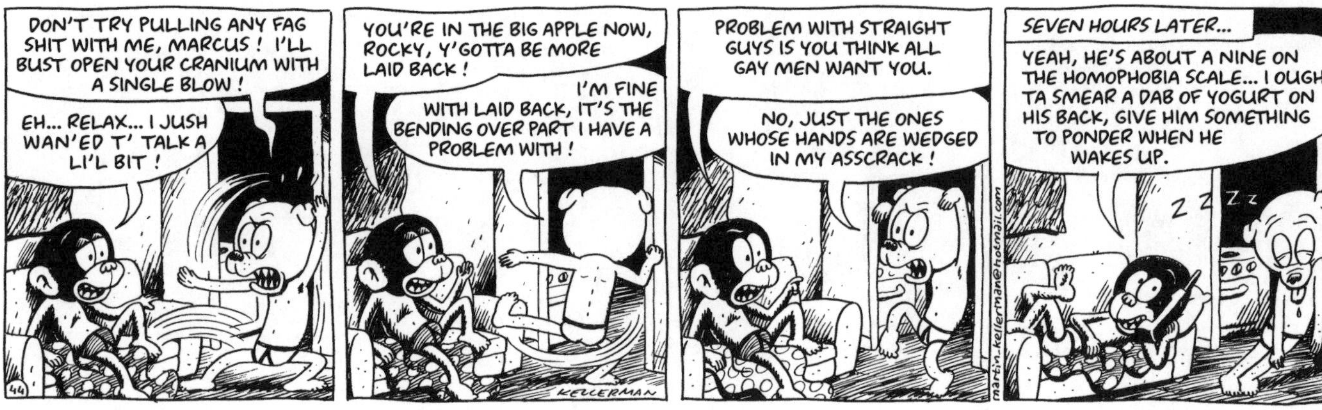
DON'T TRY PULLING ANY FAG SHIT WITH ME, MARCUS ! I'LL BUST OPEN YOUR CRANIUM WITH A SINGLE BLOW !
EH... RELAX... I JUSH WAN'ED T' TALK A LI'L BIT !
44
YOU'RE IN THE BIG APPLE NOW, ROCKY, Y'GOTTA BE MORE LAID BACK !
I'M FINE WITH LAID BACK, IT'S THE BENDING OVER PART I HAVE A PROBLEM WITH !
KELLERMAN
PROBLEM WITH STRAIGHT GUYS IS YOU THINK ALL GAY MEN WANT YOU.
NO, JUST THE ONES WHOSE HANDS ARE WEDGED IN MY ASSCRACK !
martin_kellerman@hotmail.com
SEVEN HOURS LATER...
YEAH, HE'S ABOUT A NINE ON THE HOMOPHOBIA SCALE... I OUGHTA SMEAR A DAB OF YOGURT ON HIS BACK, GIVE HIM SOMETHING TO PONDER WHEN HE WAKES UP.
Z Z Z z

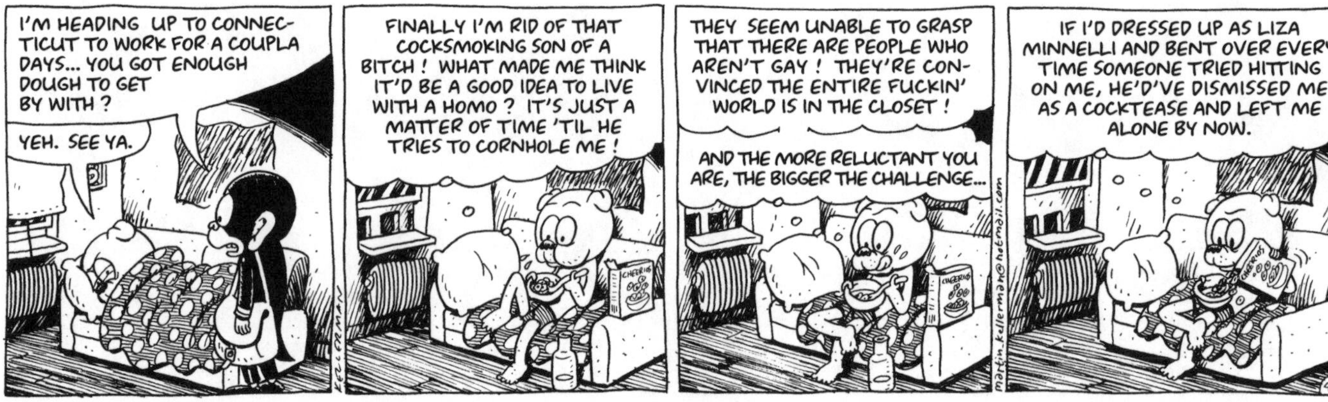
I'M HEADING UP TO CONNECTICUT TO WORK FOR A COUPLA DAYS... YOU GOT ENOUGH DOUGH TO GET BY WITH ?
YEH. SEE YA.
KELLERMAN
FINALLY I'M RID OF THAT COCKSMOKING SON OF A BITCH ! WHAT MADE ME THINK IT'D BE A GOOD IDEA TO LIVE WITH A HOMO ? IT'S JUST A MATTER OF TIME 'TIL HE TRIES TO CORNHOLE ME !
THEY SEEM UNABLE TO GRASP THAT THERE ARE PEOPLE WHO AREN'T GAY ! THEY'RE CONVINCED THE ENTIRE FUCKIN' WORLD IS IN THE CLOSET !
AND THE MORE RELUCTANT YOU ARE, THE BIGGER THE CHALLENGE...
martin_kellerman@hotmail.com
IF I'D DRESSED UP AS LIZA MINNELLI AND BENT OVER EVERY TIME SOMEONE TRIED HITTING ON ME, HE'D'VE DISMISSED ME AS A COCKTEASE AND LEFT ME ALONE BY NOW.
45

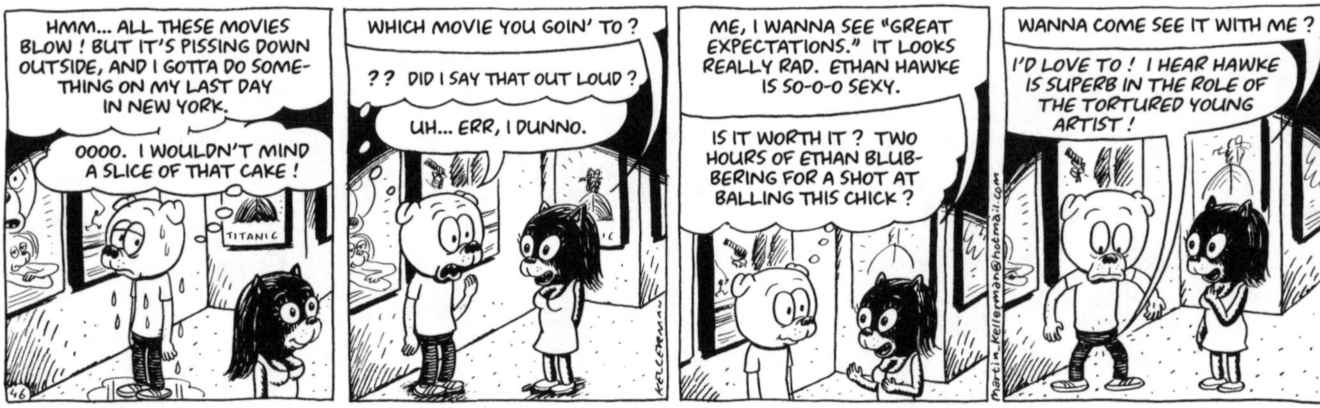
HMM... ALL THESE MOVIES BLOW ! BUT IT'S PISSING DOWN OUTSIDE, AND I GOTTA DO SOMETHING ON MY LAST DAY IN NEW YORK.
OOOO. I WOULDN'T MIND A SLICE OF THAT CAKE !
TITANIC
46
WHICH MOVIE YOU GOIN' TO ?
?? DID I SAY THAT OUT LOUD ?
UH... ERR, I DUNNO.
KELLERMAN
ME, I WANNA SEE "GREAT EXPECTATIONS." IT LOOKS REALLY RAD. ETHAN HAWKE IS SO-O-O SEXY.
IS IT WORTH IT ? TWO HOURS OF ETHAN BLUBBERING FOR A SHOT AT BALLING THIS CHICK ?
martin_kellerman@hotmail.com
WANNA COME SEE IT WITH ME ?
I'D LOVE TO ! I HEAR HAWKE IS SUPERB IN THE ROLE OF THE TORTURED YOUNG ARTIST !

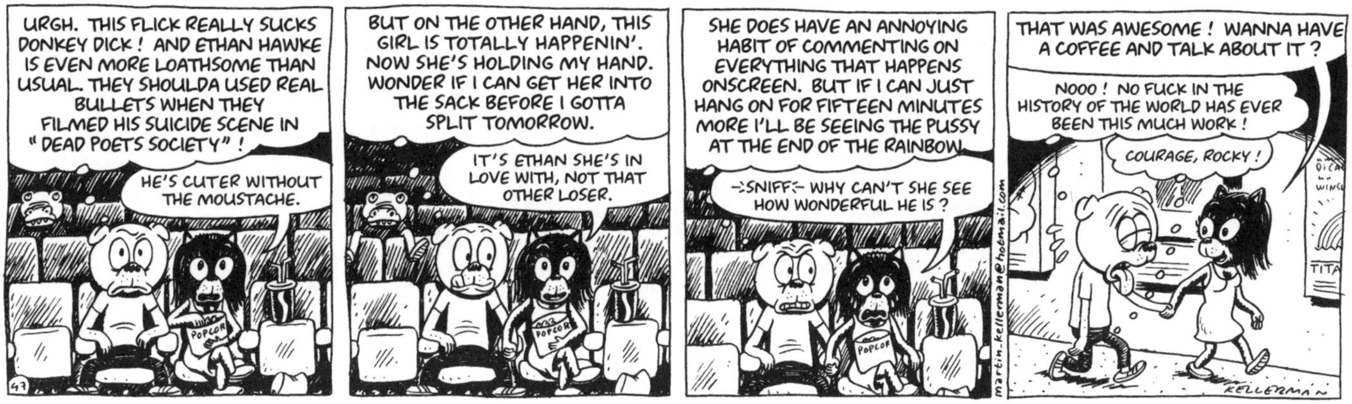
47
URGH. THIS FLICK REALLY SUCKS DONKEY DICK! AND ETHAN HAWKE IS EVEN MORE LOATHSOME THAN USUAL. THEY SHOULDA USED REAL BULLETS WHEN THEY FILMED HIS SUICIDE SCENE IN "DEAD POETS SOCIETY"!
HE'S CUTER WITHOUT THE MOUSTACHE.
BUT ON THE OTHER HAND, THIS GIRL IS TOTALLY HAPPENIN'. NOW SHE'S HOLDING MY HAND. WONDER IF I CAN GET HER INTO THE SACK BEFORE I GOTTA SPLIT TOMORROW.
IT'S ETHAN SHE'S IN LOVE WITH, NOT THAT OTHER LOSER.
SHE DOES HAVE AN ANNOYING HABIT OF COMMENTING ON EVERYTHING THAT HAPPENS ONSCREEN. BUT IF I CAN JUST HANG ON FOR FIFTEEN MINUTES MORE I'LL BE SEEING THE PUSSY AT THE END OF THE RAINBOW.
-SNIFF- WHY CAN'T SHE SEE HOW WONDERFUL HE IS?
martin.kellerman@hotmail.com
THAT WAS AWESOME! WANNA HAVE A COFFEE AND TALK ABOUT IT?
NOOO! NO FUCK IN THE HISTORY OF THE WORLD HAS EVER BEEN THIS MUCH WORK!
COURAGE, ROCKY!
KELLERMAN

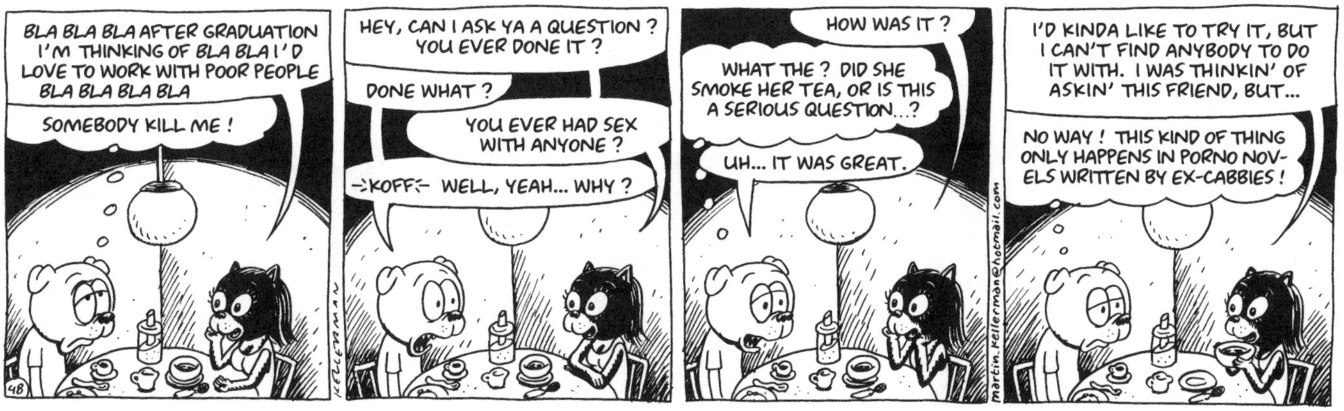
48
BLA BLA BLA AFTER GRADUATION I'M THINKING OF BLA BLA I'D LOVE TO WORK WITH POOR PEOPLE BLA BLA BLA BLA
SOMEBODY KILL ME!
KELLERMAN
HEY, CAN I ASK YA A QUESTION? YOU EVER DONE IT?
DONE WHAT?
YOU EVER HAD SEX WITH ANYONE?
-KOFF- WELL, YEAH... WHY?
HOW WAS IT?
WHAT THE? DID SHE SMOKE HER TEA, OR IS THIS A SERIOUS QUESTION...?
UH... IT WAS GREAT.
martin.kellerman@hotmail.com
I'D KINDA LIKE TO TRY IT, BUT I CAN'T FIND ANYBODY TO DO IT WITH. I WAS THINKIN' OF ASKIN' THIS FRIEND, BUT...
NO WAY! THIS KIND OF THING ONLY HAPPENS IN PORNO NOVELS WRITTEN BY EX-CABBIES!

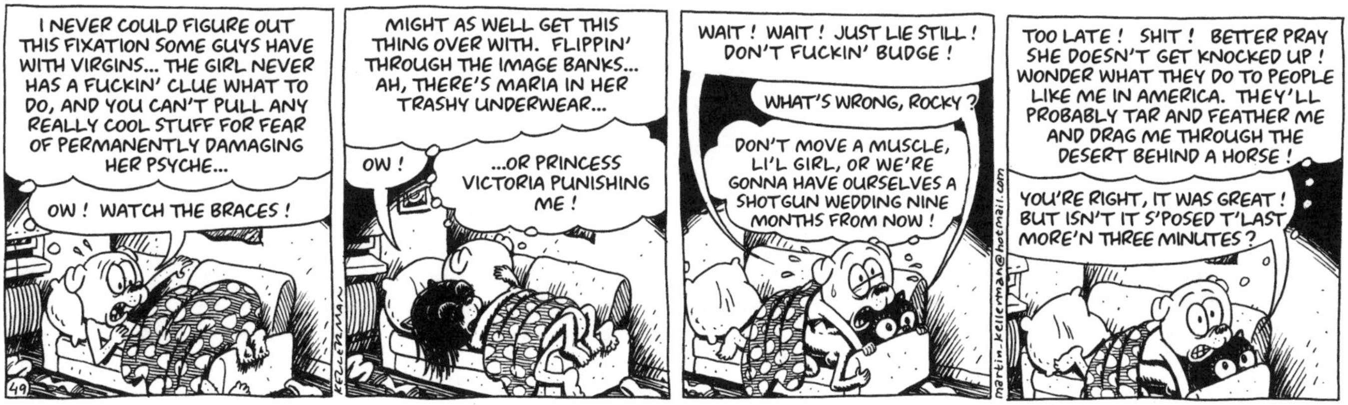
49
I NEVER COULD FIGURE OUT THIS FIXATION SOME GUYS HAVE WITH VIRGINS... THE GIRL NEVER HAS A FUCKIN' CLUE WHAT TO DO, AND YOU CAN'T PULL ANY REALLY COOL STUFF FOR FEAR OF PERMANENTLY DAMAGING HER PSYCHE...
OW! WATCH THE BRACES!
KELLERMAN
MIGHT AS WELL GET THIS THING OVER WITH. FLIPPIN' THROUGH THE IMAGE BANKS... AH, THERE'S MARIA IN HER TRASHY UNDERWEAR...
OW!
...OR PRINCESS VICTORIA PUNISHING ME!
WAIT! WAIT! JUST LIE STILL! DON'T FUCKIN' BUDGE!
WHAT'S WRONG, ROCKY?
DON'T MOVE A MUSCLE, LI'L GIRL, OR WE'RE GONNA HAVE OURSELVES A SHOTGUN WEDDING NINE MONTHS FROM NOW!
martin.kellerman@hotmail.com
TOO LATE! SHIT! BETTER PRAY SHE DOESN'T GET KNOCKED UP! WONDER WHAT THEY DO TO PEOPLE LIKE ME IN AMERICA. THEY'LL PROBABLY TAR AND FEATHER ME AND DRAG ME THROUGH THE DESERT BEHIND A HORSE!
YOU'RE RIGHT, IT WAS GREAT! BUT ISN'T IT S'POSED T'LAST MORE'N THREE MINUTES?

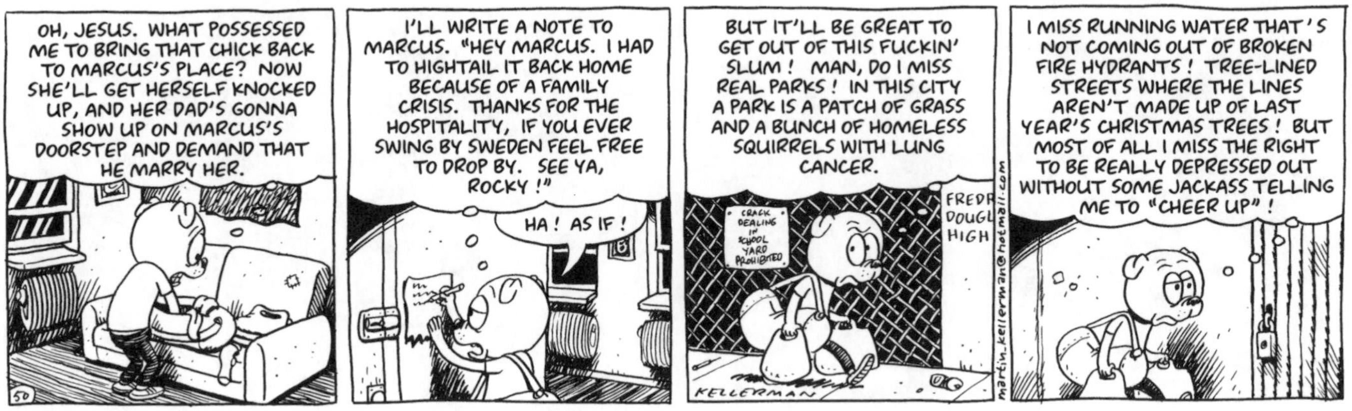
50
OH, JESUS. WHAT POSSESSED ME TO BRING THAT CHICK BACK TO MARCUS'S PLACE? NOW SHE'LL GET HERSELF KNOCKED UP, AND HER DAD'S GONNA SHOW UP ON MARCUS'S DOORSTEP AND DEMAND THAT HE MARRY HER.
I'LL WRITE A NOTE TO MARCUS. "HEY MARCUS. I HAD TO HIGHTAIL IT BACK HOME BECAUSE OF A FAMILY CRISIS. THANKS FOR THE HOSPITALITY, IF YOU EVER SWING BY SWEDEN FEEL FREE TO DROP BY. SEE YA, ROCKY !"
HA ! AS IF !
BUT IT'LL BE GREAT TO GET OUT OF THIS FUCKIN' SLUM ! MAN, DO I MISS REAL PARKS ! IN THIS CITY A PARK IS A PATCH OF GRASS AND A BUNCH OF HOMELESS SQUIRRELS WITH LUNG CANCER.
CRACK DEALING IN SCHOOL YARD PROHIBITED
FREDR DOUGL HIGH
KELLERMAN
martin_kellerman@hotmail.com
I MISS RUNNING WATER THAT'S NOT COMING OUT OF BROKEN FIRE HYDRANTS ! TREE-LINED STREETS WHERE THE LINES AREN'T MADE UP OF LAST YEAR'S CHRISTMAS TREES ! BUT MOST OF ALL I MISS THE RIGHT TO BE REALLY DEPRESSED OUT WITHOUT SOME JACKASS TELLING ME TO "CHEER UP" !

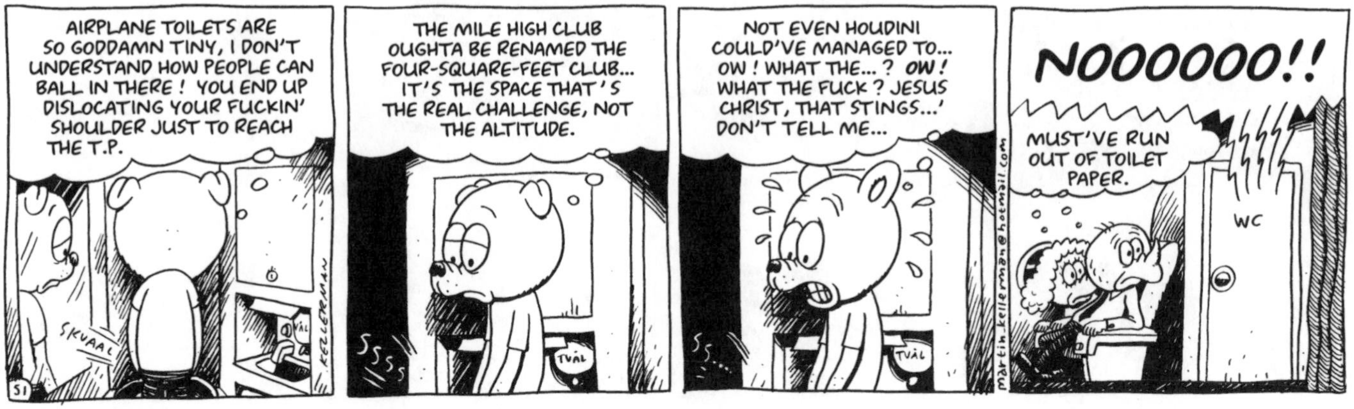
51
AIRPLANE TOILETS ARE SO GODDAMN TINY, I DON'T UNDERSTAND HOW PEOPLE CAN BALL IN THERE ! YOU END UP DISLOCATING YOUR FUCKIN' SHOULDER JUST TO REACH THE T.P.
SKVAAL
KELLERMAN
THE MILE HIGH CLUB OUGHTA BE RENAMED THE FOUR-SQUARE-FEET CLUB... IT'S THE SPACE THAT'S THE REAL CHALLENGE, NOT THE ALTITUDE.
SSSS
TVÅL
NOT EVEN HOUDINI COULD'VE MANAGED TO... OW ! WHAT THE... ? OW ! WHAT THE FUCK ? JESUS CHRIST, THAT STINGS...' DON'T TELL ME...
SS...
TVÅL
martin_kellerman@hotmail.com
NOOOOOO!!
MUST'VE RUN OUT OF TOILET PAPER.
WC

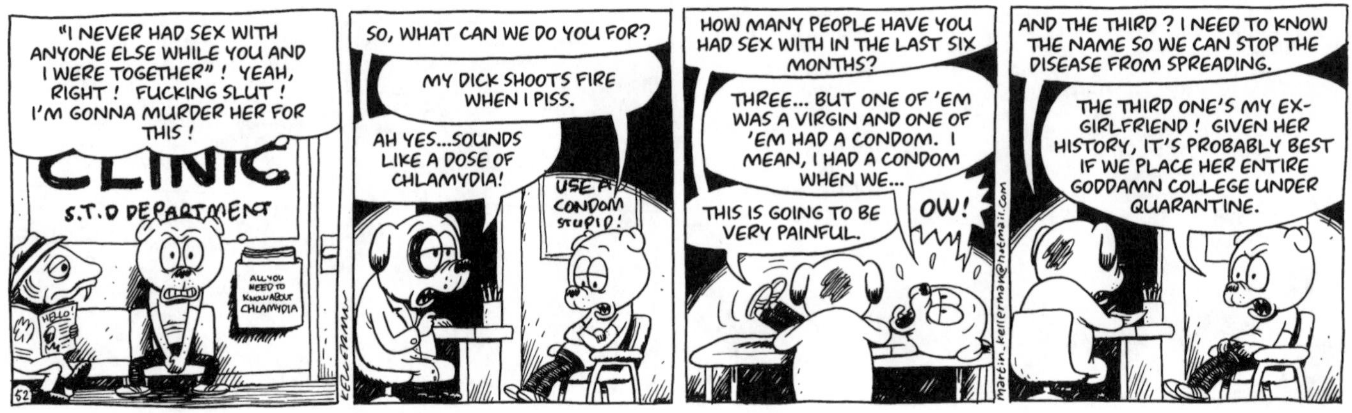
52
"I NEVER HAD SEX WITH ANYONE ELSE WHILE YOU AND I WERE TOGETHER" ! YEAH, RIGHT ! FUCKING SLUT ! I'M GONNA MURDER HER FOR THIS !
CLINIC
S.T.D DEPARTMENT
HELLO!
ALL YOU NEED TO KNOW ABOUT CHLAMYDIA
KELLERMAN
SO, WHAT CAN WE DO YOU FOR?
MY DICK SHOOTS FIRE WHEN I PISS.
AH YES...SOUNDS LIKE A DOSE OF CHLAMYDIA!
USE A CONDOM STUPID!
HOW MANY PEOPLE HAVE YOU HAD SEX WITH IN THE LAST SIX MONTHS?
THREE... BUT ONE OF 'EM WAS A VIRGIN AND ONE OF 'EM HAD A CONDOM. I MEAN, I HAD A CONDOM WHEN WE...
THIS IS GOING TO BE VERY PAINFUL.
OW!
martin_kellerman@hotmail.com
AND THE THIRD ? I NEED TO KNOW THE NAME SO WE CAN STOP THE DISEASE FROM SPREADING.
THE THIRD ONE'S MY EX-GIRLFRIEND ! GIVEN HER HISTORY, IT'S PROBABLY BEST IF WE PLACE HER ENTIRE GODDAMN COLLEGE UNDER QUARANTINE.

ON THE REBOUND

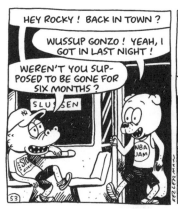

HEY ROCKY ! BACK IN TOWN ?
WUSSUP GONZO ! YEAH, I GOT IN LAST NIGHT !
WEREN'T YOU SUPPOSED TO BE GONE FOR SIX MONTHS ?
SLU SEN
NBA JAM
53
KELLERMAN
THAT WAS THE PLAN, MAN. BUT I GOT SACKED WHILE I WAS OVER THERE, AND I RAN OUT OF DOUGH. BUT THAT'S OK, I'D RATHER SPEND THE SUMMER IN STOCKHOLM.
YEAH, RIGHT. WHATEVER !
WHAT'RE YOU UP TO NOW ?
I'M HEADING DOWNTOWN, PLAY ME SOME BASKETBALL. WANNA COME ALONG ?
NAH, YOU GUYS SUCK.
ZINKENSDAMM
martin_kellerman@hotmail.com
BUT WE'RE IN TRAINING ! AND WE'LL GO SWIMMING AFTERWARD ! C'MON, HANG OUT WITH US!
THERE'LL BE GIRLS THERE !
BEER, TOO !
I'LL GIVE YA 20 KRONER !
FUNNY THING IS, NEXT WINTER I'LL REMEMBER THIS AS A COOL SUMMER OF SPONTANEOUS FUN !

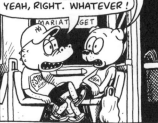

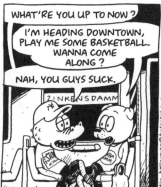

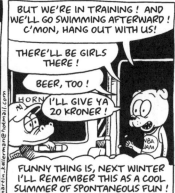

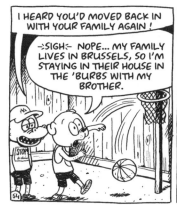

I HEARD YOU'D MOVED BACK IN WITH YOUR FAMILY AGAIN !
-SIGH- NOPE... MY FAMILY LIVES IN BRUSSELS, SO I'M STAYING IN THEIR HOUSE IN THE 'BURBS WITH MY BROTHER.
54
YOU GUYS GETTING ALONG OKAY ?
WHAT CAN I SAY ? WE'RE BROTHERS, SO IT'S ABOUT THE SAME AS IT WAS WHEN WE WERE LITTLE. I BOSS HIM AROUND 'TIL HE GETS FED UP AND BEATS THE SHIT OUTA ME.
WHEN'RE YOU GETTING YOUR OWN PLACE ?
FIRST I NEED TO GET MYSELF A NEW JOB ! OOOF !
martin_kellerman@hotmail.com
WON'T IT BE AWKWARD BRINGING GIRLS HOME, THEN ?
GONZO, IT'S ENOUGH OF A CHALLENGE TO FIND GIRLS WHO THINK GUYS WHO'VE MOVED BACK WITH THEIR PARENTS ARE SEXY.
FOPP
KELLERMAN

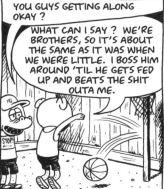

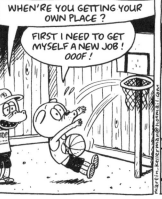

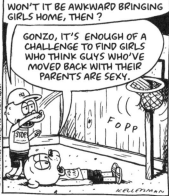

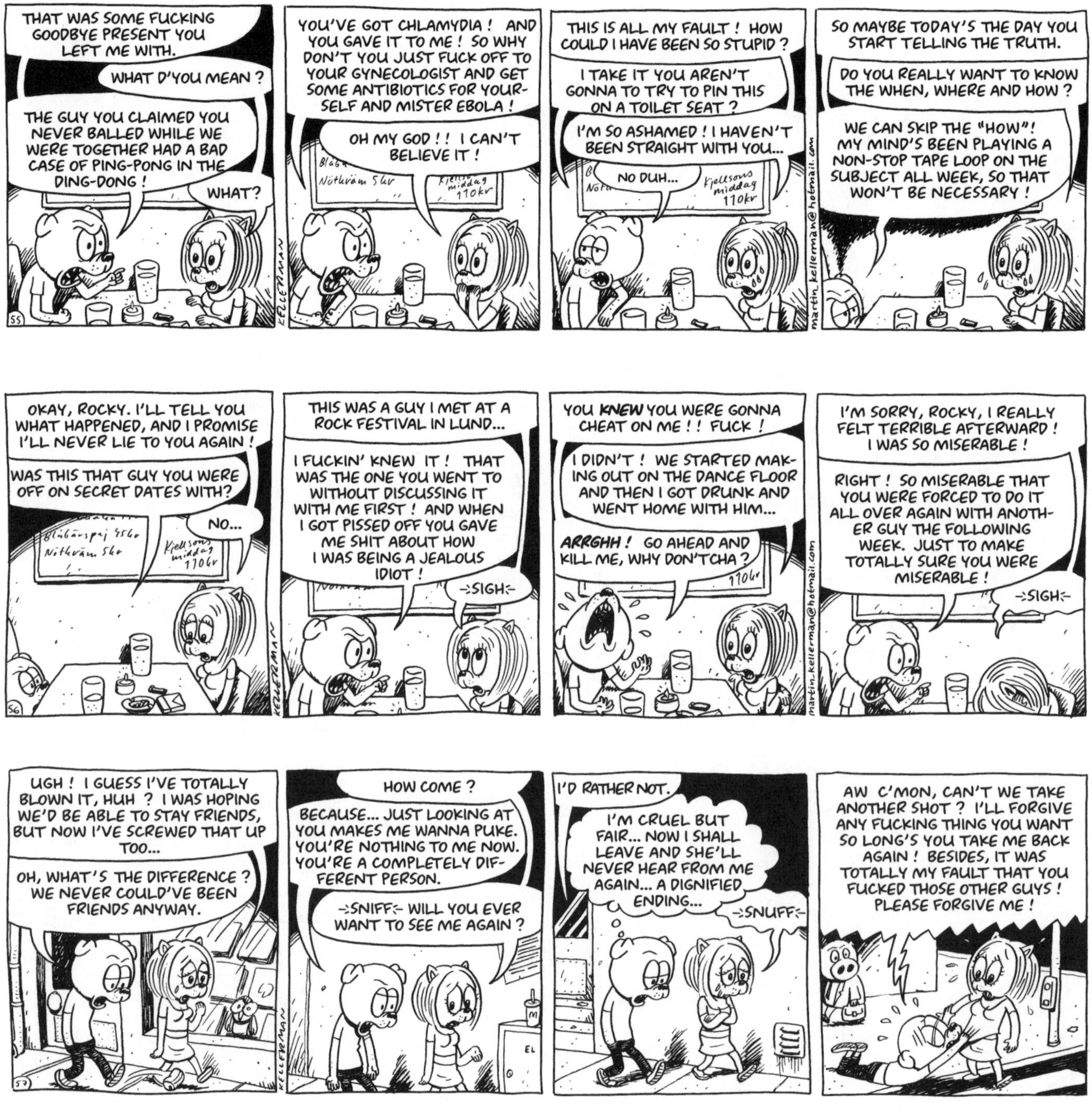
THAT WAS SOME FUCKING GOODBYE PRESENT YOU LEFT ME WITH.
WHAT D'YOU MEAN ?
THE GUY YOU CLAIMED YOU NEVER BALLED WHILE WE WERE TOGETHER HAD A BAD CASE OF PING-PONG IN THE DING-DONG !
WHAT?
KELLERMAN
YOU'VE GOT CHLAMYDIA ! AND YOU GAVE IT TO ME ! SO WHY DON'T YOU JUST FUCK OFF TO YOUR GYNECOLOGIST AND GET SOME ANTIBIOTICS FOR YOURSELF AND MISTER EBOLA !
OH MY GOD ! ! I CAN'T BELIEVE IT !
THIS IS ALL MY FAULT ! HOW COULD I HAVE BEEN SO STUPID ?
I TAKE IT YOU AREN'T GONNA TO TRY TO PIN THIS ON A TOILET SEAT ?
I'M SO ASHAMED ! I HAVEN'T BEEN STRAIGHT WITH YOU...
NO DUH...
martin_kellerman@hotmail.com
SO MAYBE TODAY'S THE DAY YOU START TELLING THE TRUTH.
DO YOU REALLY WANT TO KNOW THE WHEN, WHERE AND HOW ?
WE CAN SKIP THE "HOW"! MY MIND'S BEEN PLAYING A NON-STOP TAPE LOOP ON THE SUBJECT ALL WEEK, SO THAT WON'T BE NECESSARY !
OKAY, ROCKY. I'LL TELL YOU WHAT HAPPENED, AND I PROMISE I'LL NEVER LIE TO YOU AGAIN !
WAS THIS THAT GUY YOU WERE OFF ON SECRET DATES WITH?
NO...
KELLERMAN
THIS WAS A GUY I MET AT A ROCK FESTIVAL IN LUND...
I FUCKIN' KNEW IT ! THAT WAS THE ONE YOU WENT TO WITHOUT DISCUSSING IT WITH ME FIRST ! AND WHEN I GOT PISSED OFF YOU GAVE ME SHIT ABOUT HOW I WAS BEING A JEALOUS IDIOT !
SIGH
YOU KNEW YOU WERE GONNA CHEAT ON ME ! ! FUCK !
I DIDN'T ! WE STARTED MAKING OUT ON THE DANCE FLOOR AND THEN I GOT DRUNK AND WENT HOME WITH HIM...
ARRGHH ! GO AHEAD AND KILL ME, WHY DON'TCHA ?
martin_kellerman@hotmail.com
I'M SORRY, ROCKY, I REALLY FELT TERRIBLE AFTERWARD ! I WAS SO MISERABLE !
RIGHT ! SO MISERABLE THAT YOU WERE FORCED TO DO IT ALL OVER AGAIN WITH ANOTHER GUY THE FOLLOWING WEEK. JUST TO MAKE TOTALLY SURE YOU WERE MISERABLE !
SIGH
UGH ! I GUESS I'VE TOTALLY BLOWN IT, HUH ? I WAS HOPING WE'D BE ABLE TO STAY FRIENDS, BUT NOW I'VE SCREWED THAT UP TOO...
OH, WHAT'S THE DIFFERENCE ? WE NEVER COULD'VE BEEN FRIENDS ANYWAY.
KELLERMAN
HOW COME ?
BECAUSE... JUST LOOKING AT YOU MAKES ME WANNA PUKE. YOU'RE NOTHING TO ME NOW. YOU'RE A COMPLETELY DIFFERENT PERSON.
SNIFF WILL YOU EVER WANT TO SEE ME AGAIN ?
I'D RATHER NOT.
I'M CRUEL BUT FAIR... NOW I SHALL LEAVE AND SHE'LL NEVER HEAR FROM ME AGAIN... A DIGNIFIED ENDING...
SNUFF
AW C'MON, CAN'T WE TAKE ANOTHER SHOT ? I'LL FORGIVE ANY FUCKING THING YOU WANT SO LONG'S YOU TAKE ME BACK AGAIN ! BESIDES, IT WAS TOTALLY MY FAULT THAT YOU FUCKED THOSE OTHER GUYS ! PLEASE FORGIVE ME !

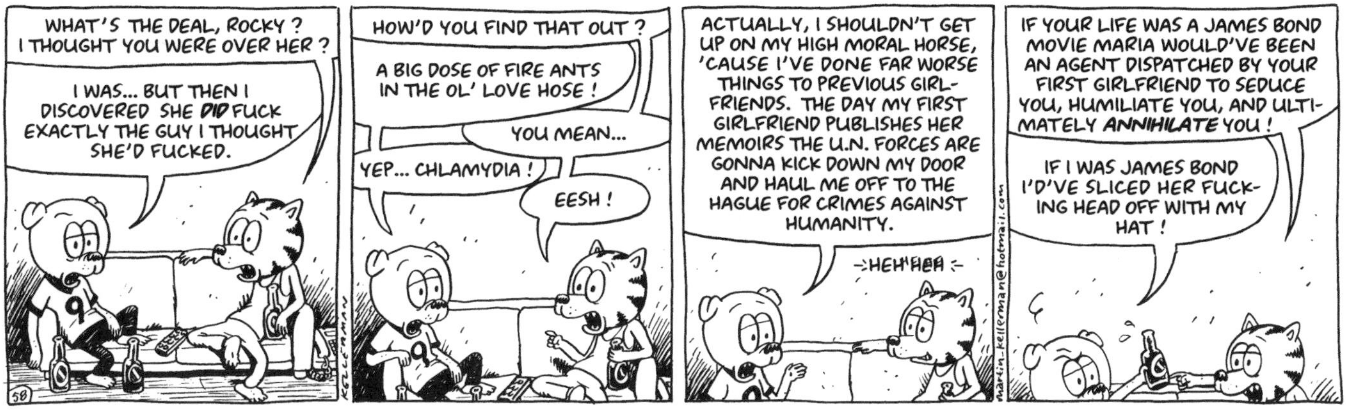
WHAT'S THE DEAL, ROCKY ? I THOUGHT YOU WERE OVER HER ?
I WAS... BUT THEN I DISCOVERED SHE DID FUCK EXACTLY THE GUY I THOUGHT SHE'D FUCKED.
58
KELLERMAN
HOW'D YOU FIND THAT OUT ?
A BIG DOSE OF FIRE ANTS IN THE OL' LOVE HOSE !
YOU MEAN...
YEP... CHLAMYDIA !
EESH !
ACTUALLY, I SHOULDN'T GET UP ON MY HIGH MORAL HORSE, 'CAUSE I'VE DONE FAR WORSE THINGS TO PREVIOUS GIRL-FRIENDS. THE DAY MY FIRST GIRLFRIEND PUBLISHES HER MEMOIRS THE U.N. FORCES ARE GONNA KICK DOWN MY DOOR AND HAUL ME OFF TO THE HAGUE FOR CRIMES AGAINST HUMANITY.
HEH HEH
martin_kellerman@hotmail.com
IF YOUR LIFE WAS A JAMES BOND MOVIE MARIA WOULD'VE BEEN AN AGENT DISPATCHED BY YOUR FIRST GIRLFRIEND TO SEDUCE YOU, HUMILIATE YOU, AND ULTIMATELY ANNIHILATE YOU !
IF I WAS JAMES BOND I'D'VE SLICED HER FUCKING HEAD OFF WITH MY HAT !

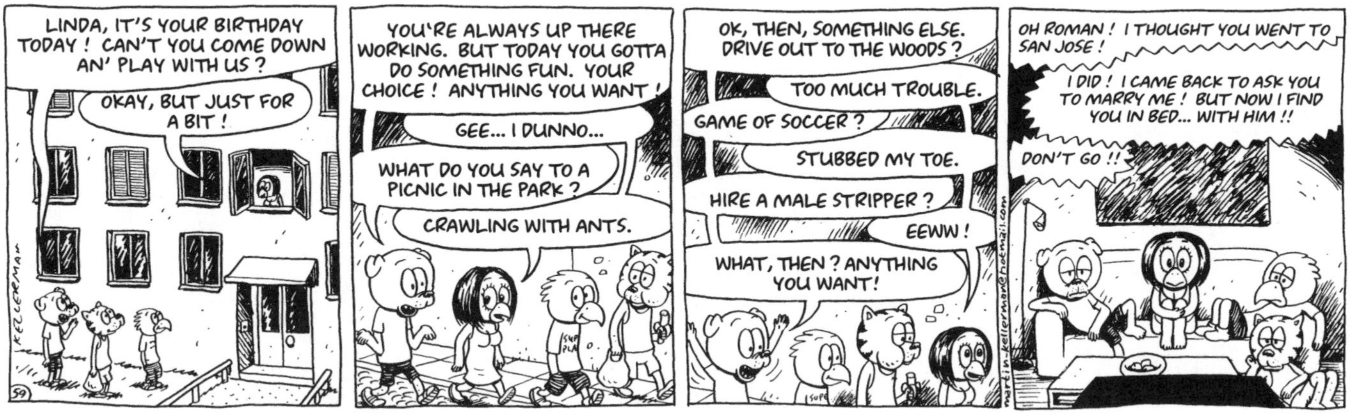
LINDA, IT'S YOUR BIRTHDAY TODAY ! CAN'T YOU COME DOWN AN' PLAY WITH US ?
OKAY, BUT JUST FOR A BIT !
KELLERMAN
59
YOU'RE ALWAYS UP THERE WORKING. BUT TODAY YOU GOTTA DO SOMETHING FUN. YOUR CHOICE ! ANYTHING YOU WANT !
GEE... I DUNNO...
WHAT DO YOU SAY TO A PICNIC IN THE PARK ?
CRAWLING WITH ANTS.
OK, THEN, SOMETHING ELSE. DRIVE OUT TO THE WOODS ?
TOO MUCH TROUBLE.
GAME OF SOCCER ?
STUBBED MY TOE.
HIRE A MALE STRIPPER ?
EEWW !
WHAT, THEN ? ANYTHING YOU WANT!
martin_kellerman@hotmail.com
OH ROMAN ! I THOUGHT YOU WENT TO SAN JOSE !
I DID ! I CAME BACK TO ASK YOU TO MARRY ME ! BUT NOW I FIND YOU IN BED... WITH HIM !!
DON'T GO !!

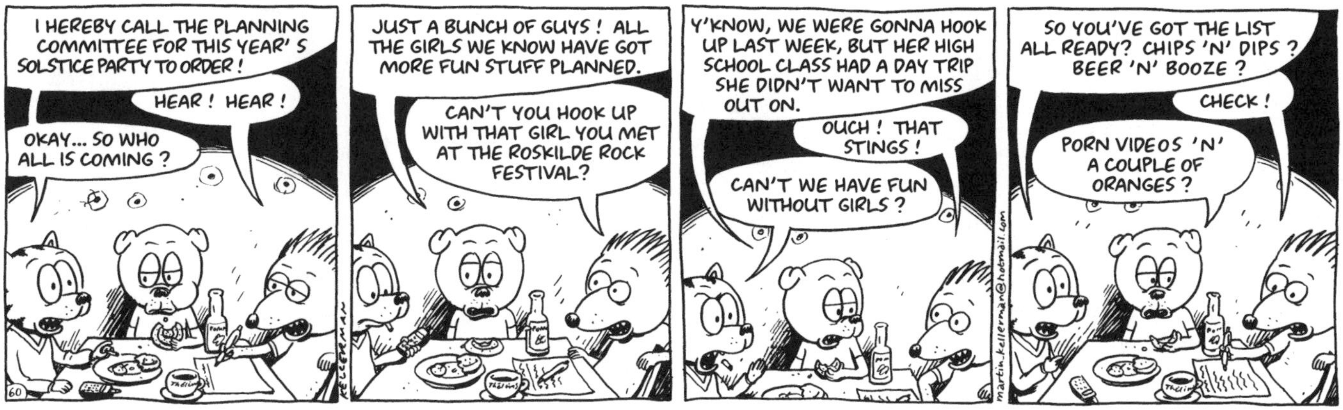
I HEREBY CALL THE PLANNING COMMITTEE FOR THIS YEAR'S SOLSTICE PARTY TO ORDER !
HEAR ! HEAR !
OKAY... SO WHO ALL IS COMING ?
60
KELLERMAN
JUST A BUNCH OF GUYS ! ALL THE GIRLS WE KNOW HAVE GOT MORE FUN STUFF PLANNED.
CAN'T YOU HOOK UP WITH THAT GIRL YOU MET AT THE ROSKILDE ROCK FESTIVAL?
Y'KNOW, WE WERE GONNA HOOK UP LAST WEEK, BUT HER HIGH SCHOOL CLASS HAD A DAY TRIP SHE DIDN'T WANT TO MISS OUT ON.
OUCH ! THAT STINGS !
CAN'T WE HAVE FUN WITHOUT GIRLS ?
martin_kellerman@hotmail.com
SO YOU'VE GOT THE LIST ALL READY? CHIPS 'N' DIPS ? BEER 'N' BOOZE ?
CHECK !
PORN VIDEOS 'N' A COUPLE OF ORANGES ?

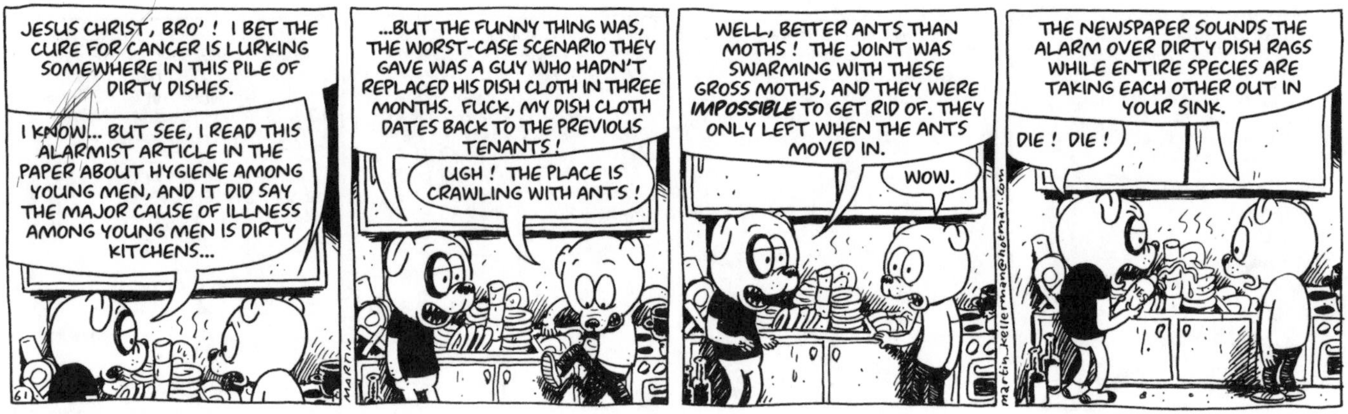
61
JESUS CHRIST, BRO' ! I BET THE CURE FOR CANCER IS LURKING SOMEWHERE IN THIS PILE OF DIRTY DISHES.
I KNOW... BUT SEE, I READ THIS ALARMIST ARTICLE IN THE PAPER ABOUT HYGIENE AMONG YOUNG MEN, AND IT DID SAY THE MAJOR CAUSE OF ILLNESS AMONG YOUNG MEN IS DIRTY KITCHENS...
MARTIN
...BUT THE FUNNY THING WAS, THE WORST-CASE SCENARIO THEY GAVE WAS A GUY WHO HADN'T REPLACED HIS DISH CLOTH IN THREE MONTHS. FUCK, MY DISH CLOTH DATES BACK TO THE PREVIOUS TENANTS !
UGH ! THE PLACE IS CRAWLING WITH ANTS !
WELL, BETTER ANTS THAN MOTHS ! THE JOINT WAS SWARMING WITH THESE GROSS MOTHS, AND THEY WERE ***IMPOSSIBLE*** TO GET RID OF. THEY ONLY LEFT WHEN THE ANTS MOVED IN.
WOW.
martin_kellerman@hotmail.com
THE NEWSPAPER SOUNDS THE ALARM OVER DIRTY DISH RAGS WHILE ENTIRE SPECIES ARE TAKING EACH OTHER OUT IN YOUR SINK.
DIE ! DIE !

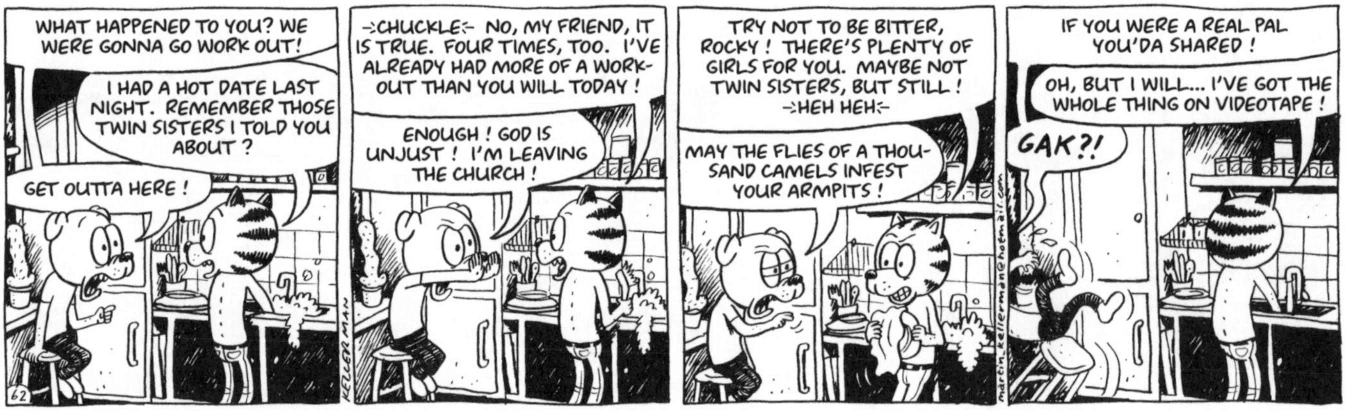
62
WHAT HAPPENED TO YOU? WE WERE GONNA GO WORK OUT!
I HAD A HOT DATE LAST NIGHT. REMEMBER THOSE TWIN SISTERS I TOLD YOU ABOUT ?
GET OUTTA HERE !
KELLERMAN
-CHUCKLE- NO, MY FRIEND, IT IS TRUE. FOUR TIMES, TOO. I'VE ALREADY HAD MORE OF A WORK-OUT THAN YOU WILL TODAY !
ENOUGH ! GOD IS UNJUST ! I'M LEAVING THE CHURCH !
TRY NOT TO BE BITTER, ROCKY ! THERE'S PLENTY OF GIRLS FOR YOU. MAYBE NOT TWIN SISTERS, BUT STILL ! -HEH HEH-
MAY THE FLIES OF A THOUSAND CAMELS INFEST YOUR ARMPITS !
martin_kellerman@hotmail.com
IF YOU WERE A REAL PAL YOU'DA SHARED !
OH, BUT I WILL... I'VE GOT THE WHOLE THING ON VIDEOTAPE !
GAK?!

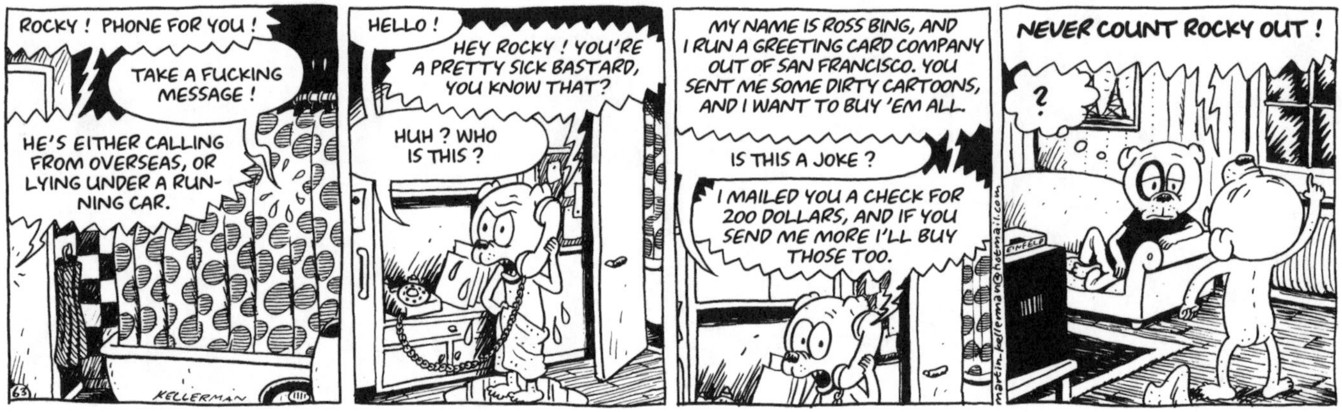
63
ROCKY ! PHONE FOR YOU !
TAKE A FUCKING MESSAGE !
HE'S EITHER CALLING FROM OVERSEAS, OR LYING UNDER A RUNNING CAR.
KELLERMAN
HELLO !
HEY ROCKY ! YOU'RE A PRETTY SICK BASTARD, YOU KNOW THAT?
HUH ? WHO IS THIS ?
MY NAME IS ROSS BING, AND I RUN A GREETING CARD COMPANY OUT OF SAN FRANCISCO. YOU SENT ME SOME DIRTY CARTOONS, AND I WANT TO BUY 'EM ALL.
IS THIS A JOKE ?
I MAILED YOU A CHECK FOR 200 DOLLARS, AND IF YOU SEND ME MORE I'LL BUY THOSE TOO.
martin_kellerman@hotmail.com
NEVER COUNT ROCKY OUT !
?

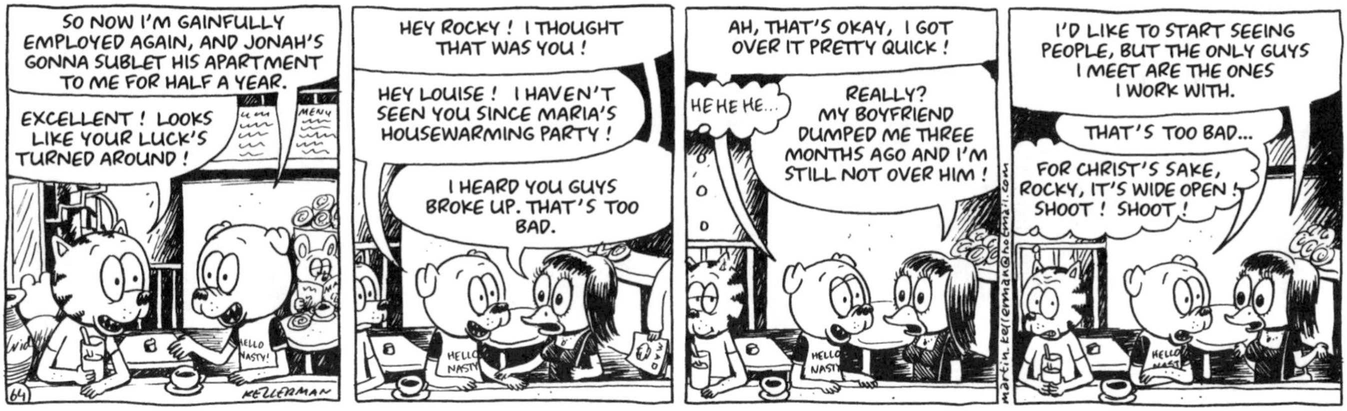
SO NOW I'M GAINFULLY EMPLOYED AGAIN, AND JONAH'S GONNA SUBLET HIS APARTMENT TO ME FOR HALF A YEAR.
EXCELLENT ! LOOKS LIKE YOUR LUCK'S TURNED AROUND !
HELLO NASTY!
64
KELLERMAN
HEY ROCKY ! I THOUGHT THAT WAS YOU !
HEY LOUISE ! I HAVEN'T SEEN YOU SINCE MARIA'S HOUSEWARMING PARTY !
I HEARD YOU GUYS BROKE UP. THAT'S TOO BAD.
AH, THAT'S OKAY, I GOT OVER IT PRETTY QUICK !
HE HE HE...
REALLY? MY BOYFRIEND DUMPED ME THREE MONTHS AGO AND I'M STILL NOT OVER HIM !
martin.kellerman@hotmail.com
I'D LIKE TO START SEEING PEOPLE, BUT THE ONLY GUYS I MEET ARE THE ONES I WORK WITH.
THAT'S TOO BAD...
FOR CHRIST'S SAKE, ROCKY, IT'S WIDE OPEN ! SHOOT ! SHOOT !

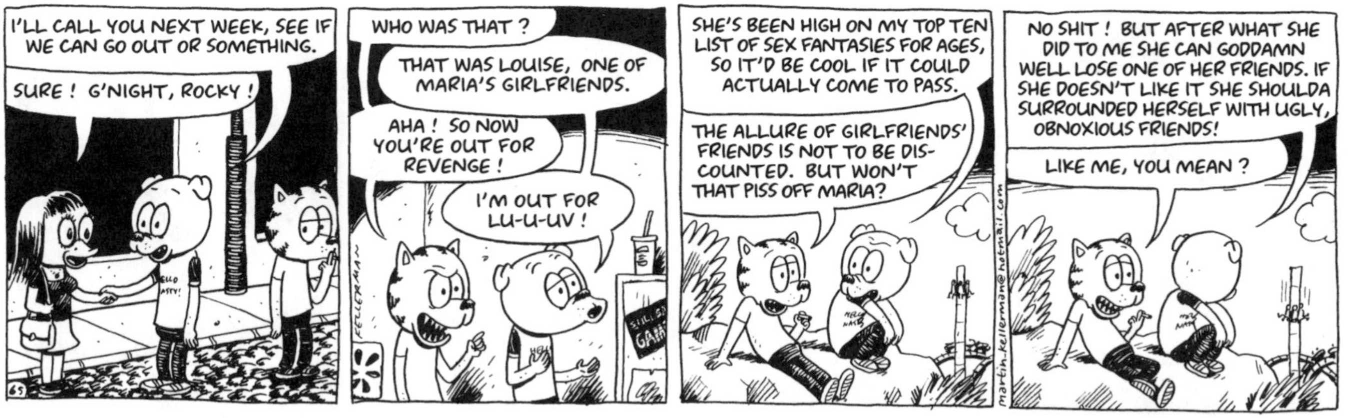
I'LL CALL YOU NEXT WEEK, SEE IF WE CAN GO OUT OR SOMETHING.
SURE ! G'NIGHT, ROCKY !
65
WHO WAS THAT ?
THAT WAS LOUISE, ONE OF MARIA'S GIRLFRIENDS.
AHA ! SO NOW YOU'RE OUT FOR REVENGE !
I'M OUT FOR LU-U-UV !
KELLERMAN
SHE'S BEEN HIGH ON MY TOP TEN LIST OF SEX FANTASIES FOR AGES, SO IT'D BE COOL IF IT COULD ACTUALLY COME TO PASS.
THE ALLURE OF GIRLFRIENDS' FRIENDS IS NOT TO BE DISCOUNTED. BUT WON'T THAT PISS OFF MARIA?
martin.kellerman@hotmail.com
NO SHIT ! BUT AFTER WHAT SHE DID TO ME SHE CAN GODDAMN WELL LOSE ONE OF HER FRIENDS. IF SHE DOESN'T LIKE IT SHE SHOULDA SURROUNDED HERSELF WITH UGLY, OBNOXIOUS FRIENDS!
LIKE ME, YOU MEAN ?

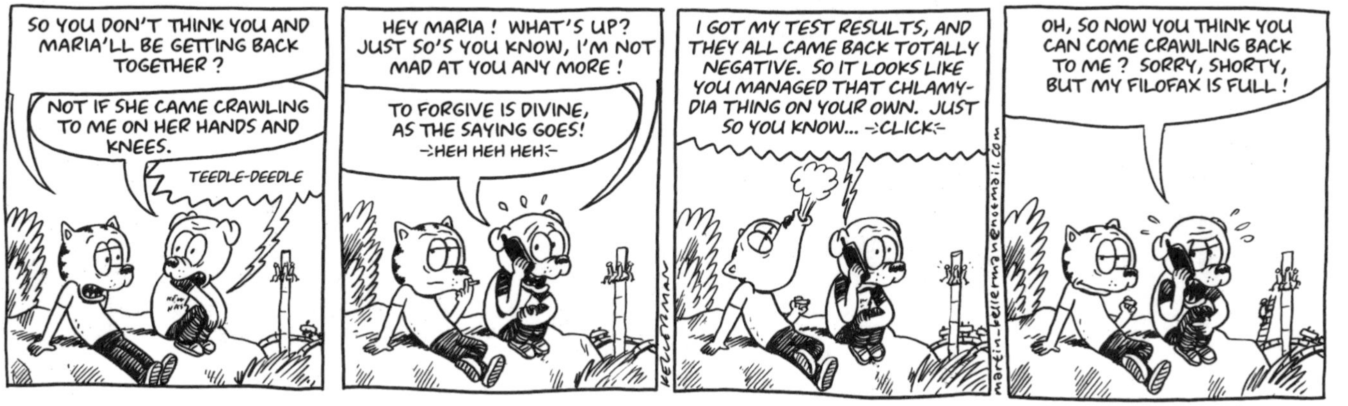
SO YOU DON'T THINK YOU AND MARIA'LL BE GETTING BACK TOGETHER ?
NOT IF SHE CAME CRAWLING TO ME ON HER HANDS AND KNEES.
TEEDLE-DEEDLE
HEY MARIA ! WHAT'S UP? JUST SO'S YOU KNOW, I'M NOT MAD AT YOU ANY MORE !
TO FORGIVE IS DIVINE, AS THE SAYING GOES! HEH HEH HEH
KELLERMAN
I GOT MY TEST RESULTS, AND THEY ALL CAME BACK TOTALLY NEGATIVE. SO IT LOOKS LIKE YOU MANAGED THAT CHLAMYDIA THING ON YOUR OWN. JUST SO YOU KNOW... CLICK
martin.kellerman@hotmail.com
OH, SO NOW YOU THINK YOU CAN COME CRAWLING BACK TO ME ? SORRY, SHORTY, BUT MY FILOFAX IS FULL !

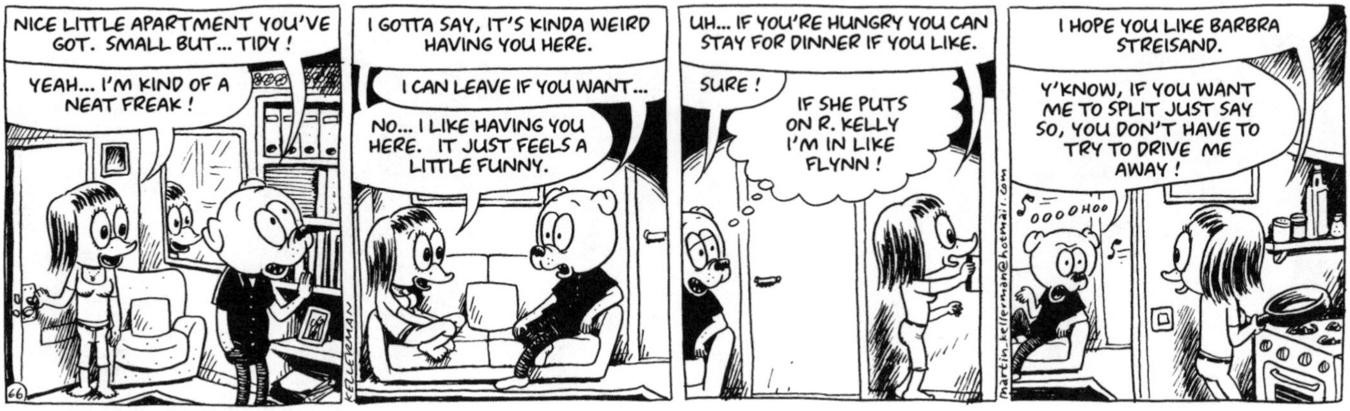
66
NICE LITTLE APARTMENT YOU'VE GOT. SMALL BUT... TIDY !
YEAH... I'M KIND OF A NEAT FREAK !
KELLERMAN
I GOTTA SAY, IT'S KINDA WEIRD HAVING YOU HERE.
I CAN LEAVE IF YOU WANT...
NO... I LIKE HAVING YOU HERE. IT JUST FEELS A LITTLE FUNNY.
UH... IF YOU'RE HUNGRY YOU CAN STAY FOR DINNER IF YOU LIKE.
SURE !
IF SHE PUTS ON R. KELLY I'M IN LIKE FLYNN !
martin.kellerman@hotmail.com
I HOPE YOU LIKE BARBRA STREISAND.
Y'KNOW, IF YOU WANT ME TO SPLIT JUST SAY SO, YOU DON'T HAVE TO TRY TO DRIVE ME AWAY !
OOOOHOO

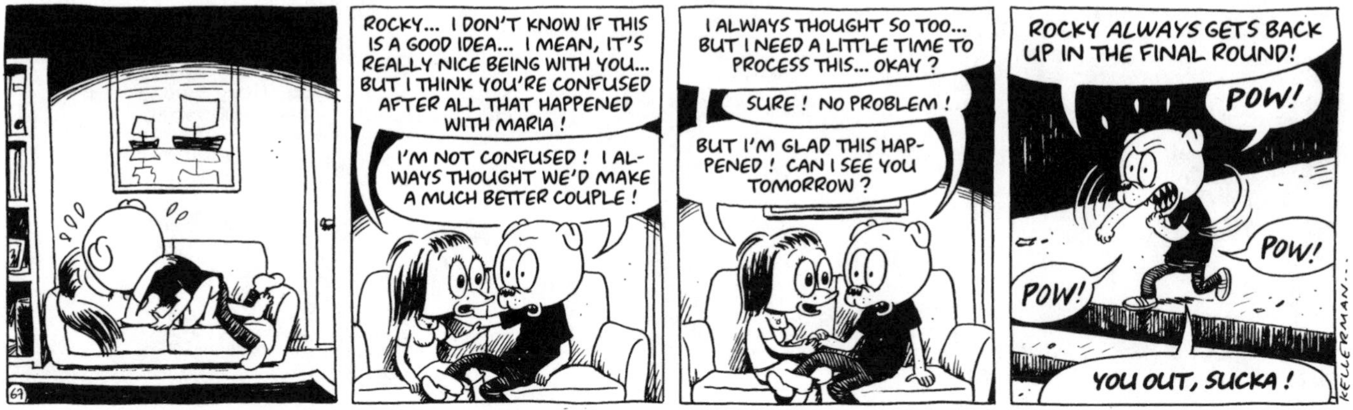
67
ROCKY... I DON'T KNOW IF THIS IS A GOOD IDEA... I MEAN, IT'S REALLY NICE BEING WITH YOU... BUT I THINK YOU'RE CONFUSED AFTER ALL THAT HAPPENED WITH MARIA !
I'M NOT CONFUSED ! I ALWAYS THOUGHT WE'D MAKE A MUCH BETTER COUPLE !
I ALWAYS THOUGHT SO TOO... BUT I NEED A LITTLE TIME TO PROCESS THIS... OKAY ?
SURE ! NO PROBLEM !
BUT I'M GLAD THIS HAPPENED ! CAN I SEE YOU TOMORROW ?
ROCKY ALWAYS GETS BACK UP IN THE FINAL ROUND!
POW!
POW!
POW!
YOU OUT, SUCKA !
KELLERMAN...

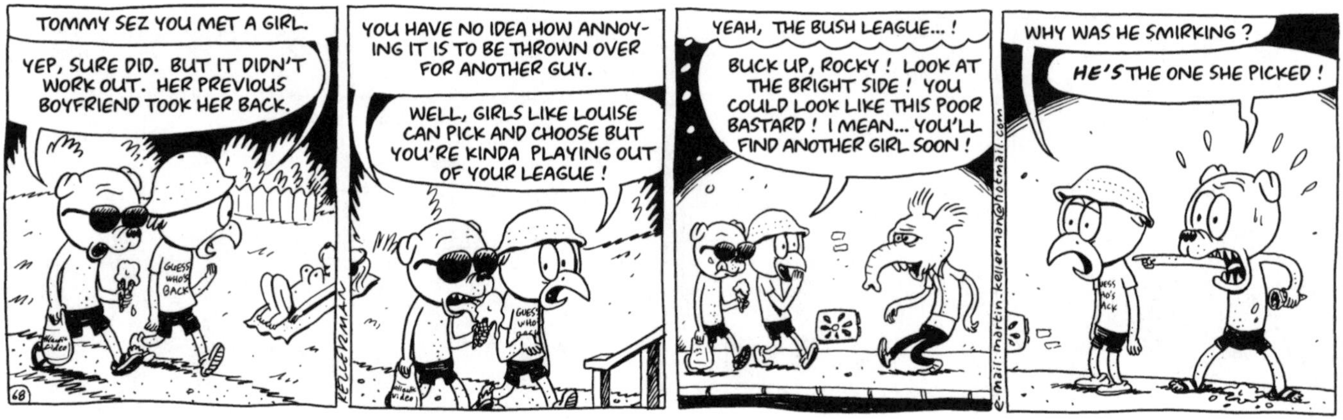
68
TOMMY SEZ YOU MET A GIRL.
YEP, SURE DID. BUT IT DIDN'T WORK OUT. HER PREVIOUS BOYFRIEND TOOK HER BACK.
GUESS WHO'S BACK
KELLERMAN
YOU HAVE NO IDEA HOW ANNOYING IT IS TO BE THROWN OVER FOR ANOTHER GUY.
WELL, GIRLS LIKE LOUISE CAN PICK AND CHOOSE BUT YOU'RE KINDA PLAYING OUT OF YOUR LEAGUE !
YEAH, THE BUSH LEAGUE... !
BUCK UP, ROCKY ! LOOK AT THE BRIGHT SIDE ! YOU COULD LOOK LIKE THIS POOR BASTARD ! I MEAN... YOU'LL FIND ANOTHER GIRL SOON !
e-mail: martin.kellerman@hotmail.com
WHY WAS HE SMIRKING ?
HE'S THE ONE SHE PICKED !

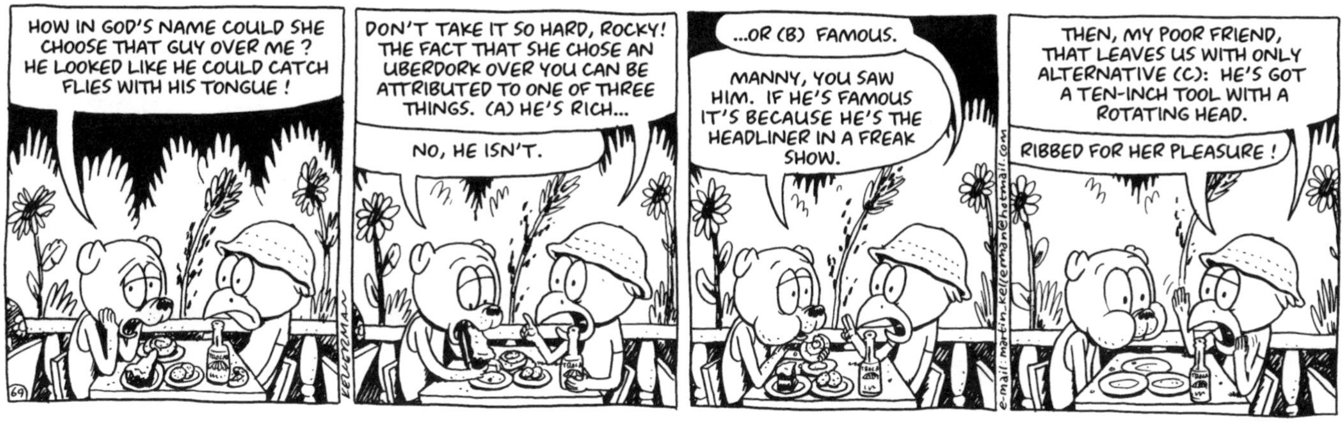
69
HOW IN GOD'S NAME COULD SHE CHOOSE THAT GUY OVER ME ? HE LOOKED LIKE HE COULD CATCH FLIES WITH HIS TONGUE !
KELLERMAN
DON'T TAKE IT SO HARD, ROCKY! THE FACT THAT SHE CHOSE AN UBERDORK OVER YOU CAN BE ATTRIBUTED TO ONE OF THREE THINGS. (A) HE'S RICH...
NO, HE ISN'T.
...OR (B) FAMOUS.
MANNY, YOU SAW HIM. IF HE'S FAMOUS IT'S BECAUSE HE'S THE HEADLINER IN A FREAK SHOW.
e-mail: martin_kellerman@hotmail.com
THEN, MY POOR FRIEND, THAT LEAVES US WITH ONLY ALTERNATIVE (C): HE'S GOT A TEN-INCH TOOL WITH A ROTATING HEAD.
RIBBED FOR HER PLEASURE !

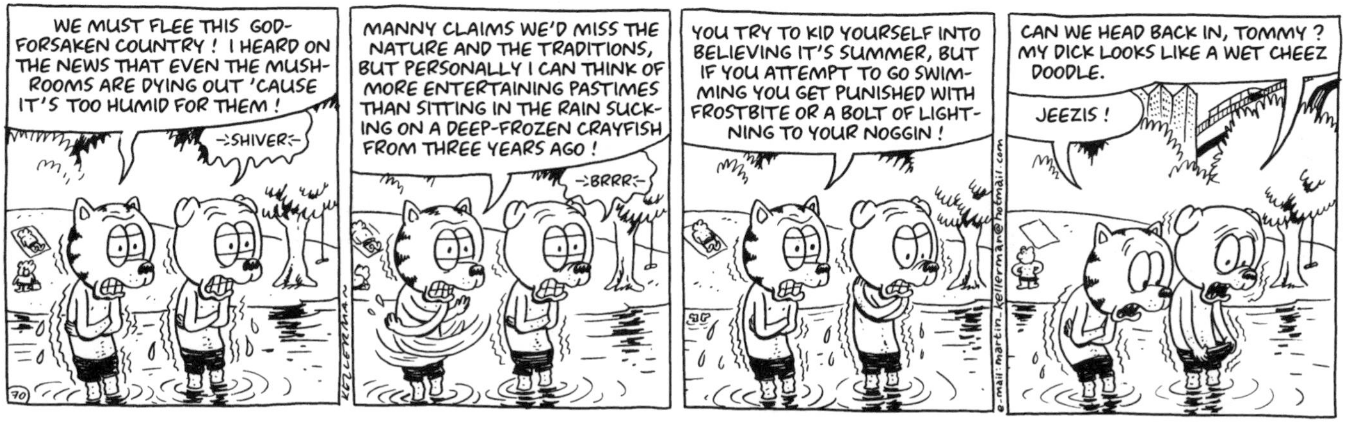
WE MUST FLEE THIS GOD-FORSAKEN COUNTRY ! I HEARD ON THE NEWS THAT EVEN THE MUSH-ROOMS ARE DYING OUT 'CAUSE IT'S TOO HUMID FOR THEM !
SHIVER
70
KELLERMAN
MANNY CLAIMS WE'D MISS THE NATURE AND THE TRADITIONS, BUT PERSONALLY I CAN THINK OF MORE ENTERTAINING PASTIMES THAN SITTING IN THE RAIN SUCK-ING ON A DEEP-FROZEN CRAYFISH FROM THREE YEARS AGO !
BRRR
YOU TRY TO KID YOURSELF INTO BELIEVING IT'S SUMMER, BUT IF YOU ATTEMPT TO GO SWIM-MING YOU GET PUNISHED WITH FROSTBITE OR A BOLT OF LIGHT-NING TO YOUR NOGGIN !
e-mail: martin_kellerman@hotmail.com
CAN WE HEAD BACK IN, TOMMY ? MY DICK LOOKS LIKE A WET CHEEZ DOODLE.
JEEZIS !

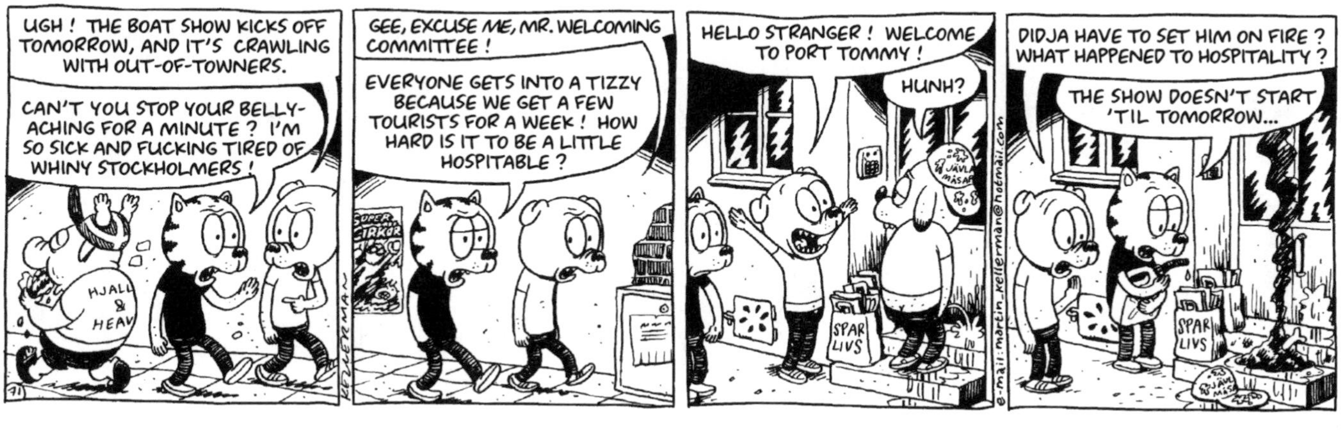
UGH ! THE BOAT SHOW KICKS OFF TOMORROW, AND IT'S CRAWLING WITH OUT-OF-TOWNERS.
CAN'T YOU STOP YOUR BELLY-ACHING FOR A MINUTE ? I'M SO SICK AND FUCKING TIRED OF WHINY STOCKHOLMERS !
71
KELLERMAN
GEE, EXCUSE ME, MR. WELCOMING COMMITTEE !
EVERYONE GETS INTO A TIZZY BECAUSE WE GET A FEW TOURISTS FOR A WEEK ! HOW HARD IS IT TO BE A LITTLE HOSPITABLE ?
HELLO STRANGER ! WELCOME TO PORT TOMMY !
HUNH?
SPAR LIVS
e-mail: martin_kellerman@hotmail.com
DIDJA HAVE TO SET HIM ON FIRE ? WHAT HAPPENED TO HOSPITALITY ?
THE SHOW DOESN'T START 'TIL TOMORROW...
SPAR LIVS

RABBIT GOES TO THE COUNTRY

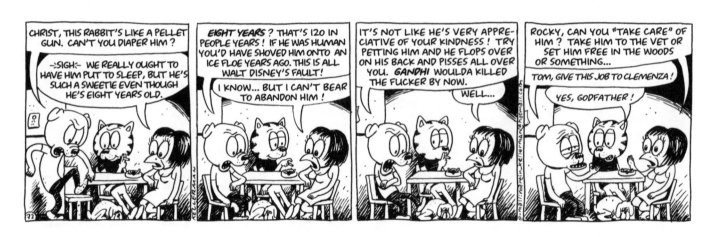

CHRIST, THIS RABBIT'S LIKE A PELLET GUN. CAN'T YOU DIAPER HIM?
-SIGH- WE REALLY OUGHT TO HAVE HIM PUT TO SLEEP, BUT HE'S SUCH A SWEETIE EVEN THOUGH HE'S EIGHT YEARS OLD.
72
KELLERMAN
EIGHT YEARS? THAT'S 120 IN PEOPLE YEARS! IF HE WAS HUMAN YOU'D HAVE SHOVED HIM ONTO AN ICE FLOE YEARS AGO. THIS IS ALL WALT DISNEY'S FAULT!
I KNOW... BUT I CAN'T BEAR TO ABANDON HIM!
IT'S NOT LIKE HE'S VERY APPRECIATIVE OF YOUR KINDNESS! TRY PETTING HIM AND HE FLOPS OVER ON HIS BACK AND PISSES ALL OVER YOU. GANDHI WOULDA KILLED THE FUCKER BY NOW.
WELL...
e-mail: martin_kellerman@hotmail.com
ROCKY, CAN YOU "TAKE CARE" OF HIM? TAKE HIM TO THE VET OR SET HIM FREE IN THE WOODS OR SOMETHING...
TOM, GIVE THIS JOB TO CLEMENZA!
YES, GODFATHER!
I'M HAVING SECOND THOUGHTS ABOUT ASKING ROCKY TO KILL MOSES. IT'S NOT ME DOING IT, BUT I GAVE THE ORDER!
MOMENT OF TRUTH
DUNE
73
KELLERMAN
WHAT I DON'T GET IS WHY YOU HIRED ROCKY AND TOMMY! THEY USED TO PLAY "ANTHILL AUSCHWITZ" WHEN THEY WERE KIDS. THAT'S HOW JEFFREY DAHMER STARTED OUT!
GOOD LORD!
AND THEIR SENSE OF HUMOR... I FOUND THIS PACKAGE OUTSIDE OUR DOOR... MOSES'S COLLAR AND A DEAD FISH.
THAT'S SICK! TELL THEM TO TAKE HIM TO THE VET!
MOSES SLEEPS WITH THE FISHES
e-mail: martin_kellerman@hotmail.com
I'M JUST SAYIN'... IF I FIND A RABBIT HEAD IN MY BED, IT'S ROCKY WHO'S GOING TO SLEEP!
MOMENT OF TRUTH
DUNE
MOSES SLEEPS WITH THE FISHES

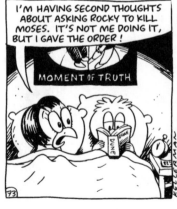

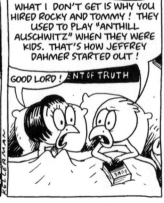

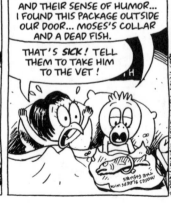

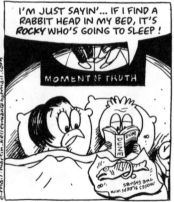

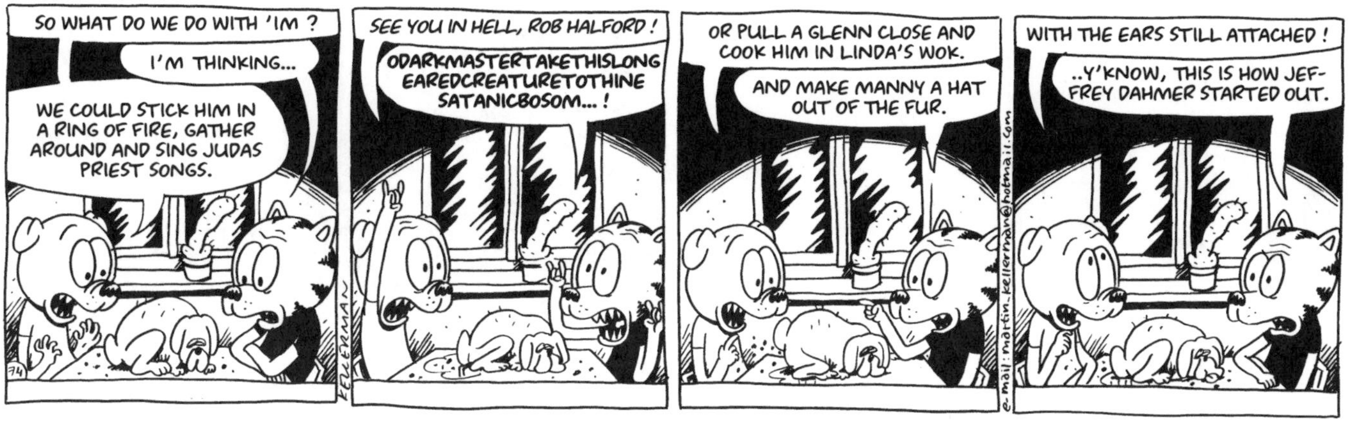
74
SO WHAT DO WE DO WITH 'IM ?
I'M THINKING...
WE COULD STICK HIM IN A RING OF FIRE, GATHER AROUND AND SING JUDAS PRIEST SONGS.
KELLERMAN
SEE YOU IN HELL, ROB HALFORD !
ODARKMASTERTAKETHISLONG EAREDCREATURETOTHINE SATANICBOSOM... !
OR PULL A GLENN CLOSE AND COOK HIM IN LINDA'S WOK.
AND MAKE MANNY A HAT OUT OF THE FUR.
e-mail: martin.kellerman@hotmail.com
WITH THE EARS STILL ATTACHED !
..Y'KNOW, THIS IS HOW JEFFREY DAHMER STARTED OUT.

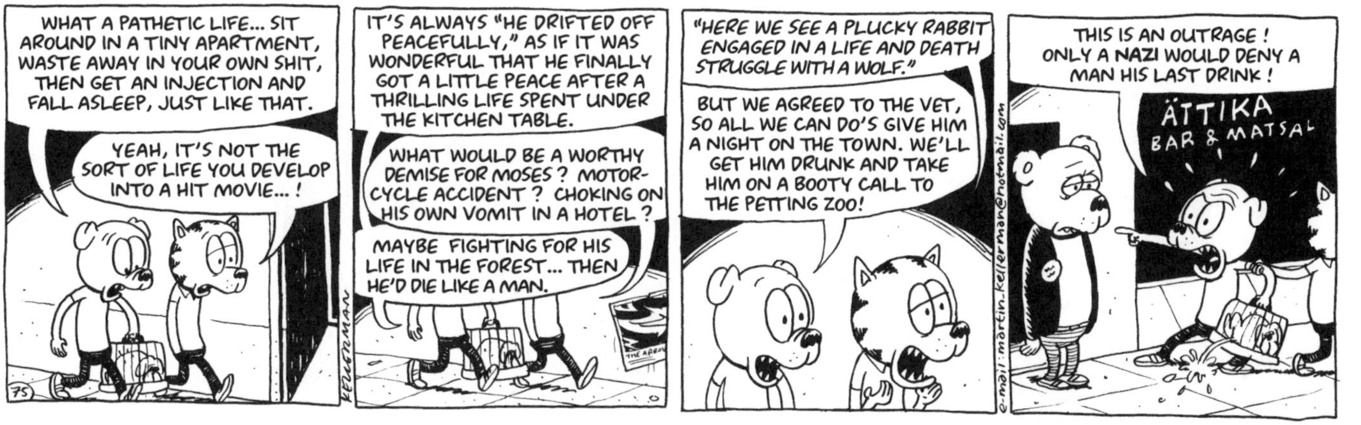
75
WHAT A PATHETIC LIFE... SIT AROUND IN A TINY APARTMENT, WASTE AWAY IN YOUR OWN SHIT, THEN GET AN INJECTION AND FALL ASLEEP, JUST LIKE THAT.
YEAH, IT'S NOT THE SORT OF LIFE YOU DEVELOP INTO A HIT MOVIE... !
KELLERMAN
IT'S ALWAYS "HE DRIFTED OFF PEACEFULLY," AS IF IT WAS WONDERFUL THAT HE FINALLY GOT A LITTLE PEACE AFTER A THRILLING LIFE SPENT UNDER THE KITCHEN TABLE.
WHAT WOULD BE A WORTHY DEMISE FOR MOSES ? MOTORCYCLE ACCIDENT ? CHOKING ON HIS OWN VOMIT IN A HOTEL ?
MAYBE FIGHTING FOR HIS LIFE IN THE FOREST... THEN HE'D DIE LIKE A MAN.
"HERE WE SEE A PLUCKY RABBIT ENGAGED IN A LIFE AND DEATH STRUGGLE WITH A WOLF."
BUT WE AGREED TO THE VET, SO ALL WE CAN DO'S GIVE HIM A NIGHT ON THE TOWN. WE'LL GET HIM DRUNK AND TAKE HIM ON A BOOTY CALL TO THE PETTING ZOO!
e-mail: martin.kellerman@hotmail.com
THIS IS AN OUTRAGE ! ONLY A **NAZI** WOULD DENY A MAN HIS LAST DRINK !
ÄTTIKA
BAR & MATSAL

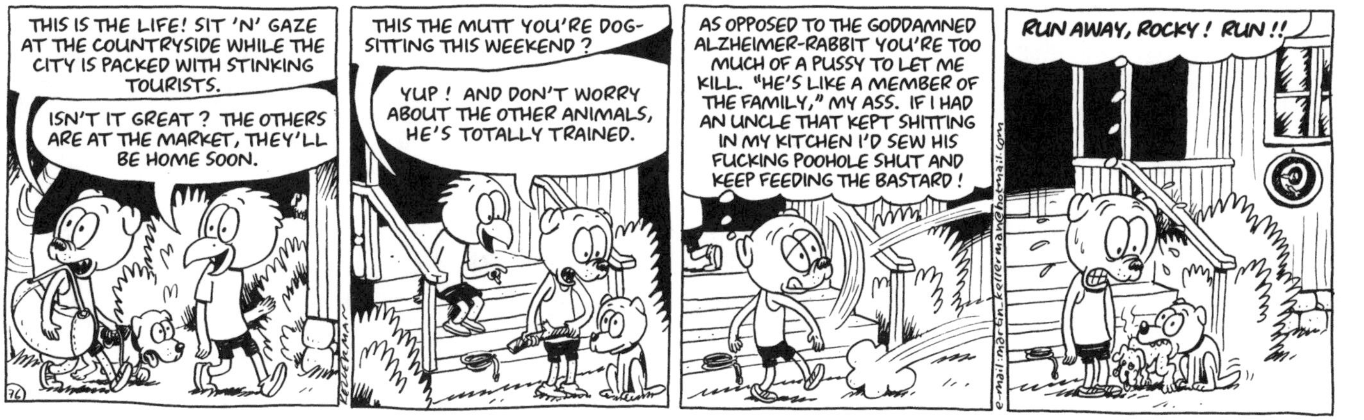
76
THIS IS THE LIFE! SIT 'N' GAZE AT THE COUNTRYSIDE WHILE THE CITY IS PACKED WITH STINKING TOURISTS.
ISN'T IT GREAT ? THE OTHERS ARE AT THE MARKET, THEY'LL BE HOME SOON.
KELLERMAN
THIS THE MUTT YOU'RE DOG-SITTING THIS WEEKEND ?
YUP ! AND DON'T WORRY ABOUT THE OTHER ANIMALS, HE'S TOTALLY TRAINED.
AS OPPOSED TO THE GODDAMNED ALZHEIMER-RABBIT YOU'RE TOO MUCH OF A PUSSY TO LET ME KILL. "HE'S LIKE A MEMBER OF THE FAMILY," MY ASS. IF I HAD AN UNCLE THAT KEPT SHITTING IN MY KITCHEN I'D SEW HIS FUCKING POOHOLE SHUT AND KEEP FEEDING THE BASTARD !
e-mail: martin.kellerman@hotmail.com
RUN AWAY, ROCKY ! RUN !!

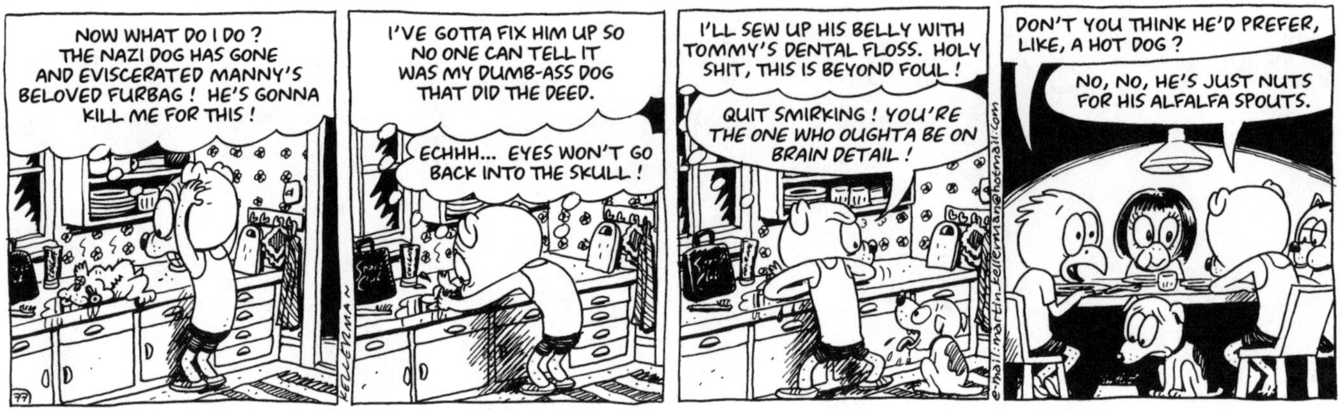
NOW WHAT DO I DO ? THE NAZI DOG HAS GONE AND EVISCERATED MANNY'S BELOVED FURBAG ! HE'S GONNA KILL ME FOR THIS !
77
KELLERMAN
I'VE GOTTA FIX HIM UP SO NO ONE CAN TELL IT WAS MY DUMB-ASS DOG THAT DID THE DEED.
ECHHH... EYES WON'T GO BACK INTO THE SKULL !
I'LL SEW UP HIS BELLY WITH TOMMY'S DENTAL FLOSS. HOLY SHIT, THIS IS BEYOND FOUL !
QUIT SMIRKING ! YOU'RE THE ONE WHO OUGHTA BE ON BRAIN DETAIL !
e-mail: martin_kellerman@hotmail.com
DON'T YOU THINK HE'D PREFER, LIKE, A HOT DOG ?
NO, NO, HE'S JUST NUTS FOR HIS ALFALFA SPOUTS.

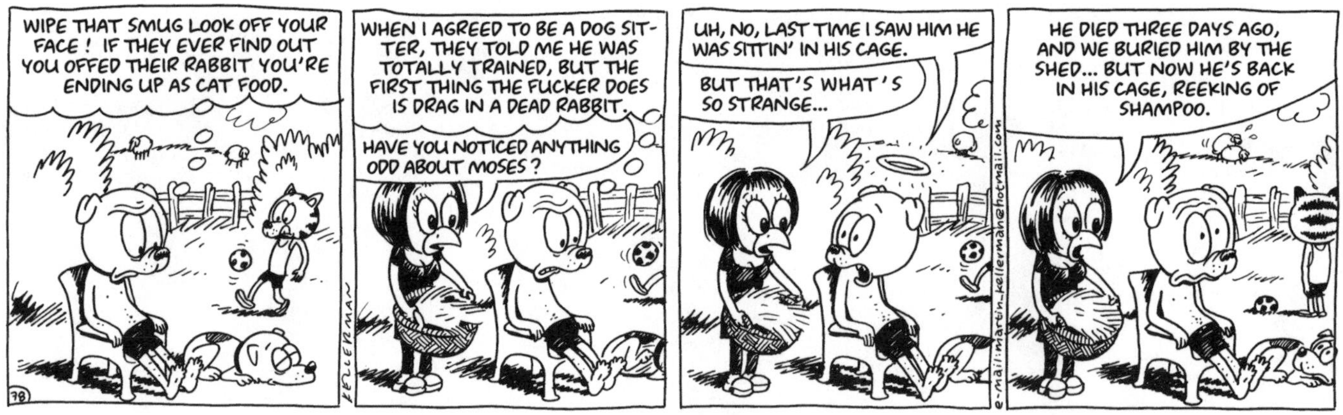
WIPE THAT SMUG LOOK OFF YOUR FACE ! IF THEY EVER FIND OUT YOU OFFED THEIR RABBIT YOU'RE ENDING UP AS CAT FOOD.
78
KELLERMAN
WHEN I AGREED TO BE A DOG SITTER, THEY TOLD ME HE WAS TOTALLY TRAINED, BUT THE FIRST THING THE FUCKER DOES IS DRAG IN A DEAD RABBIT.
HAVE YOU NOTICED ANYTHING ODD ABOUT MOSES ?
UH, NO, LAST TIME I SAW HIM HE WAS SITTIN' IN HIS CAGE.
BUT THAT'S WHAT'S SO STRANGE...
e-mail: martin_kellerman@hotmail.com
HE DIED THREE DAYS AGO, AND WE BURIED HIM BY THE SHED... BUT NOW HE'S BACK IN HIS CAGE, REEKING OF SHAMPOO.

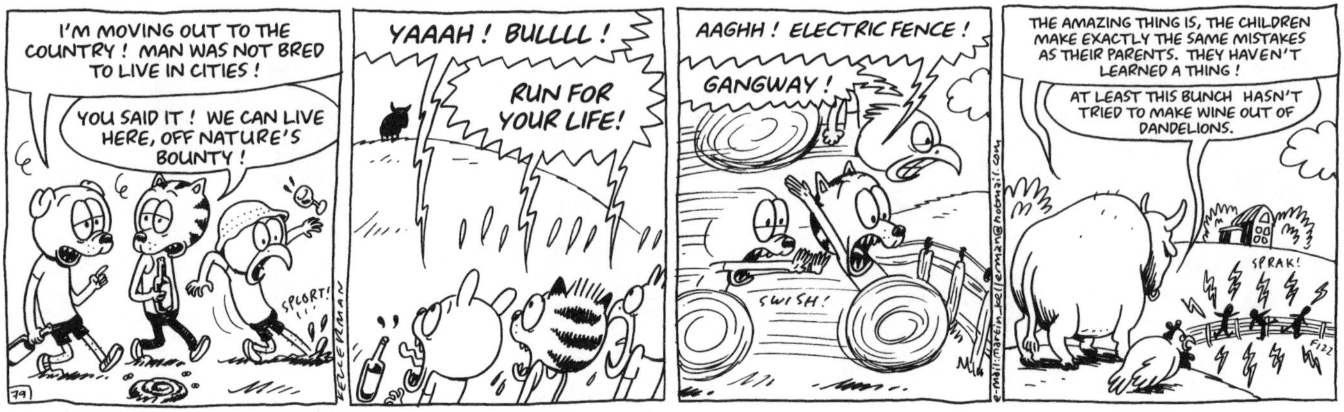
I'M MOVING OUT TO THE COUNTRY ! MAN WAS NOT BRED TO LIVE IN CITIES !
YOU SAID IT ! WE CAN LIVE HERE, OFF NATURE'S BOUNTY !
SPLORT!
79
KELLERMAN
YAAAH ! BULLLL !
RUN FOR YOUR LIFE!
AAGHH ! ELECTRIC FENCE !
GANGWAY !
SWISH!
e-mail: martin_kellerman@hotmail.com
THE AMAZING THING IS, THE CHILDREN MAKE EXACTLY THE SAME MISTAKES AS THEIR PARENTS. THEY HAVEN'T LEARNED A THING !
AT LEAST THIS BUNCH HASN'T TRIED TO MAKE WINE OUT OF DANDELIONS.
SPRAK!
FIZZ

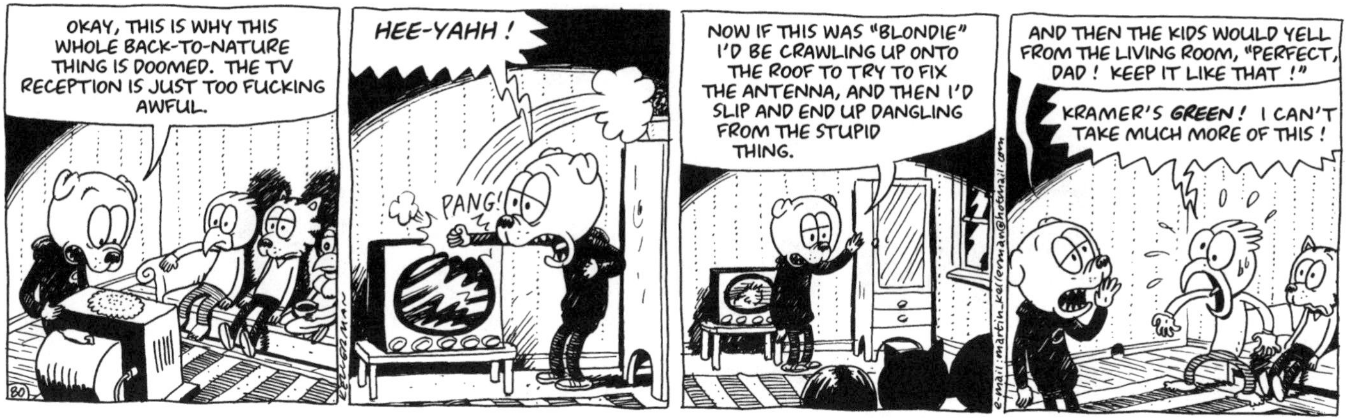
OKAY, THIS IS WHY THIS WHOLE BACK-TO-NATURE THING IS DOOMED. THE TV RECEPTION IS JUST TOO FUCKING AWFUL.
80
KELLERMAN
HEE-YAHH !
PANG!
NOW IF THIS WAS "BLONDIE" I'D BE CRAWLING UP ONTO THE ROOF TO TRY TO FIX THE ANTENNA, AND THEN I'D SLIP AND END UP DANGLING FROM THE STUPID THING.
e-mail: martin_kellerman@hotmail.com
AND THEN THE KIDS WOULD YELL FROM THE LIVING ROOM, "PERFECT, DAD ! KEEP IT LIKE THAT !"
KRAMER'S **GREEN** ! I CAN'T TAKE MUCH MORE OF THIS !

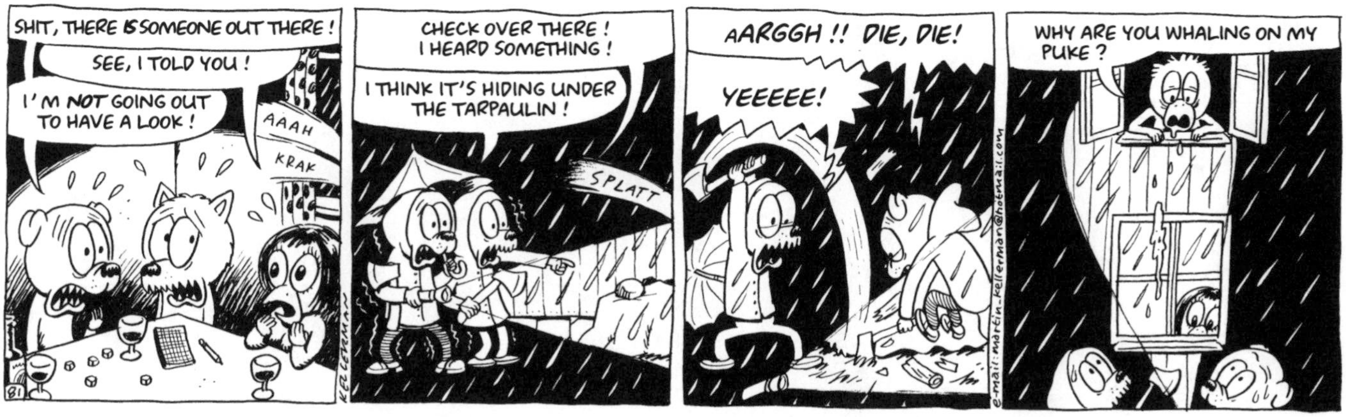
SHIT, THERE **IS** SOMEONE OUT THERE !
SEE, I TOLD YOU !
I'M **NOT** GOING OUT TO HAVE A LOOK !
AAAH
KRAK
81
KELLERMAN
CHECK OVER THERE ! I HEARD SOMETHING !
I THINK IT'S HIDING UNDER THE TARPAULIN !
SPLATT
AARGGH !! DIE, DIE!
YEEEEE!
e-mail: martin_kellerman@hotmail.com
WHY ARE YOU WHALING ON MY PUKE ?

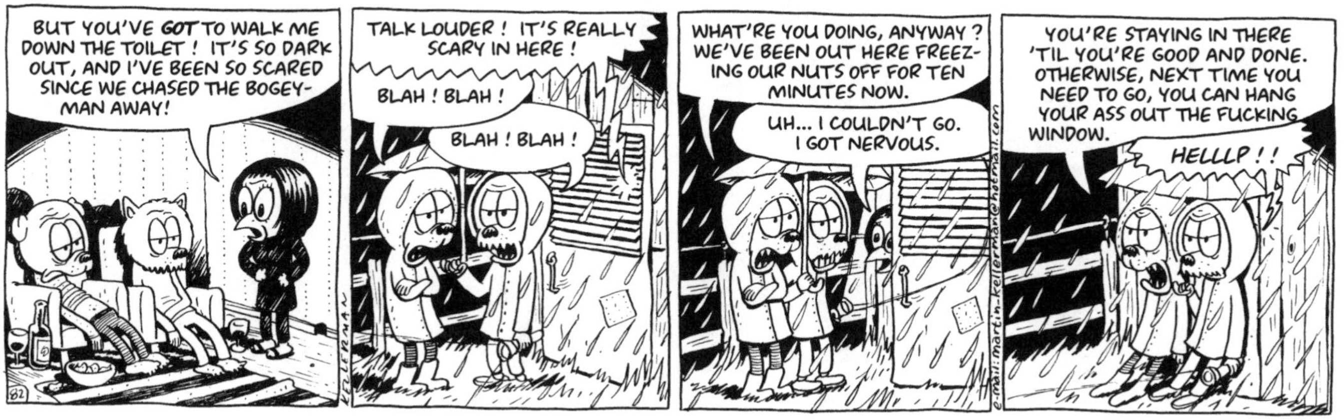
BUT YOU'VE **GOT** TO WALK ME DOWN THE TOILET ! IT'S SO DARK OUT, AND I'VE BEEN SO SCARED SINCE WE CHASED THE BOGEY-MAN AWAY!
82
KELLERMAN
TALK LOUDER ! IT'S REALLY SCARY IN HERE !
BLAH ! BLAH !
BLAH ! BLAH !
WHAT'RE YOU DOING, ANYWAY ? WE'VE BEEN OUT HERE FREEZ-ING OUR NUTS OFF FOR TEN MINUTES NOW.
UH... I COULDN'T GO. I GOT NERVOUS.
e-mail: martin_kellerman@hotmail.com
YOU'RE STAYING IN THERE 'TIL YOU'RE GOOD AND DONE. OTHERWISE, NEXT TIME YOU NEED TO GO, YOU CAN HANG YOUR ASS OUT THE FUCKING WINDOW.
HELLLP ! !

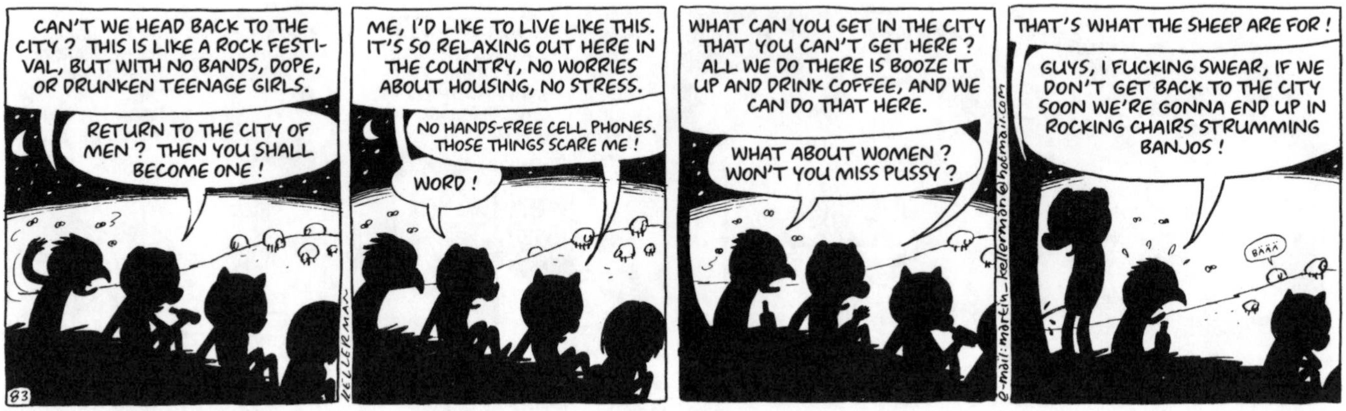
83
CAN'T WE HEAD BACK TO THE CITY ? THIS IS LIKE A ROCK FESTIVAL, BUT WITH NO BANDS, DOPE, OR DRUNKEN TEENAGE GIRLS.
RETURN TO THE CITY OF MEN ? THEN YOU SHALL BECOME ONE !
KELLERMAN
ME, I'D LIKE TO LIVE LIKE THIS. IT'S SO RELAXING OUT HERE IN THE COUNTRY, NO WORRIES ABOUT HOUSING, NO STRESS.
NO HANDS-FREE CELL PHONES. THOSE THINGS SCARE ME !
WORD !
WHAT CAN YOU GET IN THE CITY THAT YOU CAN'T GET HERE ? ALL WE DO THERE IS BOOZE IT UP AND DRINK COFFEE, AND WE CAN DO THAT HERE.
WHAT ABOUT WOMEN ? WON'T YOU MISS PUSSY ?
e-mail: martin_kellerman@hotmail.com
THAT'S WHAT THE SHEEP ARE FOR !
GUYS, I FUCKING SWEAR, IF WE DON'T GET BACK TO THE CITY SOON WE'RE GONNA END UP IN ROCKING CHAIRS STRUMMING BANJOS !
BÄÄÄ

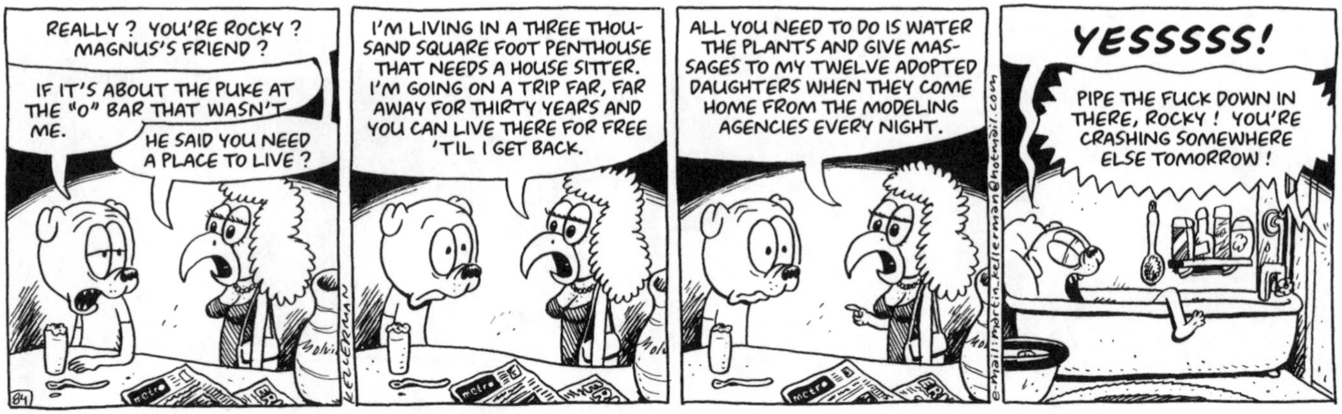
84
REALLY ? YOU'RE ROCKY ? MAGNUS'S FRIEND ?
IF IT'S ABOUT THE PUKE AT THE "O" BAR THAT WASN'T ME.
HE SAID YOU NEED A PLACE TO LIVE ?
KELLERMAN
I'M LIVING IN A THREE THOUSAND SQUARE FOOT PENTHOUSE THAT NEEDS A HOUSE SITTER. I'M GOING ON A TRIP FAR, FAR AWAY FOR THIRTY YEARS AND YOU CAN LIVE THERE FOR FREE 'TIL I GET BACK.
ALL YOU NEED TO DO IS WATER THE PLANTS AND GIVE MASSAGES TO MY TWELVE ADOPTED DAUGHTERS WHEN THEY COME HOME FROM THE MODELING AGENCIES EVERY NIGHT.
e-mail: martin.kellerman@hotmail.com
YESSSSS!
PIPE THE FUCK DOWN IN THERE, ROCKY ! YOU'RE CRASHING SOMEWHERE ELSE TOMORROW !

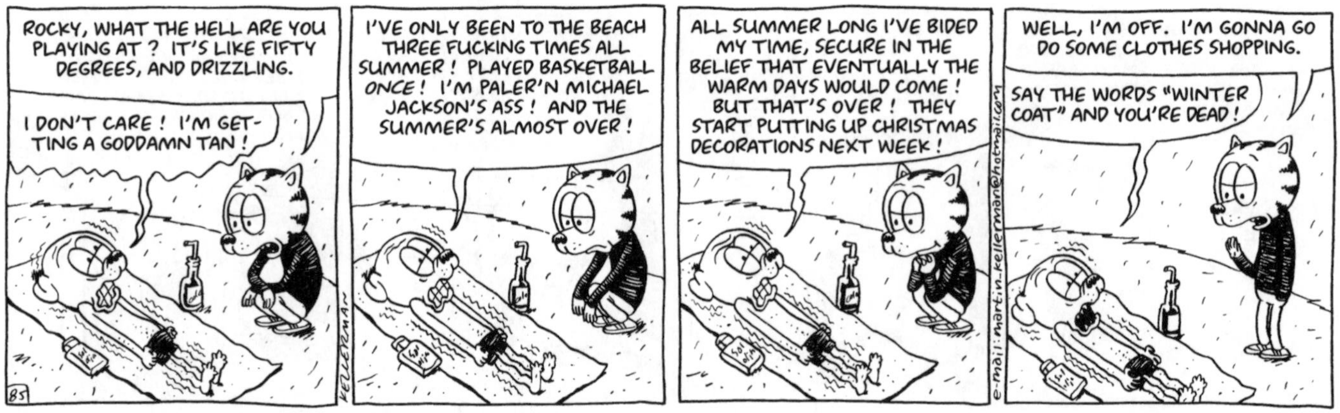
85
ROCKY, WHAT THE HELL ARE YOU PLAYING AT ? IT'S LIKE FIFTY DEGREES, AND DRIZZLING.
I DON'T CARE ! I'M GETTING A GODDAMN TAN !
KELLERMAN
I'VE ONLY BEEN TO THE BEACH THREE FUCKING TIMES ALL SUMMER ! PLAYED BASKETBALL ONCE ! I'M PALER'N MICHAEL JACKSON'S ASS ! AND THE SUMMER'S ALMOST OVER !
ALL SUMMER LONG I'VE BIDED MY TIME, SECURE IN THE BELIEF THAT EVENTUALLY THE WARM DAYS WOULD COME ! BUT THAT'S OVER ! THEY START PUTTING UP CHRISTMAS DECORATIONS NEXT WEEK !
e-mail: martin.kellerman@hotmail.com
WELL, I'M OFF. I'M GONNA GO DO SOME CLOTHES SHOPPING.
SAY THE WORDS "WINTER COAT" AND YOU'RE DEAD !

BACK IN THE SADDLE

I CANNOT BELIEVE HE BOMBED THE SHIT OUT OF TWO CITIES JUST FOR ONE MEASLY BLOWJOB !
GOOD THING HE DIDN'T FUCK HER UP THE ASS. HE WOULD'VE STARTED WORLD WAR III !
I DIDN'T INHALE!
1968
86
KELLERMAN
MAYBE IT WAS A FAIR TRADE. EYE FOR AN EYE, TOOTH FOR A TOOTH, BLOWJOB FOR A BLOWJOB.
THE "WAG THE DOG" TRICK RULES ! YOU JUST CAUSE A COMMOTION ELSEWHERE TO DIVERT THE PUBLIC'S ATTENTION.
SHE DIDN'T SWALLOW!
1998
OH, I PORKED YOUR GIRLFRIEND WHILE YOU WERE IN LONDON.
WHAT ?!
e-mail: martin_kellerman@hotmail.com
KRASH!!!

I'LL CALL YOU TOMORROW.
87
KELLERMAN
WHAT HAVE I DONE ? NO WAY CAN I AFFORD TO TAKE HER OUT ! I DON'T HAVE A POT TO PISS IN !
YOU CAN SCRAPE ENOUGH TOGETHER FOR A COFFEE.
ONE COFFEE, SURE. BUT THEN WHAT ? I'VE GOTTA AT LEAST BUY HER DINNER AND A FEW DRINKS BEFORE I NAIL HER ! THERE MUST BE SOME WAY AN ENTERPRISING YOUNG MAN CAN EARN HIMSELF SOME MONEY.
e-mail: martin_kellerman@hotmail.com
IF YOU CAN FILL IT ALL THE WAY THAT WOULD BE GREAT !

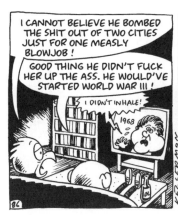

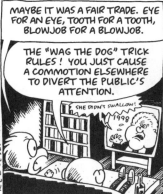

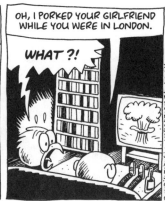

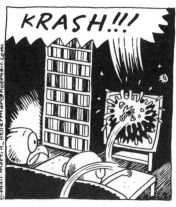

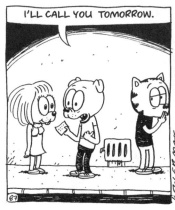

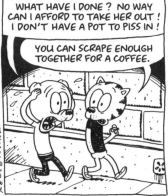

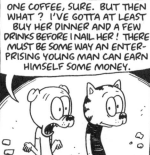

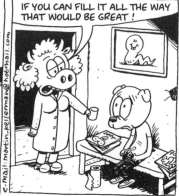

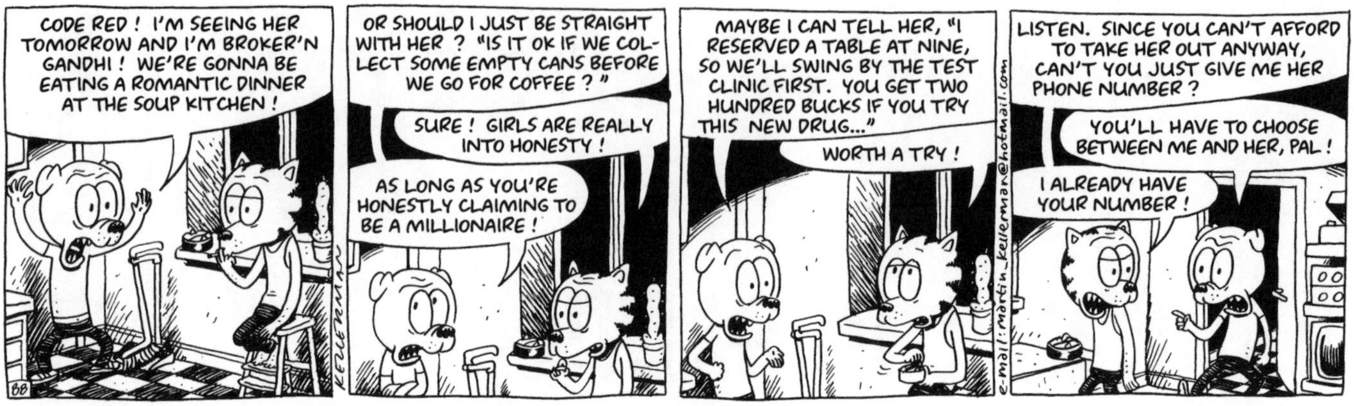
88
CODE RED ! I'M SEEING HER TOMORROW AND I'M BROKER'N GANDHI ! WE'RE GONNA BE EATING A ROMANTIC DINNER AT THE SOUP KITCHEN !
KELLERMAN
OR SHOULD I JUST BE STRAIGHT WITH HER ? "IS IT OK IF WE COLLECT SOME EMPTY CANS BEFORE WE GO FOR COFFEE ? "
SURE ! GIRLS ARE REALLY INTO HONESTY !
AS LONG AS YOU'RE HONESTLY CLAIMING TO BE A MILLIONAIRE !
MAYBE I CAN TELL HER, "I RESERVED A TABLE AT NINE, SO WE'LL SWING BY THE TEST CLINIC FIRST. YOU GET TWO HUNDRED BUCKS IF YOU TRY THIS NEW DRUG..."
WORTH A TRY !
e-mail: martin_kellerman@hotmail.com
LISTEN. SINCE YOU CAN'T AFFORD TO TAKE HER OUT ANYWAY, CAN'T YOU JUST GIVE ME HER PHONE NUMBER ?
YOU'LL HAVE TO CHOOSE BETWEEN ME AND HER, PAL !
I ALREADY HAVE YOUR NUMBER !

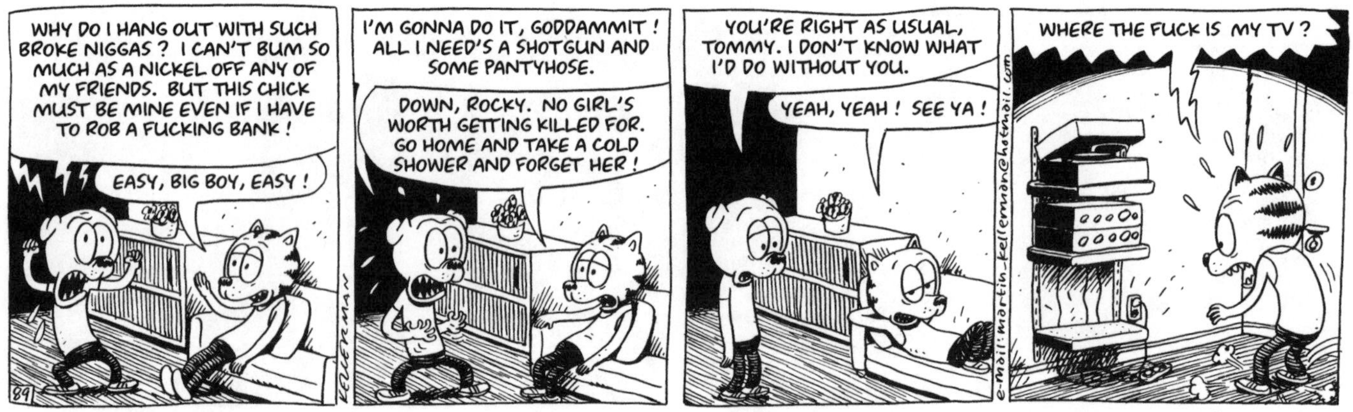
89
WHY DO I HANG OUT WITH SUCH BROKE NIGGAS ? I CAN'T BUM SO MUCH AS A NICKEL OFF ANY OF MY FRIENDS. BUT THIS CHICK MUST BE MINE EVEN IF I HAVE TO ROB A FUCKING BANK !
EASY, BIG BOY, EASY !
KELLERMAN
I'M GONNA DO IT, GODDAMMIT ! ALL I NEED'S A SHOTGUN AND SOME PANTYHOSE.
DOWN, ROCKY. NO GIRL'S WORTH GETTING KILLED FOR. GO HOME AND TAKE A COLD SHOWER AND FORGET HER !
YOU'RE RIGHT AS USUAL, TOMMY. I DON'T KNOW WHAT I'D DO WITHOUT YOU.
YEAH, YEAH ! SEE YA !
e-mail: martin_kellerman@hotmail.com
WHERE THE FUCK IS MY TV ?

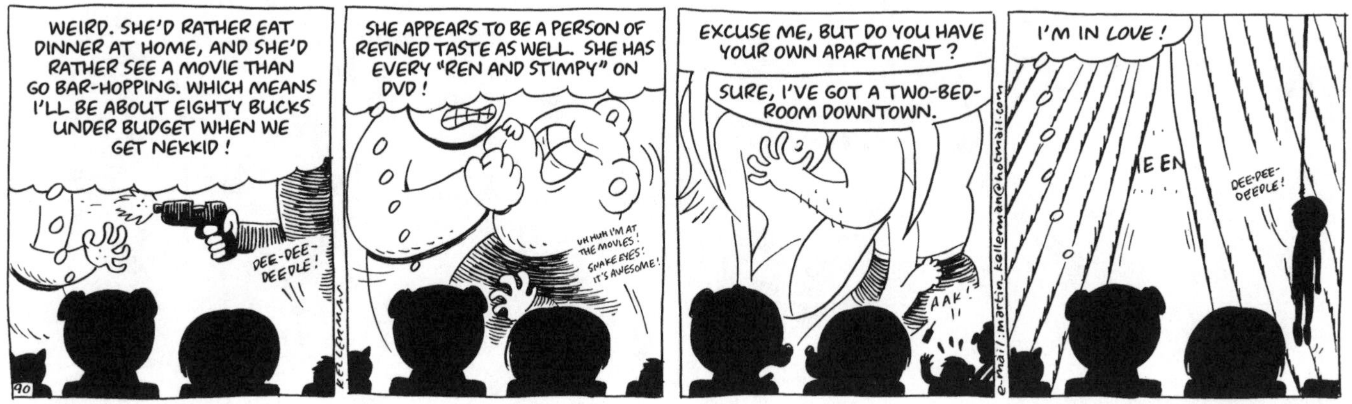
90
WEIRD. SHE'D RATHER EAT DINNER AT HOME, AND SHE'D RATHER SEE A MOVIE THAN GO BAR-HOPPING. WHICH MEANS I'LL BE ABOUT EIGHTY BUCKS UNDER BUDGET WHEN WE GET NEKKID !
DEE-DEE-DEEDLE !
KELLERMAN
SHE APPEARS TO BE A PERSON OF REFINED TASTE AS WELL. SHE HAS EVERY "REN AND STIMPY" ON DVD !
UH HUH I'M AT THE MOVIES ! SNAKE EYES ! IT'S AWESOME !
EXCUSE ME, BUT DO YOU HAVE YOUR OWN APARTMENT ?
SURE, I'VE GOT A TWO-BEDROOM DOWNTOWN.
AAK !
e-mail: martin_kellerman@hotmail.com
I'M IN LOVE !
DEE-DEE-DEEDLE !

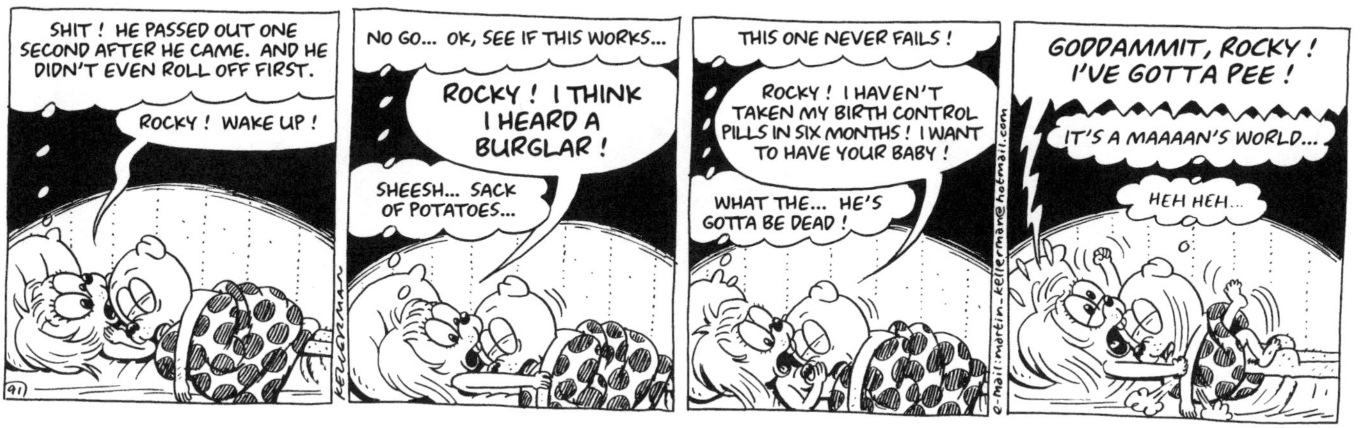
SHIT! HE PASSED OUT ONE SECOND AFTER HE CAME. AND HE DIDN'T EVEN ROLL OFF FIRST.
ROCKY! WAKE UP!
91
KELLERMAN
NO GO... OK, SEE IF THIS WORKS...
ROCKY! I THINK I HEARD A BURGLAR!
SHEESH... SACK OF POTATOES...
THIS ONE NEVER FAILS!
ROCKY! I HAVEN'T TAKEN MY BIRTH CONTROL PILLS IN SIX MONTHS! I WANT TO HAVE YOUR BABY!
WHAT THE... HE'S GOTTA BE DEAD!
e-mail: martin_kellerman@hotmail.com
GODDAMMIT, ROCKY! I'VE GOTTA PEE!
IT'S A MAAAAN'S WORLD...
HEH HEH...

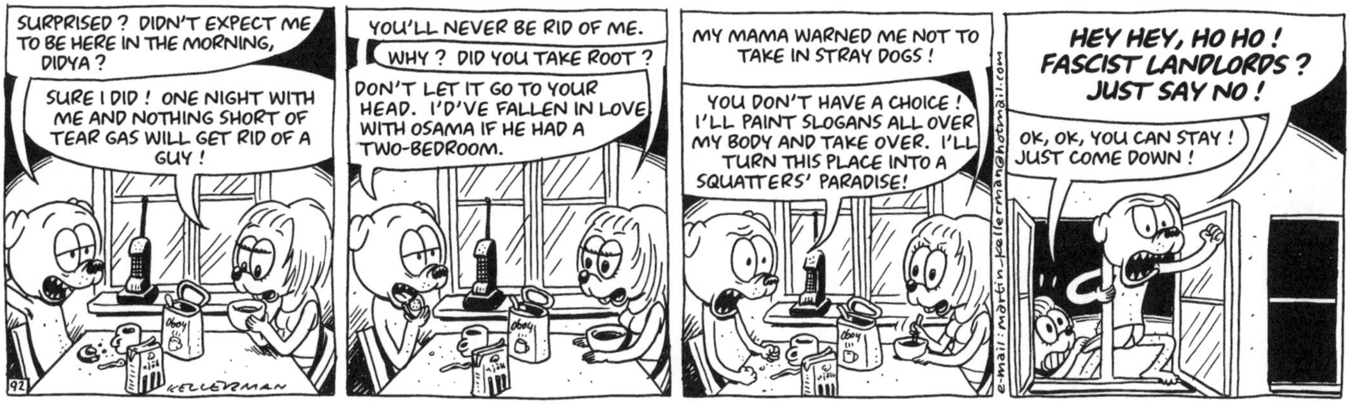
SURPRISED? DIDN'T EXPECT ME TO BE HERE IN THE MORNING, DIDYA?
SURE I DID! ONE NIGHT WITH ME AND NOTHING SHORT OF TEAR GAS WILL GET RID OF A GUY!
92
KELLERMAN
YOU'LL NEVER BE RID OF ME.
WHY? DID YOU TAKE ROOT?
DON'T LET IT GO TO YOUR HEAD. I'D'VE FALLEN IN LOVE WITH OSAMA IF HE HAD A TWO-BEDROOM.
MY MAMA WARNED ME NOT TO TAKE IN STRAY DOGS!
YOU DON'T HAVE A CHOICE! I'LL PAINT SLOGANS ALL OVER MY BODY AND TAKE OVER. I'LL TURN THIS PLACE INTO A SQUATTERS' PARADISE!
e-mail: martin_kellerman@hotmail.com
HEY HEY, HO HO! FASCIST LANDLORDS? JUST SAY NO!
OK, OK, YOU CAN STAY! JUST COME DOWN!

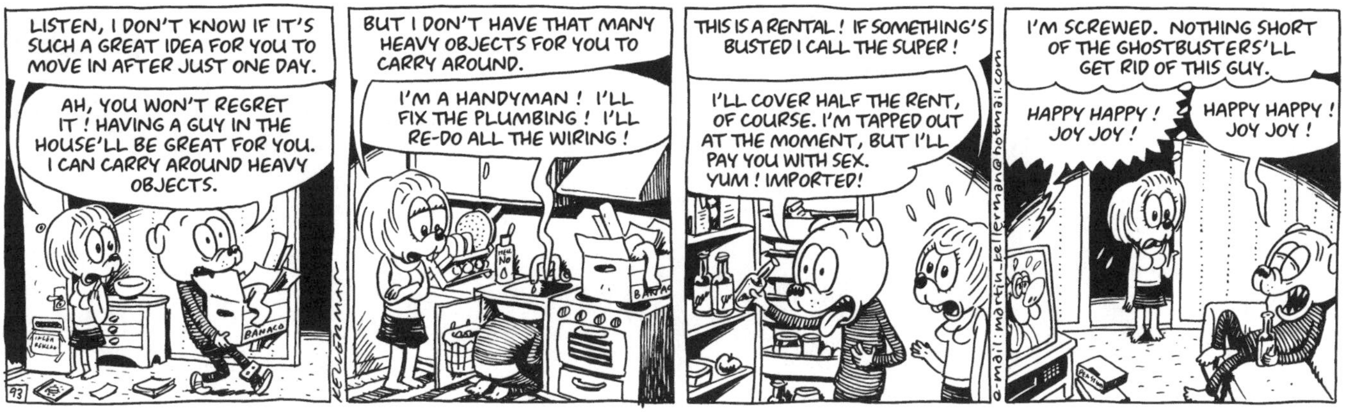
LISTEN, I DON'T KNOW IF IT'S SUCH A GREAT IDEA FOR YOU TO MOVE IN AFTER JUST ONE DAY.
AH, YOU WON'T REGRET IT! HAVING A GUY IN THE HOUSE'LL BE GREAT FOR YOU. I CAN CARRY AROUND HEAVY OBJECTS.
93
KELLERMAN
BUT I DON'T HAVE THAT MANY HEAVY OBJECTS FOR YOU TO CARRY AROUND.
I'M A HANDYMAN! I'LL FIX THE PLUMBING! I'LL RE-DO ALL THE WIRING!
THIS IS A RENTAL! IF SOMETHING'S BUSTED I CALL THE SUPER!
I'LL COVER HALF THE RENT, OF COURSE. I'M TAPPED OUT AT THE MOMENT, BUT I'LL PAY YOU WITH SEX. YUM! IMPORTED!
e-mail: martin_kellerman@hotmail.com
I'M SCREWED. NOTHING SHORT OF THE GHOSTBUSTERS'LL GET RID OF THIS GUY.
HAPPY HAPPY! JOY JOY!
HAPPY HAPPY! JOY JOY!

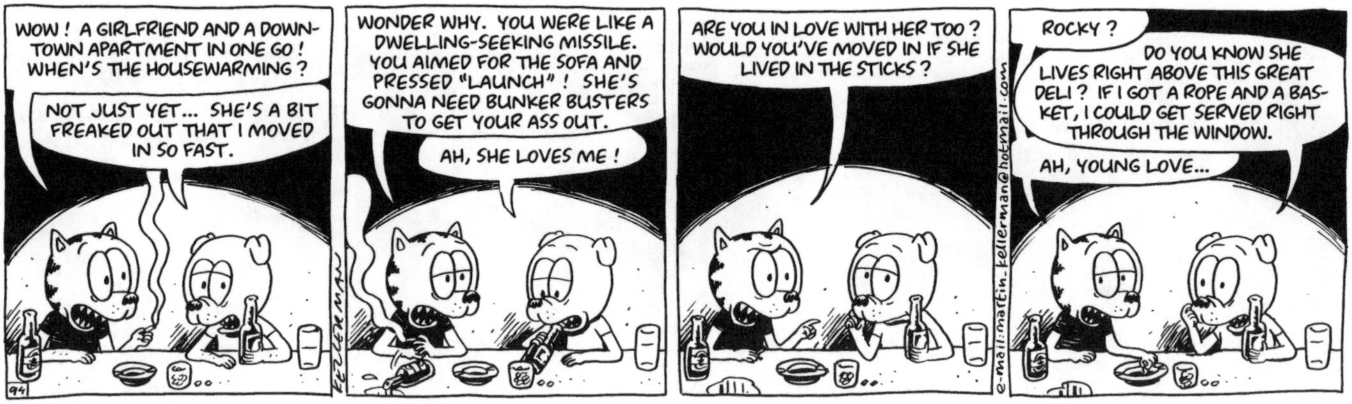
94
WOW ! A GIRLFRIEND AND A DOWN-TOWN APARTMENT IN ONE GO ! WHEN'S THE HOUSEWARMING ?
NOT JUST YET... SHE'S A BIT FREAKED OUT THAT I MOVED IN SO FAST.
KELLERMAN
WONDER WHY. YOU WERE LIKE A DWELLING-SEEKING MISSILE. YOU AIMED FOR THE SOFA AND PRESSED "LAUNCH" ! SHE'S GONNA NEED BUNKER BUSTERS TO GET YOUR ASS OUT.
AH, SHE LOVES ME !
ARE YOU IN LOVE WITH HER TOO ? WOULD YOU'VE MOVED IN IF SHE LIVED IN THE STICKS ?
e-mail: martin.kellerman@hotmail.com
ROCKY ?
DO YOU KNOW SHE LIVES RIGHT ABOVE THIS GREAT DELI ? IF I GOT A ROPE AND A BAS-KET, I COULD GET SERVED RIGHT THROUGH THE WINDOW.
AH, YOUNG LOVE...

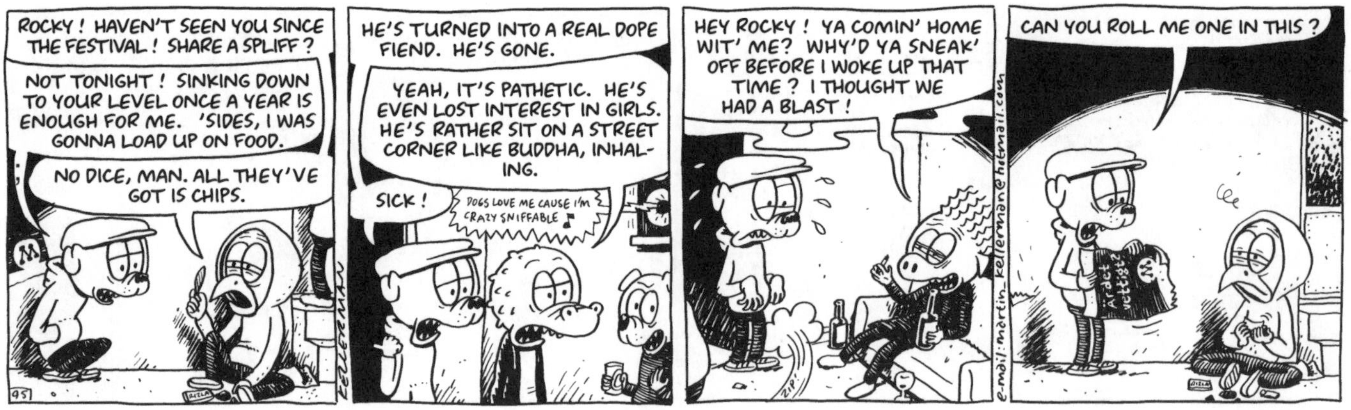
95
ROCKY ! HAVEN'T SEEN YOU SINCE THE FESTIVAL ! SHARE A SPLIFF ?
NOT TONIGHT ! SINKING DOWN TO YOUR LEVEL ONCE A YEAR IS ENOUGH FOR ME. 'SIDES, I WAS GONNA LOAD UP ON FOOD.
NO DICE, MAN. ALL THEY'VE GOT IS CHIPS.
KELLERMAN
HE'S TURNED INTO A REAL DOPE FIEND. HE'S GONE.
YEAH, IT'S PATHETIC. HE'S EVEN LOST INTEREST IN GIRLS. HE'S RATHER SIT ON A STREET CORNER LIKE BUDDHA, INHAL-ING.
SICK !
DOGS LOVE ME CAUSE I'M CRAZY SNIFFABLE
HEY ROCKY ! YA COMIN' HOME WIT' ME? WHY'D YA SNEAK' OFF BEFORE I WOKE UP THAT TIME ? I THOUGHT WE HAD A BLAST !
ZIP!
e-mail: martin_kellerman@hotmail.com
CAN YOU ROLL ME ONE IN THIS ?

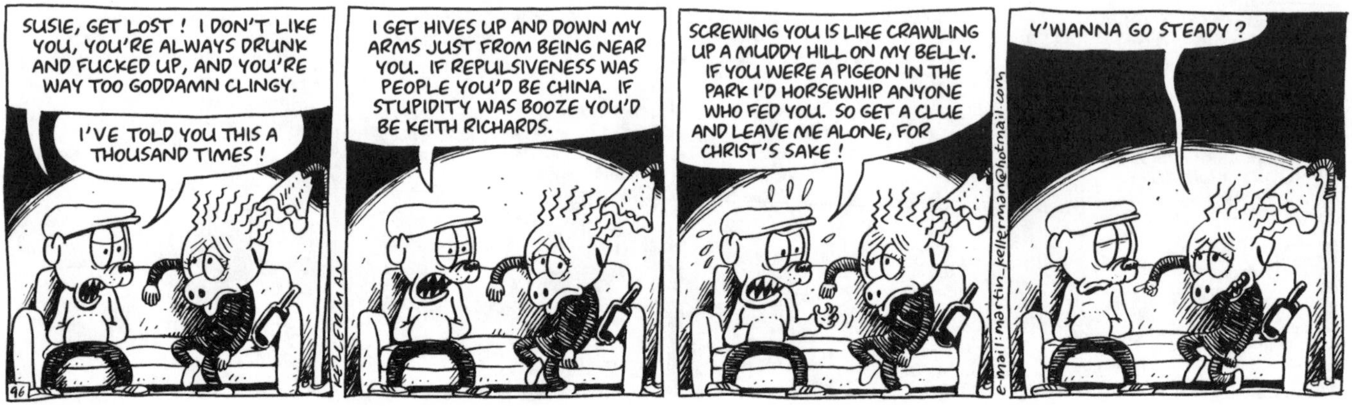
96
SUSIE, GET LOST ! I DON'T LIKE YOU, YOU'RE ALWAYS DRUNK AND FUCKED UP, AND YOU'RE WAY TOO GODDAMN CLINGY.
I'VE TOLD YOU THIS A THOUSAND TIMES !
KELLERMAN
I GET HIVES UP AND DOWN MY ARMS JUST FROM BEING NEAR YOU. IF REPULSIVENESS WAS PEOPLE YOU'D BE CHINA. IF STUPIDITY WAS BOOZE YOU'D BE KEITH RICHARDS.
SCREWING YOU IS LIKE CRAWLING UP A MUDDY HILL ON MY BELLY. IF YOU WERE A PIGEON IN THE PARK I'D HORSEWHIP ANYONE WHO FED YOU. SO GET A CLUE AND LEAVE ME ALONE, FOR CHRIST'S SAKE !
e-mail: martin_kellerman@hotmail.com
Y'WANNA GO STEADY ?

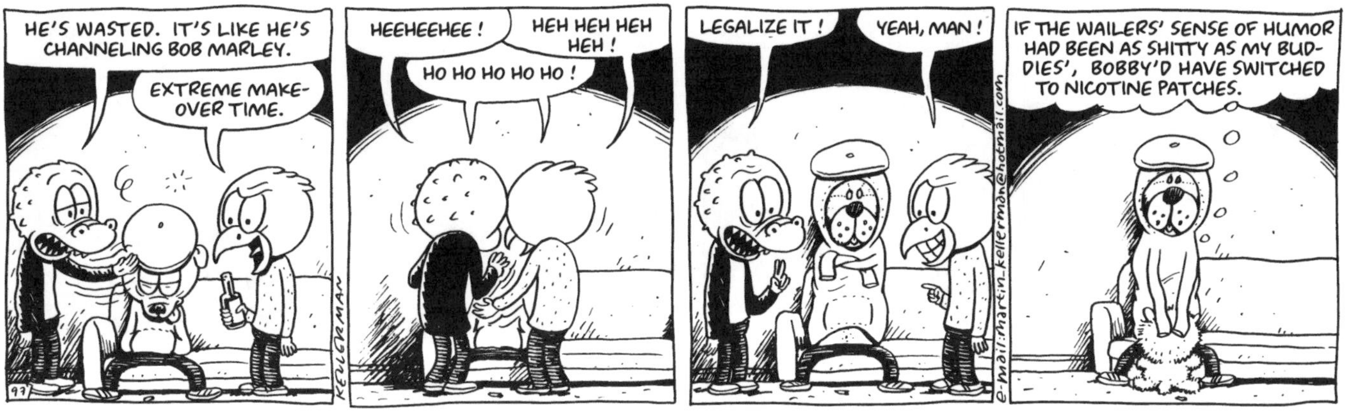
97
HE'S WASTED. IT'S LIKE HE'S CHANNELING BOB MARLEY.
EXTREME MAKE-OVER TIME.
KELLERMAN
HEEHEEHEE!
HEH HEH HEH HEH!
HO HO HO HO HO!
LEGALIZE IT!
YEAH, MAN!
e-mail: martin_kellerman@hotmail.com
IF THE WAILERS' SENSE OF HUMOR HAD BEEN AS SHITTY AS MY BUD-DIES', BOBBY'D HAVE SWITCHED TO NICOTINE PATCHES.

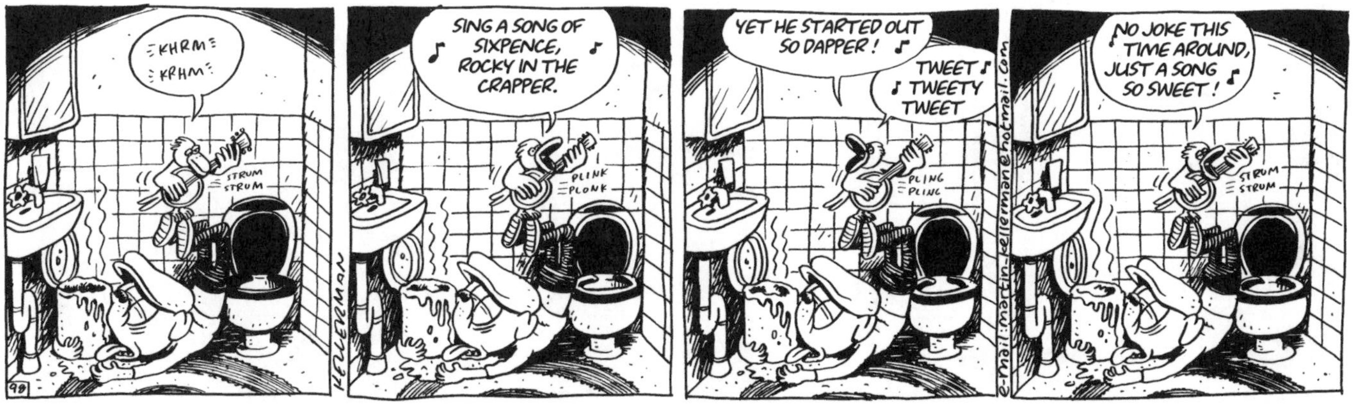
98
KHRM
KRHM
STRUM
STRUM
KELLERMAN
SING A SONG OF SIXPENCE, ROCKY IN THE CRAPPER.
PLINK
PLONK
YET HE STARTED OUT SO DAPPER!
TWEET TWEETY TWEET
PLING
PLING
e-mail: martin_kellerman@hotmail.com
NO JOKE THIS TIME AROUND, JUST A SONG SO SWEET!
STRUM
STRUM

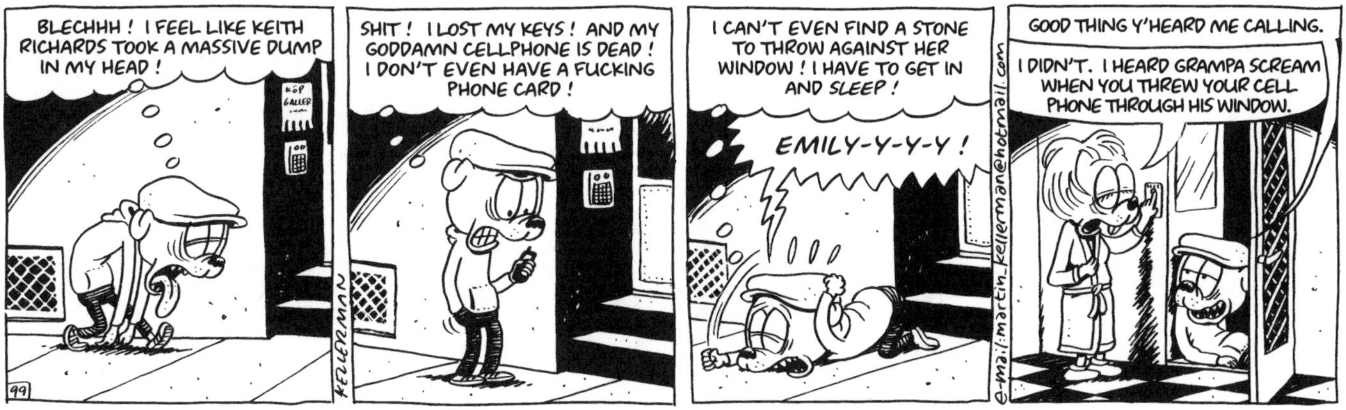
99
BLECHHH! I FEEL LIKE KEITH RICHARDS TOOK A MASSIVE DUMP IN MY HEAD!
KELLERMAN
SHIT! I LOST MY KEYS! AND MY GODDAMN CELLPHONE IS DEAD! I DON'T EVEN HAVE A FUCKING PHONE CARD!
I CAN'T EVEN FIND A STONE TO THROW AGAINST HER WINDOW! I HAVE TO GET IN AND SLEEP!
EMILY-Y-Y-Y!
e-mail: martin_kellerman@hotmail.com
GOOD THING Y'HEARD ME CALLING.
I DIDN'T. I HEARD GRAMPA SCREAM WHEN YOU THREW YOUR CELL PHONE THROUGH HIS WINDOW.

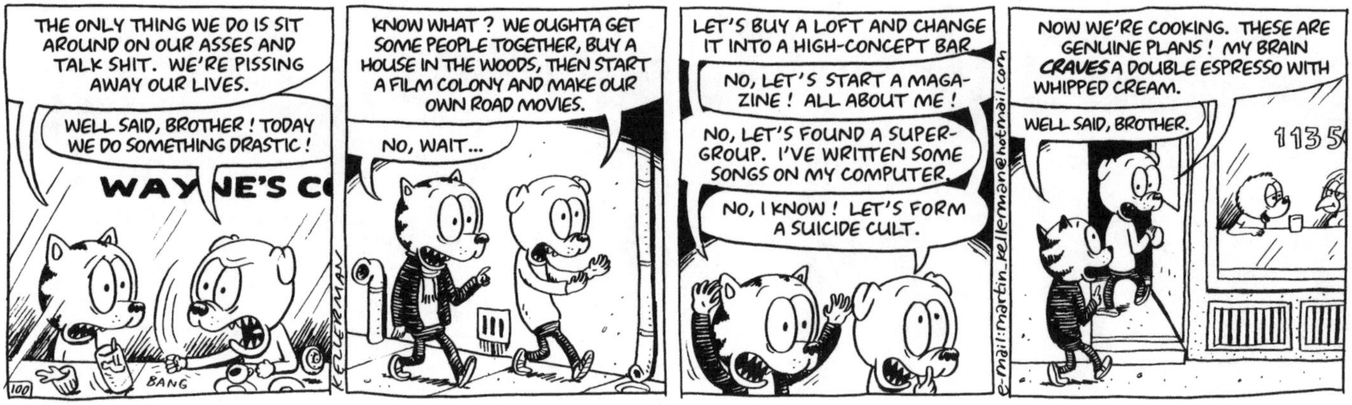
THE ONLY THING WE DO IS SIT AROUND ON OUR ASSES AND TALK SHIT. WE'RE PISSING AWAY OUR LIVES.
WELL SAID, BROTHER! TODAY WE DO SOMETHING DRASTIC!
WAYNE'S C
BANG
100
KELLERMAN
KNOW WHAT? WE OUGHTA GET SOME PEOPLE TOGETHER, BUY A HOUSE IN THE WOODS, THEN START A FILM COLONY AND MAKE OUR OWN ROAD MOVIES.
NO, WAIT...
LET'S BUY A LOFT AND CHANGE IT INTO A HIGH-CONCEPT BAR.
NO, LET'S START A MAGAZINE! ALL ABOUT ME!
NO, LET'S FOUND A SUPERGROUP. I'VE WRITTEN SOME SONGS ON MY COMPUTER.
NO, I KNOW! LET'S FORM A SUICIDE CULT.
e-mail:martin_kellerman@hotmail.com
NOW WE'RE COOKING. THESE ARE GENUINE PLANS! MY BRAIN CRAVES A DOUBLE ESPRESSO WITH WHIPPED CREAM.
WELL SAID, BROTHER.

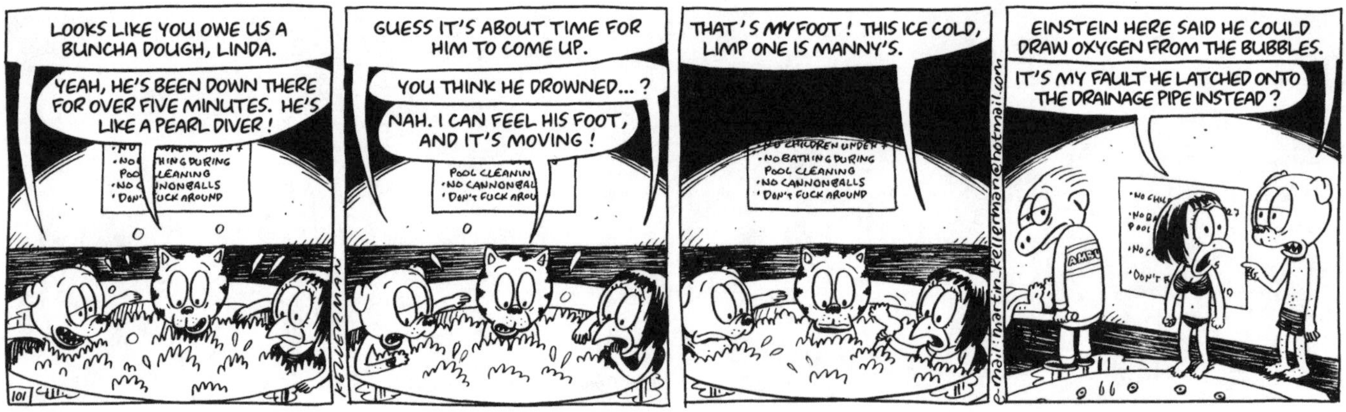
LOOKS LIKE YOU OWE US A BUNCHA DOUGH, LINDA.
YEAH, HE'S BEEN DOWN THERE FOR OVER FIVE MINUTES. HE'S LIKE A PEARL DIVER!
101
KELLERMAN
GUESS IT'S ABOUT TIME FOR HIM TO COME UP.
YOU THINK HE DROWNED...?
NAH. I CAN FEEL HIS FOOT, AND IT'S MOVING!
THAT'S MY FOOT! THIS ICE COLD, LIMP ONE IS MANNY'S.
• NO BATHING DURING POOL CLEANING
• NO CANNONBALLS
• DON'T FUCK AROUND
e-mail:martin_kellerman@hotmail.com
EINSTEIN HERE SAID HE COULD DRAW OXYGEN FROM THE BUBBLES.
IT'S MY FAULT HE LATCHED ONTO THE DRAINAGE PIPE INSTEAD?

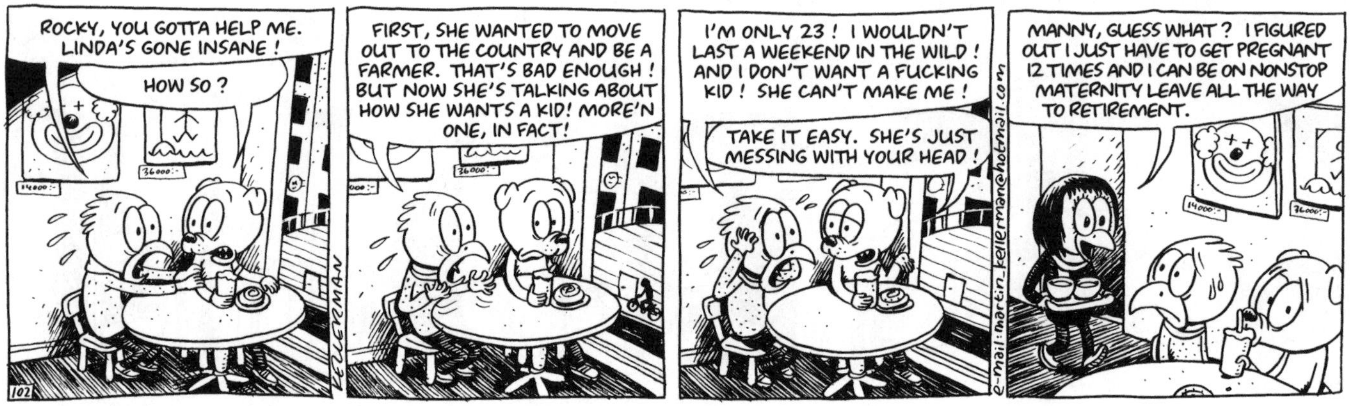
ROCKY, YOU GOTTA HELP ME. LINDA'S GONE INSANE!
HOW SO?
14000:-
36000:-
102
KELLERMAN
FIRST, SHE WANTED TO MOVE OUT TO THE COUNTRY AND BE A FARMER. THAT'S BAD ENOUGH! BUT NOW SHE'S TALKING ABOUT HOW SHE WANTS A KID! MORE'N ONE, IN FACT!
I'M ONLY 23! I WOULDN'T LAST A WEEKEND IN THE WILD! AND I DON'T WANT A FUCKING KID! SHE CAN'T MAKE ME!
TAKE IT EASY. SHE'S JUST MESSING WITH YOUR HEAD!
e-mail:martin_kellerman@hotmail.com
MANNY, GUESS WHAT? I FIGURED OUT I JUST HAVE TO GET PREGNANT 12 TIMES AND I CAN BE ON NONSTOP MATERNITY LEAVE ALL THE WAY TO RETIREMENT.

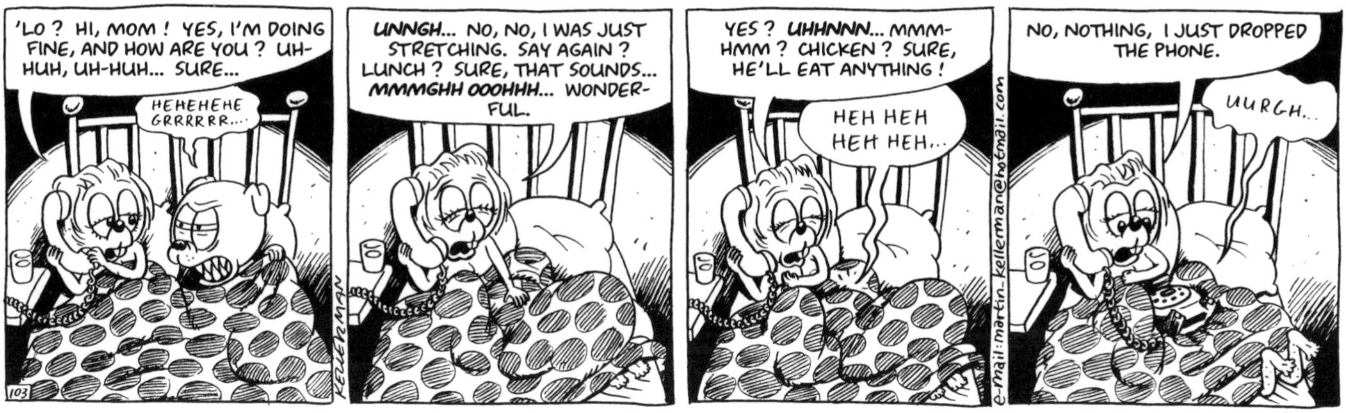
'LO ? HI, MOM ! YES, I'M DOING FINE, AND HOW ARE YOU ? UH-HUH, UH-HUH... SURE...
HEHEHEHE GRRRRRR...
UNNGH... NO, NO, I WAS JUST STRETCHING. SAY AGAIN ? LUNCH ? SURE, THAT SOUNDS... MMMGHH OOOHHH... WONDERFUL.
YES ? UHHNNN... MMM-HMM ? CHICKEN ? SURE, HE'LL EAT ANYTHING !
HEH HEH HEH HEH...
NO, NOTHING, I JUST DROPPED THE PHONE.
UURGH...
103
KELLERMAN
e-mail: martin_kellerman@hotmail.com

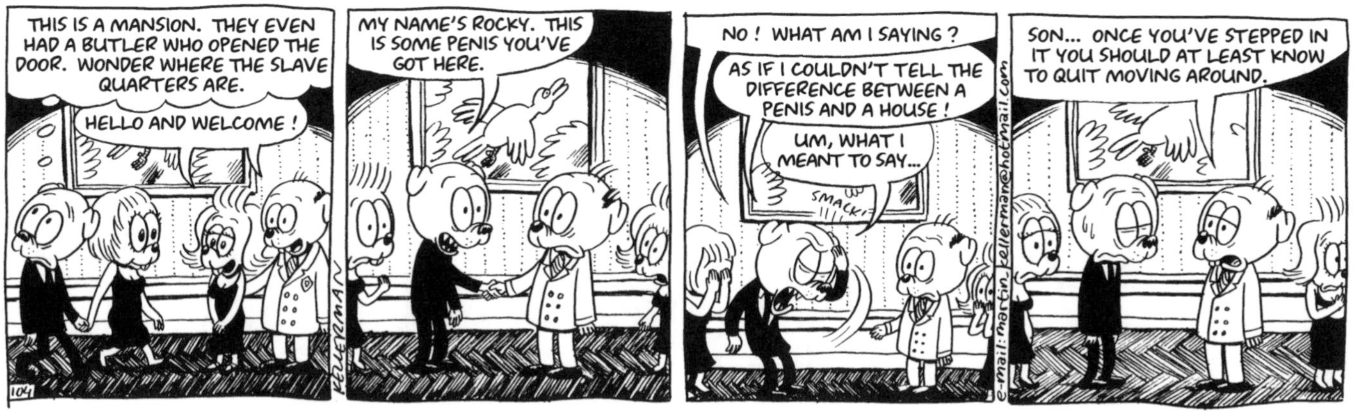
THIS IS A MANSION. THEY EVEN HAD A BUTLER WHO OPENED THE DOOR. WONDER WHERE THE SLAVE QUARTERS ARE.
HELLO AND WELCOME !
MY NAME'S ROCKY. THIS IS SOME PENIS YOU'VE GOT HERE.
NO ! WHAT AM I SAYING ?
AS IF I COULDN'T TELL THE DIFFERENCE BETWEEN A PENIS AND A HOUSE !
UM, WHAT I MEANT TO SAY...
SMACK!
SON... ONCE YOU'VE STEPPED IN IT YOU SHOULD AT LEAST KNOW TO QUIT MOVING AROUND.
104
KELLERMAN
e-mail: martin_kellerman@hotmail.com

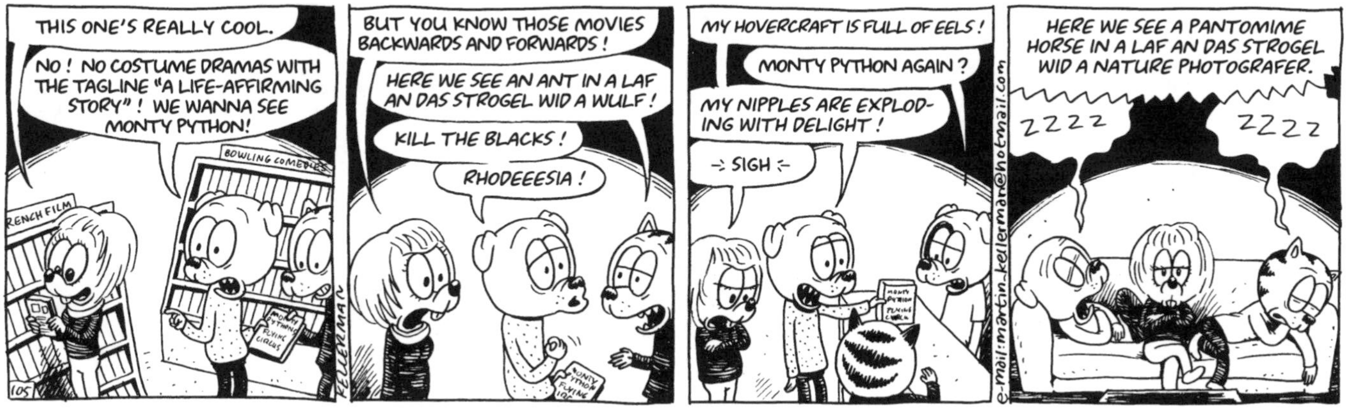
THIS ONE'S REALLY COOL.
NO ! NO COSTUME DRAMAS WITH THE TAGLINE "A LIFE-AFFIRMING STORY" ! WE WANNA SEE MONTY PYTHON!
BUT YOU KNOW THOSE MOVIES BACKWARDS AND FORWARDS !
HERE WE SEE AN ANT IN A LAF AN DAS STROGEL WID A WULF !
KILL THE BLACKS !
RHODEEESIA !
MY HOVERCRAFT IS FULL OF EELS !
MONTY PYTHON AGAIN ?
MY NIPPLES ARE EXPLODING WITH DELIGHT !
SIGH
HERE WE SEE A PANTOMIME HORSE IN A LAF AN DAS STROGEL WID A NATURE PHOTOGRAFER.
ZZZZ
ZZZZ
105
KELLERMAN
e-mail: martin.kellerman@hotmail.com

THE SWITCH

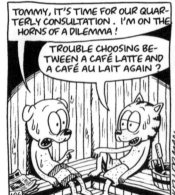

TOMMY, IT'S TIME FOR OUR QUARTERLY CONSULTATION. I'M ON THE HORNS OF A DILEMMA!
TROUBLE CHOOSING BETWEEN A CAFÉ LATTE AND A CAFÉ AU LAIT AGAIN?
106
KELLERMAN
NO, WORSE! I WAS OVER AT EMILY'S PARENTS YESTERDAY FOR DINNER...
SOUNDS LIKE YOU'RE GETTIN' SERIOUS...
ANYWAY, HER FAMILY'S REALLY STRAIGHT... HER DAD CALLED ME "YOUNG MAN"!
FSSSH
IT TURNS OUT THAT EMILY HAS A SISTER, TWO YEARS YOUNGER. I THINK I LIKE HER BETTER!
FORGET IT, ROCKY. I'M WITH SEINFELD. NO ONE HAS EVER MADE THE SWITCH.
e-mail:martin_kellerman@hotmail.com
I DON'T KNOW WHAT IT IS. SHE'S A LOT LIKE EMILY, BUT SHE'S GOT A CERTAIN... *JE NE SAIS QUOI.*
IS THAT FRENCH FOR MASSIVE JUGS?

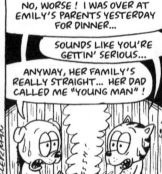

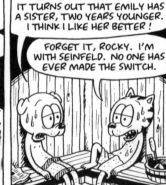

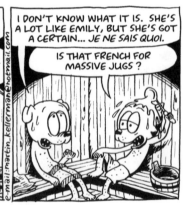

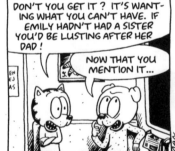

DON'T YOU GET IT? IT'S WANTING WHAT YOU CAN'T HAVE. IF EMILY HADN'T HAD A SISTER YOU'D BE LUSTING AFTER HER DAD!
NOW THAT YOU MENTION IT...
107
KELLERMAN
NO, SERIOUSLY. WHEN YOU WERE DATING MARIA ALWAYS OBSESSED ON HER FRIENDS, BUT NOW THAT YOU'VE BROKEN UP THEY FELL OFF YOUR RADAR.
AS LECTER PUT IT, YOU DESIRE WHAT YOU SEE EVERY DAY.
YOUR PLAN OF NAILING THE DEBUTANTE BY ATTENDING THAT EXPENSIVE RIDING SCHOOL, HOW'D THATGO?
IT FAILED 'CAUSE IT TURNS OUT HORSES PETRIFY ME. I JUST STOOD THERE WHILE THEY LICKED ME.
e-mail:martin_kellerman@hotmail.com
ALSO, ONCE SHE STARTED DOING SPICE GIRLS IMPRESSIONS IN PUBLIC I LOST INTEREST.
SHE MUST BE INCONSOLABLE.

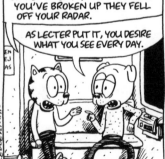

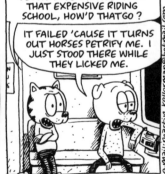

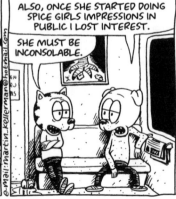

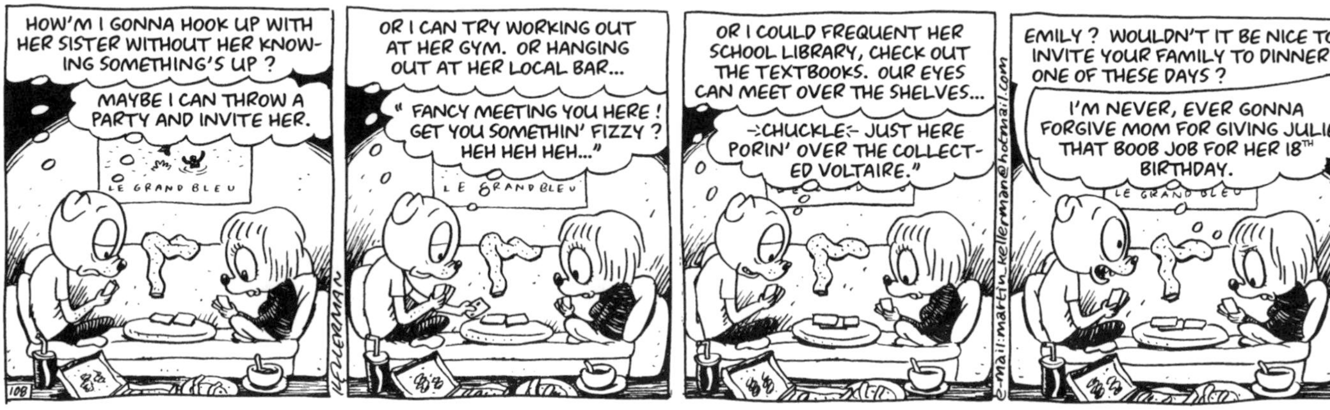
HOW'M I GONNA HOOK UP WITH HER SISTER WITHOUT HER KNOWING SOMETHING'S UP ?
MAYBE I CAN THROW A PARTY AND INVITE HER.
LE GRAND BLEU
108
KELLERMAN
OR I CAN TRY WORKING OUT AT HER GYM. OR HANGING OUT AT HER LOCAL BAR...
" FANCY MEETING YOU HERE ! GET YOU SOMETHIN' FIZZY ? HEH HEH HEH..."
LE GRAND BLEU
OR I COULD FREQUENT HER SCHOOL LIBRARY, CHECK OUT THE TEXTBOOKS. OUR EYES CAN MEET OVER THE SHELVES...
-CHUCKLE- JUST HERE PORIN' OVER THE COLLECTED VOLTAIRE."
e-mail:martin_kellerman@hotmail.com
EMILY ? WOULDN'T IT BE NICE TO INVITE YOUR FAMILY TO DINNER ONE OF THESE DAYS ?
I'M NEVER, EVER GONNA FORGIVE MOM FOR GIVING JULIE THAT BOOB JOB FOR HER 18TH BIRTHDAY.
LE GRAND BLEU

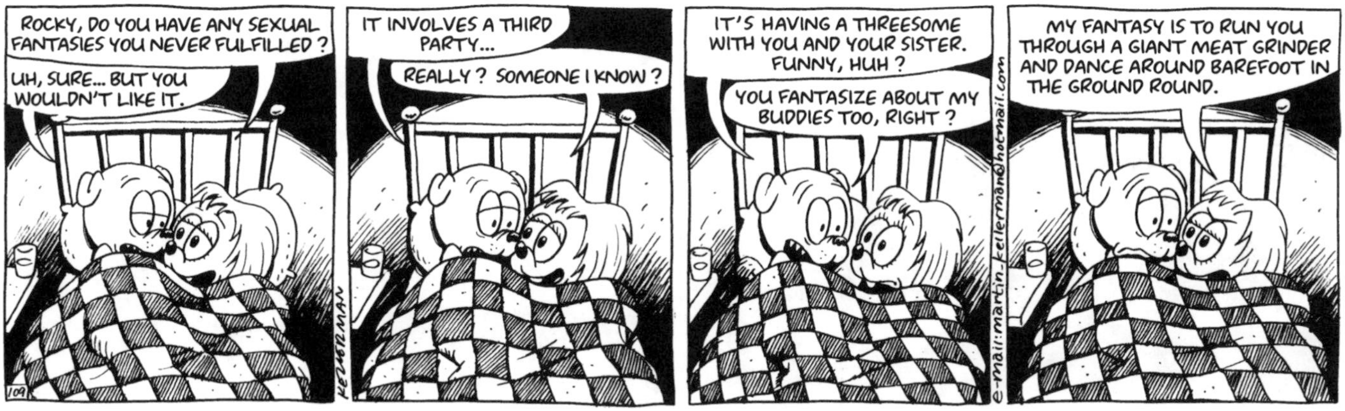
ROCKY, DO YOU HAVE ANY SEXUAL FANTASIES YOU NEVER FULFILLED ?
UH, SURE... BUT YOU WOULDN'T LIKE IT.
109
KELLERMAN
IT INVOLVES A THIRD PARTY...
REALLY ? SOMEONE I KNOW ?
IT'S HAVING A THREESOME WITH YOU AND YOUR SISTER. FUNNY, HUH ?
YOU FANTASIZE ABOUT MY BUDDIES TOO, RIGHT ?
e-mail:martin_kellerman@hotmail.com
MY FANTASY IS TO RUN YOU THROUGH A GIANT MEAT GRINDER AND DANCE AROUND BAREFOOT IN THE GROUND ROUND.

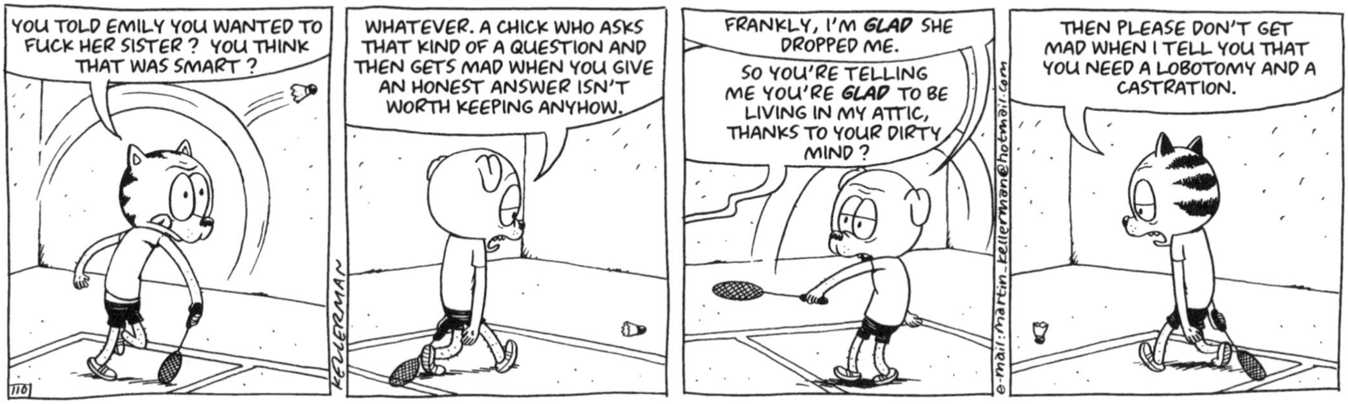
YOU TOLD EMILY YOU WANTED TO FUCK HER SISTER ? YOU THINK THAT WAS SMART ?
110
KELLERMAN
WHATEVER. A CHICK WHO ASKS THAT KIND OF A QUESTION AND THEN GETS MAD WHEN YOU GIVE AN HONEST ANSWER ISN'T WORTH KEEPING ANYHOW.
FRANKLY, I'M GLAD SHE DROPPED ME.
SO YOU'RE TELLING ME YOU'RE GLAD TO BE LIVING IN MY ATTIC, THANKS TO YOUR DIRTY MIND ?
e-mail:martin_kellerman@hotmail.com
THEN PLEASE DON'T GET MAD WHEN I TELL YOU THAT YOU NEED A LOBOTOMY AND A CASTRATION.

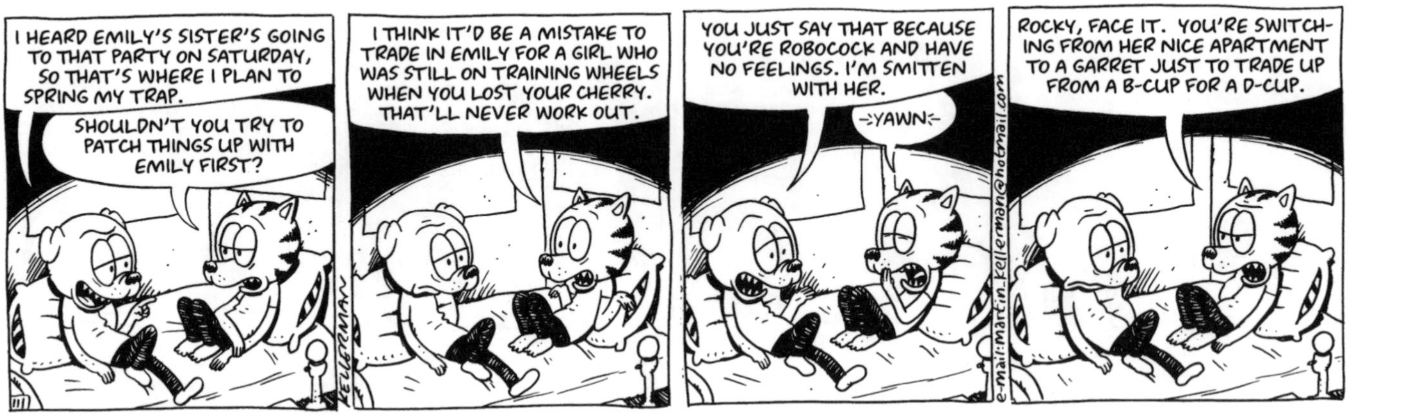
I HEARD EMILY'S SISTER'S GOING TO THAT PARTY ON SATURDAY, SO THAT'S WHERE I PLAN TO SPRING MY TRAP.
SHOULDN'T YOU TRY TO PATCH THINGS UP WITH EMILY FIRST?
111
KELLERMAN
I THINK IT'D BE A MISTAKE TO TRADE IN EMILY FOR A GIRL WHO WAS STILL ON TRAINING WHEELS WHEN YOU LOST YOUR CHERRY. THAT'LL NEVER WORK OUT.
YOU JUST SAY THAT BECAUSE YOU'RE ROBOCOCK AND HAVE NO FEELINGS. I'M SMITTEN WITH HER.
YAWN
e-mail:martin_kellerman@hotmail.com
ROCKY, FACE IT. YOU'RE SWITCHING FROM HER NICE APARTMENT TO A GARRET JUST TO TRADE UP FROM A B-CUP FOR A D-CUP.

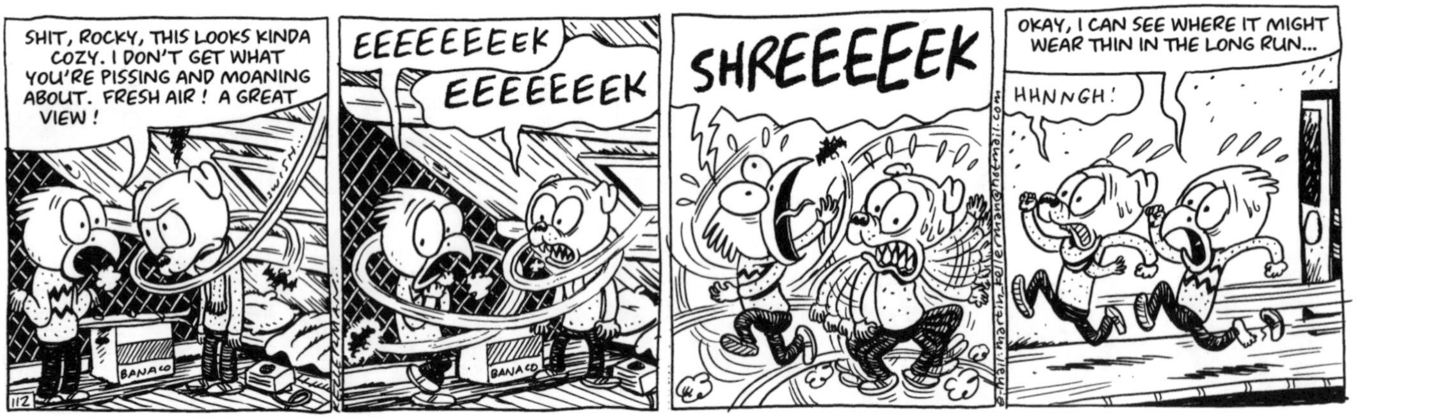
SHIT, ROCKY, THIS LOOKS KINDA COZY. I DON'T GET WHAT YOU'RE PISSING AND MOANING ABOUT. FRESH AIR! A GREAT VIEW!
SWISH
BANACO
112
KELLERMAN
EEEEEEEEEK
EEEEEEEK
SHREEEEEK
OKAY, I CAN SEE WHERE IT MIGHT WEAR THIN IN THE LONG RUN...
HHNNGH!

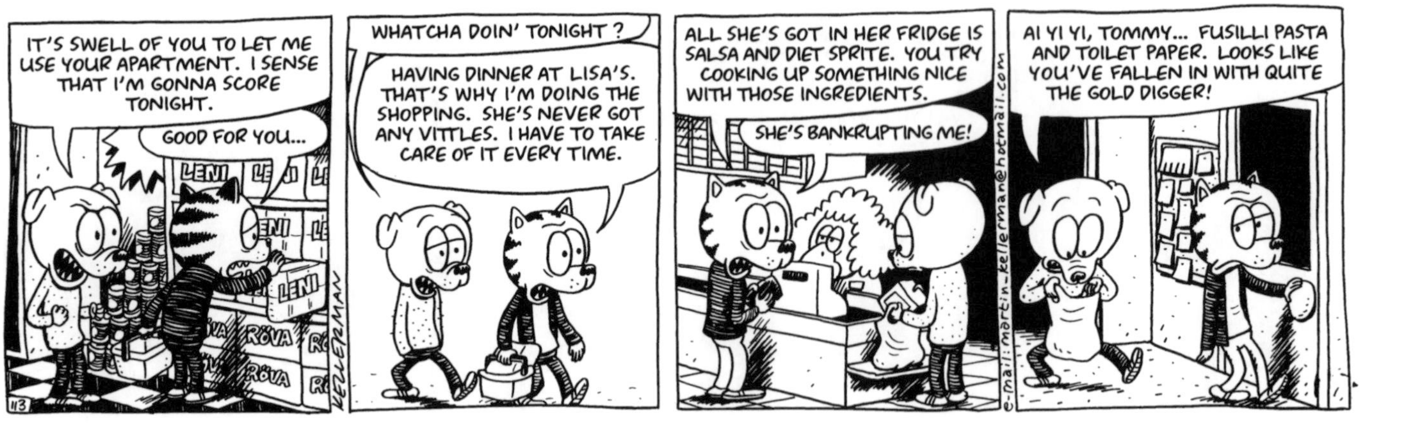
IT'S SWELL OF YOU TO LET ME USE YOUR APARTMENT. I SENSE THAT I'M GONNA SCORE TONIGHT.
GOOD FOR YOU...
LENI
RÖVA
113
KELLERMAN
WHATCHA DOIN' TONIGHT?
HAVING DINNER AT LISA'S. THAT'S WHY I'M DOING THE SHOPPING. SHE'S NEVER GOT ANY VITTLES. I HAVE TO TAKE CARE OF IT EVERY TIME.
ALL SHE'S GOT IN HER FRIDGE IS SALSA AND DIET SPRITE. YOU TRY COOKING UP SOMETHING NICE WITH THOSE INGREDIENTS.
SHE'S BANKRUPTING ME!
e-mail:martin_kellerman@hotmail.com
AI YI YI, TOMMY... FUSILLI PASTA AND TOILET PAPER. LOOKS LIKE YOU'VE FALLEN IN WITH QUITE THE GOLD DIGGER!

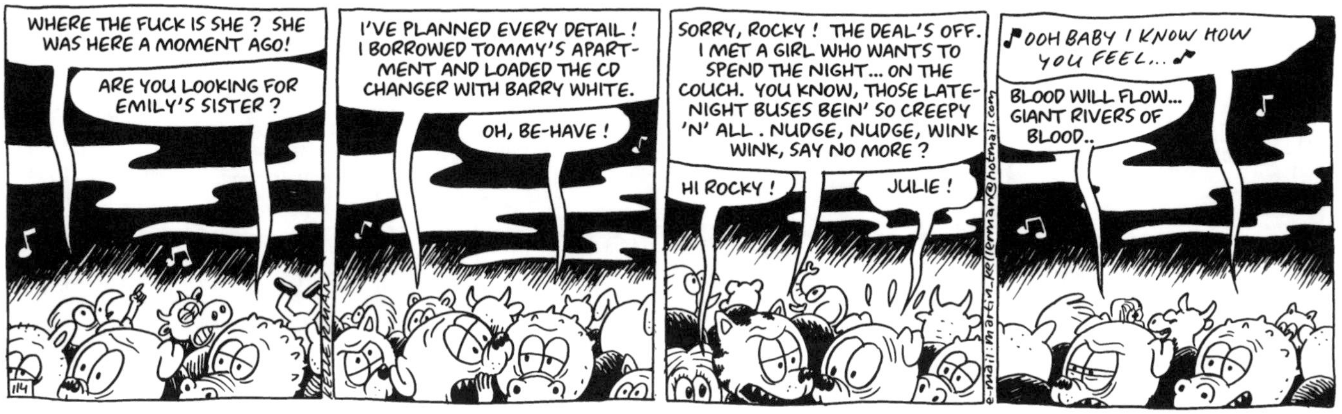
WHERE THE FUCK IS SHE ? SHE WAS HERE A MOMENT AGO!
ARE YOU LOOKING FOR EMILY'S SISTER ?
I'VE PLANNED EVERY DETAIL ! I BORROWED TOMMY'S APARTMENT AND LOADED THE CD CHANGER WITH BARRY WHITE.
OH, BE-HAVE !
SORRY, ROCKY ! THE DEAL'S OFF. I MET A GIRL WHO WANTS TO SPEND THE NIGHT... ON THE COUCH. YOU KNOW, THOSE LATE-NIGHT BUSES BEIN' SO CREEPY 'N' ALL . NUDGE, NUDGE, WINK WINK, SAY NO MORE ?
HI ROCKY !
JULIE !
OOH BABY I KNOW HOW YOU FEEL...
BLOOD WILL FLOW... GIANT RIVERS OF BLOOD..
e-mail: martin_kellerman@hotmail.com

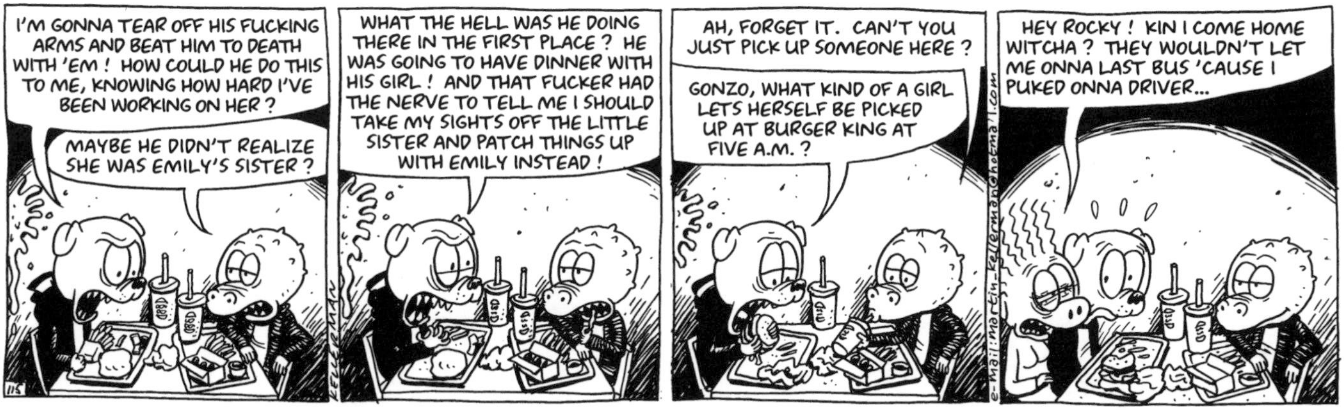
I'M GONNA TEAR OFF HIS FUCKING ARMS AND BEAT HIM TO DEATH WITH 'EM ! HOW COULD HE DO THIS TO ME, KNOWING HOW HARD I'VE BEEN WORKING ON HER ?
MAYBE HE DIDN'T REALIZE SHE WAS EMILY'S SISTER ?
WHAT THE HELL WAS HE DOING THERE IN THE FIRST PLACE ? HE WAS GOING TO HAVE DINNER WITH HIS GIRL ! AND THAT FUCKER HAD THE NERVE TO TELL ME I SHOULD TAKE MY SIGHTS OFF THE LITTLE SISTER AND PATCH THINGS UP WITH EMILY INSTEAD !
AH, FORGET IT. CAN'T YOU JUST PICK UP SOMEONE HERE ?
GONZO, WHAT KIND OF A GIRL LETS HERSELF BE PICKED UP AT BURGER KING AT FIVE A.M. ?
HEY ROCKY ! KIN I COME HOME WITCHA ? THEY WOULDN'T LET ME ONNA LAST BUS 'CAUSE I PUKED ONNA DRIVER...
e-mail: martin_kellerman@hotmail.com

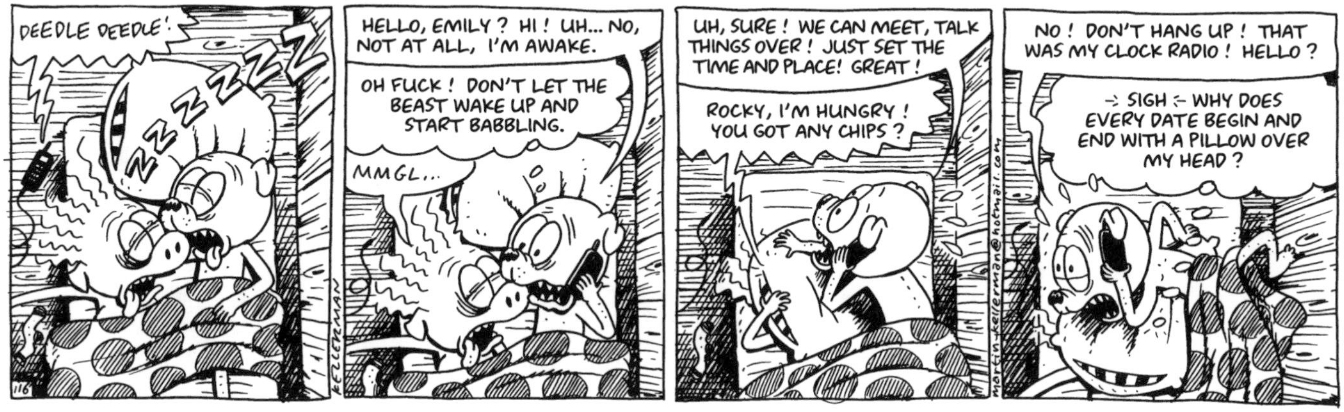
DEEDLE DEEDLE
ZZZZZZ
HELLO, EMILY ? HI ! UH... NO, NOT AT ALL, I'M AWAKE.
OH FUCK ! DON'T LET THE BEAST WAKE UP AND START BABBLING.
MMGL...
UH, SURE ! WE CAN MEET, TALK THINGS OVER ! JUST SET THE TIME AND PLACE! GREAT !
ROCKY, I'M HUNGRY ! YOU GOT ANY CHIPS ?
NO ! DON'T HANG UP ! THAT WAS MY CLOCK RADIO ! HELLO ?
SIGH WHY DOES EVERY DATE BEGIN AND END WITH A PILLOW OVER MY HEAD ?
martin_kellerman@hotmail.com

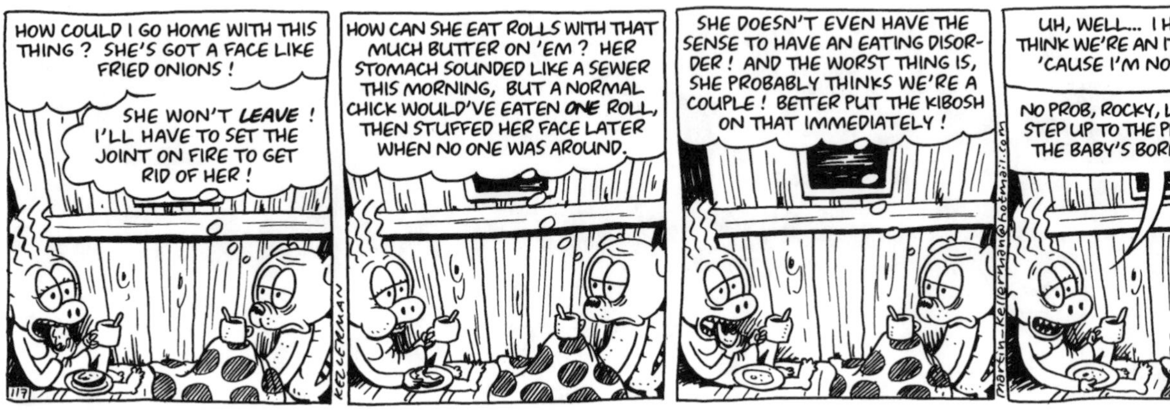
117
HOW COULD I GO HOME WITH THIS THING ? SHE'S GOT A FACE LIKE FRIED ONIONS !
SHE WON'T LEAVE ! I'LL HAVE TO SET THE JOINT ON FIRE TO GET RID OF HER !
KELLERMAN
HOW CAN SHE EAT ROLLS WITH THAT MUCH BUTTER ON 'EM ? HER STOMACH SOUNDED LIKE A SEWER THIS MORNING, BUT A NORMAL CHICK WOULD'VE EATEN ONE ROLL, THEN STUFFED HER FACE LATER WHEN NO ONE WAS AROUND.
SHE DOESN'T EVEN HAVE THE SENSE TO HAVE AN EATING DISORDER ! AND THE WORST THING IS, SHE PROBABLY THINKS WE'RE A COUPLE ! BETTER PUT THE KIBOSH ON THAT IMMEDIATELY !
martin_kellerman@hotmail.com
UH, WELL... I HOPE YOU DON'T THINK WE'RE AN ITEM OR ANYTHING, 'CAUSE I'M NOT INTERESTED.
NO PROB, ROCKY, LONG AS YOU STEP UP TO THE PLATE WHEN THE BABY'S BORN !

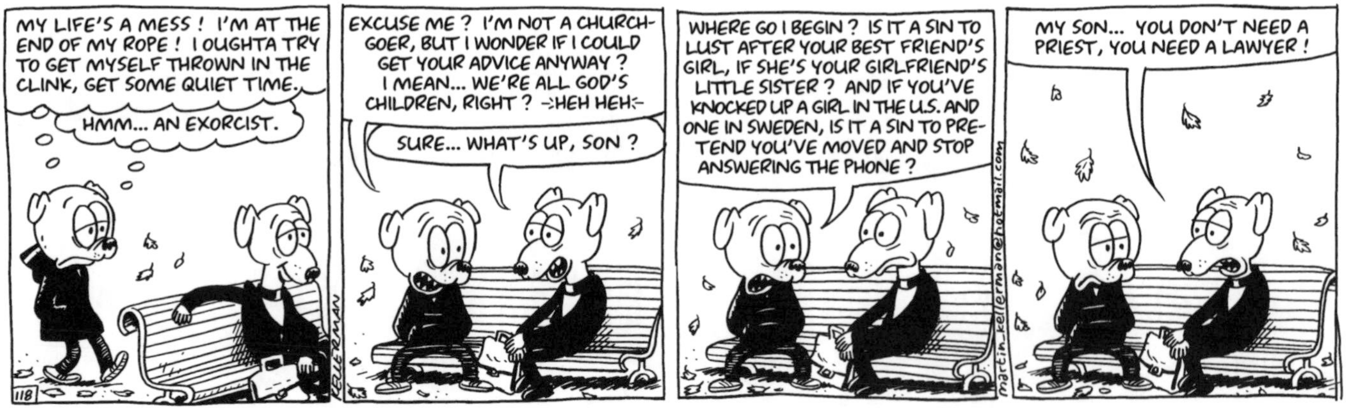
118
MY LIFE'S A MESS ! I'M AT THE END OF MY ROPE ! I OUGHTA TRY TO GET MYSELF THROWN IN THE CLINK, GET SOME QUIET TIME.
HMM... AN EXORCIST.
KELLERMAN
EXCUSE ME ? I'M NOT A CHURCHGOER, BUT I WONDER IF I COULD GET YOUR ADVICE ANYWAY ? I MEAN... WE'RE ALL GOD'S CHILDREN, RIGHT ? HEH HEH
SURE... WHAT'S UP, SON ?
WHERE DO I BEGIN ? IS IT A SIN TO LUST AFTER YOUR BEST FRIEND'S GIRL, IF SHE'S YOUR GIRLFRIEND'S LITTLE SISTER ? AND IF YOU'VE KNOCKED UP A GIRL IN THE U.S. AND ONE IN SWEDEN, IS IT A SIN TO PRETEND YOU'VE MOVED AND STOP ANSWERING THE PHONE ?
martin_kellerman@hotmail.com
MY SON... YOU DON'T NEED A PRIEST, YOU NEED A LAWYER !

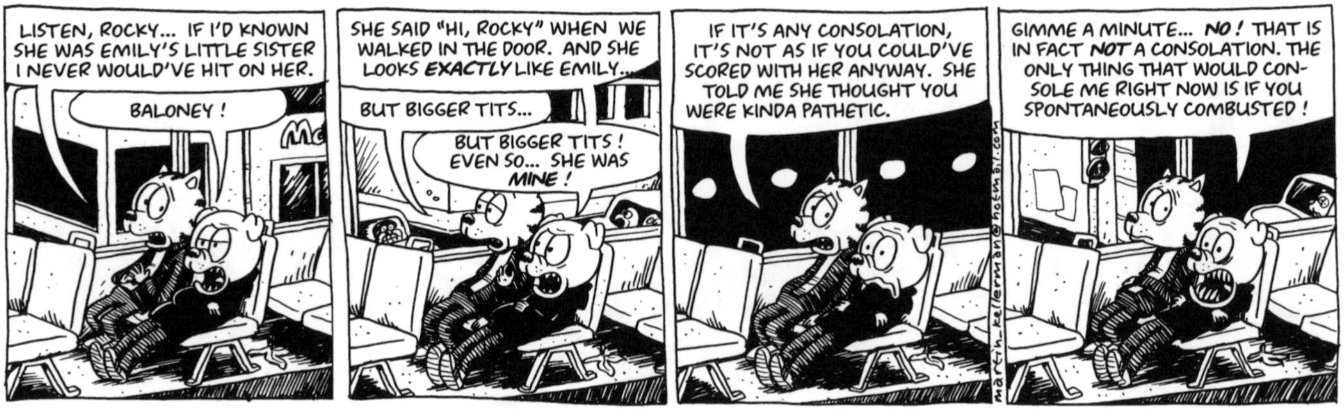
LISTEN, ROCKY... IF I'D KNOWN SHE WAS EMILY'S LITTLE SISTER I NEVER WOULD'VE HIT ON HER.
BALONEY !
SHE SAID "HI, ROCKY" WHEN WE WALKED IN THE DOOR. AND SHE LOOKS EXACTLY LIKE EMILY...
BUT BIGGER TITS...
BUT BIGGER TITS ! EVEN SO... SHE WAS MINE !
IF IT'S ANY CONSOLATION, IT'S NOT AS IF YOU COULD'VE SCORED WITH HER ANYWAY. SHE TOLD ME SHE THOUGHT YOU WERE KINDA PATHETIC.
martin_kellerman@hotmail.com
GIMME A MINUTE... NO ! THAT IS IN FACT NOT A CONSOLATION. THE ONLY THING THAT WOULD CONSOLE ME RIGHT NOW IS IF YOU SPONTANEOUSLY COMBUSTED !

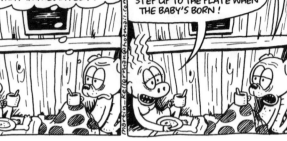

NINE TO FIVE, THE SEQUEL

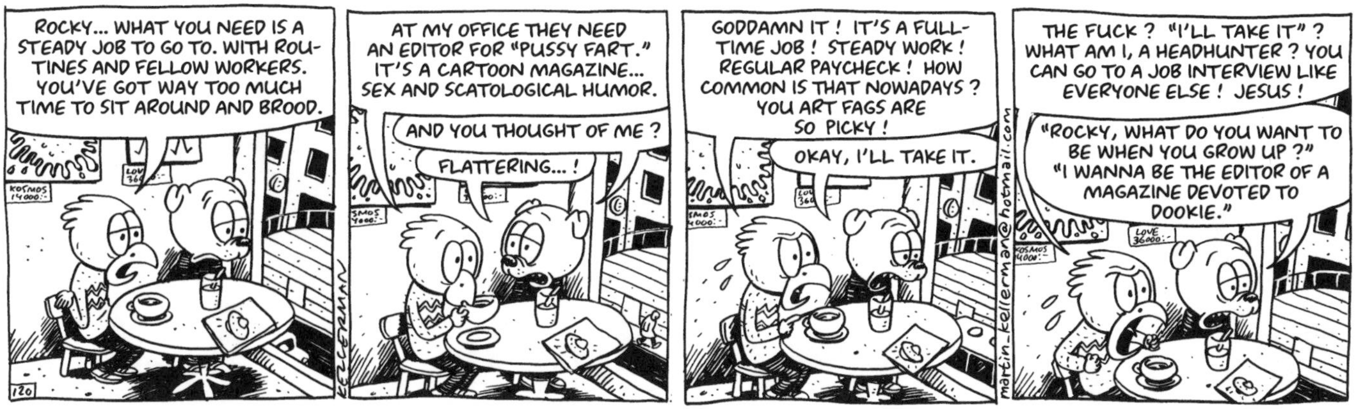
ROCKY... WHAT YOU NEED IS A STEADY JOB TO GO TO. WITH ROUTINES AND FELLOW WORKERS. YOU'VE GOT WAY TOO MUCH TIME TO SIT AROUND AND BROOD.
120
KELLERMAN
AT MY OFFICE THEY NEED AN EDITOR FOR "PUSSY FART." IT'S A CARTOON MAGAZINE... SEX AND SCATOLOGICAL HUMOR.
AND YOU THOUGHT OF ME ?
FLATTERING... !
GODDAMN IT ! IT'S A FULL-TIME JOB ! STEADY WORK ! REGULAR PAYCHECK ! HOW COMMON IS THAT NOWADAYS ? YOU ART FAGS ARE SO PICKY !
OKAY, I'LL TAKE IT.
martin_kellerman@hotmail.com
THE FUCK ? "I'LL TAKE IT" ? WHAT AM I, A HEADHUNTER ? YOU CAN GO TO A JOB INTERVIEW LIKE EVERYONE ELSE ! JESUS !
"ROCKY, WHAT DO YOU WANT TO BE WHEN YOU GROW UP ?" "I WANNA BE THE EDITOR OF A MAGAZINE DEVOTED TO DOOKIE."

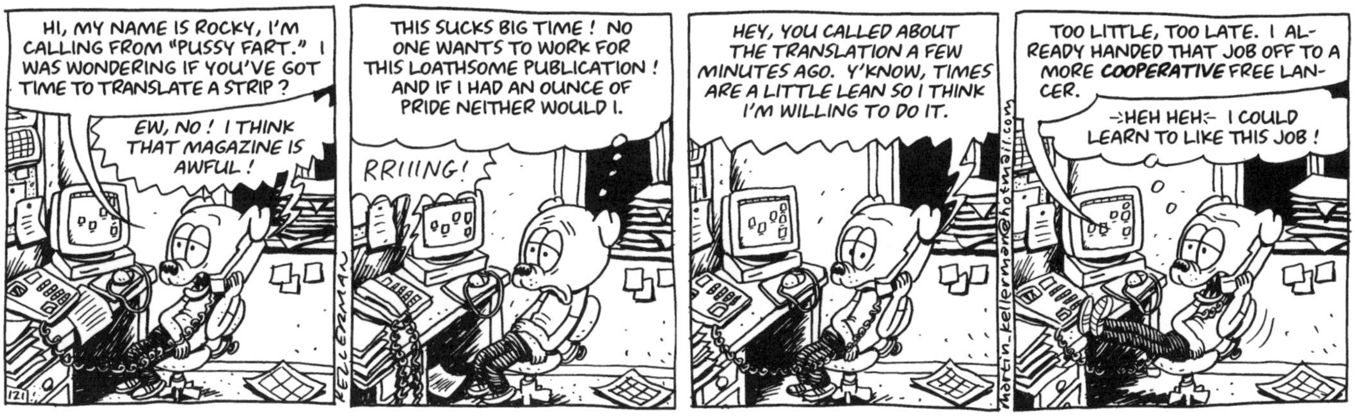
HI, MY NAME IS ROCKY, I'M CALLING FROM "PUSSY FART." I WAS WONDERING IF YOU'VE GOT TIME TO TRANSLATE A STRIP ?
EW, NO ! I THINK THAT MAGAZINE IS AWFUL !
121
KELLERMAN
THIS SUCKS BIG TIME ! NO ONE WANTS TO WORK FOR THIS LOATHSOME PUBLICATION ! AND IF I HAD AN OUNCE OF PRIDE NEITHER WOULD I.
RRIIING !
HEY, YOU CALLED ABOUT THE TRANSLATION A FEW MINUTES AGO. Y'KNOW, TIMES ARE A LITTLE LEAN SO I THINK I'M WILLING TO DO IT.
martin_kellerman@hotmail.com
TOO LITTLE, TOO LATE. I ALREADY HANDED THAT JOB OFF TO A MORE COOPERATIVE FREE LANCER.
HEH HEH I COULD LEARN TO LIKE THIS JOB !

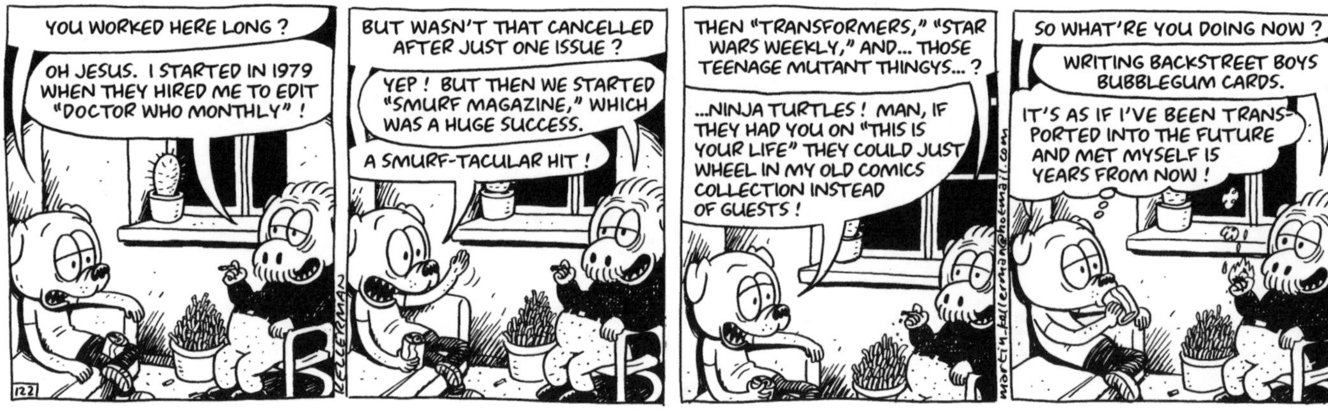
YOU WORKED HERE LONG ?
OH JESUS. I STARTED IN 1979 WHEN THEY HIRED ME TO EDIT "DOCTOR WHO MONTHLY" !
122
KELLERMAN
BUT WASN'T THAT CANCELLED AFTER JUST ONE ISSUE ?
YEP ! BUT THEN WE STARTED "SMURF MAGAZINE," WHICH WAS A HUGE SUCCESS.
A SMURF-TACULAR HIT !
THEN "TRANSFORMERS," "STAR WARS WEEKLY," AND... THOSE TEENAGE MUTANT THINGYS... ?
...NINJA TURTLES ! MAN, IF THEY HAD YOU ON "THIS IS YOUR LIFE" THEY COULD JUST WHEEL IN MY OLD COMICS COLLECTION INSTEAD OF GUESTS !
martin_kellerman@hotmail.com
SO WHAT'RE YOU DOING NOW ?
WRITING BACKSTREET BOYS BUBBLEGUM CARDS.
IT'S AS IF I'VE BEEN TRANSPORTED INTO THE FUTURE AND MET MYSELF 15 YEARS FROM NOW !

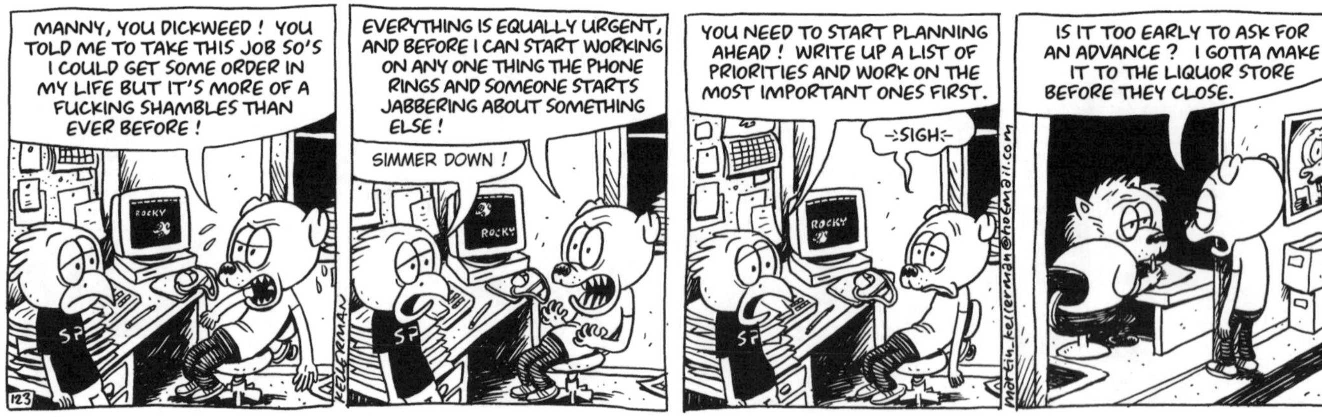
MANNY, YOU DICKWEED ! YOU TOLD ME TO TAKE THIS JOB SO'S I COULD GET SOME ORDER IN MY LIFE BUT IT'S MORE OF A FUCKING SHAMBLES THAN EVER BEFORE !
ROCKY
123
KELLERMAN
EVERYTHING IS EQUALLY URGENT, AND BEFORE I CAN START WORKING ON ANY ONE THING THE PHONE RINGS AND SOMEONE STARTS JABBERING ABOUT SOMETHING ELSE !
SIMMER DOWN !
ROCKY
YOU NEED TO START PLANNING AHEAD ! WRITE UP A LIST OF PRIORITIES AND WORK ON THE MOST IMPORTANT ONES FIRST.
SIGH
ROCKY
martin_kellerman@hotmail.com
IS IT TOO EARLY TO ASK FOR AN ADVANCE ? I GOTTA MAKE IT TO THE LIQUOR STORE BEFORE THEY CLOSE.

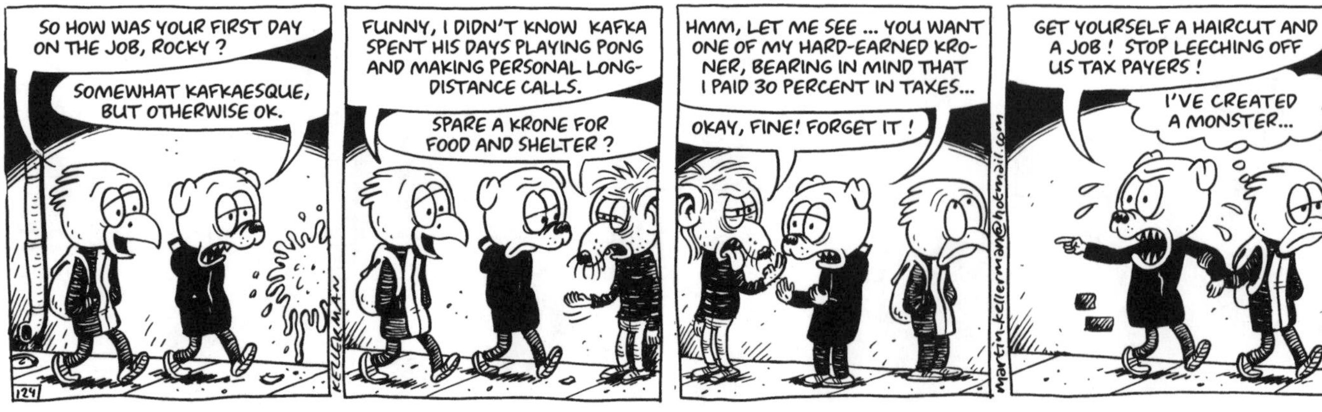
SO HOW WAS YOUR FIRST DAY ON THE JOB, ROCKY ?
SOMEWHAT KAFKAESQUE, BUT OTHERWISE OK.
124
KELLERMAN
FUNNY, I DIDN'T KNOW KAFKA SPENT HIS DAYS PLAYING PONG AND MAKING PERSONAL LONG-DISTANCE CALLS.
SPARE A KRONE FOR FOOD AND SHELTER ?
HMM, LET ME SEE ... YOU WANT ONE OF MY HARD-EARNED KRONER, BEARING IN MIND THAT I PAID 30 PERCENT IN TAXES...
OKAY, FINE! FORGET IT !
martin_kellerman@hotmail.com
GET YOURSELF A HAIRCUT AND A JOB ! STOP LEECHING OFF US TAX PAYERS !
I'VE CREATED A MONSTER...

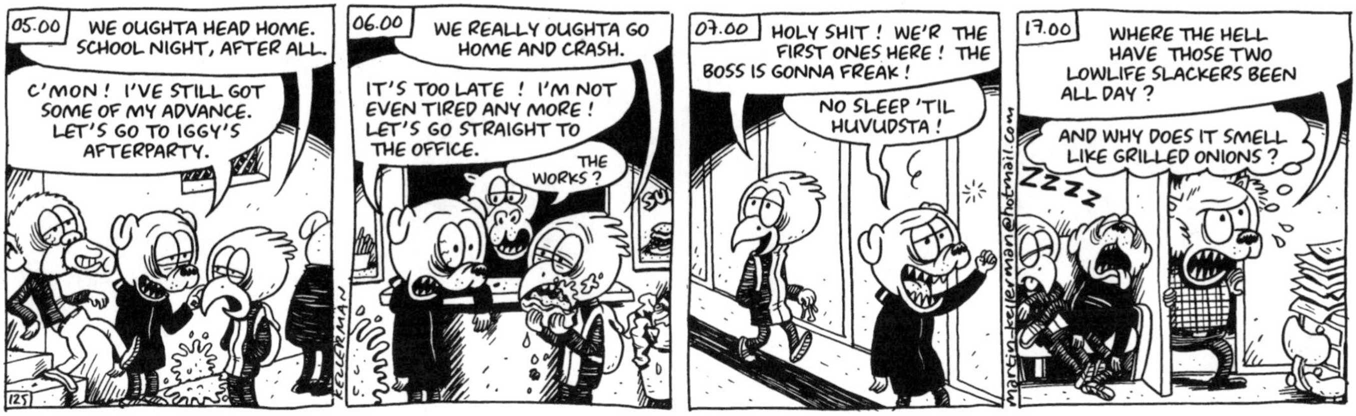
125
05.00
WE OUGHTA HEAD HOME. SCHOOL NIGHT, AFTER ALL.
C'MON! I'VE STILL GOT SOME OF MY ADVANCE. LET'S GO TO IGGY'S AFTERPARTY.
KELLERMAN
06.00
WE REALLY OUGHTA GO HOME AND CRASH.
IT'S TOO LATE! I'M NOT EVEN TIRED ANY MORE! LET'S GO STRAIGHT TO THE OFFICE.
THE WORKS?
07.00
HOLY SHIT! WE'R THE FIRST ONES HERE! THE BOSS IS GONNA FREAK!
NO SLEEP 'TIL HUVUDSTA!
martin_kellerman@hotmail.com
17.00
WHERE THE HELL HAVE THOSE TWO LOWLIFE SLACKERS BEEN ALL DAY?
AND WHY DOES IT SMELL LIKE GRILLED ONIONS?
ZZZZ

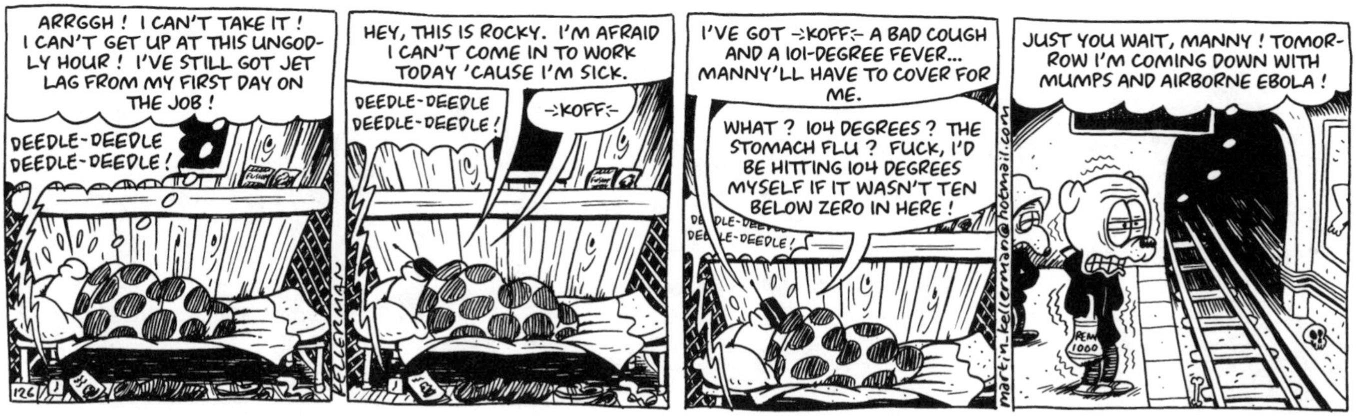
126
ARRGGH! I CAN'T TAKE IT! I CAN'T GET UP AT THIS UNGODLY HOUR! I'VE STILL GOT JET LAG FROM MY FIRST DAY ON THE JOB!
DEEDLE-DEEDLE DEEDLE-DEEDLE!
KELLERMAN
HEY, THIS IS ROCKY. I'M AFRAID I CAN'T COME IN TO WORK TODAY 'CAUSE I'M SICK.
DEEDLE-DEEDLE DEEDLE-DEEDLE!
-KOFF-
I'VE GOT -KOFF- A BAD COUGH AND A 101-DEGREE FEVER... MANNY'LL HAVE TO COVER FOR ME.
WHAT? 104 DEGREES? THE STOMACH FLU? FUCK, I'D BE HITTING 104 DEGREES MYSELF IF IT WASN'T TEN BELOW ZERO IN HERE!
martin_kellerman@hotmail.com
JUST YOU WAIT, MANNY! TOMORROW I'M COMING DOWN WITH MUMPS AND AIRBORNE EBOLA!
REMA 1000

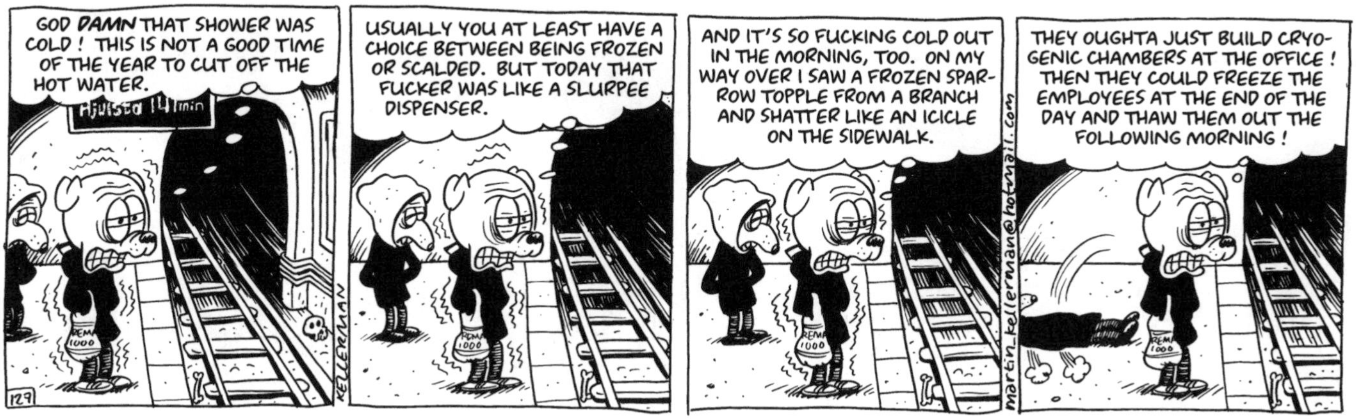
127
GOD DAMN THAT SHOWER WAS COLD! THIS IS NOT A GOOD TIME OF THE YEAR TO CUT OFF THE HOT WATER.
REMA 1000
KELLERMAN
USUALLY YOU AT LEAST HAVE A CHOICE BETWEEN BEING FROZEN OR SCALDED. BUT TODAY THAT FUCKER WAS LIKE A SLURPEE DISPENSER.
AND IT'S SO FUCKING COLD OUT IN THE MORNING, TOO. ON MY WAY OVER I SAW A FROZEN SPARROW TOPPLE FROM A BRANCH AND SHATTER LIKE AN ICICLE ON THE SIDEWALK.
martin_kellerman@hotmail.com
THEY OUGHTA JUST BUILD CRYOGENIC CHAMBERS AT THE OFFICE! THEN THEY COULD FREEZE THE EMPLOYEES AT THE END OF THE DAY AND THAW THEM OUT THE FOLLOWING MORNING!

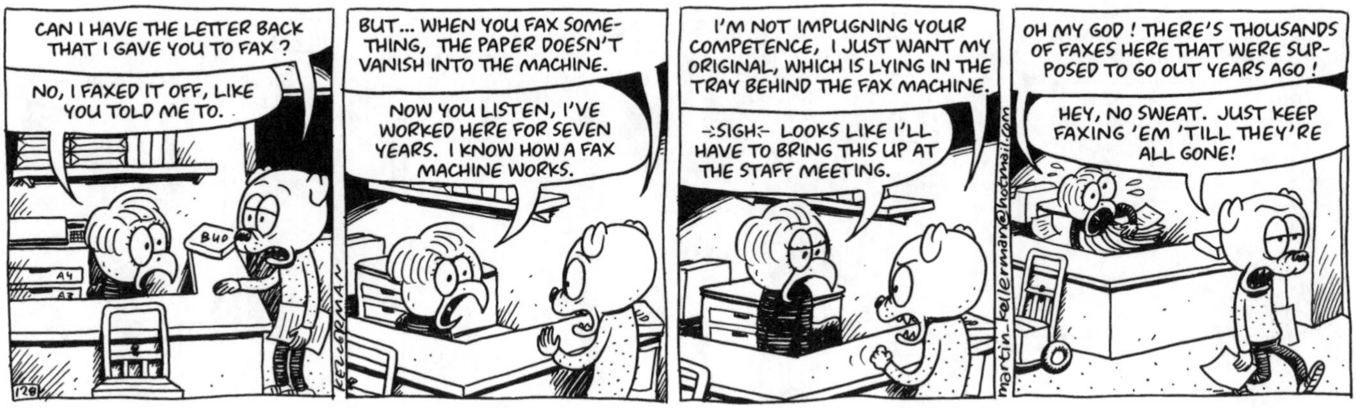
CAN I HAVE THE LETTER BACK THAT I GAVE YOU TO FAX ?
NO, I FAXED IT OFF, LIKE YOU TOLD ME TO.
BUD
A4
A3
128
KELLERMAN
BUT... WHEN YOU FAX SOMETHING, THE PAPER DOESN'T VANISH INTO THE MACHINE.
NOW YOU LISTEN, I'VE WORKED HERE FOR SEVEN YEARS. I KNOW HOW A FAX MACHINE WORKS.
I'M NOT IMPUGNING YOUR COMPETENCE, I JUST WANT MY ORIGINAL, WHICH IS LYING IN THE TRAY BEHIND THE FAX MACHINE.
→SIGH← LOOKS LIKE I'LL HAVE TO BRING THIS UP AT THE STAFF MEETING.
martin_kellerman@hotmail.com
OH MY GOD ! THERE'S THOUSANDS OF FAXES HERE THAT WERE SUPPOSED TO GO OUT YEARS AGO !
HEY, NO SWEAT. JUST KEEP FAXING 'EM 'TILL THEY'RE ALL GONE!

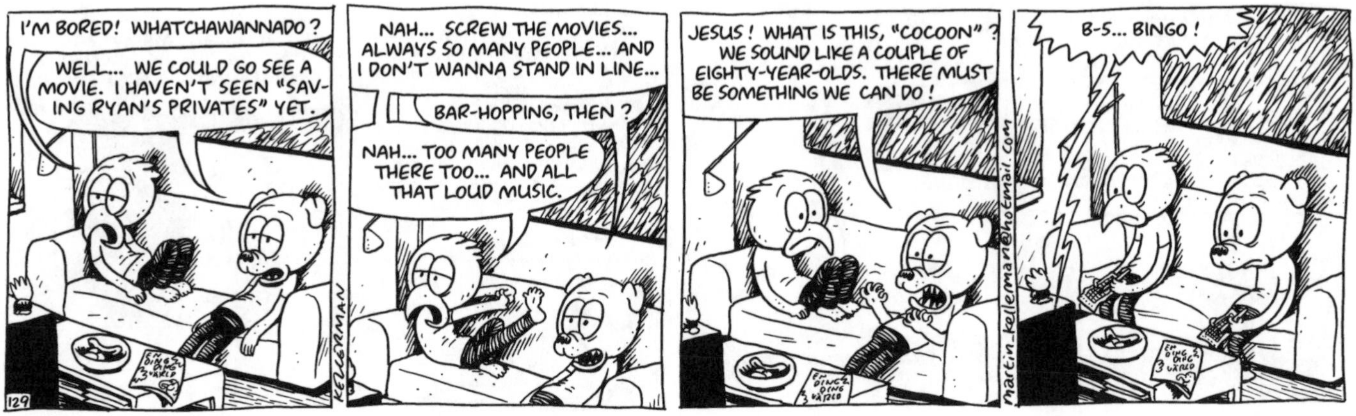
I'M BORED! WHATCHAWANNADO ?
WELL... WE COULD GO SEE A MOVIE. I HAVEN'T SEEN "SAVING RYAN'S PRIVATES" YET.
129
KELLERMAN
NAH... SCREW THE MOVIES... ALWAYS SO MANY PEOPLE... AND I DON'T WANNA STAND IN LINE...
BAR-HOPPING, THEN ?
NAH... TOO MANY PEOPLE THERE TOO... AND ALL THAT LOUD MUSIC.
JESUS ! WHAT IS THIS, "COCOON" ? WE SOUND LIKE A COUPLE OF EIGHTY-YEAR-OLDS. THERE MUST BE SOMETHING WE CAN DO !
martin_kellerman@hotmail.com
B-5... BINGO !

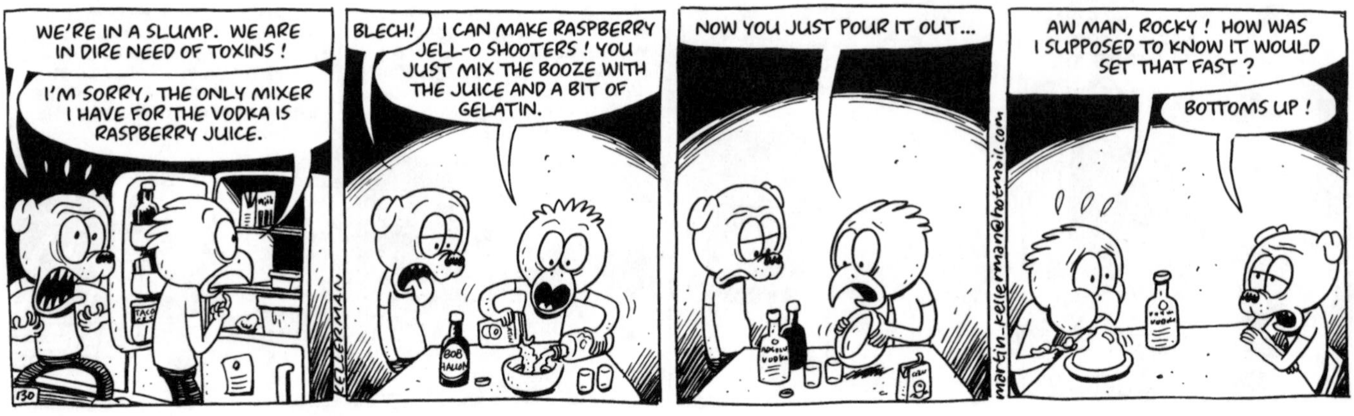
WE'RE IN A SLUMP. WE ARE IN DIRE NEED OF TOXINS !
I'M SORRY, THE ONLY MIXER I HAVE FOR THE VODKA IS RASPBERRY JUICE.
130
KELLERMAN
BLECH!
I CAN MAKE RASPBERRY JELL-O SHOOTERS ! YOU JUST MIX THE BOOZE WITH THE JUICE AND A BIT OF GELATIN.
BOB HALLON
NOW YOU JUST POUR IT OUT...
VODKA
martin_kellerman@hotmail.com
AW MAN, ROCKY ! HOW WAS I SUPPOSED TO KNOW IT WOULD SET THAT FAST ?
BOTTOMS UP !

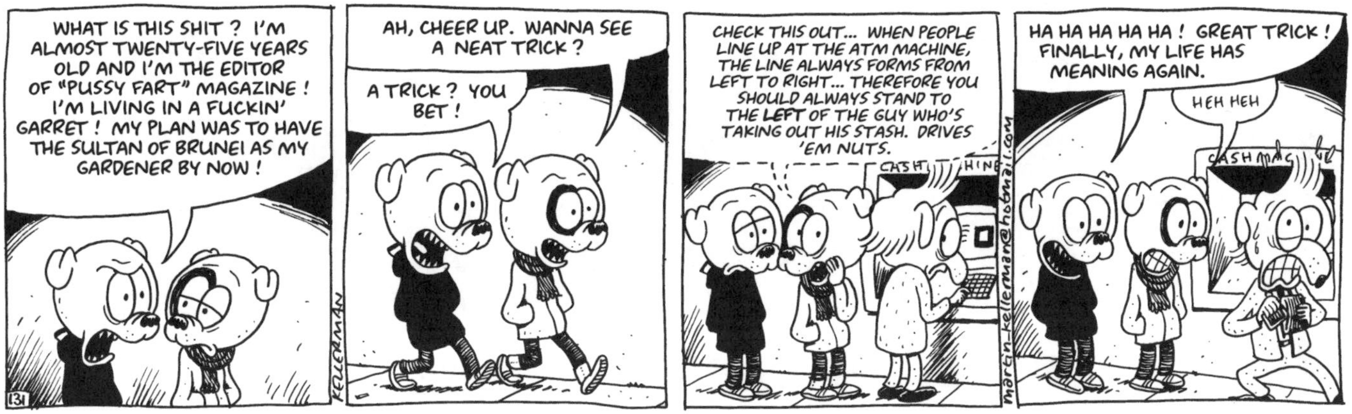
131
WHAT IS THIS SHIT ? I'M ALMOST TWENTY-FIVE YEARS OLD AND I'M THE EDITOR OF "PUSSY FART" MAGAZINE ! I'M LIVING IN A FUCKIN' GARRET ! MY PLAN WAS TO HAVE THE SULTAN OF BRUNEI AS MY GARDENER BY NOW !
KELLERMAN
AH, CHEER UP. WANNA SEE A NEAT TRICK ?
A TRICK ? YOU BET !
CHECK THIS OUT... WHEN PEOPLE LINE UP AT THE ATM MACHINE, THE LINE ALWAYS FORMS FROM LEFT TO RIGHT... THEREFORE YOU SHOULD ALWAYS STAND TO THE LEFT OF THE GUY WHO'S TAKING OUT HIS STASH. DRIVES 'EM NUTS.
martin_kellerman@hotmail.com
HA HA HA HA HA ! GREAT TRICK ! FINALLY, MY LIFE HAS MEANING AGAIN.
HEH HEH

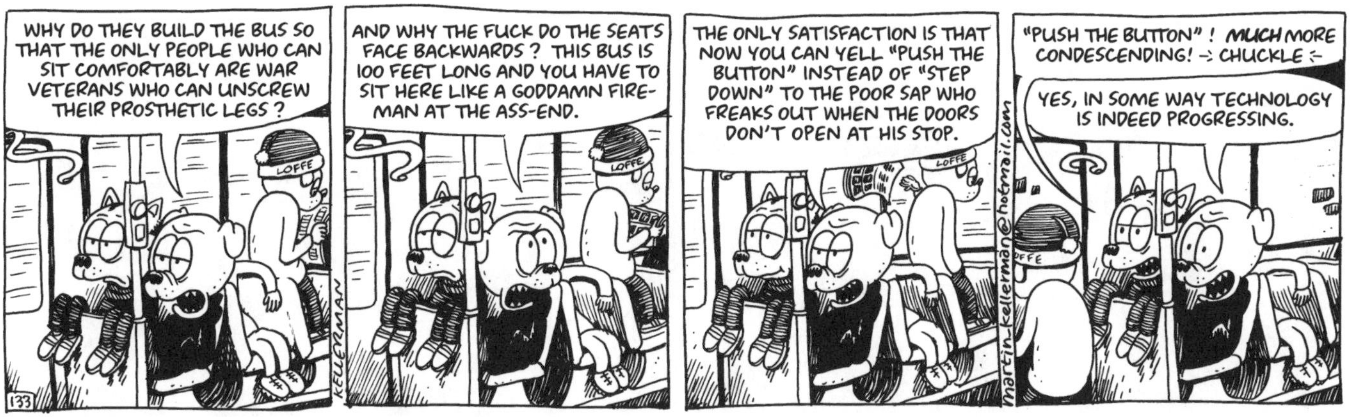
133
WHY DO THEY BUILD THE BUS SO THAT THE ONLY PEOPLE WHO CAN SIT COMFORTABLY ARE WAR VETERANS WHO CAN UNSCREW THEIR PROSTHETIC LEGS ?
LOFFE
KELLERMAN
AND WHY THE FUCK DO THE SEATS FACE BACKWARDS ? THIS BUS IS 100 FEET LONG AND YOU HAVE TO SIT HERE LIKE A GODDAMN FIRE-MAN AT THE ASS-END.
THE ONLY SATISFACTION IS THAT NOW YOU CAN YELL "PUSH THE BUTTON" INSTEAD OF "STEP DOWN" TO THE POOR SAP WHO FREAKS OUT WHEN THE DOORS DON'T OPEN AT HIS STOP.
martin_kellerman@hotmail.com
"PUSH THE BUTTON" ! MUCH MORE CONDESCENDING! ⇾ CHUCKLE ⇽
YES, IN SOME WAY TECHNOLOGY IS INDEED PROGRESSING.

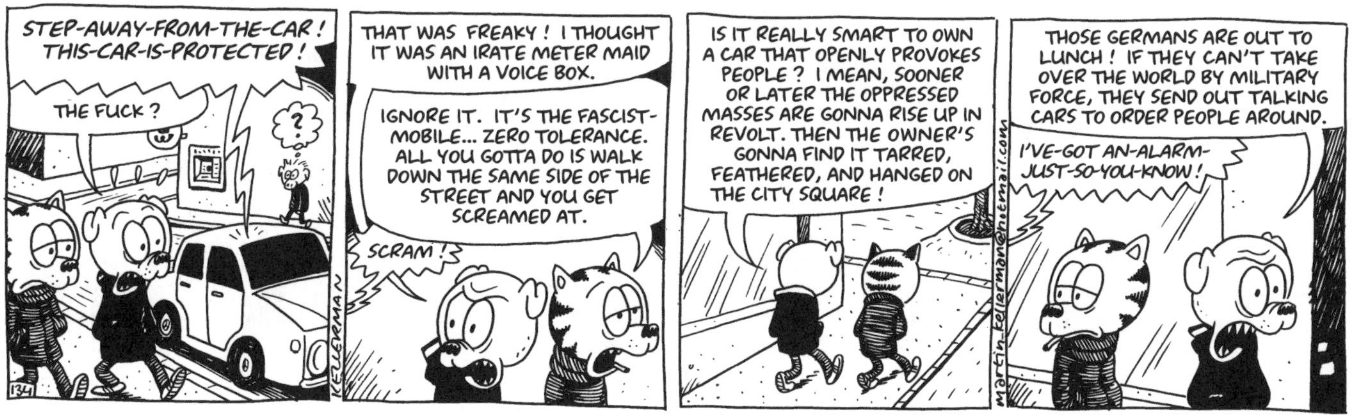
134
STEP-AWAY-FROM-THE-CAR ! THIS-CAR-IS-PROTECTED !
THE FUCK ?
?
KELLERMAN
THAT WAS FREAKY ! I THOUGHT IT WAS AN IRATE METER MAID WITH A VOICE BOX.
IGNORE IT. IT'S THE FASCIST-MOBILE... ZERO TOLERANCE. ALL YOU GOTTA DO IS WALK DOWN THE SAME SIDE OF THE STREET AND YOU GET SCREAMED AT.
SCRAM !
IS IT REALLY SMART TO OWN A CAR THAT OPENLY PROVOKES PEOPLE ? I MEAN, SOONER OR LATER THE OPPRESSED MASSES ARE GONNA RISE UP IN REVOLT. THEN THE OWNER'S GONNA FIND IT TARRED, FEATHERED, AND HANGED ON THE CITY SQUARE !
martin_kellerman@hotmail.com
THOSE GERMANS ARE OUT TO LUNCH ! IF THEY CAN'T TAKE OVER THE WORLD BY MILITARY FORCE, THEY SEND OUT TALKING CARS TO ORDER PEOPLE AROUND.
I'VE-GOT AN-ALARM-JUST-SO-YOU-KNOW !

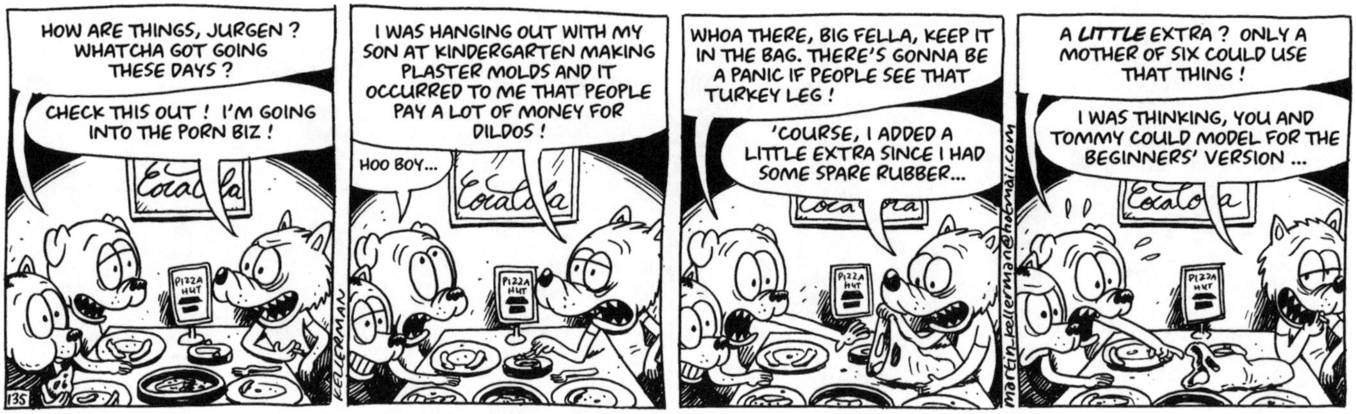
HOW ARE THINGS, JURGEN ? WHATCHA GOT GOING THESE DAYS ?
CHECK THIS OUT ! I'M GOING INTO THE PORN BIZ !
PIZZA HUT
135
KELLERMAN
I WAS HANGING OUT WITH MY SON AT KINDERGARTEN MAKING PLASTER MOLDS AND IT OCCURRED TO ME THAT PEOPLE PAY A LOT OF MONEY FOR DILDOS !
HOO BOY...
PIZZA HUT
WHOA THERE, BIG FELLA, KEEP IT IN THE BAG. THERE'S GONNA BE A PANIC IF PEOPLE SEE THAT TURKEY LEG !
'COURSE, I ADDED A LITTLE EXTRA SINCE I HAD SOME SPARE RUBBER...
PIZZA HUT
martin_kellerman@hotmail.com
A LITTLE EXTRA ? ONLY A MOTHER OF SIX COULD USE THAT THING !
I WAS THINKING, YOU AND TOMMY COULD MODEL FOR THE BEGINNERS' VERSION ...
PIZZA HUT

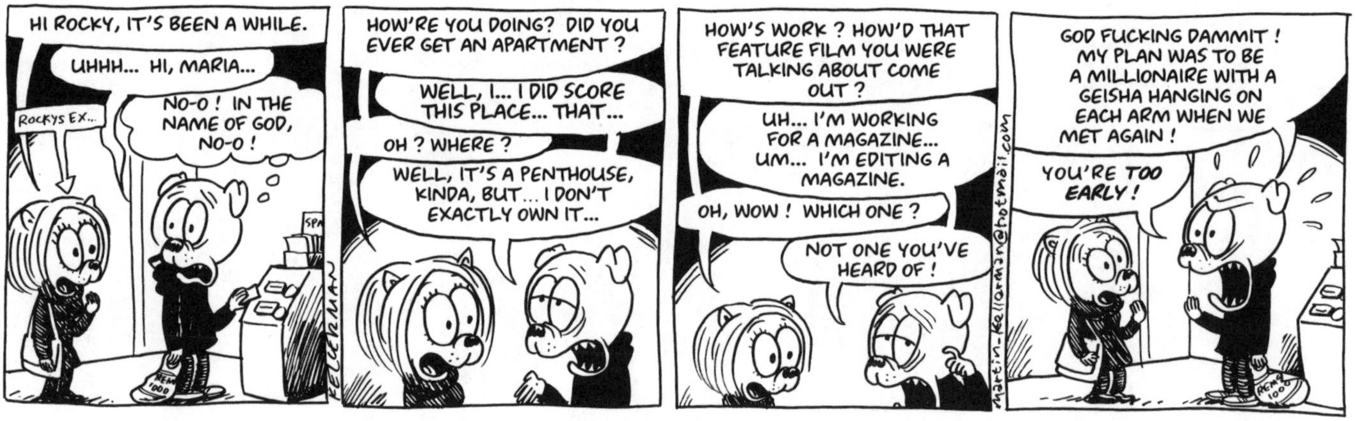
HI ROCKY, IT'S BEEN A WHILE.
UHHH... HI, MARIA...
ROCKYS EX..
NO-O ! IN THE NAME OF GOD, NO-O !
KELLERMAN
HOW'RE YOU DOING? DID YOU EVER GET AN APARTMENT ?
WELL, I... I DID SCORE THIS PLACE... THAT...
OH ? WHERE ?
WELL, IT'S A PENTHOUSE, KINDA, BUT... I DON'T EXACTLY OWN IT...
HOW'S WORK ? HOW'D THAT FEATURE FILM YOU WERE TALKING ABOUT COME OUT ?
UH... I'M WORKING FOR A MAGAZINE... UM... I'M EDITING A MAGAZINE.
OH, WOW ! WHICH ONE ?
NOT ONE YOU'VE HEARD OF !
martin_kellerman@hotmail.com
GOD FUCKING DAMMIT ! MY PLAN WAS TO BE A MILLIONAIRE WITH A GEISHA HANGING ON EACH ARM WHEN WE MET AGAIN !
YOU'RE TOO EARLY !

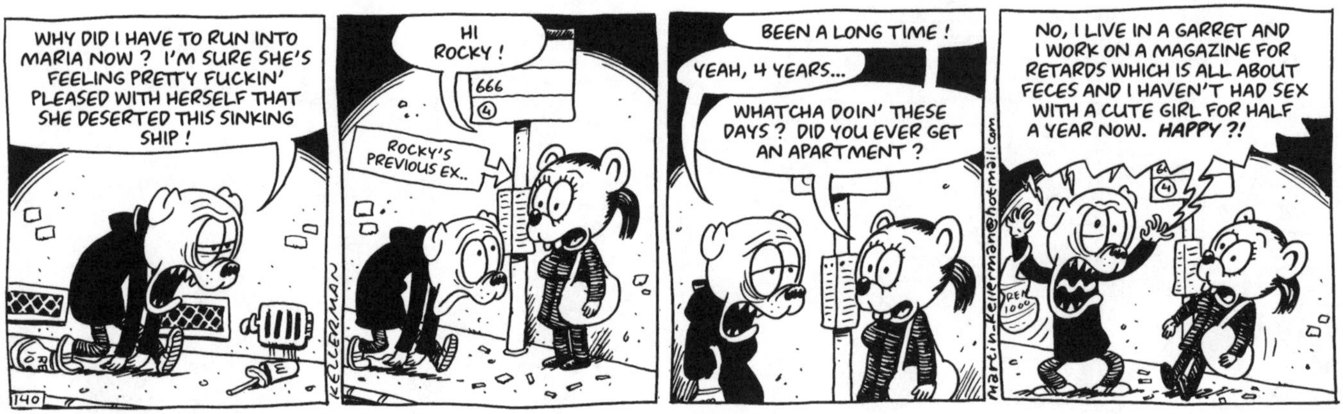
WHY DID I HAVE TO RUN INTO MARIA NOW ? I'M SURE SHE'S FEELING PRETTY FUCKIN' PLEASED WITH HERSELF THAT SHE DESERTED THIS SINKING SHIP !
140
KELLERMAN
HI ROCKY !
666
4
ROCKY'S PREVIOUS EX..
BEEN A LONG TIME !
YEAH, 4 YEARS...
WHATCHA DOIN' THESE DAYS ? DID YOU EVER GET AN APARTMENT ?
martin_kellerman@hotmail.com
NO, I LIVE IN A GARRET AND I WORK ON A MAGAZINE FOR RETARDS WHICH IS ALL ABOUT FECES AND I HAVEN'T HAD SEX WITH A CUTE GIRL FOR HALF A YEAR NOW. HAPPY ?!

SICK, SICK, SICK

WHAT THE HELL ARE YOU DOING AT HOME ? "PUSSY FART" WAS SUPPOSED TO WRAP LAST WEEK !
BUT I'M SI-I-I-ICK.
EVERY TIME WE'RE ON DEADLINE YOU'RE SICK !
141
KELLERMAN
CAN'T MANNY FINISH IT UP ?
HE'S IN TOKYO ! HE'S BEEN SCHEDULING HIS TRIPS AROUND YOUR PUBLICATION SCHEDULE SO HE DOESN'T END UP DOING YOUR JOB FOR YOU !
FUCKER...
MUST HANG UP NOW... I THINK I'M GONNA PUKE.
NO !
martin_kellerman@hotmail.com
I'M MOVING TO THE COUNTRY... I CAN LIVE ON POTATOES THAT I GROW MYSELF... NO MORE STRESS... I CAN ALWAYS CALL UP MANNY WHEN IT'S HARVEST TIME...
DEEDLEDEEDLE !

JESUS CHRIST, ROCKY, WHAT HAPPENED TO YOU ? YOU LOOK LIKE TOM HANKS IN "PHILADELPHIA" !
MY STOMACH BLEW UP ! I WAS SUFFERING FROM JOB-RELATED STRESS.
142
KELLERMAN
WHAT STRESS ? ALL YOU DO IS TAKE NAPS AND SURF THE NET!
TRUE, BUT I'D BE STRESSIN' ABOUT ALL THE STUFF I WASN'T DOING, AND TOWARDS THE END OF THE MONTH WHEN IT HAD TO GET DONE I STRESSED OUT SO MUCH I GOT SICK !
THEY GOT YOU DOPED UP ?
YEAH, THEY'RE TRYING ALL SORTS OF JUNK ! BUT THE ONLY RESULT SO FAR IS THAT I'M SUPER CONSTIPATED. I FEEL LIKE ONE OF THOSE JIFFY POP STOVETOP CONTAINERS.
martin_kellerman@hotmail.com
THEY'RE GONNA HAVE TO GIVE ME A CAESAREAN TO EXCAVATE ALL THAT SHIT ! IT FEELS LIKE I'VE GOT THAT FOSSILIZED T. REX TURD IN MY GUT!

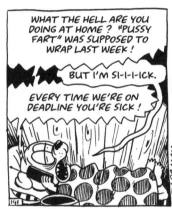

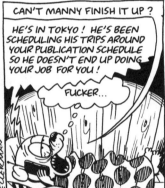

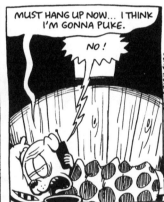

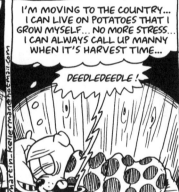

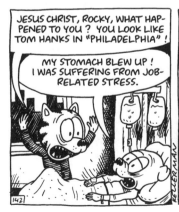

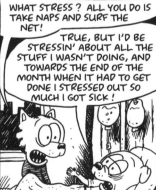

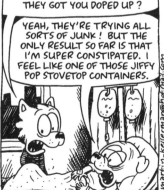

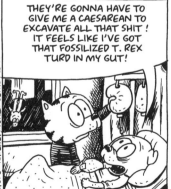

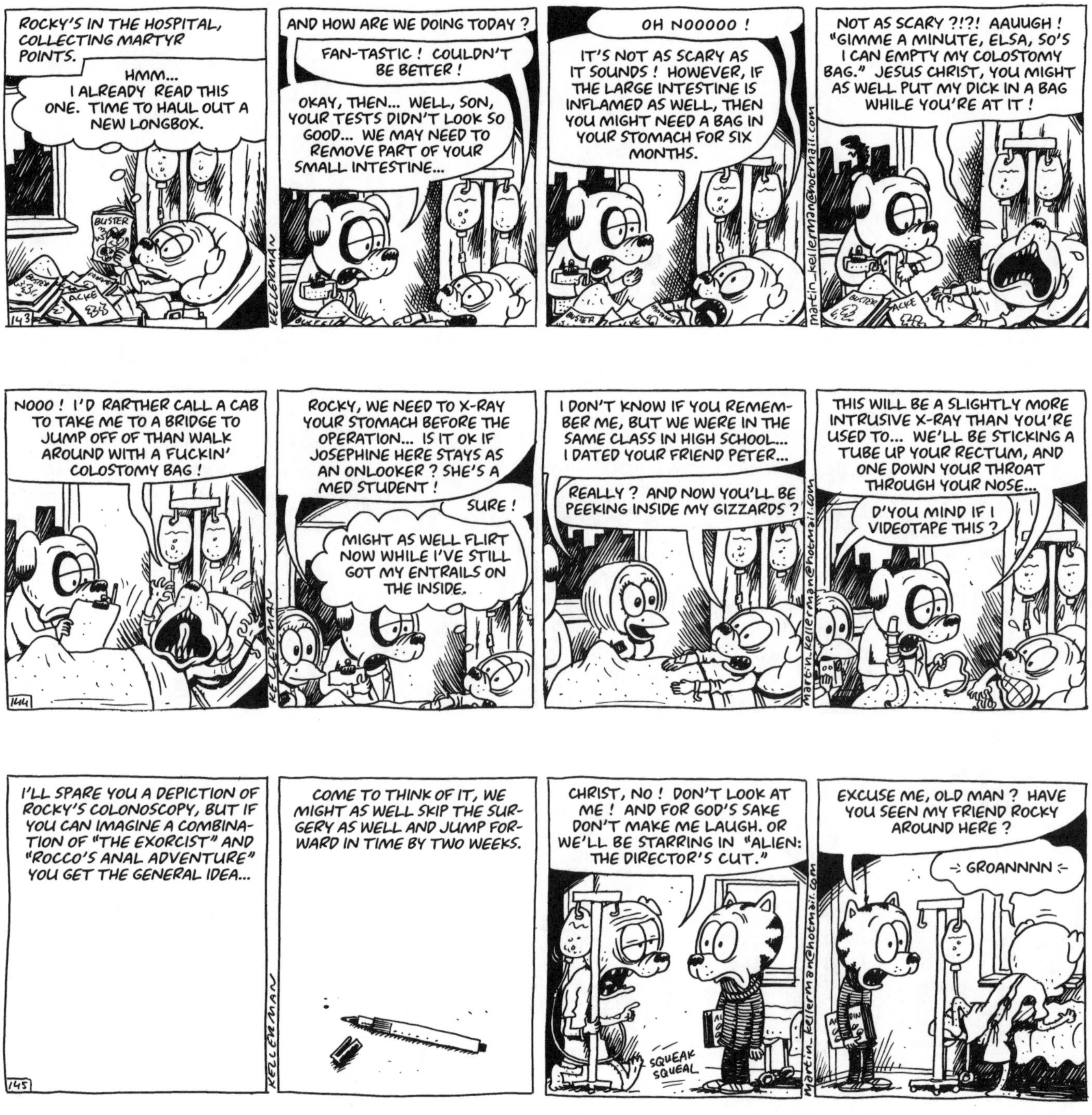
ROCKY'S IN THE HOSPITAL, COLLECTING MARTYR POINTS.
HMM... I ALREADY READ THIS ONE. TIME TO HAUL OUT A NEW LONGBOX.
BUSTER
143
KELLERMAN
AND HOW ARE WE DOING TODAY ?
FAN-TASTIC ! COULDN'T BE BETTER !
OKAY, THEN... WELL, SON, YOUR TESTS DIDN'T LOOK SO GOOD... WE MAY NEED TO REMOVE PART OF YOUR SMALL INTESTINE...
OH NOOOOO !
IT'S NOT AS SCARY AS IT SOUNDS ! HOWEVER, IF THE LARGE INTESTINE IS INFLAMED AS WELL, THEN YOU MIGHT NEED A BAG IN YOUR STOMACH FOR SIX MONTHS.
martin_kellerman@hotmail.com
NOT AS SCARY ?!?! AAUUGH ! "GIMME A MINUTE, ELSA, SO'S I CAN EMPTY MY COLOSTOMY BAG." JESUS CHRIST, YOU MIGHT AS WELL PUT MY DICK IN A BAG WHILE YOU'RE AT IT !
NOOO ! I'D RARTHER CALL A CAB TO TAKE ME TO A BRIDGE TO JUMP OFF OF THAN WALK AROUND WITH A FUCKIN' COLOSTOMY BAG !
144
KELLERMAN
ROCKY, WE NEED TO X-RAY YOUR STOMACH BEFORE THE OPERATION... IS IT OK IF JOSEPHINE HERE STAYS AS AN ONLOOKER ? SHE'S A MED STUDENT !
SURE !
MIGHT AS WELL FLIRT NOW WHILE I'VE STILL GOT MY ENTRAILS ON THE INSIDE.
I DON'T KNOW IF YOU REMEMBER ME, BUT WE WERE IN THE SAME CLASS IN HIGH SCHOOL... I DATED YOUR FRIEND PETER...
REALLY ? AND NOW YOU'LL BE PEEKING INSIDE MY GIZZARDS ?
martin_kellerman@hotmail.com
THIS WILL BE A SLIGHTLY MORE INTRUSIVE X-RAY THAN YOU'RE USED TO... WE'LL BE STICKING A TUBE UP YOUR RECTUM, AND ONE DOWN YOUR THROAT THROUGH YOUR NOSE...
D'YOU MIND IF I VIDEOTAPE THIS ?
I'LL SPARE YOU A DEPICTION OF ROCKY'S COLONOSCOPY, BUT IF YOU CAN IMAGINE A COMBINATION OF "THE EXORCIST" AND "ROCCO'S ANAL ADVENTURE" YOU GET THE GENERAL IDEA...
145
KELLERMAN
COME TO THINK OF IT, WE MIGHT AS WELL SKIP THE SURGERY AS WELL AND JUMP FORWARD IN TIME BY TWO WEEKS.
CHRIST, NO ! DON'T LOOK AT ME ! AND FOR GOD'S SAKE DON'T MAKE ME LAUGH. OR WE'LL BE STARRING IN "ALIEN: THE DIRECTOR'S CUT."
SQUEAK SQUEAL
martin_kellerman@hotmail.com
EXCUSE ME, OLD MAN ? HAVE YOU SEEN MY FRIEND ROCKY AROUND HERE ?
GROANNNN

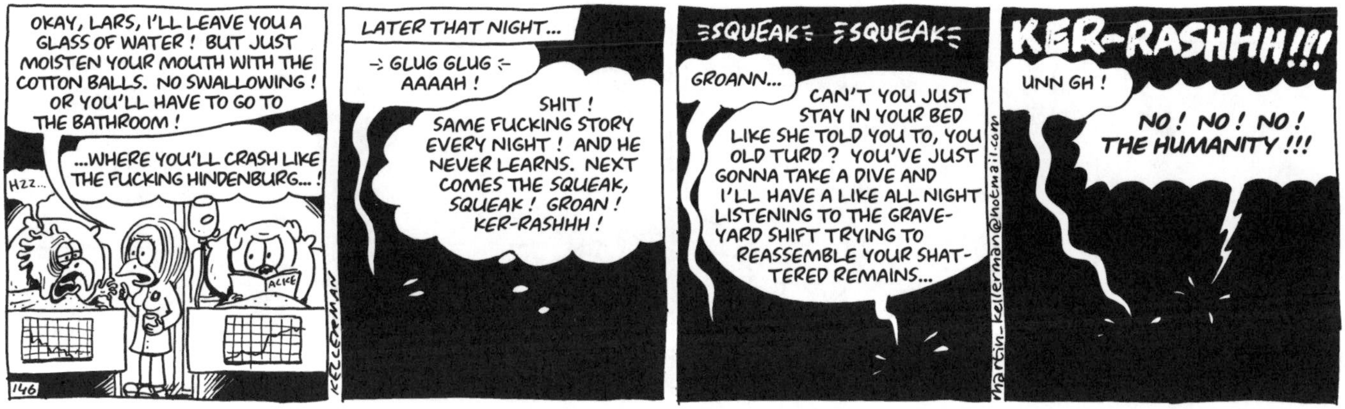
OKAY, LARS, I'LL LEAVE YOU A GLASS OF WATER ! BUT JUST MOISTEN YOUR MOUTH WITH THE COTTON BALLS. NO SWALLOWING ! OR YOU'LL HAVE TO GO TO THE BATHROOM !
...WHERE YOU'LL CRASH LIKE THE FUCKING HINDENBURG... !
HZZ...
ACKE
146
KELLERMAN
LATER THAT NIGHT...
GLUG GLUG AAAAH !
SHIT ! SAME FUCKING STORY EVERY NIGHT ! AND HE NEVER LEARNS. NEXT COMES THE SQUEAK, SQUEAK ! GROAN ! KER-RASHHH !
SQUEAK SQUEAK
GROANN...
CAN'T YOU JUST STAY IN YOUR BED LIKE SHE TOLD YOU TO, YOU OLD TURD ? YOU'VE JUST GONNA TAKE A DIVE AND I'LL HAVE A LIKE ALL NIGHT LISTENING TO THE GRAVEYARD SHIFT TRYING TO REASSEMBLE YOUR SHATTERED REMAINS...
martin_kellerman@hotmail.com
KER-RASHHH!!!
UNN GH !
NO ! NO ! NO ! THE HUMANITY !!!

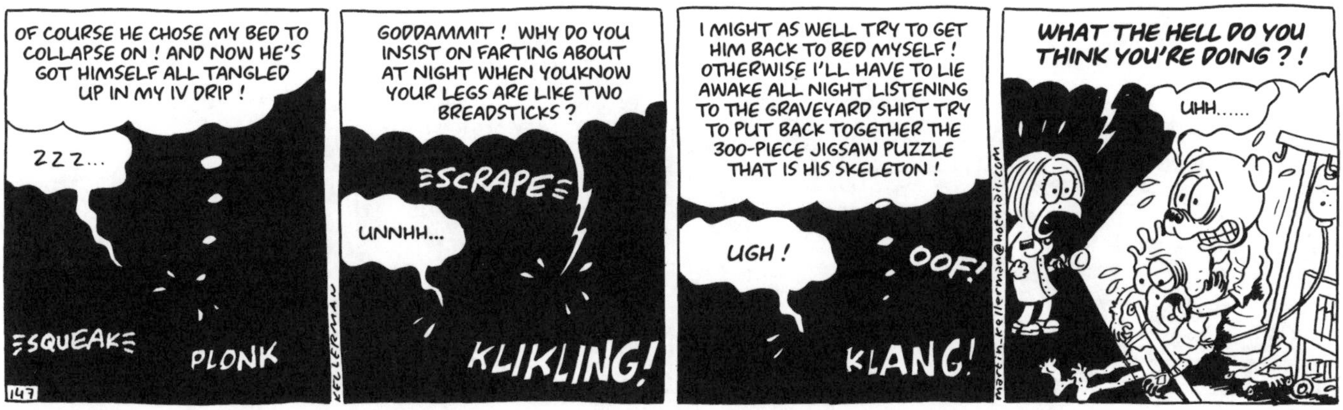
OF COURSE HE CHOSE MY BED TO COLLAPSE ON ! AND NOW HE'S GOT HIMSELF ALL TANGLED UP IN MY IV DRIP !
ZZZ...
SQUEAK
PLONK
147
KELLERMAN
GODDAMMIT ! WHY DO YOU INSIST ON FARTING ABOUT AT NIGHT WHEN YOUKNOW YOUR LEGS ARE LIKE TWO BREADSTICKS ?
SCRAPE
UNNHH...
KLIKLING!
I MIGHT AS WELL TRY TO GET HIM BACK TO BED MYSELF ! OTHERWISE I'LL HAVE TO LIE AWAKE ALL NIGHT LISTENING TO THE GRAVEYARD SHIFT TRY TO PUT BACK TOGETHER THE 300-PIECE JIGSAW PUZZLE THAT IS HIS SKELETON !
UGH !
OOF!
KLANG!
martin.kellerman@hotmail.com
WHAT THE HELL DO YOU THINK YOU'RE DOING ? !
UHH......

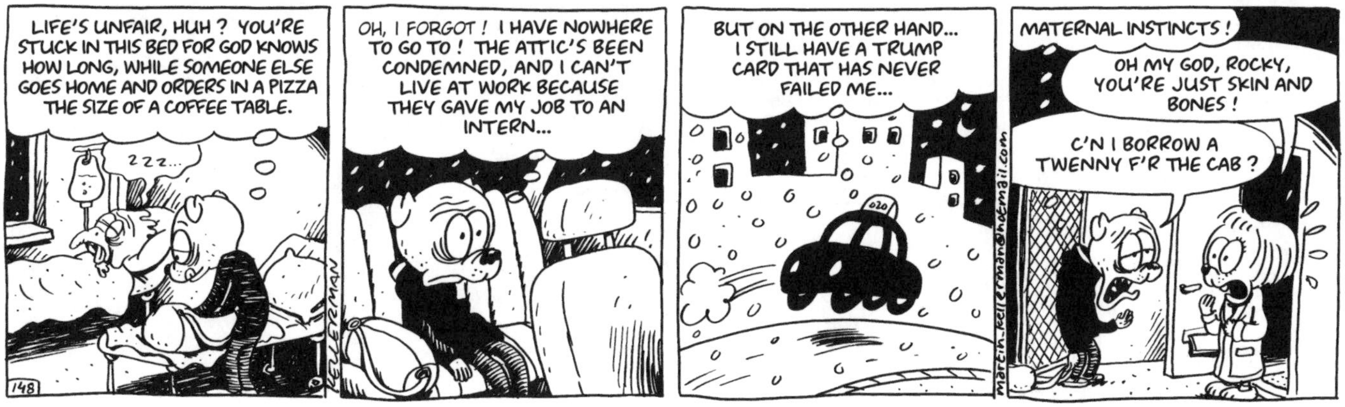
LIFE'S UNFAIR, HUH ? YOU'RE STUCK IN THIS BED FOR GOD KNOWS HOW LONG, WHILE SOMEONE ELSE GOES HOME AND ORDERS IN A PIZZA THE SIZE OF A COFFEE TABLE.
ZZZ...
148
KELLERMAN
OH, I FORGOT ! I HAVE NOWHERE TO GO TO ! THE ATTIC'S BEEN CONDEMNED, AND I CAN'T LIVE AT WORK BECAUSE THEY GAVE MY JOB TO AN INTERN...
BUT ON THE OTHER HAND... I STILL HAVE A TRUMP CARD THAT HAS NEVER FAILED ME...
martin.kellerman@hotmail.com
MATERNAL INSTINCTS !
OH MY GOD, ROCKY, YOU'RE JUST SKIN AND BONES !
C'N I BORROW A TWENNY F'R THE CAB ?

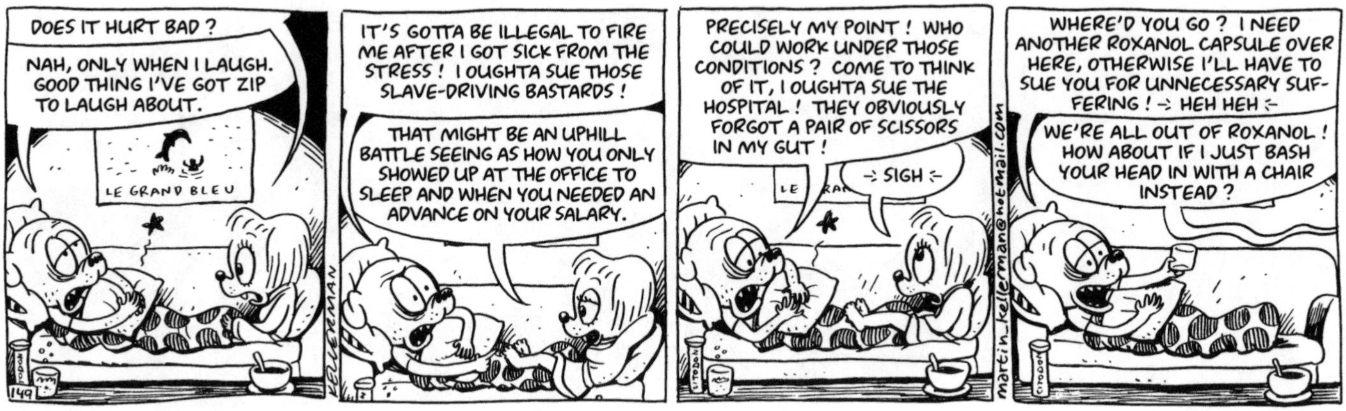
DOES IT HURT BAD ?
NAH, ONLY WHEN I LAUGH. GOOD THING I'VE GOT ZIP TO LAUGH ABOUT.
LE GRAND BLEU
149
KELLERMAN
IT'S GOTTA BE ILLEGAL TO FIRE ME AFTER I GOT SICK FROM THE STRESS ! I OUGHTA SUE THOSE SLAVE-DRIVING BASTARDS !
THAT MIGHT BE AN UPHILL BATTLE SEEING AS HOW YOU ONLY SHOWED UP AT THE OFFICE TO SLEEP AND WHEN YOU NEEDED AN ADVANCE ON YOUR SALARY.
PRECISELY MY POINT ! WHO COULD WORK UNDER THOSE CONDITIONS ? COME TO THINK OF IT, I OUGHTA SUE THE HOSPITAL ! THEY OBVIOUSLY FORGOT A PAIR OF SCISSORS IN MY GUT !
SIGH
martin_kellerman@hotmail.com
WHERE'D YOU GO ? I NEED ANOTHER ROXANOL CAPSULE OVER HERE, OTHERWISE I'LL HAVE TO SUE YOU FOR UNNECESSARY SUFFERING ! HEH HEH
WE'RE ALL OUT OF ROXANOL ! HOW ABOUT IF I JUST BASH YOUR HEAD IN WITH A CHAIR INSTEAD ?

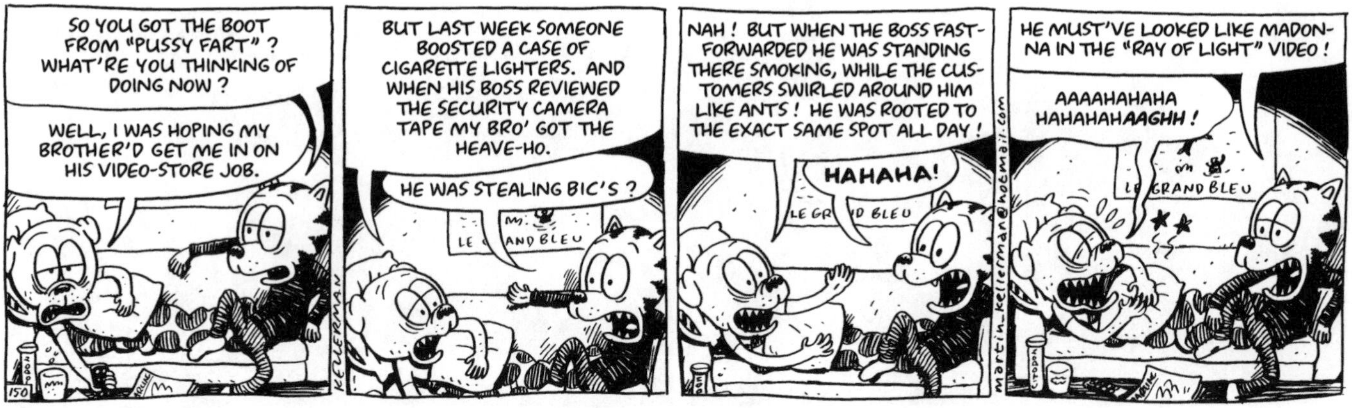
SO YOU GOT THE BOOT FROM "PUSSY FART" ? WHAT'RE YOU THINKING OF DOING NOW ?
WELL, I WAS HOPING MY BROTHER'D GET ME IN ON HIS VIDEO-STORE JOB.
150
KELLERMAN
BUT LAST WEEK SOMEONE BOOSTED A CASE OF CIGARETTE LIGHTERS. AND WHEN HIS BOSS REVIEWED THE SECURITY CAMERA TAPE MY BRO' GOT THE HEAVE-HO.
HE WAS STEALING BIC'S ?
NAH ! BUT WHEN THE BOSS FAST-FORWARDED HE WAS STANDING THERE SMOKING, WHILE THE CUSTOMERS SWIRLED AROUND HIM LIKE ANTS ! HE WAS ROOTED TO THE EXACT SAME SPOT ALL DAY !
HAHAHA!
martin_kellerman@hotmail.com
HE MUST'VE LOOKED LIKE MADONNA IN THE "RAY OF LIGHT" VIDEO !
AAAAHAHAHA HAHAHAH**AAGHH** !
LE GRAND BLEU

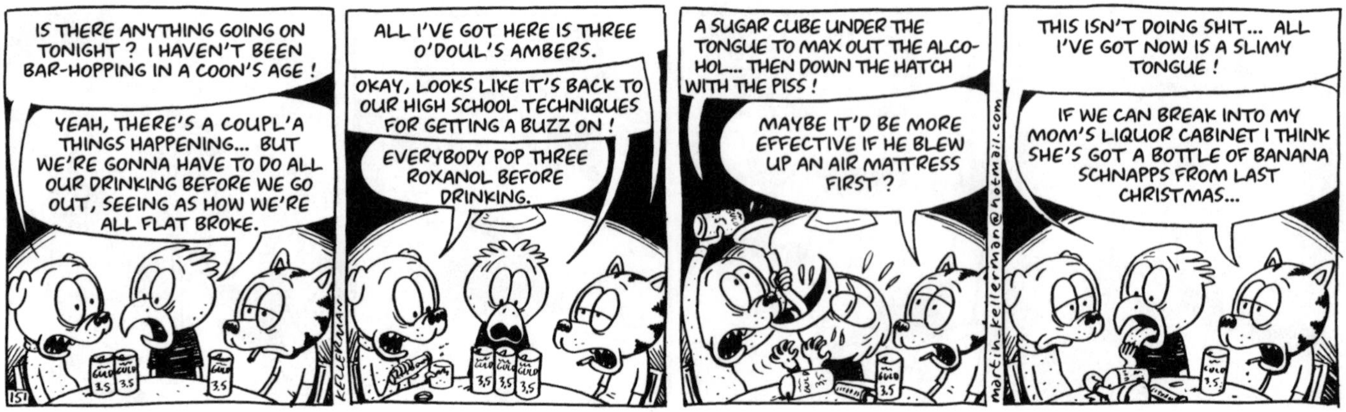
IS THERE ANYTHING GOING ON TONIGHT ? I HAVEN'T BEEN BAR-HOPPING IN A COON'S AGE !
YEAH, THERE'S A COUPL'A THINGS HAPPENING... BUT WE'RE GONNA HAVE TO DO ALL OUR DRINKING BEFORE WE GO OUT, SEEING AS HOW WE'RE ALL FLAT BROKE.
151
KELLERMAN
ALL I'VE GOT HERE IS THREE O'DOUL'S AMBERS.
OKAY, LOOKS LIKE IT'S BACK TO OUR HIGH SCHOOL TECHNIQUES FOR GETTING A BUZZ ON !
EVERYBODY POP THREE ROXANOL BEFORE DRINKING.
A SUGAR CUBE UNDER THE TONGUE TO MAX OUT THE ALCOHOL... THEN DOWN THE HATCH WITH THE PISS !
MAYBE IT'D BE MORE EFFECTIVE IF HE BLEW UP AN AIR MATTRESS FIRST ?
martin_kellerman@hotmail.com
THIS ISN'T DOING SHIT... ALL I'VE GOT NOW IS A SLIMY TONGUE !
IF WE CAN BREAK INTO MY MOM'S LIQUOR CABINET I THINK SHE'S GOT A BOTTLE OF BANANA SCHNAPPS FROM LAST CHRISTMAS...

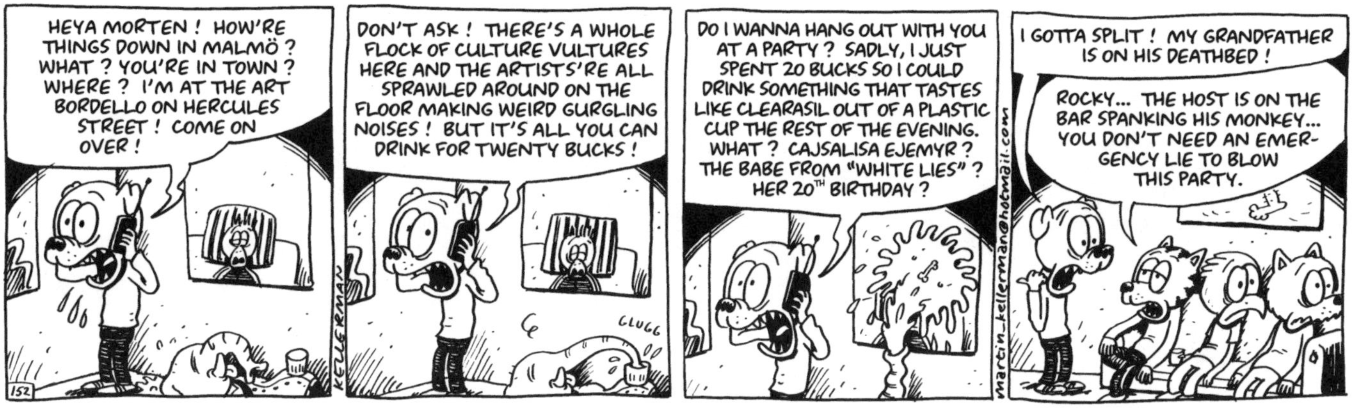
HEYA MORTEN ! HOW'RE THINGS DOWN IN MALMÖ ? WHAT ? YOU'RE IN TOWN ? WHERE ? I'M AT THE ART BORDELLO ON HERCULES STREET ! COME ON OVER !
152
KELLERMAN
DON'T ASK ! THERE'S A WHOLE FLOCK OF CULTURE VULTURES HERE AND THE ARTISTS'RE ALL SPRAWLED AROUND ON THE FLOOR MAKING WEIRD GURGLING NOISES ! BUT IT'S ALL YOU CAN DRINK FOR TWENTY BUCKS !
CLUGG
DO I WANNA HANG OUT WITH YOU AT A PARTY ? SADLY, I JUST SPENT 20 BUCKS SO I COULD DRINK SOMETHING THAT TASTES LIKE CLEARASIL OUT OF A PLASTIC CUP THE REST OF THE EVENING. WHAT ? CAJSALISA EJEMYR ? THE BABE FROM "WHITE LIES" ? HER 20TH BIRTHDAY ?
martin_kellerman@hotmail.com
I GOTTA SPLIT ! MY GRANDFATHER IS ON HIS DEATHBED !
ROCKY... THE HOST IS ON THE BAR SPANKING HIS MONKEY... YOU DON'T NEED AN EMERGENCY LIE TO BLOW THIS PARTY.

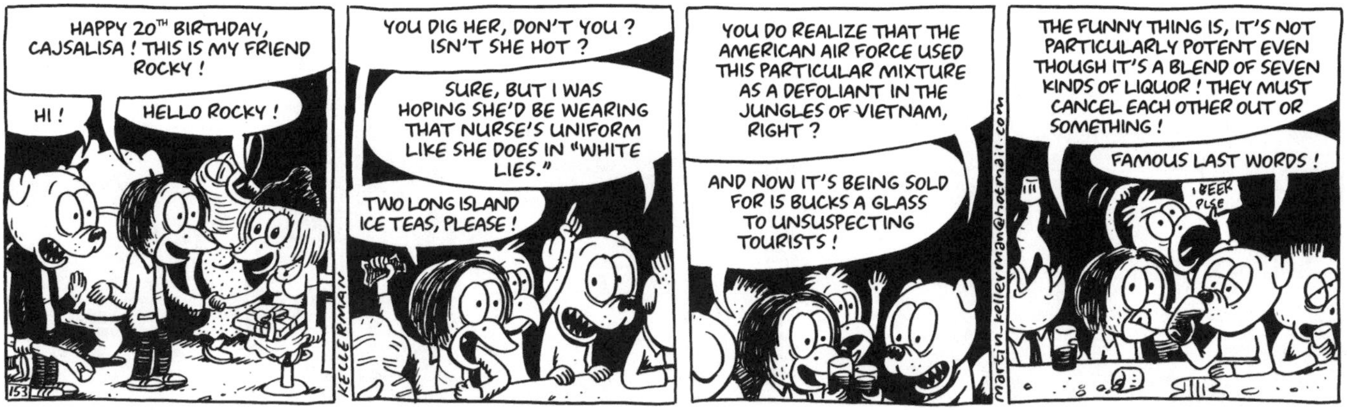
HAPPY 20TH BIRTHDAY, CAJSALISA ! THIS IS MY FRIEND ROCKY !
HI !
HELLO ROCKY !
153
KELLERMAN
YOU DIG HER, DON'T YOU ? ISN'T SHE HOT ?
SURE, BUT I WAS HOPING SHE'D BE WEARING THAT NURSE'S UNIFORM LIKE SHE DOES IN "WHITE LIES."
TWO LONG ISLAND ICE TEAS, PLEASE !
YOU DO REALIZE THAT THE AMERICAN AIR FORCE USED THIS PARTICULAR MIXTURE AS A DEFOLIANT IN THE JUNGLES OF VIETNAM, RIGHT ?
AND NOW IT'S BEING SOLD FOR 15 BUCKS A GLASS TO UNSUSPECTING TOURISTS !
martin_kellerman@hotmail.com
THE FUNNY THING IS, IT'S NOT PARTICULARLY POTENT EVEN THOUGH IT'S A BLEND OF SEVEN KINDS OF LIQUOR ! THEY MUST CANCEL EACH OTHER OUT OR SOMETHING !
FAMOUS LAST WORDS !
1 BEER PLSE

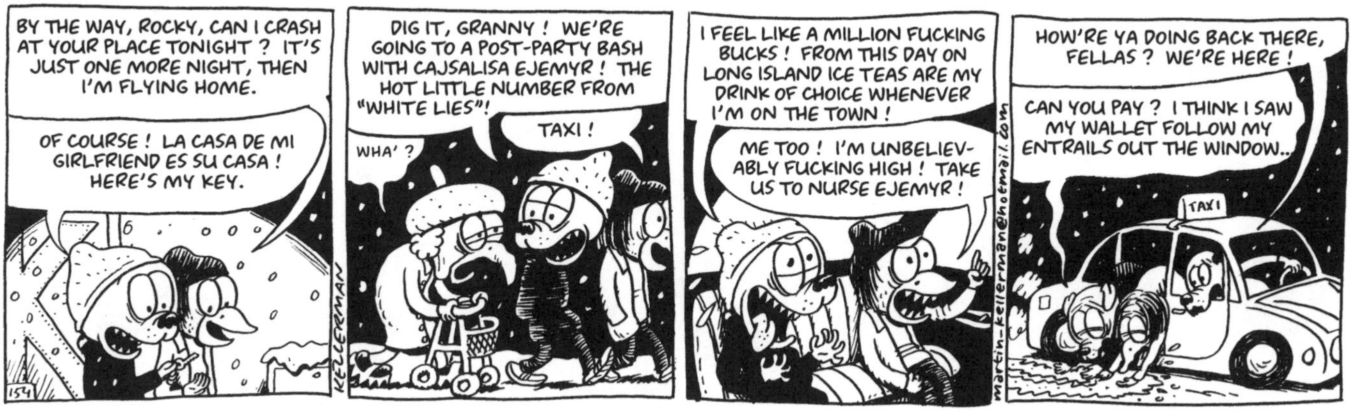
BY THE WAY, ROCKY, CAN I CRASH AT YOUR PLACE TONIGHT ? IT'S JUST ONE MORE NIGHT, THEN I'M FLYING HOME.
OF COURSE ! LA CASA DE MI GIRLFRIEND ES SU CASA ! HERE'S MY KEY.
154
KELLERMAN
DIG IT, GRANNY ! WE'RE GOING TO A POST-PARTY BASH WITH CAJSALISA EJEMYR ! THE HOT LITTLE NUMBER FROM "WHITE LIES"!
WHA' ?
TAXI !
I FEEL LIKE A MILLION FUCKING BUCKS ! FROM THIS DAY ON LONG ISLAND ICE TEAS ARE MY DRINK OF CHOICE WHENEVER I'M ON THE TOWN !
ME TOO ! I'M UNBELIEVABLY FUCKING HIGH ! TAKE US TO NURSE EJEMYR !
martin_kellerman@hotmail.com
HOW'RE YA DOING BACK THERE, FELLAS ? WE'RE HERE !
CAN YOU PAY ? I THINK I SAW MY WALLET FOLLOW MY ENTRAILS OUT THE WINDOW...
TAXI

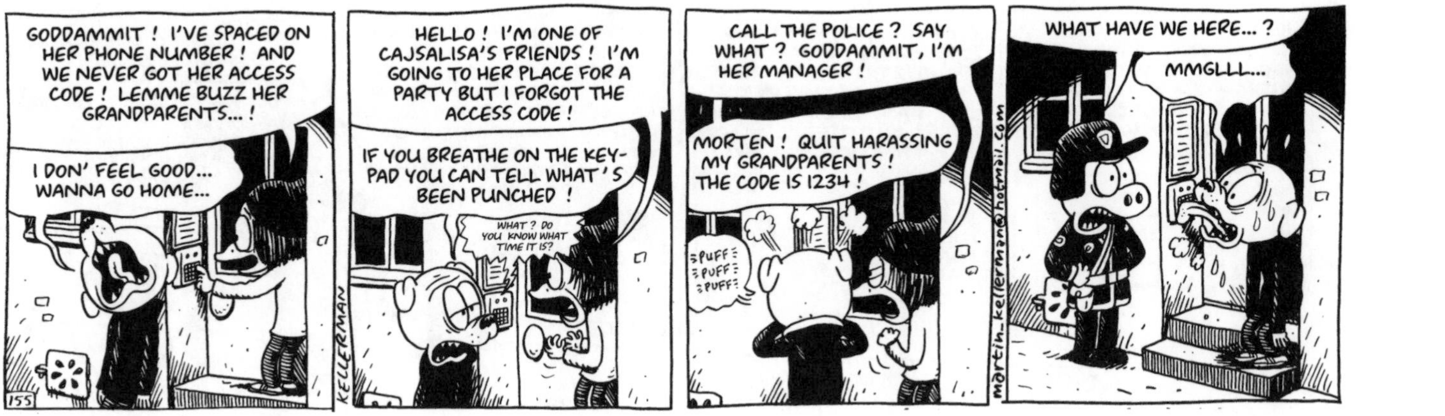
GODDAMMIT ! I'VE SPACED ON HER PHONE NUMBER ! AND WE NEVER GOT HER ACCESS CODE ! LEMME BUZZ HER GRANDPARENTS... !
I DON' FEEL GOOD... WANNA GO HOME...
155
HELLO ! I'M ONE OF CAJSALISA'S FRIENDS ! I'M GOING TO HER PLACE FOR A PARTY BUT I FORGOT THE ACCESS CODE !
IF YOU BREATHE ON THE KEY-PAD YOU CAN TELL WHAT'S BEEN PUNCHED !
WHAT ? DO YOU KNOW WHAT TIME IT IS?
KELLERMAN
CALL THE POLICE ? SAY WHAT ? GODDAMMIT, I'M HER MANAGER !
MORTEN ! QUIT HARASSING MY GRANDPARENTS ! THE CODE IS 1234 !
PUFF PUFF PUFF
martin_kellerman@hotmail.com
WHAT HAVE WE HERE... ?
MMGLLL...

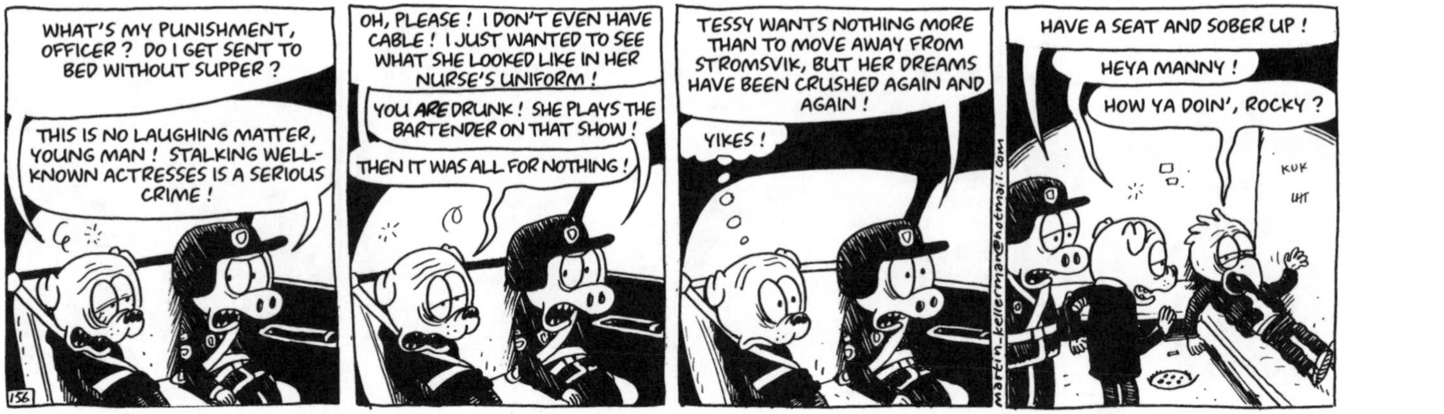
WHAT'S MY PUNISHMENT, OFFICER ? DO I GET SENT TO BED WITHOUT SUPPER ?
THIS IS NO LAUGHING MATTER, YOUNG MAN ! STALKING WELL-KNOWN ACTRESSES IS A SERIOUS CRIME !
156
OH, PLEASE ! I DON'T EVEN HAVE CABLE ! I JUST WANTED TO SEE WHAT SHE LOOKED LIKE IN HER NURSE'S UNIFORM !
YOU ARE DRUNK ! SHE PLAYS THE BARTENDER ON THAT SHOW !
THEN IT WAS ALL FOR NOTHING !
TESSY WANTS NOTHING MORE THAN TO MOVE AWAY FROM STROMSVIK, BUT HER DREAMS HAVE BEEN CRUSHED AGAIN AND AGAIN !
YIKES !
martin_kellerman@hotmail.com
HAVE A SEAT AND SOBER UP !
HEYA MANNY !
HOW YA DOIN', ROCKY ?
KUK

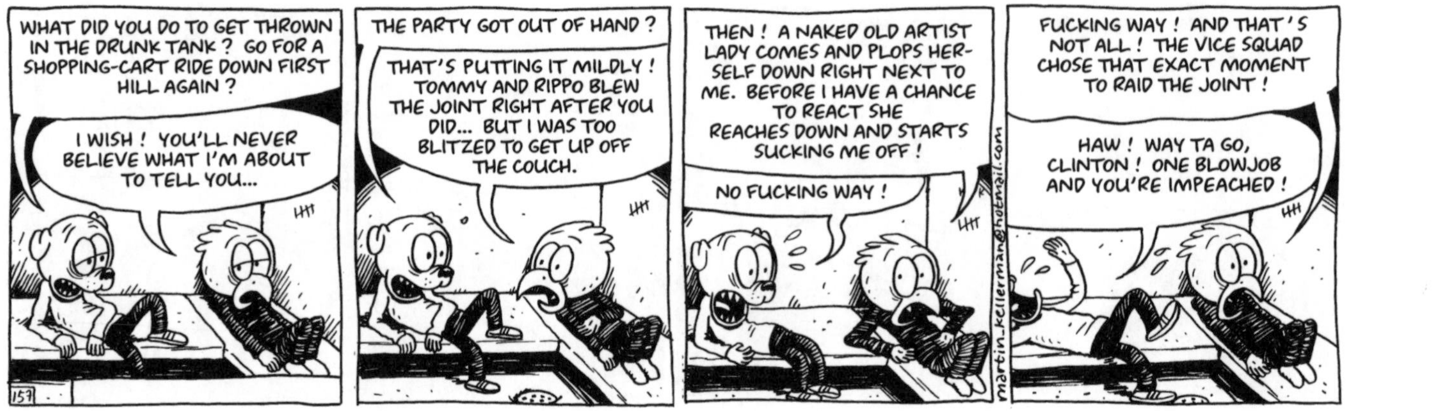
WHAT DID YOU DO TO GET THROWN IN THE DRUNK TANK ? GO FOR A SHOPPING-CART RIDE DOWN FIRST HILL AGAIN ?
I WISH ! YOU'LL NEVER BELIEVE WHAT I'M ABOUT TO TELL YOU...
157
THE PARTY GOT OUT OF HAND ?
THAT'S PUTTING IT MILDLY ! TOMMY AND RIPPO BLEW THE JOINT RIGHT AFTER YOU DID... BUT I WAS TOO BLITZED TO GET UP OFF THE COUCH.
THEN ! A NAKED OLD ARTIST LADY COMES AND PLOPS HER-SELF DOWN RIGHT NEXT TO ME. BEFORE I HAVE A CHANCE TO REACT SHE REACHES DOWN AND STARTS SUCKING ME OFF !
NO FUCKING WAY !
martin_kellerman@hotmail.com
FUCKING WAY ! AND THAT'S NOT ALL ! THE VICE SQUAD CHOSE THAT EXACT MOMENT TO RAID THE JOINT !
HAW ! WAY TA GO, CLINTON ! ONE BLOWJOB AND YOU'RE IMPEACHED !

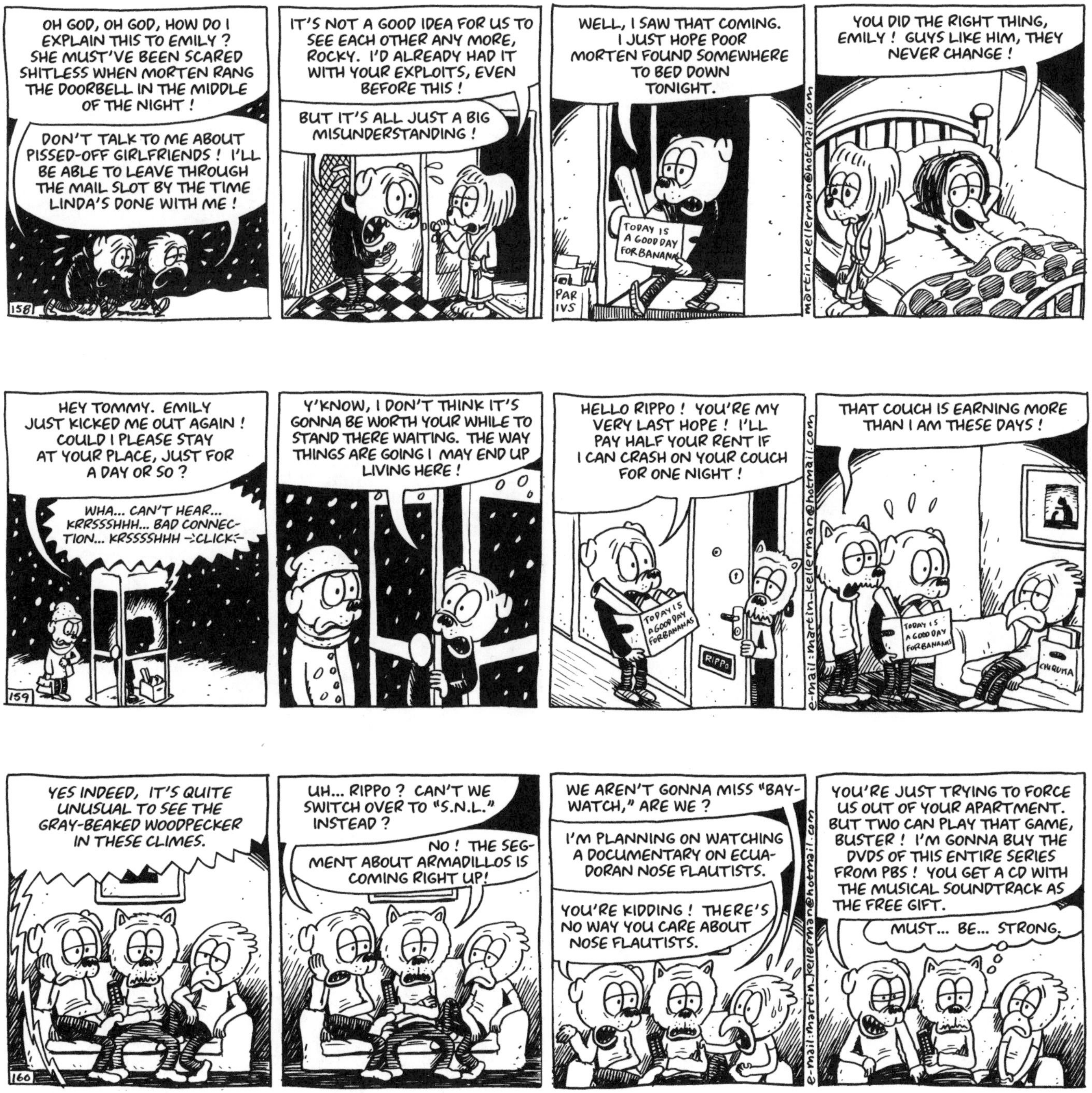
158
OH GOD, OH GOD, HOW DO I EXPLAIN THIS TO EMILY? SHE MUST'VE BEEN SCARED SHITLESS WHEN MORTEN RANG THE DOORBELL IN THE MIDDLE OF THE NIGHT!
DON'T TALK TO ME ABOUT PISSED-OFF GIRLFRIENDS! I'LL BE ABLE TO LEAVE THROUGH THE MAIL SLOT BY THE TIME LINDA'S DONE WITH ME!
IT'S NOT A GOOD IDEA FOR US TO SEE EACH OTHER ANY MORE, ROCKY. I'D ALREADY HAD IT WITH YOUR EXPLOITS, EVEN BEFORE THIS!
BUT IT'S ALL JUST A BIG MISUNDERSTANDING!
WELL, I SAW THAT COMING. I JUST HOPE POOR MORTEN FOUND SOMEWHERE TO BED DOWN TONIGHT.
TODAY IS A GOOD DAY FOR BANANA
PAR IVS
martin-kellerman@hotmail.com
YOU DID THE RIGHT THING, EMILY! GUYS LIKE HIM, THEY NEVER CHANGE!
159
HEY TOMMY. EMILY JUST KICKED ME OUT AGAIN! COULD I PLEASE STAY AT YOUR PLACE, JUST FOR A DAY OR SO?
WHA... CAN'T HEAR... KRRSSSHHH... BAD CONNECTION... KRSSSSHHH –CLICK–
Y'KNOW, I DON'T THINK IT'S GONNA BE WORTH YOUR WHILE TO STAND THERE WAITING. THE WAY THINGS ARE GOING I MAY END UP LIVING HERE!
HELLO RIPPO! YOU'RE MY VERY LAST HOPE! I'LL PAY HALF YOUR RENT IF I CAN CRASH ON YOUR COUCH FOR ONE NIGHT!
TODAY IS A GOOD DAY FOR BANANAS
RIPPO
e-mail: martin-kellerman@hotmail.com
THAT COUCH IS EARNING MORE THAN I AM THESE DAYS!
TODAY IS A GOOD DAY FOR BANANAS
CHIQUITA
160
YES INDEED, IT'S QUITE UNUSUAL TO SEE THE GRAY-BEAKED WOODPECKER IN THESE CLIMES.
UH... RIPPO? CAN'T WE SWITCH OVER TO "S.N.L." INSTEAD?
NO! THE SEGMENT ABOUT ARMADILLOS IS COMING RIGHT UP!
WE AREN'T GONNA MISS "BAYWATCH," ARE WE?
I'M PLANNING ON WATCHING A DOCUMENTARY ON ECUADORAN NOSE FLAUTISTS.
YOU'RE KIDDING! THERE'S NO WAY YOU CARE ABOUT NOSE FLAUTISTS.
e-mail: martin-kellerman@hotmail.com
YOU'RE JUST TRYING TO FORCE US OUT OF YOUR APARTMENT. BUT TWO CAN PLAY THAT GAME, BUSTER! I'M GONNA BUY THE DVDS OF THIS ENTIRE SERIES FROM PBS! YOU GET A CD WITH THE MUSICAL SOUNDTRACK AS THE FREE GIFT.
MUST... BE... STRONG.

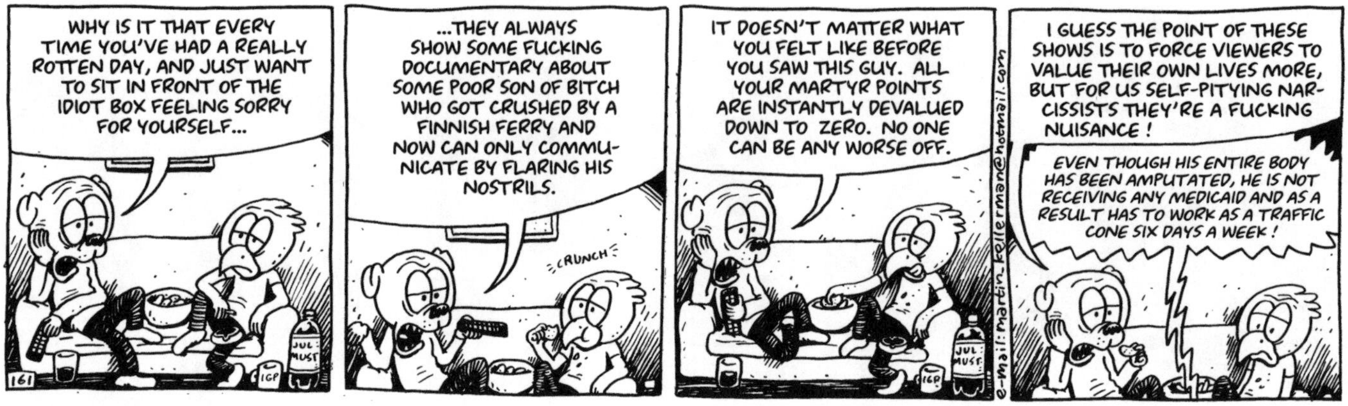
161
WHY IS IT THAT EVERY TIME YOU'VE HAD A REALLY ROTTEN DAY, AND JUST WANT TO SIT IN FRONT OF THE IDIOT BOX FEELING SORRY FOR YOURSELF...
JUL MUST
...THEY ALWAYS SHOW SOME FUCKING DOCUMENTARY ABOUT SOME POOR SON OF BITCH WHO GOT CRUSHED BY A FINNISH FERRY AND NOW CAN ONLY COMMUNICATE BY FLARING HIS NOSTRILS.
CRUNCH
IT DOESN'T MATTER WHAT YOU FELT LIKE BEFORE YOU SAW THIS GUY. ALL YOUR MARTYR POINTS ARE INSTANTLY DEVALUED DOWN TO ZERO. NO ONE CAN BE ANY WORSE OFF.
JUL MUST
e-mail: martin_kellerman@hotmail.com
I GUESS THE POINT OF THESE SHOWS IS TO FORCE VIEWERS TO VALUE THEIR OWN LIVES MORE, BUT FOR US SELF-PITYING NARCISSISTS THEY'RE A FUCKING NUISANCE !
EVEN THOUGH HIS ENTIRE BODY HAS BEEN AMPUTATED, HE IS NOT RECEIVING ANY MEDICAID AND AS A RESULT HAS TO WORK AS A TRAFFIC CONE SIX DAYS A WEEK !

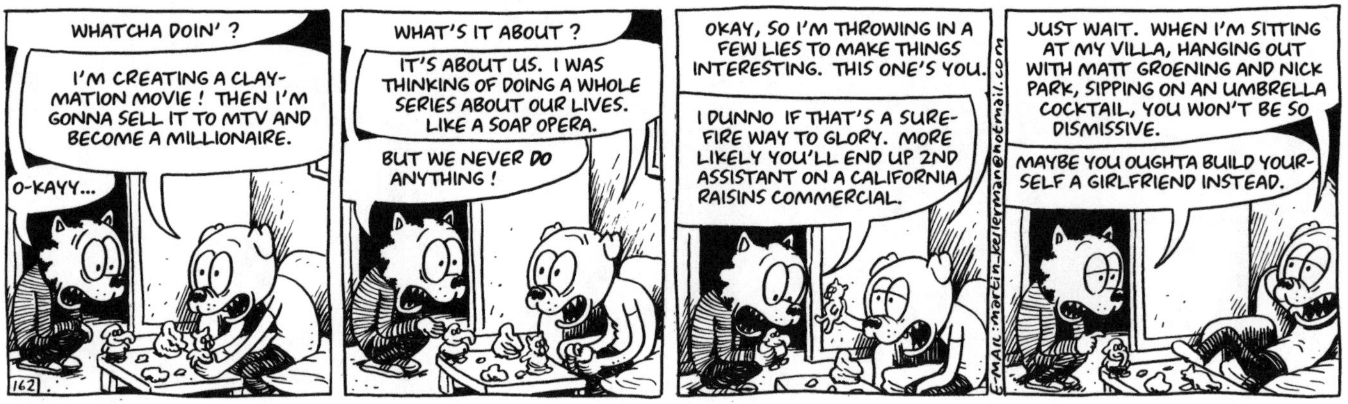
162
WHATCHA DOIN' ?
I'M CREATING A CLAYMATION MOVIE ! THEN I'M GONNA SELL IT TO MTV AND BECOME A MILLIONAIRE.
O-KAYY...
WHAT'S IT ABOUT ?
IT'S ABOUT US. I WAS THINKING OF DOING A WHOLE SERIES ABOUT OUR LIVES. LIKE A SOAP OPERA.
BUT WE NEVER DO ANYTHING !
OKAY, SO I'M THROWING IN A FEW LIES TO MAKE THINGS INTERESTING. THIS ONE'S YOU.
I DUNNO IF THAT'S A SURE-FIRE WAY TO GLORY. MORE LIKELY YOU'LL END UP 2ND ASSISTANT ON A CALIFORNIA RAISINS COMMERCIAL.
E-MAIL: martin_kellerman@hotmail.com
JUST WAIT. WHEN I'M SITTING AT MY VILLA, HANGING OUT WITH MATT GROENING AND NICK PARK, SIPPING ON AN UMBRELLA COCKTAIL, YOU WON'T BE SO DISMISSIVE.
MAYBE YOU OUGHTA BUILD YOURSELF A GIRLFRIEND INSTEAD.

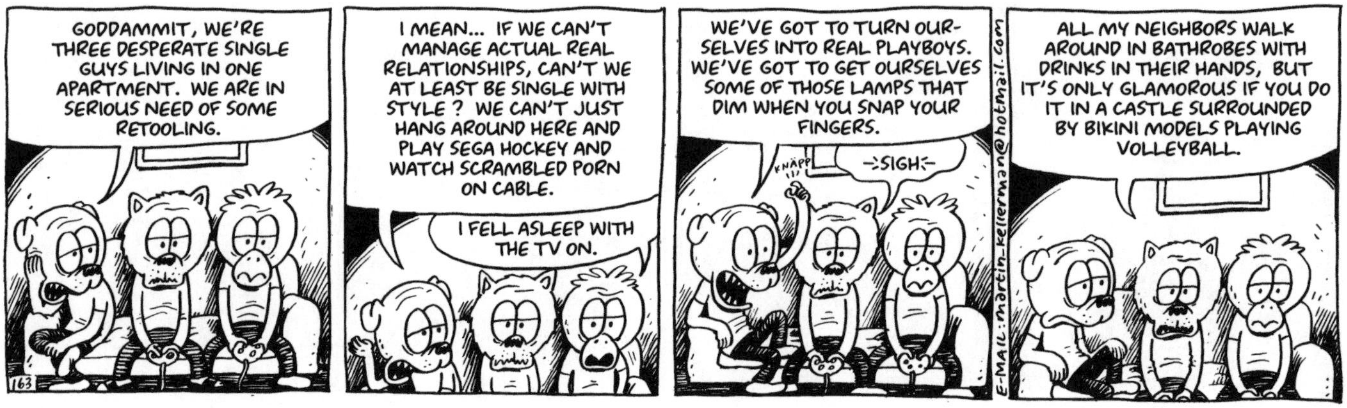
163
GODDAMMIT, WE'RE THREE DESPERATE SINGLE GUYS LIVING IN ONE APARTMENT. WE ARE IN SERIOUS NEED OF SOME RETOOLING.
I MEAN... IF WE CAN'T MANAGE ACTUAL REAL RELATIONSHIPS, CAN'T WE AT LEAST BE SINGLE WITH STYLE ? WE CAN'T JUST HANG AROUND HERE AND PLAY SEGA HOCKEY AND WATCH SCRAMBLED PORN ON CABLE.
I FELL ASLEEP WITH THE TV ON.
WE'VE GOT TO TURN OURSELVES INTO REAL PLAYBOYS. WE'VE GOT TO GET OURSELVES SOME OF THOSE LAMPS THAT DIM WHEN YOU SNAP YOUR FINGERS.
KNÄPP
SIGH
E-MAIL: martin_kellerman@hotmail.com
ALL MY NEIGHBORS WALK AROUND IN BATHROBES WITH DRINKS IN THEIR HANDS, BUT IT'S ONLY GLAMOROUS IF YOU DO IT IN A CASTLE SURROUNDED BY BIKINI MODELS PLAYING VOLLEYBALL.

FRIENDS AND LOVERS

WHAT ARE YOU TRYING TO TELL ME ? YOU WANT *US* TO START GOING OUT ?

SURE ! WHY NOT ? WE ALWAYS HAVE A GREAT TIME WHEN WE'RE TOGETHER !

BUT WE'VE BEEN FRIEND FOR TEN YEARS ! IF WE STARTED DATING WE MIGHT RUIN IT !

WHY WOULD WE ? IT'LL JUST BE EXACTLY LIKE NOW, EXCEPT WE'D BE SLEEPING TOGETHER ON TOP OF IT !

THAT IS SO YOU ! JUST BECAUSE YOU'RE TOO LAZY TO GET YOUR ASS OUT TO A BAR AND PICK UP A GIRL YOU'RE TRYING TO NAIL YOUR FRIENDS INSTEAD.

BUT I PROMISE YOU I'LL RESPECT YOU IN THE MORNING, DARLIN'...

AIN'T HAPPENING, ROCKY !

SOME FRIEND YOU TURNED OUT TO BE ! AND AFTER I HELPED YOU MOVE AND EVERYTHING !

E-MAIL: martin_kellerman@hotmail.com

SO, DID IT WORK OUT ? ARE YOU IN NOW ?

WELL, NOT QUITE. IT TAKES MORE THAN ONE NIGHT TO SEAL THIS KIND OF DEAL ! BUT IT'LL BE GREAT HAVING A GIRL NOW THAT THE NIGHTS ARE STARTING TO GET COLDER !

SO YOU'RE WILLING TO SACRI-FICE A TEN-YEAR FRIENDSHIP BECAUSE YOU'RE COLD AT NIGHT ? GET YOURSELF SOME PAJAMAS, FOR CHRIST'S SAKE !

YOU THINK THIS ISN'T SERIOUS ! BUT WE'RE EVEN TALKING ABOUT MOVING IN TOGETHER.

YOU SHOULDN'T RUSH INTO THIS SORT OF THING, ROCKY ! YOU HAVE TO MAKE SURE IT'S RIGHT FIRST.

WELL, YOU MAY HAVE A POINT THERE... AND ACTUALLY, I'M REALLY HAVING A BLAST STAYING HERE WITH YOU AND RIPPO.

I THINK YOU MAKE A GREAT COUPLE AND YOU SHOULD MOVE IN TOGETHER RIGHT NOW ! BUT IF THAT DOESN'T WORK OUT, COULD YOU ASK HER IF SHE WOULD AT LEAST TAKE IN MANNY ?

E-MAIL: martin_kellerman@hotmail.com

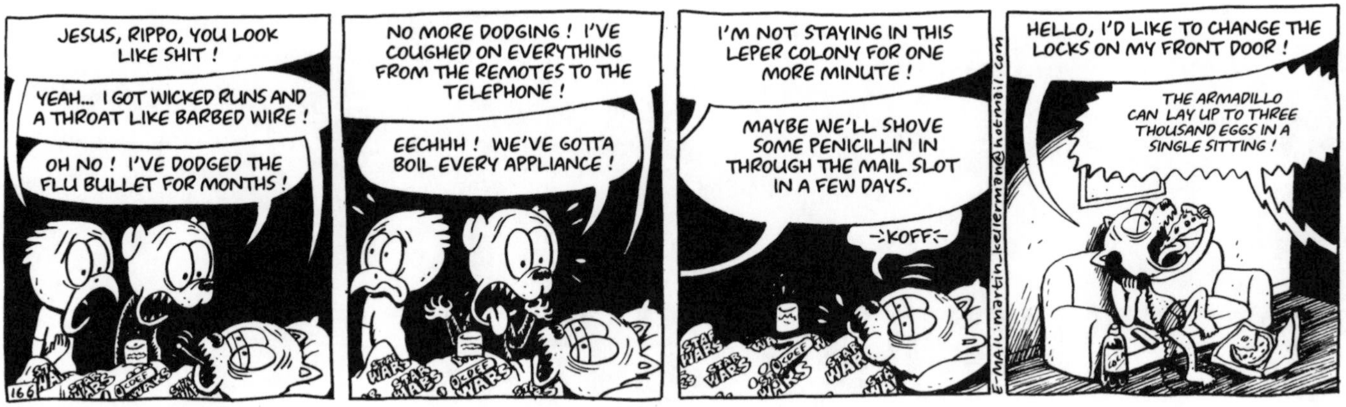
166
JESUS, RIPPO, YOU LOOK LIKE SHIT !
YEAH... I GOT WICKED RUNS AND A THROAT LIKE BARBED WIRE !
OH NO ! I'VE DODGED THE FLU BULLET FOR MONTHS !
NO MORE DODGING ! I'VE COUGHED ON EVERYTHING FROM THE REMOTES TO THE TELEPHONE !
EECHHH ! WE'VE GOTTA BOIL EVERY APPLIANCE !
I'M NOT STAYING IN THIS LEPER COLONY FOR ONE MORE MINUTE !
MAYBE WE'LL SHOVE SOME PENICILLIN IN THROUGH THE MAIL SLOT IN A FEW DAYS.
KOFF
E-MAIL: martin_kellerman@hotmail.com
HELLO, I'D LIKE TO CHANGE THE LOCKS ON MY FRONT DOOR !
THE ARMADILLO CAN LAY UP TO THREE THOUSAND EGGS IN A SINGLE SITTING !

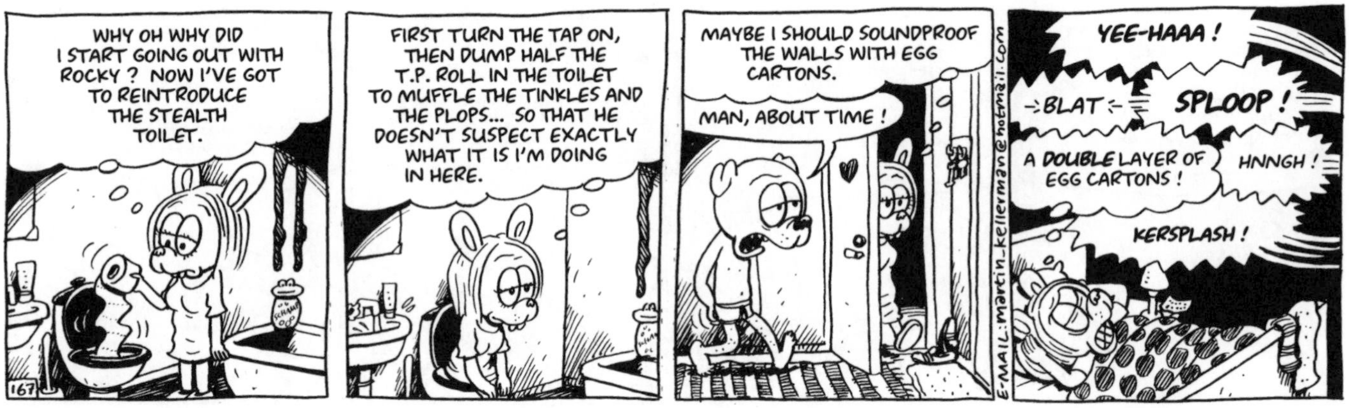
167
WHY OH WHY DID I START GOING OUT WITH ROCKY ? NOW I'VE GOT TO REINTRODUCE THE STEALTH TOILET.
FIRST TURN THE TAP ON, THEN DUMP HALF THE T.P. ROLL IN THE TOILET TO MUFFLE THE TINKLES AND THE PLOPS... SO THAT HE DOESN'T SUSPECT EXACTLY WHAT IT IS I'M DOING IN HERE.
MAYBE I SHOULD SOUNDPROOF THE WALLS WITH EGG CARTONS.
MAN, ABOUT TIME !
E-MAIL: martin_kellerman@hotmail.com
YEE-HAAA !
BLAT
SPLOOP !
A DOUBLE LAYER OF EGG CARTONS !
HNNGH !
KERSPLASH !

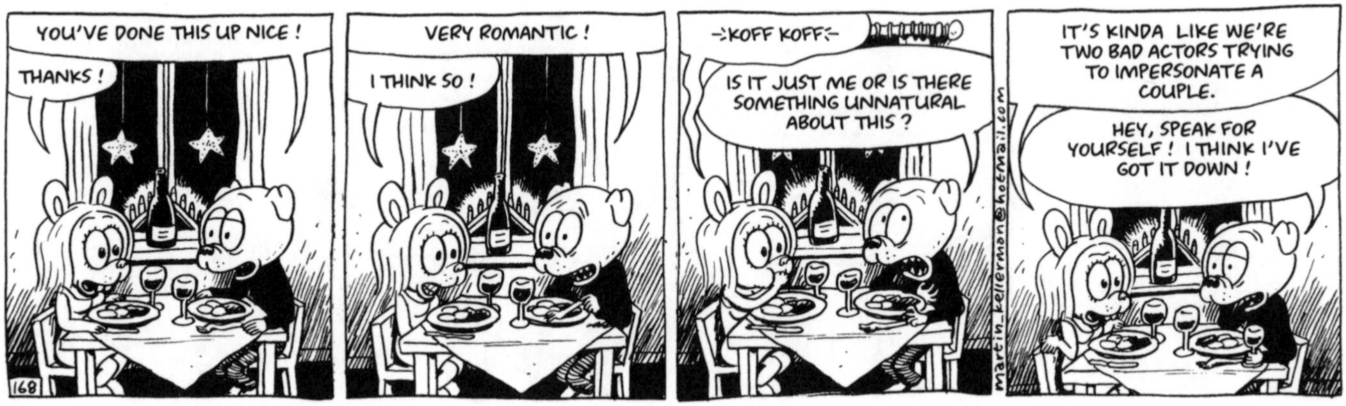
168
YOU'VE DONE THIS UP NICE !
THANKS !
VERY ROMANTIC !
I THINK SO !
KOFF KOFF
IS IT JUST ME OR IS THERE SOMETHING UNNATURAL ABOUT THIS ?
martin_kellerman@hotmail.com
IT'S KINDA LIKE WE'RE TWO BAD ACTORS TRYING TO IMPERSONATE A COUPLE.
HEY, SPEAK FOR YOURSELF ! I THINK I'VE GOT IT DOWN !

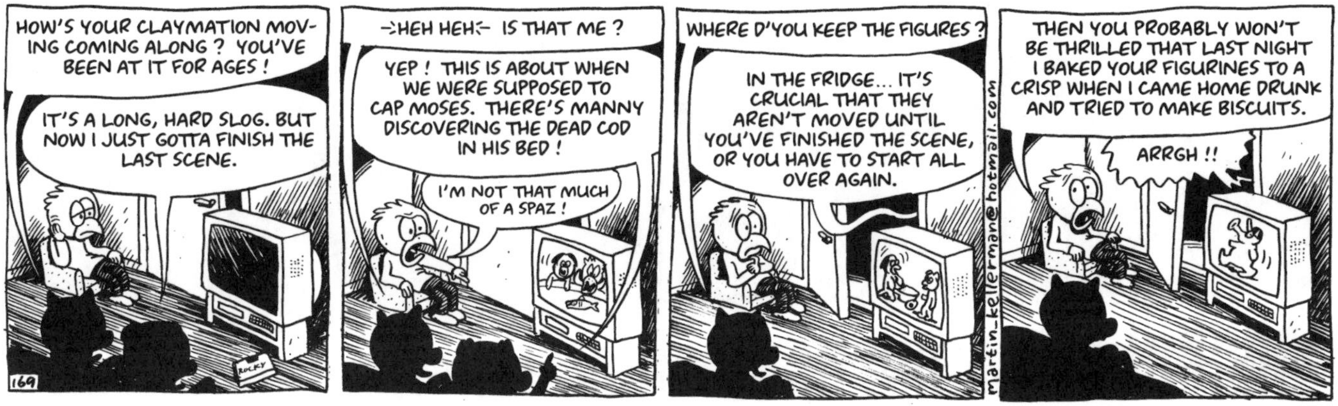

169
HOW'S YOUR CLAYMATION MOVING COMING ALONG? YOU'VE BEEN AT IT FOR AGES!
IT'S A LONG, HARD SLOG. BUT NOW I JUST GOTTA FINISH THE LAST SCENE.
ROCKY
-HEH HEH- IS THAT ME?
YEP! THIS IS ABOUT WHEN WE WERE SUPPOSED TO CAP MOSES. THERE'S MANNY DISCOVERING THE DEAD COD IN HIS BED!
I'M NOT THAT MUCH OF A SPAZ!
WHERE D'YOU KEEP THE FIGURES?
IN THE FRIDGE... IT'S CRUCIAL THAT THEY AREN'T MOVED UNTIL YOU'VE FINISHED THE SCENE, OR YOU HAVE TO START ALL OVER AGAIN.
martin_kellerman@hotmail.com
THEN YOU PROBABLY WON'T BE THRILLED THAT LAST NIGHT I BAKED YOUR FIGURINES TO A CRISP WHEN I CAME HOME DRUNK AND TRIED TO MAKE BISCUITS.
ARRGH!!

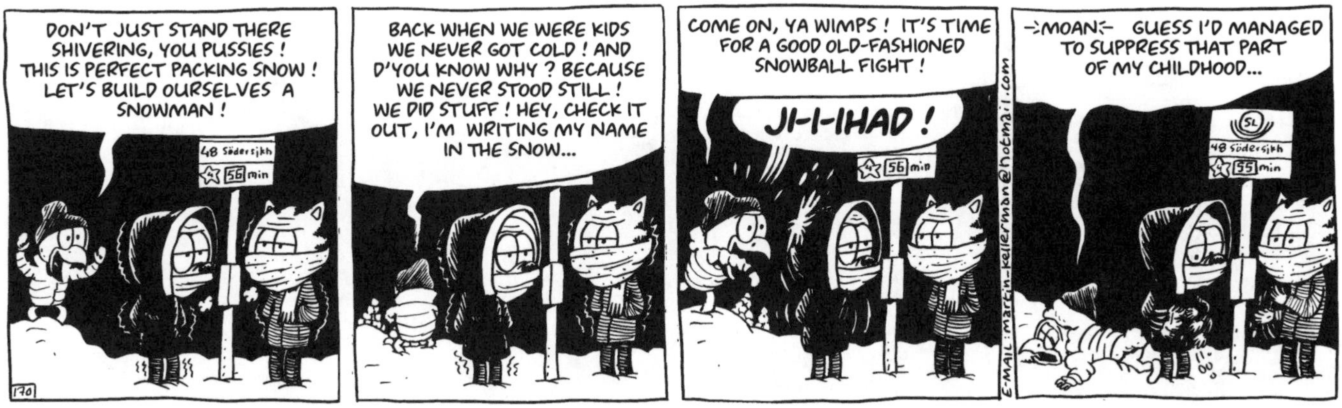

170
DON'T JUST STAND THERE SHIVERING, YOU PUSSIES! THIS IS PERFECT PACKING SNOW! LET'S BUILD OURSELVES A SNOWMAN!
56 min
BACK WHEN WE WERE KIDS WE NEVER GOT COLD! AND D'YOU KNOW WHY? BECAUSE WE NEVER STOOD STILL! WE DID STUFF! HEY, CHECK IT OUT, I'M WRITING MY NAME IN THE SNOW...
COME ON, YA WIMPS! IT'S TIME FOR A GOOD OLD-FASHIONED SNOWBALL FIGHT!
JI-I-IHAD!
56 min
E-MAIL: martin_kellerman@hotmail.com
-MOAN- GUESS I'D MANAGED TO SUPPRESS THAT PART OF MY CHILDHOOD...
SL
55 min

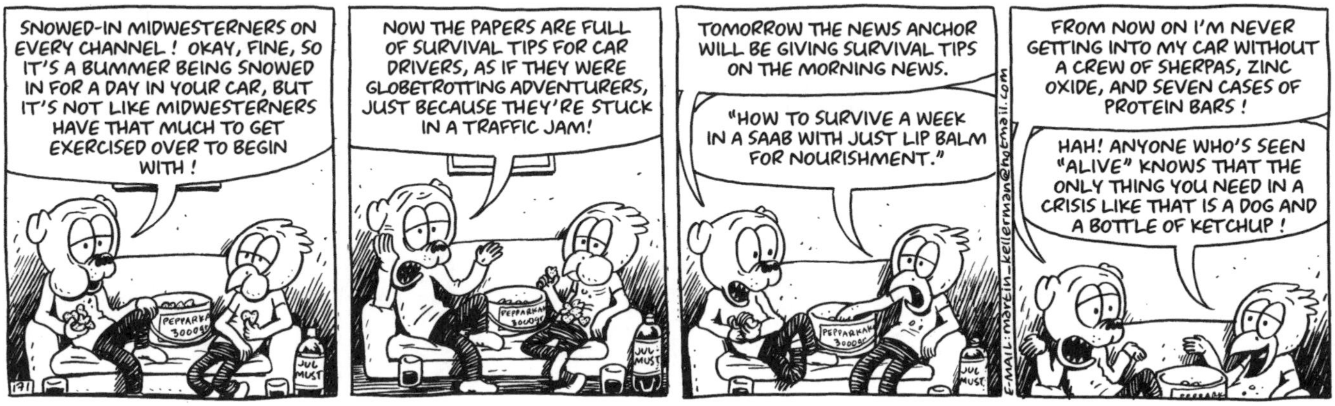

171
SNOWED-IN MIDWESTERNERS ON EVERY CHANNEL! OKAY, FINE, SO IT'S A BUMMER BEING SNOWED IN FOR A DAY IN YOUR CAR, BUT IT'S NOT LIKE MIDWESTERNERS HAVE THAT MUCH TO GET EXERCISED OVER TO BEGIN WITH!
JUL MUST
NOW THE PAPERS ARE FULL OF SURVIVAL TIPS FOR CAR DRIVERS, AS IF THEY WERE GLOBETROTTING ADVENTURERS, JUST BECAUSE THEY'RE STUCK IN A TRAFFIC JAM!
JUL MUST
TOMORROW THE NEWS ANCHOR WILL BE GIVING SURVIVAL TIPS ON THE MORNING NEWS.
"HOW TO SURVIVE A WEEK IN A SAAB WITH JUST LIP BALM FOR NOURISHMENT."
JUL MUST
E-MAIL: martin_kellerman@hotmail.com
FROM NOW ON I'M NEVER GETTING INTO MY CAR WITHOUT A CREW OF SHERPAS, ZINC OXIDE, AND SEVEN CASES OF PROTEIN BARS!
HAH! ANYONE WHO'S SEEN "ALIVE" KNOWS THAT THE ONLY THING YOU NEED IN A CRISIS LIKE THAT IS A DOG AND A BOTTLE OF KETCHUP!

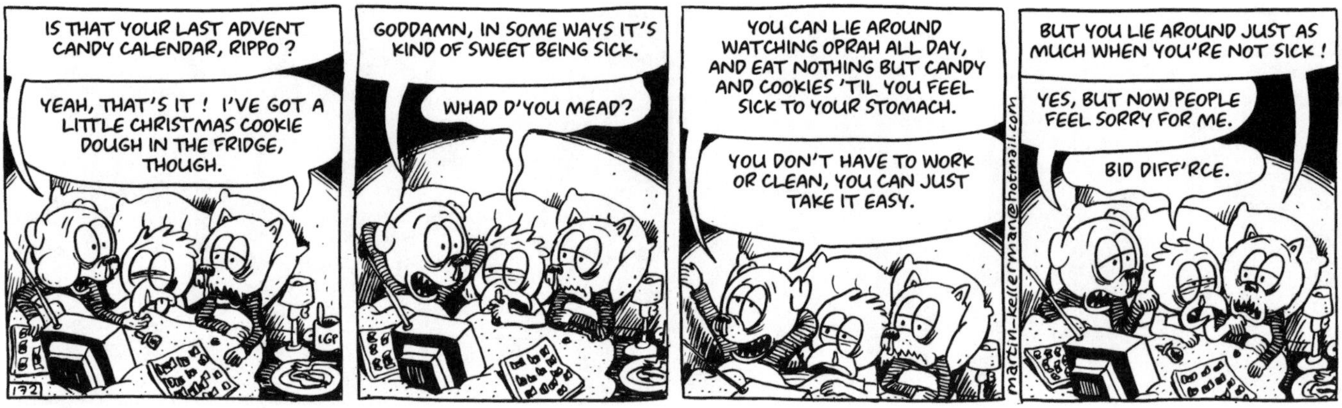
IS THAT YOUR LAST ADVENT CANDY CALENDAR, RIPPO ?
YEAH, THAT'S IT ! I'VE GOT A LITTLE CHRISTMAS COOKIE DOUGH IN THE FRIDGE, THOUGH.
172
GODDAMN, IN SOME WAYS IT'S KIND OF SWEET BEING SICK.
WHAD D'YOU MEAD?
YOU CAN LIE AROUND WATCHING OPRAH ALL DAY, AND EAT NOTHING BUT CANDY AND COOKIES 'TIL YOU FEEL SICK TO YOUR STOMACH.
YOU DON'T HAVE TO WORK OR CLEAN, YOU CAN JUST TAKE IT EASY.
martin_kellerman@hotmail.com
BUT YOU LIE AROUND JUST AS MUCH WHEN YOU'RE NOT SICK !
YES, BUT NOW PEOPLE FEEL SORRY FOR ME.
BID DIFF'RCE.

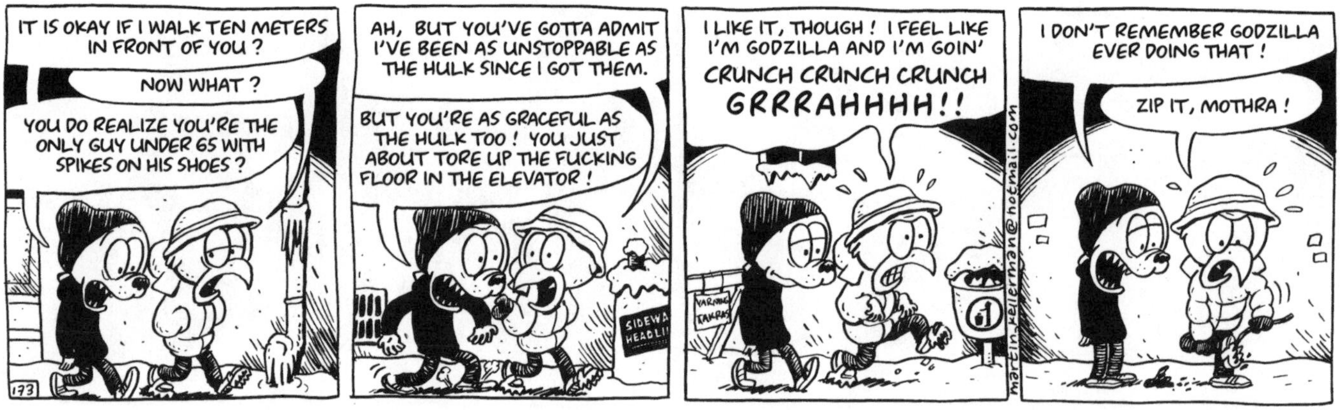
IT IS OKAY IF I WALK TEN METERS IN FRONT OF YOU ?
NOW WHAT ?
YOU DO REALIZE YOU'RE THE ONLY GUY UNDER 65 WITH SPIKES ON HIS SHOES ?
173
AH, BUT YOU'VE GOTTA ADMIT I'VE BEEN AS UNSTOPPABLE AS THE HULK SINCE I GOT THEM.
BUT YOU'RE AS GRACEFUL AS THE HULK TOO ! YOU JUST ABOUT TORE UP THE FUCKING FLOOR IN THE ELEVATOR !
I LIKE IT, THOUGH ! I FEEL LIKE I'M GODZILLA AND I'M GOIN'
CRUNCH CRUNCH CRUNCH
GRRRAHHHH!!
martin_kellerman@hotmail.com
I DON'T REMEMBER GODZILLA EVER DOING THAT !
ZIP IT, MOTHRA !

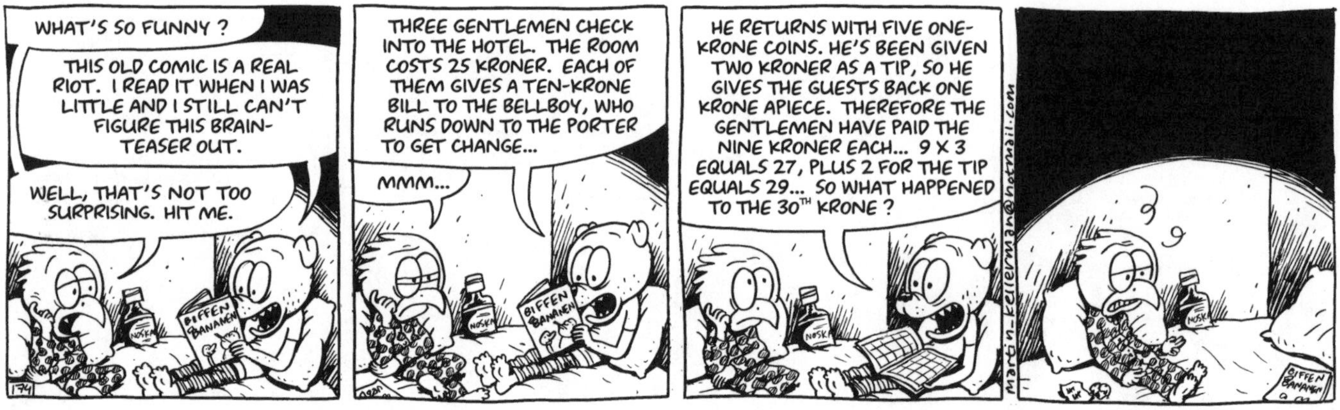
WHAT'S SO FUNNY ?
THIS OLD COMIC IS A REAL RIOT. I READ IT WHEN I WAS LITTLE AND I STILL CAN'T FIGURE THIS BRAIN-TEASER OUT.
WELL, THAT'S NOT TOO SURPRISING. HIT ME.
BIFFEN BANANEN
174
THREE GENTLEMEN CHECK INTO THE HOTEL. THE ROOM COSTS 25 KRONER. EACH OF THEM GIVES A TEN-KRONE BILL TO THE BELLBOY, WHO RUNS DOWN TO THE PORTER TO GET CHANGE...
MMM...
BIFFEN BANANEN
HE RETURNS WITH FIVE ONE-KRONE COINS. HE'S BEEN GIVEN TWO KRONER AS A TIP, SO HE GIVES THE GUESTS BACK ONE KRONE APIECE. THEREFORE THE GENTLEMEN HAVE PAID THE NINE KRONER EACH... 9 X 3 EQUALS 27, PLUS 2 FOR THE TIP EQUALS 29... SO WHAT HAPPENED TO THE 30TH KRONE ?
martin_kellerman@hotmail.com
BIFFEN BANANEN

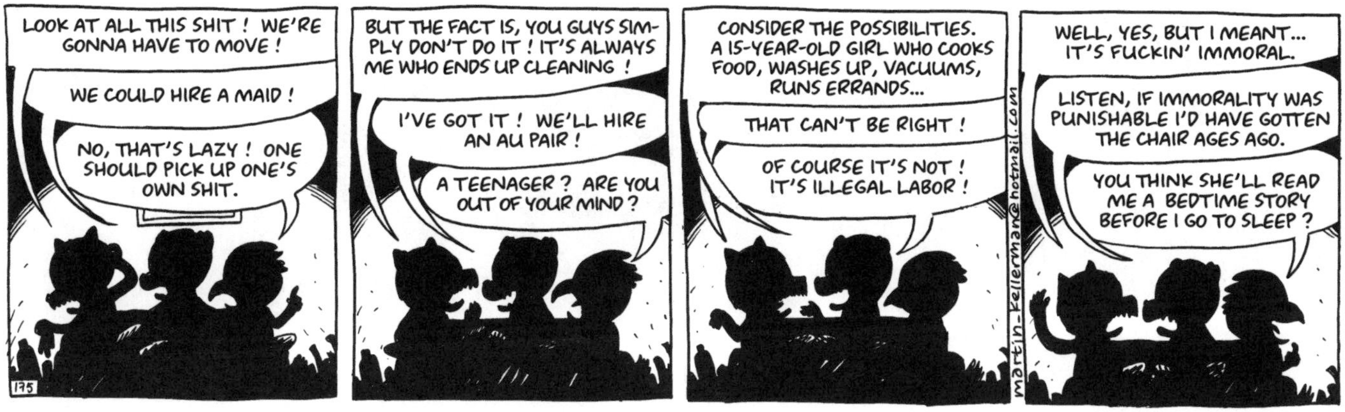
175
LOOK AT ALL THIS SHIT ! WE'RE GONNA HAVE TO MOVE !
WE COULD HIRE A MAID !
NO, THAT'S LAZY ! ONE SHOULD PICK UP ONE'S OWN SHIT.
BUT THE FACT IS, YOU GUYS SIMPLY DON'T DO IT ! IT'S ALWAYS ME WHO ENDS UP CLEANING !
I'VE GOT IT ! WE'LL HIRE AN AU PAIR !
A TEENAGER ? ARE YOU OUT OF YOUR MIND ?
CONSIDER THE POSSIBILITIES. A 15-YEAR-OLD GIRL WHO COOKS FOOD, WASHES UP, VACUUMS, RUNS ERRANDS...
THAT CAN'T BE RIGHT !
OF COURSE IT'S NOT ! IT'S ILLEGAL LABOR !
martin_kellerman@hotmail.com
WELL, YES, BUT I MEANT... IT'S FUCKIN' IMMORAL.
LISTEN, IF IMMORALITY WAS PUNISHABLE I'D HAVE GOTTEN THE CHAIR AGES AGO.
YOU THINK SHE'LL READ ME A BEDTIME STORY BEFORE I GO TO SLEEP ?

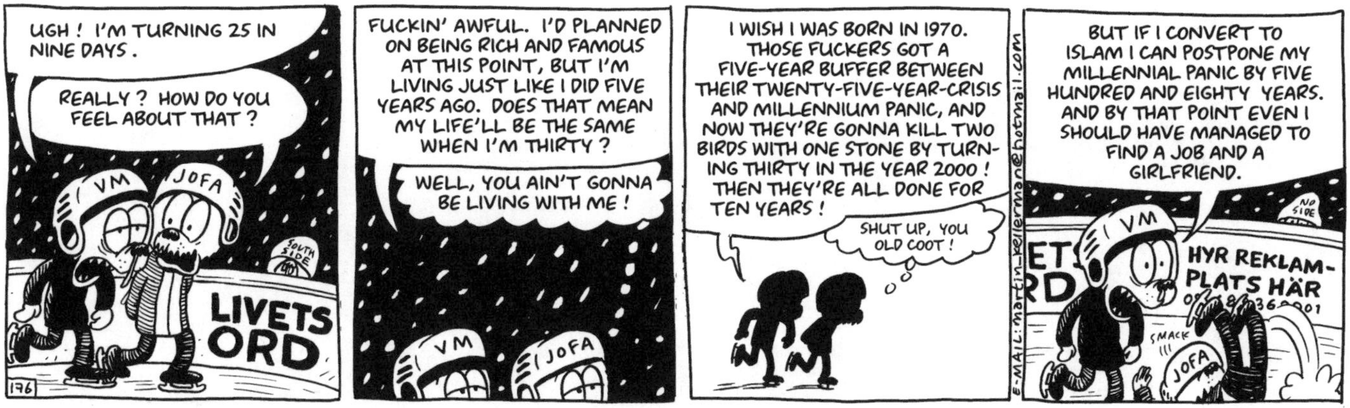
176
UGH ! I'M TURNING 25 IN NINE DAYS .
REALLY ? HOW DO YOU FEEL ABOUT THAT ?
VM
JOFA
SOUTH SIDE
LIVETS ORD
FUCKIN' AWFUL. I'D PLANNED ON BEING RICH AND FAMOUS AT THIS POINT, BUT I'M LIVING JUST LIKE I DID FIVE YEARS AGO. DOES THAT MEAN MY LIFE'LL BE THE SAME WHEN I'M THIRTY ?
WELL, YOU AIN'T GONNA BE LIVING WITH ME !
VM
JOFA
I WISH I WAS BORN IN 1970. THOSE FUCKERS GOT A FIVE-YEAR BUFFER BETWEEN THEIR TWENTY-FIVE-YEAR-CRISIS AND MILLENNIUM PANIC, AND NOW THEY'RE GONNA KILL TWO BIRDS WITH ONE STONE BY TURNING THIRTY IN THE YEAR 2000 ! THEN THEY'RE ALL DONE FOR TEN YEARS !
SHUT UP, YOU OLD COOT !
E-MAIL: martin_kellerman@hotmail.com
BUT IF I CONVERT TO ISLAM I CAN POSTPONE MY MILLENNIAL PANIC BY FIVE HUNDRED AND EIGHTY YEARS. AND BY THAT POINT EVEN I SHOULD HAVE MANAGED TO FIND A JOB AND A GIRLFRIEND.
NO SIDE
VM
HYR REKLAM-PLATS HÄR
SMACK
JOFA

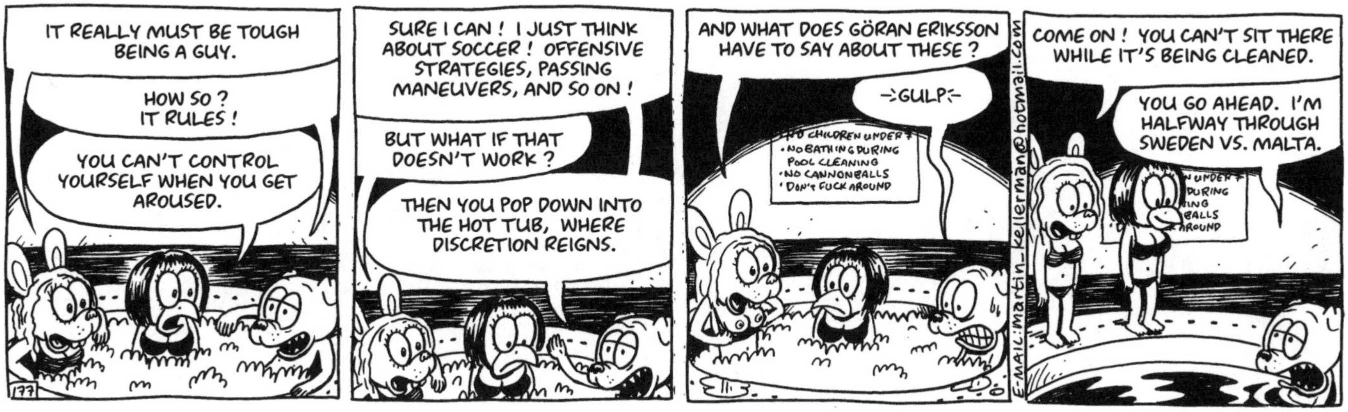
177
IT REALLY MUST BE TOUGH BEING A GUY.
HOW SO ? IT RULES !
YOU CAN'T CONTROL YOURSELF WHEN YOU GET AROUSED.
SURE I CAN ! I JUST THINK ABOUT SOCCER ! OFFENSIVE STRATEGIES, PASSING MANEUVERS, AND SO ON !
BUT WHAT IF THAT DOESN'T WORK ?
THEN YOU POP DOWN INTO THE HOT TUB, WHERE DISCRETION REIGNS.
AND WHAT DOES GÖRAN ERIKSSON HAVE TO SAY ABOUT THESE ?
-GULP-
NO CHILDREN UNDER 7
NO BATHING DURING POOL CLEANING
NO CANNONBALLS
DON'T FUCK AROUND
E-MAIL: martin_kellerman@hotmail.com
COME ON ! YOU CAN'T SIT THERE WHILE IT'S BEING CLEANED.
YOU GO AHEAD. I'M HALFWAY THROUGH SWEDEN VS. MALTA.

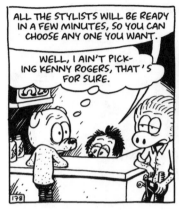

ALL THE STYLISTS WILL BE READY IN A FEW MINUTES, SO YOU CAN CHOOSE ANY ONE YOU WANT.
WELL, I AIN'T PICKING KENNY ROGERS, THAT'S FOR SURE.
178
THE PROBLEM WITH HAIR STYLISTS IS THAT THEY HAVE THE POWER TO CHANGE YOUR PERSONALITY COMPLETELY, FROM ROCKY TO...
BERT FROM SESAME STREET.
BOBBY EWING.
DEMOLITION MAN.
HOMINA HOMINA ! SHE LOOKS COMPETENT ! THAT'S THE ONE I WANT !
martin_kellerman@hotmail.com
WHATCHA GOT IN THE BAG, ROCKY ?
MY EARS !
ROCKY
16
THIS RELATIONSHIP'S ABOUT AS THRILLING AS A MacGYVER RERUN. WE KNEW EACH OTHER BEFOREHAND, SO NOW IT'S EXACTLY LIKE WHEN WE WERE PALS EXCEPT WE'RE SHARING A TOOTHBRUSH GLASS.
179
OKAY, IT'S ACTUALLY PRETTY SWEET BEING ABLE TO HAVE SEX EVERY DAY, BUT IT'D BE NICE IF THE RELATIONSHIP COULD OFFER SOMETHING BEYOND WHAT YOU CAN ACHIEVE YOURSELF WITH THE NAKED CHANNEL AND A THERMOS FULL OF WARM NOODLES.
BUT IF I BREAK UP WITH HER SHE'S GOING TO MAKE IT SOUND LIKE I DUMPED HER AS SOON AS I GOT HER INTO BED, AND BLA BLA BLA. "WAS THAT ALL OUR FRIENDSHIP WAS WORTH TO YOU ?" AND BLA BLA BLA. I'M GONNA HAVE TO FAKE MY OWN DEATH TO GET OUT OF THIS SITUATION.
martin_kellerman@hotmail.com
ROCKY, I'M BREAKING UP WITH YOU.
WHAT ?! AFTER A DECADE-LONG FRIENDSHIP YOU THROW ME OUT LIKE A USED CONDOM !
WHY THE LONG FACE ? YOU WANTED TO BREAK UP TOO, ADMIT IT !
WELL, YEAH... IT'S JUST THAT YOU BEAT ME TO THE PUNCH. AND IT'S ALWAYS EASIER BEING THE DUMPER THAN THE DUMPEE. I NEVER GET TO DUMP ANYONE !
180
OKAY, THEN, I'LL TAKE IT BACK, AND YOU CAN DUMP ME INSTEAD.
DON'T DO ME ANY FAVORS !
NO, REALLY ! IF IT MAKES THINGS EASIER FOR YOU, YOU CAN DO IT.
I TAKE BACK MY DUMPING, WE'RE STILL TOGETHER.
FORGET IT, BABY, IT'S OVER ! GATHER ALL YOUR SHIT TOGETHER AND GET THE HELL OUTTA HERE RIGHT NOW !
UH... BUT THIS IS MY APARTMENT.
martin_kellerman@hotmail.com
COOL IT, ROCKY ! YOU'RE GOING TO HAVE TO CONTENT YOURSELF WITH DUMPING ME. YOU DON'T GET TO THROW MY CLOTHES OUT ON THE STREET.
AW, C'MON ! I JUST WANT TO SEE HOW IT FEELS !

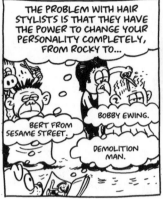

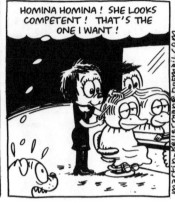

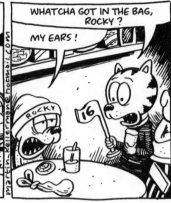

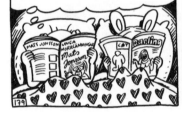

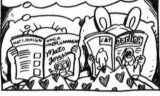

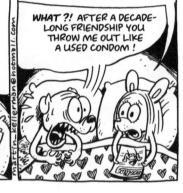

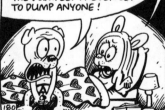

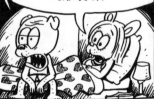

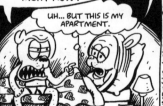

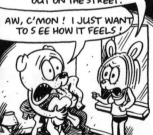

AUTEUR! AUTEUR!

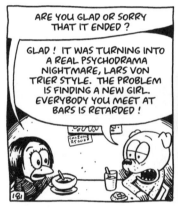

181
ARE YOU GLAD OR SORRY THAT IT ENDED ?
GLAD ! IT WAS TURNING INTO A REAL PSYCHODRAMA NIGHTMARE, LARS VON TRIER STYLE. THE PROBLEM IS FINDING A NEW GIRL. EVERYBODY YOU MEET AT BARS IS RETARDED !
YOU COULD TRY RIDING SCHOOL.
NAAHH...
HA HA HA HA HA
EEEEP...
OR HANG OUT AT THE LOCAL COLLEGE.
NAAHH...
I REALLY FIND CALCULUS FASCINATING, DON'T YOU ?
HUH ?
martin_kellerman@hotmail.com
OR... MAKE A MOVIE ABOUT 14-YEAR-OLD GIRLS !
EXPRESS
DIRECTOR TOUCHED MY BREASTS! READ ALL ABOUT IT.
NAAHH...
YES !

182
HAVE YOU BOUGHT ANY CHRISTMAS PRESENTS YET?
NO... I DON'T HAVE A POT TO PISS IN OR A WINDOW TO THROW IT OUT OF. BUT SINCE MY BIRTHDAY FALLS ON CHRISTMAS EVE, I FIGURE I'LL JUST RE-GIFT ALL MY PRESENTS.
ISN'T IT ABOUT TIME FOR YOU TO FIND ANOTHER JOB?
I ACTUALLY SENT IN A STRIP YESTERDAY, WE'LL SEE IF THAT TURNS INTO SOMETHING.
WELL, I MEANT A REAL JOB. WITH, LIKE, A SALARY.
AH, SOMETHING'S BOUND TO TURN UP. IF I'M TO BE A MULTI-MILLIONAIRE BY THE YEAR 2000, I CAN'T AFFORD TO TIE MYSELF DOWN WITH A 9-TO-5 JOB..
martin_kellerman@hotmail.com
DO YOU REMEMBER A TV SHOW CALLED "FANTASY ISLAND" ? IT WAS ABOUT THIS GUY AND A DWARF WHO LIVED ON AN ISLAND WHERE ALL DREAMS TURNED INTO REALITY.
YES ! "FANTASY ISLAND" ! THAT WAS MY FAVORITE SHOW EVER !
NO KIDDING !

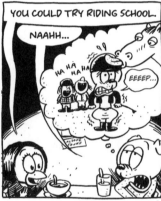

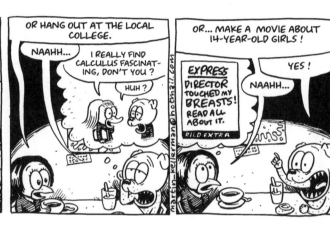

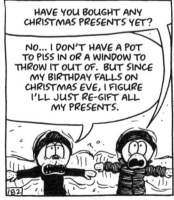

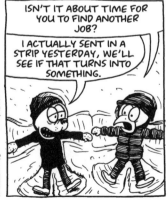

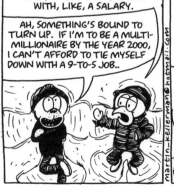

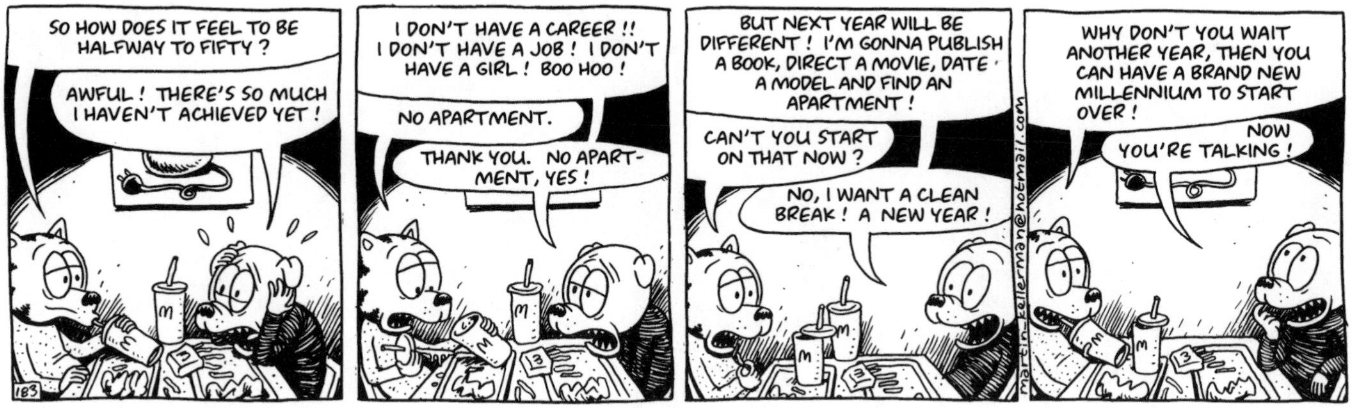
SO HOW DOES IT FEEL TO BE HALFWAY TO FIFTY ?
AWFUL ! THERE'S SO MUCH I HAVEN'T ACHIEVED YET !
183
I DON'T HAVE A CAREER !! I DON'T HAVE A JOB ! I DON'T HAVE A GIRL ! BOO HOO !
NO APARTMENT.
THANK YOU. NO APARTMENT, YES !
BUT NEXT YEAR WILL BE DIFFERENT ! I'M GONNA PUBLISH A BOOK, DIRECT A MOVIE, DATE A MODEL AND FIND AN APARTMENT !
CAN'T YOU START ON THAT NOW ?
NO, I WANT A CLEAN BREAK ! A NEW YEAR !
martin_kellerman@hotmail.com
WHY DON'T YOU WAIT ANOTHER YEAR, THEN YOU CAN HAVE A BRAND NEW MILLENNIUM TO START OVER !
NOW YOU'RE TALKING !

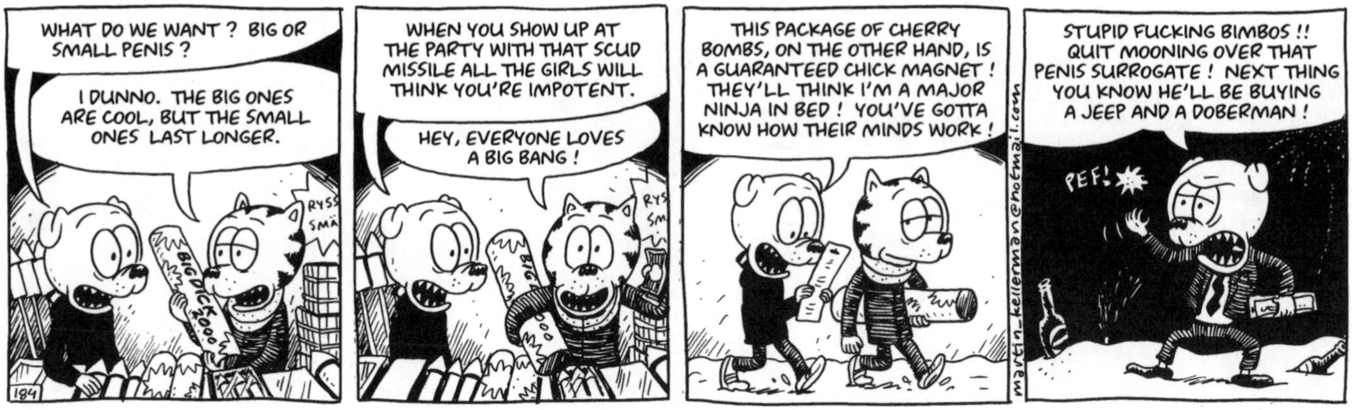
WHAT DO WE WANT ? BIG OR SMALL PENIS ?
I DUNNO. THE BIG ONES ARE COOL, BUT THE SMALL ONES LAST LONGER.
RYSS SMÄ
BIG DICK 2000
184
WHEN YOU SHOW UP AT THE PARTY WITH THAT SCUD MISSILE ALL THE GIRLS WILL THINK YOU'RE IMPOTENT.
HEY, EVERYONE LOVES A BIG BANG !
THIS PACKAGE OF CHERRY BOMBS, ON THE OTHER HAND, IS A GUARANTEED CHICK MAGNET ! THEY'LL THINK I'M A MAJOR NINJA IN BED ! YOU'VE GOTTA KNOW HOW THEIR MINDS WORK !
martin_kellerman@hotmail.com
STUPID FUCKING BIMBOS !! QUIT MOONING OVER THAT PENIS SURROGATE ! NEXT THING YOU KNOW HE'LL BE BUYING A JEEP AND A DOBERMAN !
PEF!

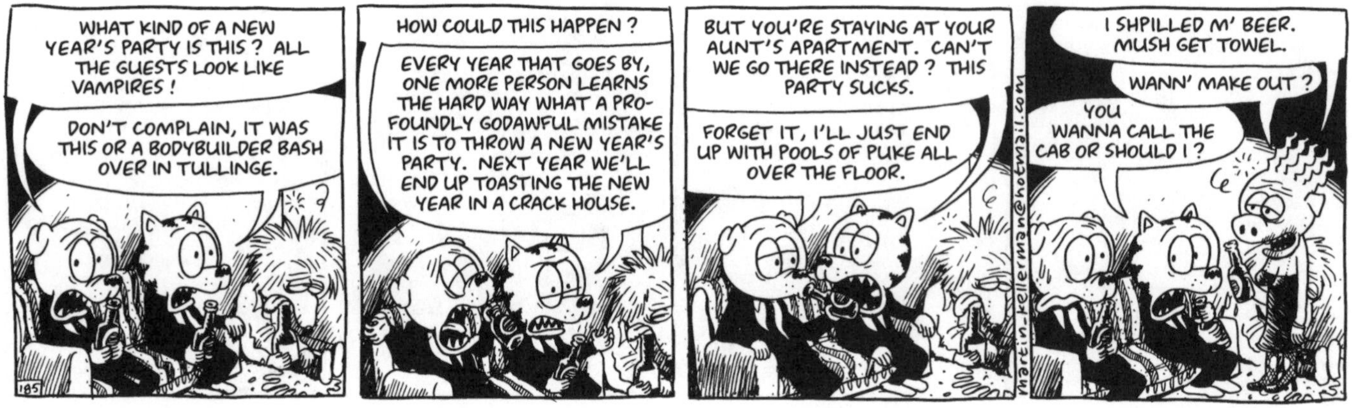
WHAT KIND OF A NEW YEAR'S PARTY IS THIS ? ALL THE GUESTS LOOK LIKE VAMPIRES !
DON'T COMPLAIN, IT WAS THIS OR A BODYBUILDER BASH OVER IN TULLINGE.
185
HOW COULD THIS HAPPEN ?
EVERY YEAR THAT GOES BY, ONE MORE PERSON LEARNS THE HARD WAY WHAT A PROFOUNDLY GODAWFUL MISTAKE IT IS TO THROW A NEW YEAR'S PARTY. NEXT YEAR WE'LL END UP TOASTING THE NEW YEAR IN A CRACK HOUSE.
BUT YOU'RE STAYING AT YOUR AUNT'S APARTMENT. CAN'T WE GO THERE INSTEAD ? THIS PARTY SUCKS.
FORGET IT, I'LL JUST END UP WITH POOLS OF PUKE ALL OVER THE FLOOR.
martin_kellerman@hotmail.com
I SHPILLED M' BEER. MUSH GET TOWEL.
WANN' MAKE OUT ?
YOU WANNA CALL THE CAB OR SHOULD I ?

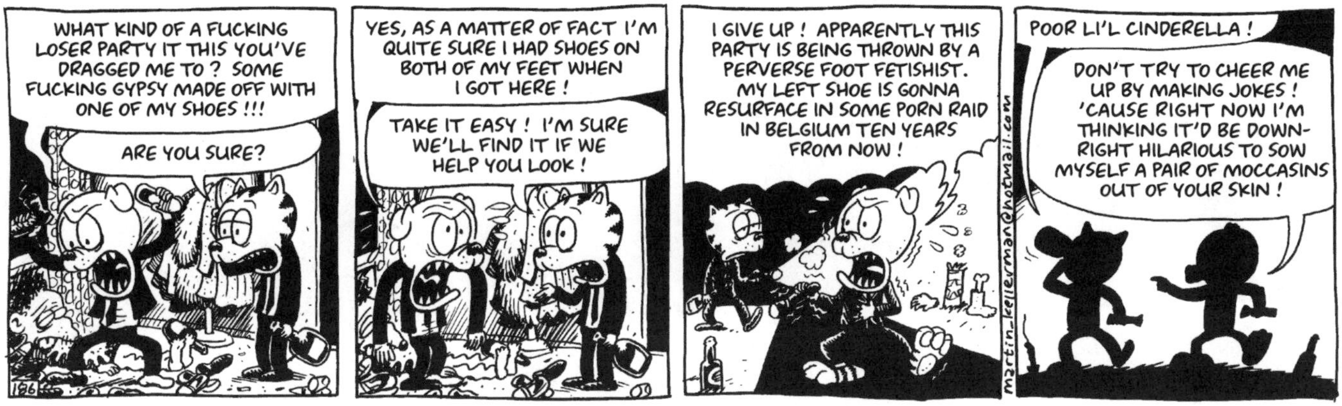
WHAT KIND OF A FUCKING LOSER PARTY IT THIS YOU'VE DRAGGED ME TO? SOME FUCKING GYPSY MADE OFF WITH ONE OF MY SHOES !!!
ARE YOU SURE?
186
YES, AS A MATTER OF FACT I'M QUITE SURE I HAD SHOES ON BOTH OF MY FEET WHEN I GOT HERE !
TAKE IT EASY ! I'M SURE WE'LL FIND IT IF WE HELP YOU LOOK !
I GIVE UP ! APPARENTLY THIS PARTY IS BEING THROWN BY A PERVERSE FOOT FETISHIST. MY LEFT SHOE IS GONNA RESURFACE IN SOME PORN RAID IN BELGIUM TEN YEARS FROM NOW !
martin_kellerman@hotmail.com
POOR LI'L CINDERELLA !
DON'T TRY TO CHEER ME UP BY MAKING JOKES ! 'CAUSE RIGHT NOW I'M THINKING IT'D BE DOWN-RIGHT HILARIOUS TO SOW MYSELF A PAIR OF MOCCASINS OUT OF YOUR SKIN !

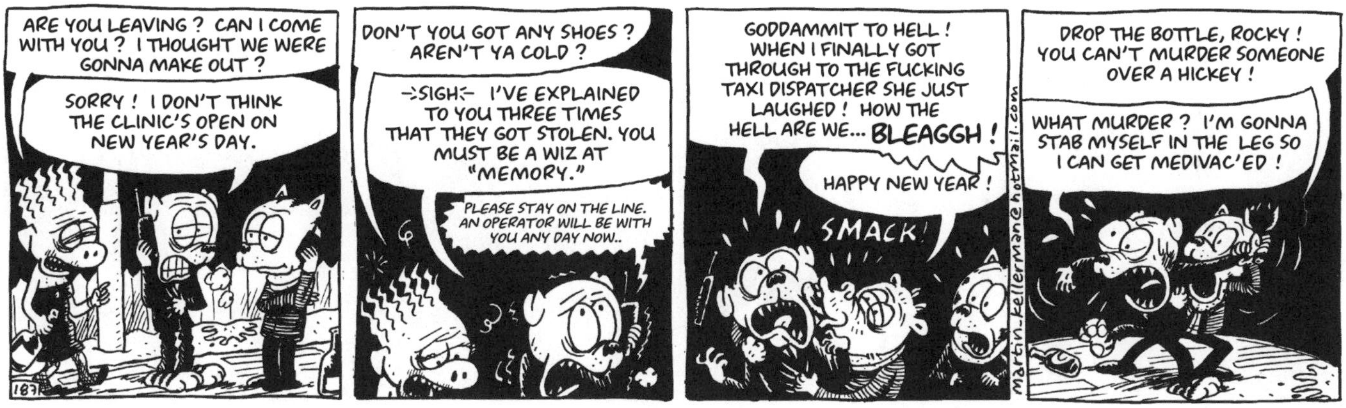
ARE YOU LEAVING? CAN I COME WITH YOU? I THOUGHT WE WERE GONNA MAKE OUT?
SORRY ! I DON'T THINK THE CLINIC'S OPEN ON NEW YEAR'S DAY.
187
DON'T YOU GOT ANY SHOES? AREN'T YA COLD?
-SIGH- I'VE EXPLAINED TO YOU THREE TIMES THAT THEY GOT STOLEN. YOU MUST BE A WIZ AT "MEMORY."
PLEASE STAY ON THE LINE. AN OPERATOR WILL BE WITH YOU ANY DAY NOW..
GODDAMMIT TO HELL ! WHEN I FINALLY GOT THROUGH TO THE FUCKING TAXI DISPATCHER SHE JUST LAUGHED ! HOW THE HELL ARE WE... BLEAGGH !
HAPPY NEW YEAR !
SMACK !
martin_kellerman@hotmail.com
DROP THE BOTTLE, ROCKY ! YOU CAN'T MURDER SOMEONE OVER A HICKEY !
WHAT MURDER? I'M GONNA STAB MYSELF IN THE LEG SO I CAN GET MEDIVAC'ED !

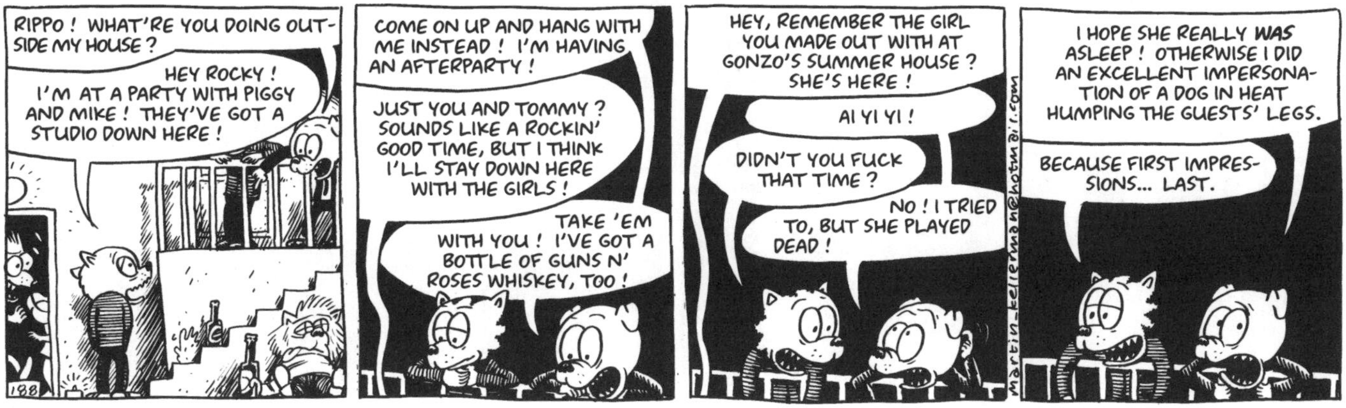
RIPPO ! WHAT'RE YOU DOING OUTSIDE MY HOUSE?
HEY ROCKY ! I'M AT A PARTY WITH PIGGY AND MIKE ! THEY'VE GOT A STUDIO DOWN HERE !
188
COME ON UP AND HANG WITH ME INSTEAD ! I'M HAVING AN AFTERPARTY !
JUST YOU AND TOMMY? SOUNDS LIKE A ROCKIN' GOOD TIME, BUT I THINK I'LL STAY DOWN HERE WITH THE GIRLS !
TAKE 'EM WITH YOU ! I'VE GOT A BOTTLE OF GUNS N' ROSES WHISKEY, TOO !
HEY, REMEMBER THE GIRL YOU MADE OUT WITH AT GONZO'S SUMMER HOUSE? SHE'S HERE !
AI YI YI !
DIDN'T YOU FUCK THAT TIME?
NO ! I TRIED TO, BUT SHE PLAYED DEAD !
martin_kellerman@hotmail.com
I HOPE SHE REALLY WAS ASLEEP ! OTHERWISE I DID AN EXCELLENT IMPERSONATION OF A DOG IN HEAT HUMPING THE GUESTS' LEGS.
BECAUSE FIRST IMPRESSIONS... LAST.

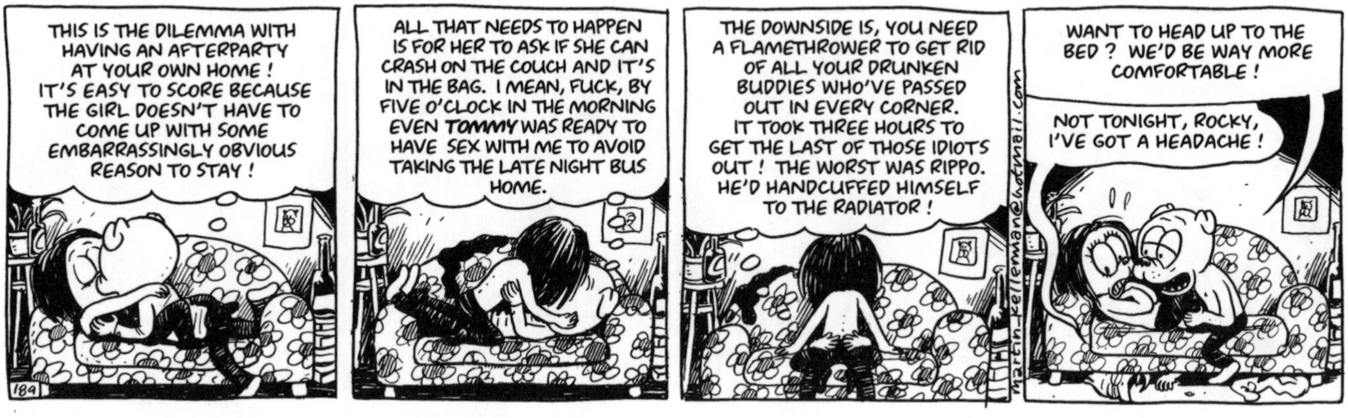
THIS IS THE DILEMMA WITH HAVING AN AFTERPARTY AT YOUR OWN HOME ! IT'S EASY TO SCORE BECAUSE THE GIRL DOESN'T HAVE TO COME UP WITH SOME EMBARRASSINGLY OBVIOUS REASON TO STAY !
189
ALL THAT NEEDS TO HAPPEN IS FOR HER TO ASK IF SHE CAN CRASH ON THE COUCH AND IT'S IN THE BAG. I MEAN, FUCK, BY FIVE O'CLOCK IN THE MORNING EVEN TOMMY WAS READY TO HAVE SEX WITH ME TO AVOID TAKING THE LATE NIGHT BUS HOME.
THE DOWNSIDE IS, YOU NEED A FLAMETHROWER TO GET RID OF ALL YOUR DRUNKEN BUDDIES WHO'VE PASSED OUT IN EVERY CORNER. IT TOOK THREE HOURS TO GET THE LAST OF THOSE IDIOTS OUT ! THE WORST WAS RIPPO. HE'D HANDCUFFED HIMSELF TO THE RADIATOR !
martin_kellerman@hotmail.com
WANT TO HEAD UP TO THE BED ? WE'D BE WAY MORE COMFORTABLE !
NOT TONIGHT, ROCKY, I'VE GOT A HEADACHE !

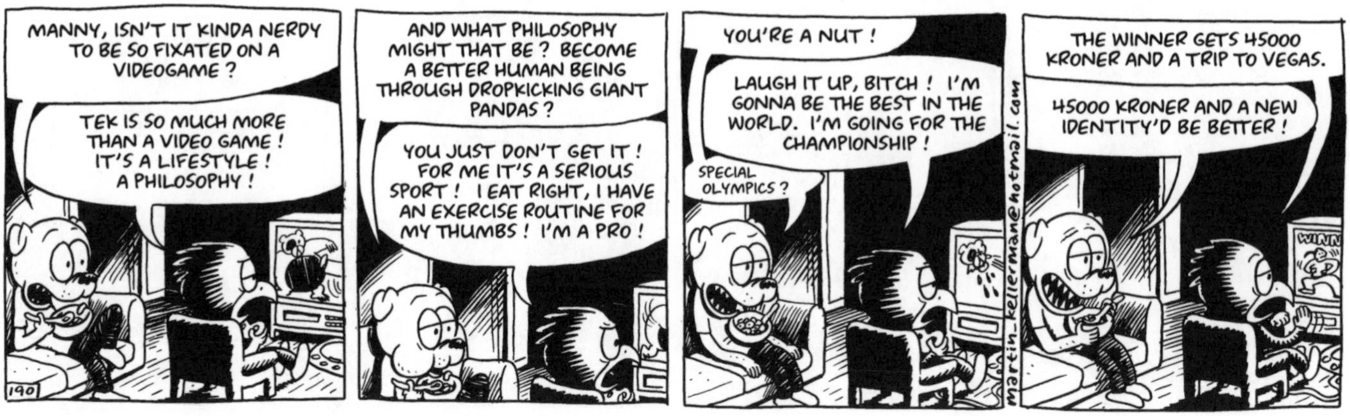
MANNY, ISN'T IT KINDA NERDY TO BE SO FIXATED ON A VIDEOGAME ?
TEK IS SO MUCH MORE THAN A VIDEO GAME ! IT'S A LIFESTYLE ! A PHILOSOPHY !
190
AND WHAT PHILOSOPHY MIGHT THAT BE ? BECOME A BETTER HUMAN BEING THROUGH DROPKICKING GIANT PANDAS ?
YOU JUST DON'T GET IT ! FOR ME IT'S A SERIOUS SPORT ! I EAT RIGHT, I HAVE AN EXERCISE ROUTINE FOR MY THUMBS ! I'M A PRO !
YOU'RE A NUT !
LAUGH IT UP, BITCH ! I'M GONNA BE THE BEST IN THE WORLD. I'M GOING FOR THE CHAMPIONSHIP !
SPECIAL OLYMPICS ?
martin_kellerman@hotmail.com
THE WINNER GETS 45000 KRONER AND A TRIP TO VEGAS.
45000 KRONER AND A NEW IDENTITY'D BE BETTER !

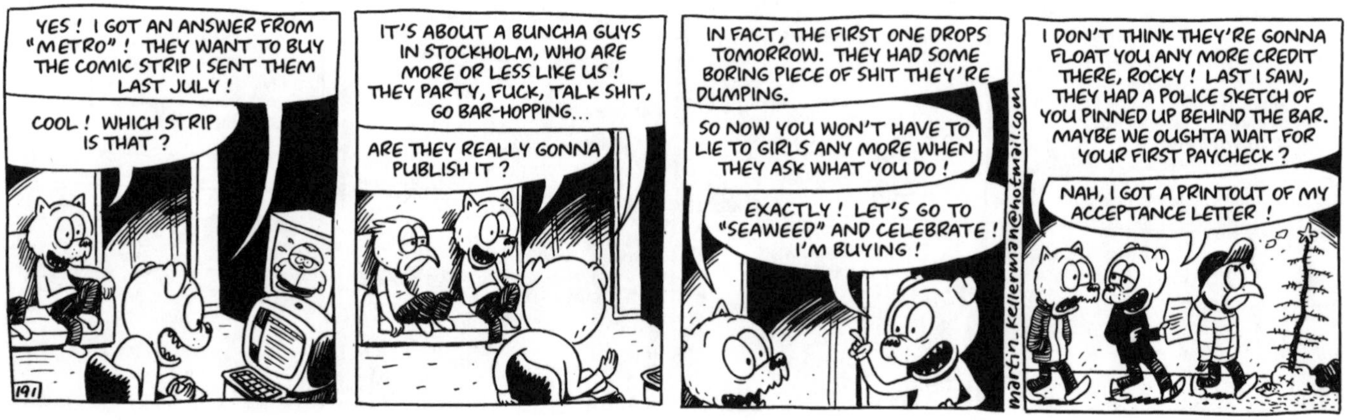
YES ! I GOT AN ANSWER FROM "METRO" ! THEY WANT TO BUY THE COMIC STRIP I SENT THEM LAST JULY !
COOL ! WHICH STRIP IS THAT ?
191
IT'S ABOUT A BUNCHA GUYS IN STOCKHOLM, WHO ARE MORE OR LESS LIKE US ! THEY PARTY, FUCK, TALK SHIT, GO BAR-HOPPING...
ARE THEY REALLY GONNA PUBLISH IT ?
IN FACT, THE FIRST ONE DROPS TOMORROW. THEY HAD SOME BORING PIECE OF SHIT THEY'RE DUMPING.
SO NOW YOU WON'T HAVE TO LIE TO GIRLS ANY MORE WHEN THEY ASK WHAT YOU DO !
EXACTLY ! LET'S GO TO "SEAWEED" AND CELEBRATE ! I'M BUYING !
martin_kellerman@hotmail.com
I DON'T THINK THEY'RE GONNA FLOAT YOU ANY MORE CREDIT THERE, ROCKY ! LAST I SAW, THEY HAD A POLICE SKETCH OF YOU PINNED UP BEHIND THE BAR. MAYBE WE OUGHTA WAIT FOR YOUR FIRST PAYCHECK ?
NAH, I GOT A PRINTOUT OF MY ACCEPTANCE LETTER !

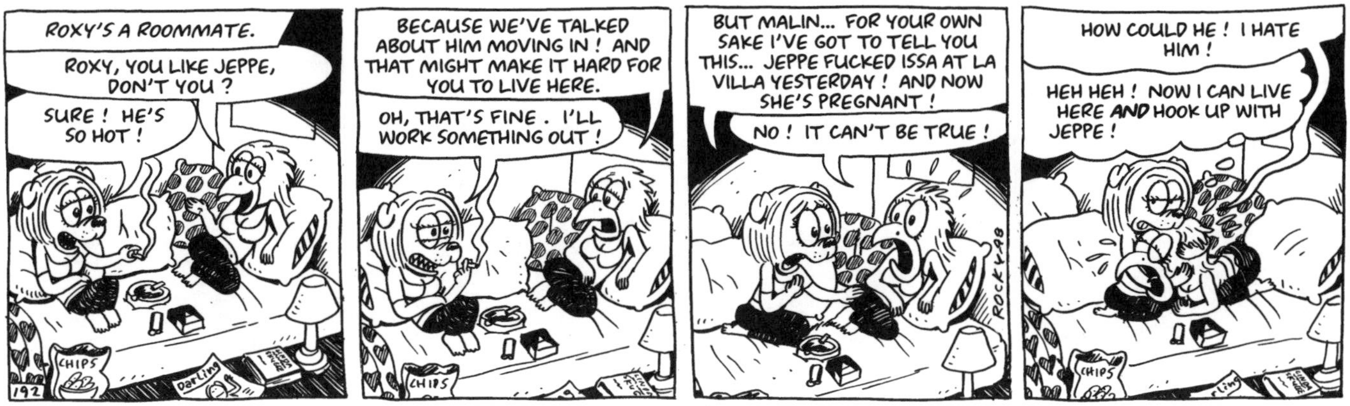
ROXY'S A ROOMMATE.
ROXY, YOU LIKE JEPPE, DON'T YOU ?
SURE ! HE'S SO HOT !
BECAUSE WE'VE TALKED ABOUT HIM MOVING IN ! AND THAT MIGHT MAKE IT HARD FOR YOU TO LIVE HERE.
OH, THAT'S FINE . I'LL WORK SOMETHING OUT !
BUT MALIN... FOR YOUR OWN SAKE I'VE GOT TO TELL YOU THIS... JEPPE FUCKED ISSA AT LA VILLA YESTERDAY ! AND NOW SHE'S PREGNANT !
NO ! IT CAN'T BE TRUE !
ROCKY 98
HOW COULD HE ! I HATE HIM !
HEH HEH ! NOW I CAN LIVE HERE AND HOOK UP WITH JEPPE !
CHIPS
192

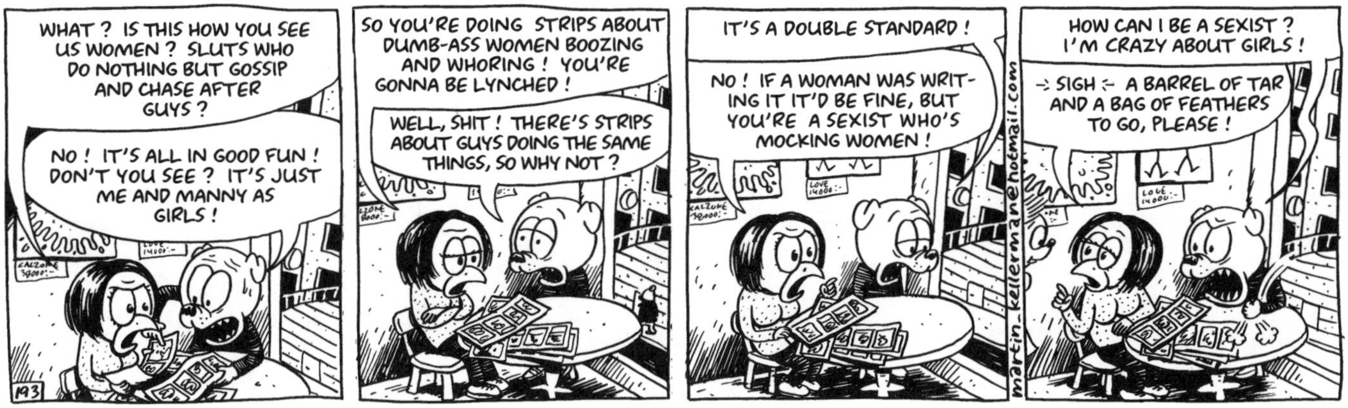
WHAT ? IS THIS HOW YOU SEE US WOMEN ? SLUTS WHO DO NOTHING BUT GOSSIP AND CHASE AFTER GUYS ?
NO ! IT'S ALL IN GOOD FUN ! DON'T YOU SEE ? IT'S JUST ME AND MANNY AS GIRLS !
SO YOU'RE DOING STRIPS ABOUT DUMB-ASS WOMEN BOOZING AND WHORING ! YOU'RE GONNA BE LYNCHED !
WELL, SHIT ! THERE'S STRIPS ABOUT GUYS DOING THE SAME THINGS, SO WHY NOT ?
IT'S A DOUBLE STANDARD !
NO ! IF A WOMAN WAS WRITING IT IT'D BE FINE, BUT YOU'RE A SEXIST WHO'S MOCKING WOMEN !
martin_kellerman@hotmail.com
HOW CAN I BE A SEXIST ? I'M CRAZY ABOUT GIRLS !
-:- SIGH -:- A BARREL OF TAR AND A BAG OF FEATHERS TO GO, PLEASE !
193

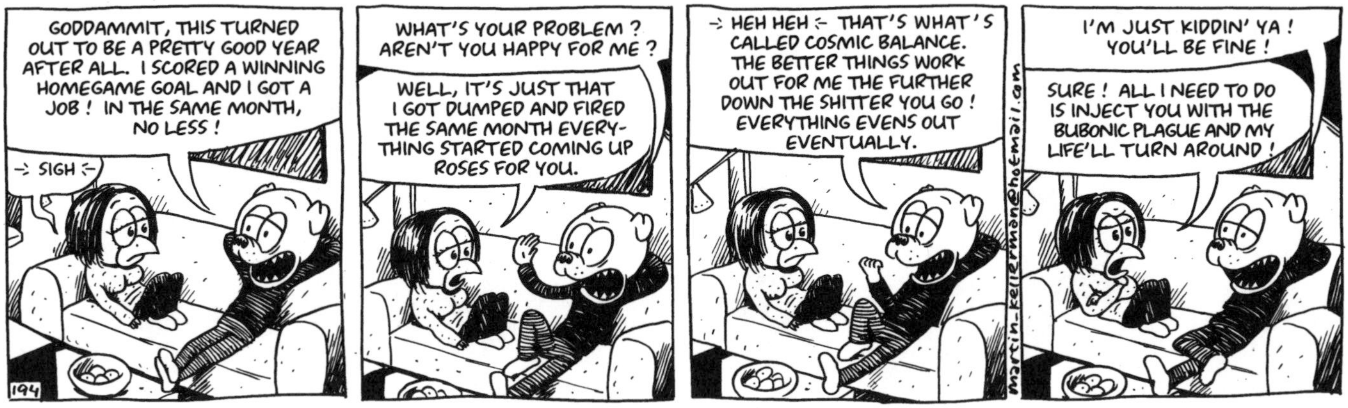
GODDAMMIT, THIS TURNED OUT TO BE A PRETTY GOOD YEAR AFTER ALL. I SCORED A WINNING HOMEGAME GOAL AND I GOT A JOB ! IN THE SAME MONTH, NO LESS !
-:- SIGH -:-
WHAT'S YOUR PROBLEM ? AREN'T YOU HAPPY FOR ME ?
WELL, IT'S JUST THAT I GOT DUMPED AND FIRED THE SAME MONTH EVERYTHING STARTED COMING UP ROSES FOR YOU.
-:- HEH HEH -:- THAT'S WHAT'S CALLED COSMIC BALANCE. THE BETTER THINGS WORK OUT FOR ME THE FURTHER DOWN THE SHITTER YOU GO ! EVERYTHING EVENS OUT EVENTUALLY.
martin_kellerman@hotmail.com
I'M JUST KIDDIN' YA ! YOU'LL BE FINE !
SURE ! ALL I NEED TO DO IS INJECT YOU WITH THE BUBONIC PLAGUE AND MY LIFE'LL TURN AROUND !
194

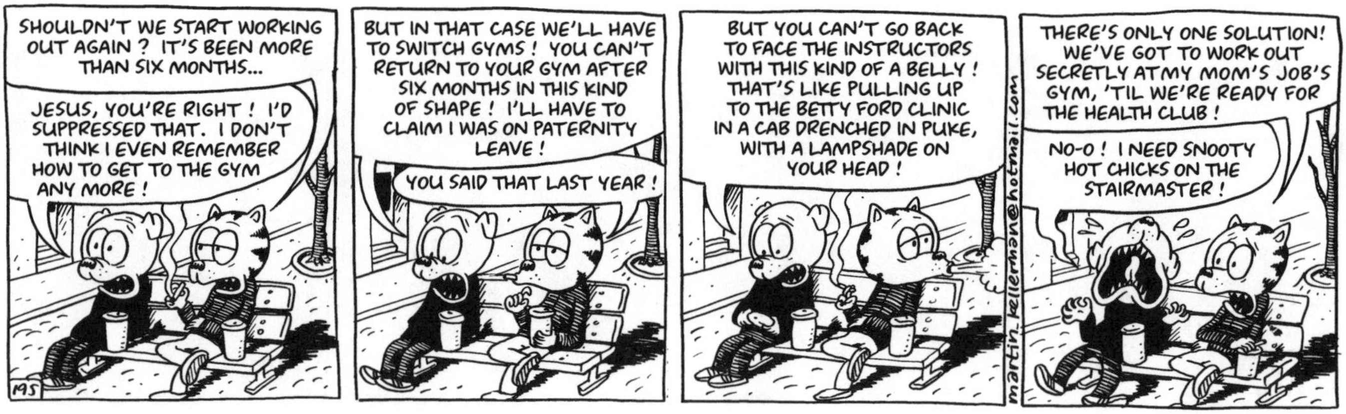
195
SHOULDN'T WE START WORKING OUT AGAIN ? IT'S BEEN MORE THAN SIX MONTHS...
JESUS, YOU'RE RIGHT ! I'D SUPPRESSED THAT. I DON'T THINK I EVEN REMEMBER HOW TO GET TO THE GYM ANY MORE !
BUT IN THAT CASE WE'LL HAVE TO SWITCH GYMS ! YOU CAN'T RETURN TO YOUR GYM AFTER SIX MONTHS IN THIS KIND OF SHAPE ! I'LL HAVE TO CLAIM I WAS ON PATERNITY LEAVE !
YOU SAID THAT LAST YEAR !
BUT YOU CAN'T GO BACK TO FACE THE INSTRUCTORS WITH THIS KIND OF A BELLY ! THAT'S LIKE PULLING UP TO THE BETTY FORD CLINIC IN A CAB DRENCHED IN PUKE, WITH A LAMPSHADE ON YOUR HEAD !
martin_kellerman@hotmail.com
THERE'S ONLY ONE SOLUTION ! WE'VE GOT TO WORK OUT SECRETLY AT MY MOM'S JOB'S GYM, 'TIL WE'RE READY FOR THE HEALTH CLUB !
NO-O ! I NEED SNOOTY HOT CHICKS ON THE STAIRMASTER !

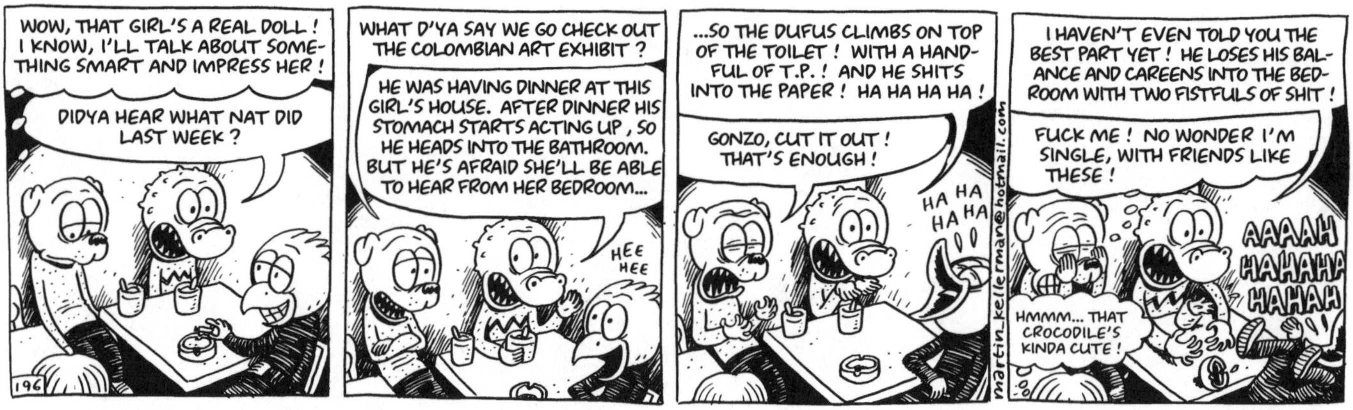
196
WOW, THAT GIRL'S A REAL DOLL ! I KNOW, I'LL TALK ABOUT SOMETHING SMART AND IMPRESS HER !
DIDYA HEAR WHAT NAT DID LAST WEEK ?
WHAT D'YA SAY WE GO CHECK OUT THE COLOMBIAN ART EXHIBIT ?
HE WAS HAVING DINNER AT THIS GIRL'S HOUSE. AFTER DINNER HIS STOMACH STARTS ACTING UP , SO HE HEADS INTO THE BATHROOM. BUT HE'S AFRAID SHE'LL BE ABLE TO HEAR FROM HER BEDROOM...
HEE HEE
...SO THE DUFUS CLIMBS ON TOP OF THE TOILET ! WITH A HANDFUL OF T.P. ! AND HE SHITS INTO THE PAPER ! HA HA HA HA !
GONZO, CUT IT OUT ! THAT'S ENOUGH !
HA HA HA HA
martin_kellerman@hotmail.com
I HAVEN'T EVEN TOLD YOU THE BEST PART YET ! HE LOSES HIS BALANCE AND CAREENS INTO THE BEDROOM WITH TWO FISTFULS OF SHIT !
FUCK ME ! NO WONDER I'M SINGLE, WITH FRIENDS LIKE THESE !
AAAAH HAHAHA HAHAH
HMMM... THAT CROCODILE'S KINDA CUTE !

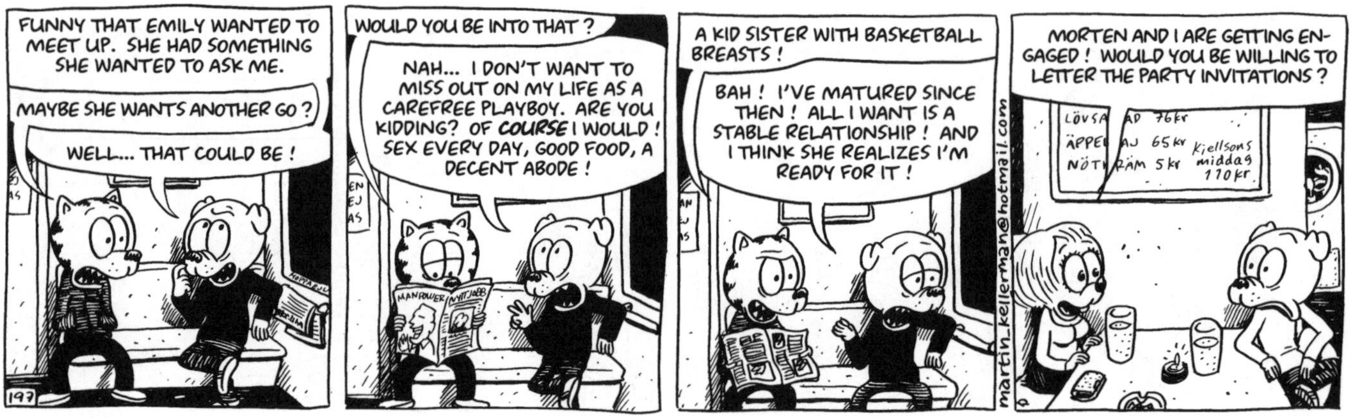
197
FUNNY THAT EMILY WANTED TO MEET UP. SHE HAD SOMETHING SHE WANTED TO ASK ME.
MAYBE SHE WANTS ANOTHER GO ?
WELL... THAT COULD BE !
WOULD YOU BE INTO THAT ?
NAH... I DON'T WANT TO MISS OUT ON MY LIFE AS A CAREFREE PLAYBOY. ARE YOU KIDDING? OF COURSE I WOULD ! SEX EVERY DAY, GOOD FOOD, A DECENT ABODE !
MANPOWER
NYTT JOBB
A KID SISTER WITH BASKETBALL BREASTS !
BAH ! I'VE MATURED SINCE THEN ! ALL I WANT IS A STABLE RELATIONSHIP ! AND I THINK SHE REALIZES I'M READY FOR IT !
martin_kellerman@hotmail.com
MORTEN AND I ARE GETTING ENGAGED ! WOULD YOU BE WILLING TO LETTER THE PARTY INVITATIONS ?
Kjellsons middag 110kr

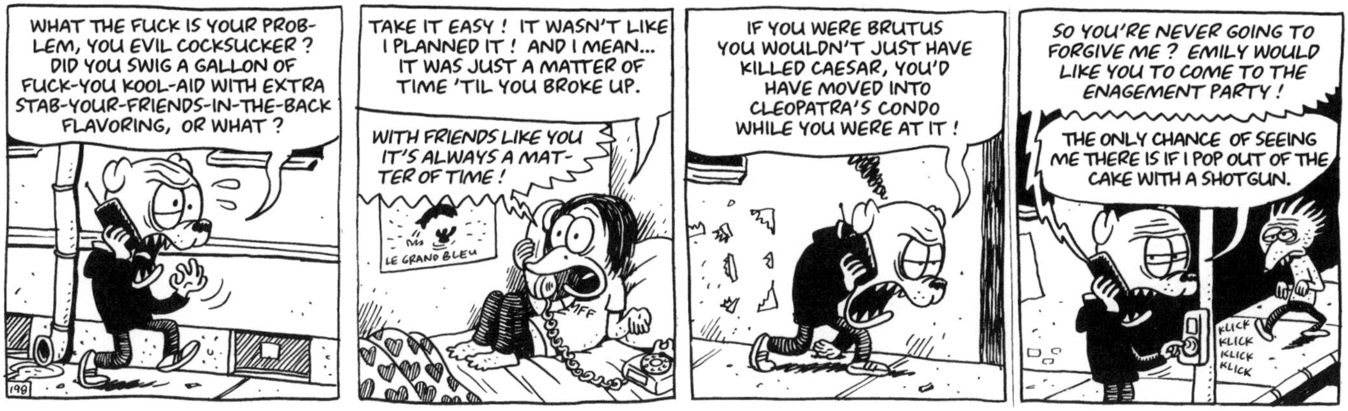
WHAT THE FUCK IS YOUR PROBLEM, YOU EVIL COCKSUCKER? DID YOU SWIG A GALLON OF FUCK-YOU KOOL-AID WITH EXTRA STAB-YOUR-FRIENDS-IN-THE-BACK FLAVORING, OR WHAT?
198
TAKE IT EASY! IT WASN'T LIKE I PLANNED IT! AND I MEAN... IT WAS JUST A MATTER OF TIME 'TIL YOU BROKE UP.
WITH FRIENDS LIKE YOU IT'S ALWAYS A MATTER OF TIME!
LE GRAND BLEU
IF YOU WERE BRUTUS YOU WOULDN'T JUST HAVE KILLED CAESAR, YOU'D HAVE MOVED INTO CLEOPATRA'S CONDO WHILE YOU WERE AT IT!
SO YOU'RE NEVER GOING TO FORGIVE ME? EMILY WOULD LIKE YOU TO COME TO THE ENAGEMENT PARTY!
THE ONLY CHANCE OF SEEING ME THERE IS IF I POP OUT OF THE CAKE WITH A SHOTGUN.
KLICK KLICK KLICK KLICK

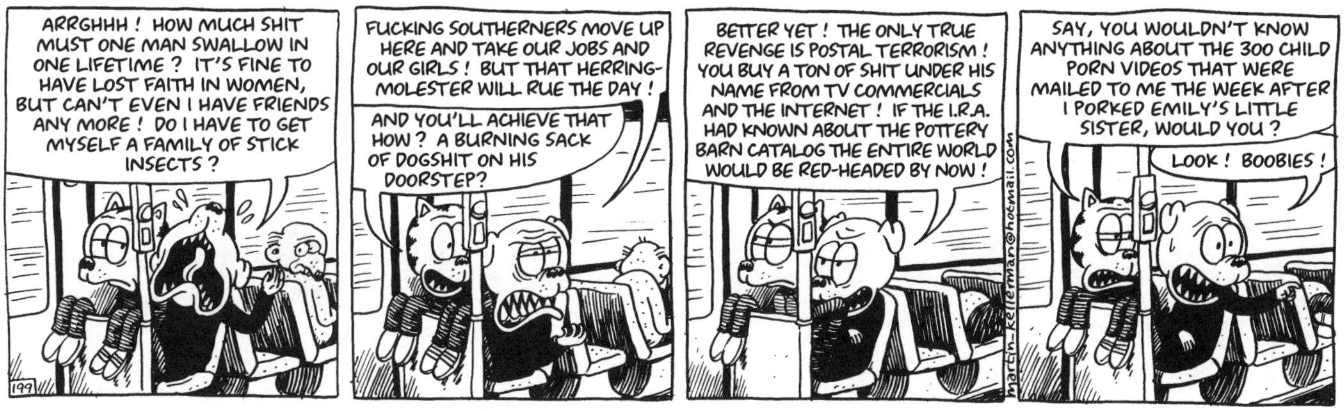
ARRGHHH! HOW MUCH SHIT MUST ONE MAN SWALLOW IN ONE LIFETIME? IT'S FINE TO HAVE LOST FAITH IN WOMEN, BUT CAN'T EVEN I HAVE FRIENDS ANY MORE! DO I HAVE TO GET MYSELF A FAMILY OF STICK INSECTS?
199
FUCKING SOUTHERNERS MOVE UP HERE AND TAKE OUR JOBS AND OUR GIRLS! BUT THAT HERRING-MOLESTER WILL RUE THE DAY!
AND YOU'LL ACHIEVE THAT HOW? A BURNING SACK OF DOGSHIT ON HIS DOORSTEP?
BETTER YET! THE ONLY TRUE REVENGE IS POSTAL TERRORISM! YOU BUY A TON OF SHIT UNDER HIS NAME FROM TV COMMERCIALS AND THE INTERNET! IF THE I.R.A. HAD KNOWN ABOUT THE POTTERY BARN CATALOG THE ENTIRE WORLD WOULD BE RED-HEADED BY NOW!
martin-kellerman@hotmail.com
SAY, YOU WOULDN'T KNOW ANYTHING ABOUT THE 300 CHILD PORN VIDEOS THAT WERE MAILED TO ME THE WEEK AFTER I PORKED EMILY'S LITTLE SISTER, WOULD YOU?
LOOK! BOOBIES!

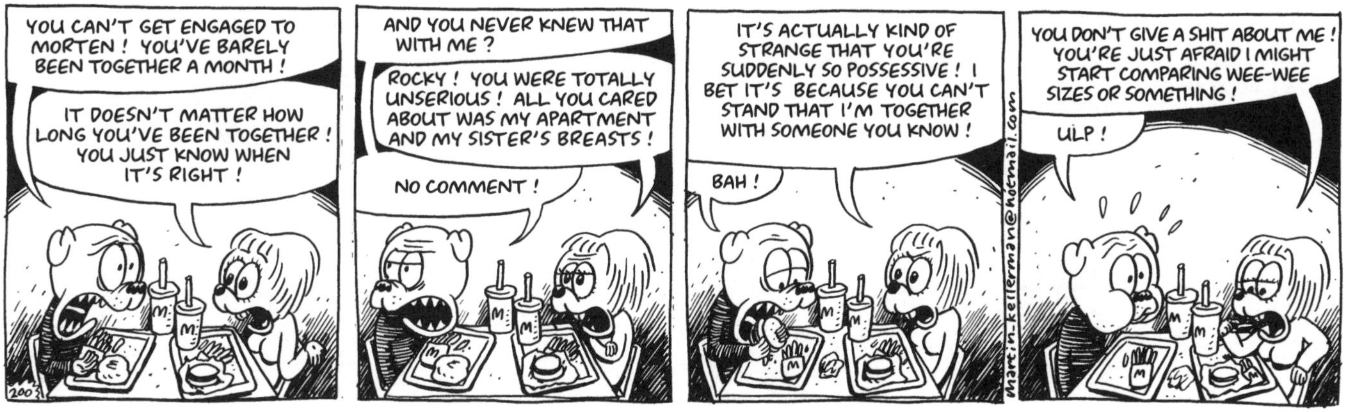
YOU CAN'T GET ENGAGED TO MORTEN! YOU'VE BARELY BEEN TOGETHER A MONTH!
IT DOESN'T MATTER HOW LONG YOU'VE BEEN TOGETHER! YOU JUST KNOW WHEN IT'S RIGHT!
AND YOU NEVER KNEW THAT WITH ME?
ROCKY! YOU WERE TOTALLY UNSERIOUS! ALL YOU CARED ABOUT WAS MY APARTMENT AND MY SISTER'S BREASTS!
NO COMMENT!
IT'S ACTUALLY KIND OF STRANGE THAT YOU'RE SUDDENLY SO POSSESSIVE! I BET IT'S BECAUSE YOU CAN'T STAND THAT I'M TOGETHER WITH SOMEONE YOU KNOW!
BAH!
martin-kellerman@hotmail.com
YOU DON'T GIVE A SHIT ABOUT ME! YOU'RE JUST AFRAID I MIGHT START COMPARING WEE-WEE SIZES OR SOMETHING!
ULP!

THE GRIND

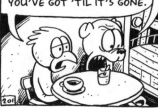

WHY? HOW COULD I HAVE BEEN SO STUPID? IF I'D JUST KEPT MY YAP SHUT ABOUT WANTING TO BOINK HER SISTER WE'D STILL BE TOGETHER.
YOU DON'T KNOW WHAT YOU'VE GOT 'TIL IT'S GONE.
201
PLEASE, GOD! IF I JUST GET HER BACK I WILL NEVER EVER AGAIN SO MUCH AS LOOK AT ANOTHER WOMAN! I'LL LAY OFF THE FUCKING CURSING, TOO, AND PUT A HALT TO THE MASTURBATION!
DON'T COUNT YOUR CHICKENS BEFORE THEY'RE HATCHED.
GODDAMMIT, MANNY, QUIT SPITTING OUT FORTUNE COOKIE SLOGANS EVERY TIME I OPEN MY FUCKING MOUTH!
I'M SORRY, ROCKY. BUT IT'S HARD TO WORK UP TOO MUCH SYMPATHY FOR YOU SINCE IT'S ALL YOUR OWN FAULT.
martin_kellerman@hotmail.com
FACE IT, SHE'S GETTING ENGAGED NEXT WEEK. IT'S OVER.
WAY TO GO, GOD! YOU HAD A SHOT AT MAKING A BETTER MAN OF ME, BUT NO-O-O! JUST FOR THAT I'M GONNA MORPH INTO A SWEARING, WEED-SMOKING, WILDLY MASTURBATING SATANIST.

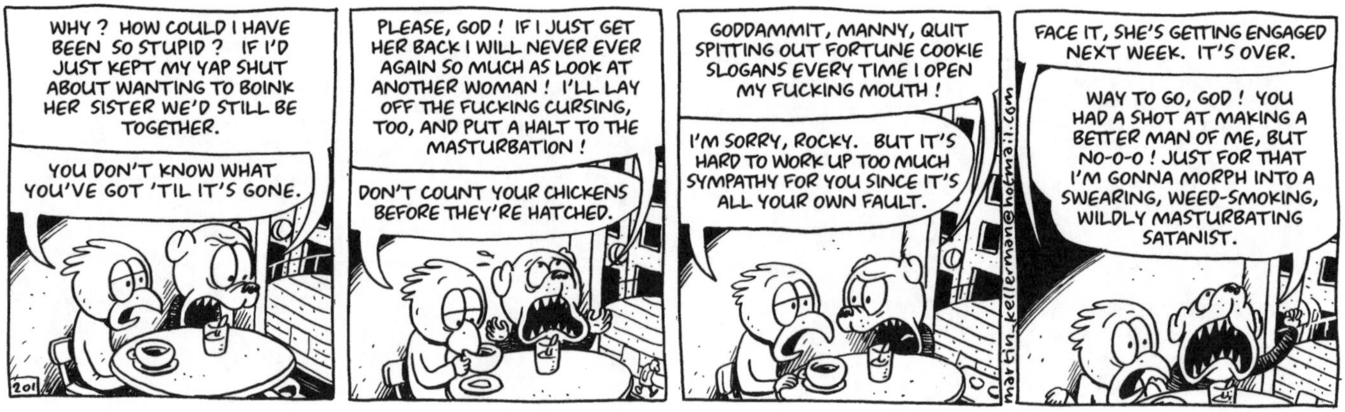

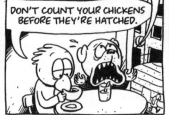

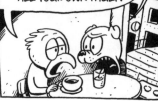

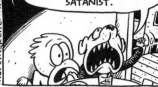

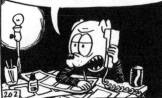

NO, I DON'T HAVE TIME TO GO OUT FOR COFFEE! FROM THIS POINT ON I WILL LEAVE THE LIFE OF AN ASCETIC, WITH TONS OF WORK AND STRICT DISCIPLINE. MY ONLY PLEASURE SHALL BE A GAME OF "MASTERMIND" EVERY SUNDAY AFTERNOON!
202
KELLERMAN
I'M NOT STOPPING 'TIL I'M RICH AND FAMOUS. WHEN EMILY REALIZES THAT I'VE BECOME A BETTER MAN SHE'LL BREAK OFF HER ENGAGEMENT TO MORTEN!
JESUS, YOU SOUND REALLY FOCUSED!
YES, I MUST GET HER BACK! I REALIZE NOW THAT WE'RE PERFECT FOR EACH OTHER! I HAVEN'T EVEN THOUGHT ABOUT ANYONE ELSE FOR A WEEK! ALL I'VE DONE IS WORK, WORK, WORK!
martin_kellerman@hotmail.com
WHAT'S THIS WEEK'S STRIP ABOUT?
IT'S ABOUT THE WHOREMONGERING SON OF A BITCH EMIL, WHO BETRAYS HIS GIRLFRIEND ROXY IN HER TIME OF NEED AND GETS ENGAGED TO HER SLUTTY FRIEND FROM THE SOUTH.

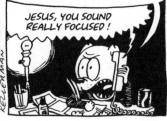

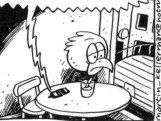

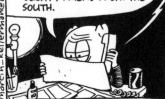

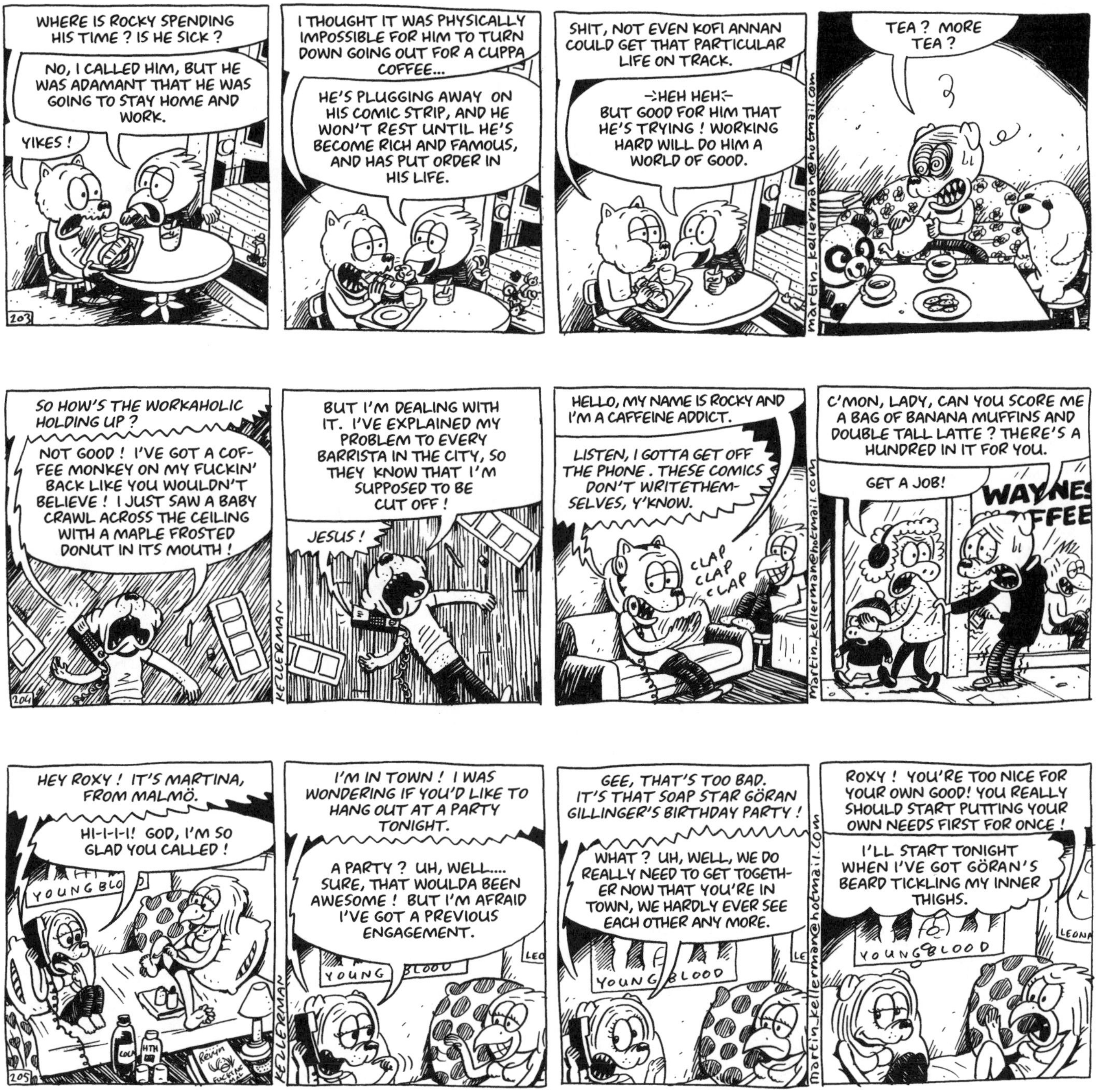
WHERE IS ROCKY SPENDING HIS TIME ? IS HE SICK ?
NO, I CALLED HIM, BUT HE WAS ADAMANT THAT HE WAS GOING TO STAY HOME AND WORK.
YIKES !
203
I THOUGHT IT WAS PHYSICALLY IMPOSSIBLE FOR HIM TO TURN DOWN GOING OUT FOR A CUPPA COFFEE...
HE'S PLUGGING AWAY ON HIS COMIC STRIP, AND HE WON'T REST UNTIL HE'S BECOME RICH AND FAMOUS, AND HAS PUT ORDER IN HIS LIFE.
SHIT, NOT EVEN KOFI ANNAN COULD GET THAT PARTICULAR LIFE ON TRACK.
HEH HEH
BUT GOOD FOR HIM THAT HE'S TRYING ! WORKING HARD WILL DO HIM A WORLD OF GOOD.
martin_kellerman@hotmail.com
TEA ? MORE TEA ?
SO HOW'S THE WORKAHOLIC HOLDING UP ?
NOT GOOD ! I'VE GOT A COFFEE MONKEY ON MY FUCKIN' BACK LIKE YOU WOULDN'T BELIEVE ! I JUST SAW A BABY CRAWL ACROSS THE CEILING WITH A MAPLE FROSTED DONUT IN ITS MOUTH !
204
KELLERMAN
BUT I'M DEALING WITH IT. I'VE EXPLAINED MY PROBLEM TO EVERY BARRISTA IN THE CITY, SO THEY KNOW THAT I'M SUPPOSED TO BE CUT OFF !
JESUS !
HELLO, MY NAME IS ROCKY AND I'M A CAFFEINE ADDICT.
LISTEN, I GOTTA GET OFF THE PHONE. THESE COMICS DON'T WRITETHEMSELVES, Y'KNOW.
CLAP CLAP CLAP
martin_kellerman@hotmail.com
C'MON, LADY, CAN YOU SCORE ME A BAG OF BANANA MUFFINS AND DOUBLE TALL LATTE ? THERE'S A HUNDRED IN IT FOR YOU.
GET A JOB!
HEY ROXY ! IT'S MARTINA, FROM MALMÖ.
HI-I-I-I! GOD, I'M SO GLAD YOU CALLED !
YOUNG BLOOD
205
KELLERMAN
I'M IN TOWN ! I WAS WONDERING IF YOU'D LIKE TO HANG OUT AT A PARTY TONIGHT.
A PARTY ? UH, WELL.... SURE, THAT WOULDA BEEN AWESOME ! BUT I'M AFRAID I'VE GOT A PREVIOUS ENGAGEMENT.
YOUNG BLOOD
GEE, THAT'S TOO BAD. IT'S THAT SOAP STAR GÖRAN GILLINGER'S BIRTHDAY PARTY !
WHAT ? UH, WELL, WE DO REALLY NEED TO GET TOGETHER NOW THAT YOU'RE IN TOWN, WE HARDLY EVER SEE EACH OTHER ANY MORE.
YOUNG BLOOD
martin_kellerman@hotmail.com
ROXY ! YOU'RE TOO NICE FOR YOUR OWN GOOD! YOU REALLY SHOULD START PUTTING YOUR OWN NEEDS FIRST FOR ONCE !
I'LL START TONIGHT WHEN I'VE GOT GÖRAN'S BEARD TICKLING MY INNER THIGHS.
YOUNG BLOOD

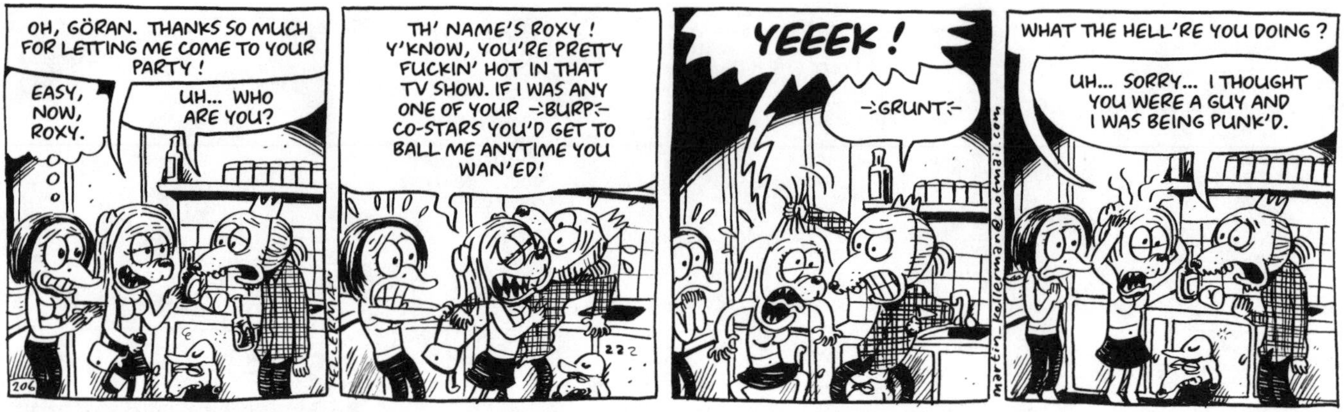
OH, GÖRAN. THANKS SO MUCH FOR LETTING ME COME TO YOUR PARTY !
EASY, NOW, ROXY.
UH... WHO ARE YOU?
206
KELLERMAN
TH' NAME'S ROXY ! Y'KNOW, YOU'RE PRETTY FUCKIN' HOT IN THAT TV SHOW. IF I WAS ANY ONE OF YOUR -BURP- CO-STARS YOU'D GET TO BALL ME ANYTIME YOU WAN'ED!
ZZZ
YEEEK !
-GRUNT-
martin_kellerman@hotmail.com
WHAT THE HELL'RE YOU DOING ?
UH... SORRY... I THOUGHT YOU WERE A GUY AND I WAS BEING PUNK'D.

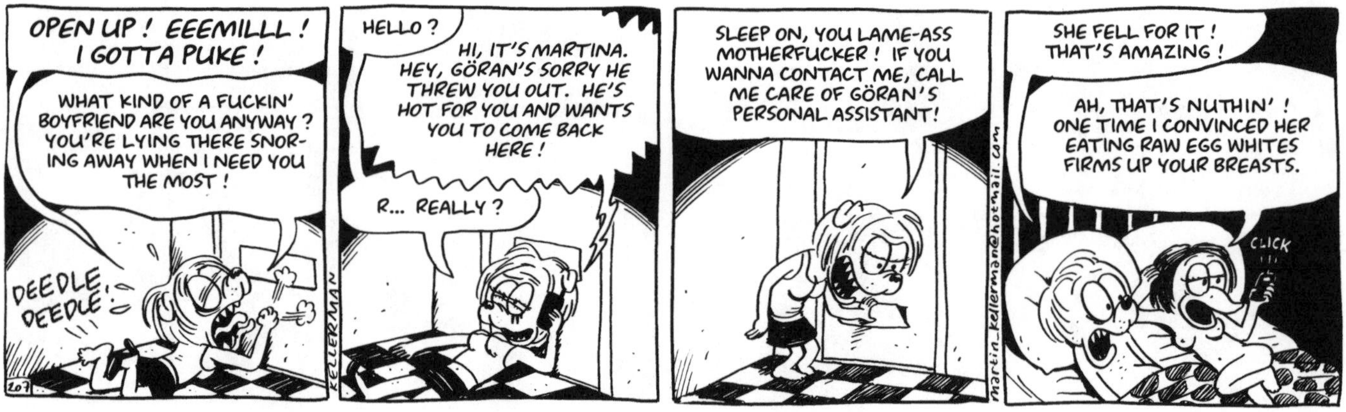
OPEN UP ! EEEMILLL ! I GOTTA PUKE !
WHAT KIND OF A FUCKIN' BOYFRIEND ARE YOU ANYWAY ? YOU'RE LYING THERE SNORING AWAY WHEN I NEED YOU THE MOST !
DEEDLE DEEDLE
207
KELLERMAN
HELLO ?
HI, IT'S MARTINA. HEY, GÖRAN'S SORRY HE THREW YOU OUT. HE'S HOT FOR YOU AND WANTS YOU TO COME BACK HERE !
R... REALLY ?
SLEEP ON, YOU LAME-ASS MOTHERFUCKER ! IF YOU WANNA CONTACT ME, CALL ME CARE OF GÖRAN'S PERSONAL ASSISTANT!
martin_kellerman@hotmail.com
SHE FELL FOR IT ! THAT'S AMAZING !
AH, THAT'S NUTHIN' ! ONE TIME I CONVINCED HER EATING RAW EGG WHITES FIRMS UP YOUR BREASTS.
CLICK

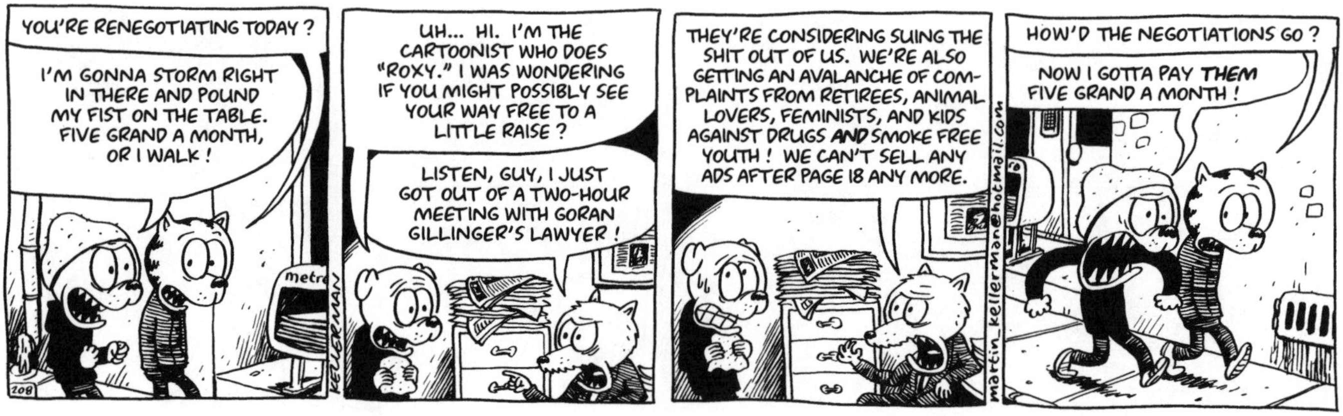
YOU'RE RENEGOTIATING TODAY ?
I'M GONNA STORM RIGHT IN THERE AND POUND MY FIST ON THE TABLE. FIVE GRAND A MONTH, OR I WALK !
208
KELLERMAN
UH... HI. I'M THE CARTOONIST WHO DOES "ROXY." I WAS WONDERING IF YOU MIGHT POSSIBLY SEE YOUR WAY FREE TO A LITTLE RAISE ?
LISTEN, GUY, I JUST GOT OUT OF A TWO-HOUR MEETING WITH GORAN GILLINGER'S LAWYER !
THEY'RE CONSIDERING SUING THE SHIT OUT OF US. WE'RE ALSO GETTING AN AVALANCHE OF COMPLAINTS FROM RETIREES, ANIMAL LOVERS, FEMINISTS, AND KIDS AGAINST DRUGS AND SMOKE FREE YOUTH ! WE CAN'T SELL ANY ADS AFTER PAGE 18 ANY MORE.
martin_kellerman@hotmail.com
HOW'D THE NEGOTIATIONS GO ?
NOW I GOTTA PAY THEM FIVE GRAND A MONTH !

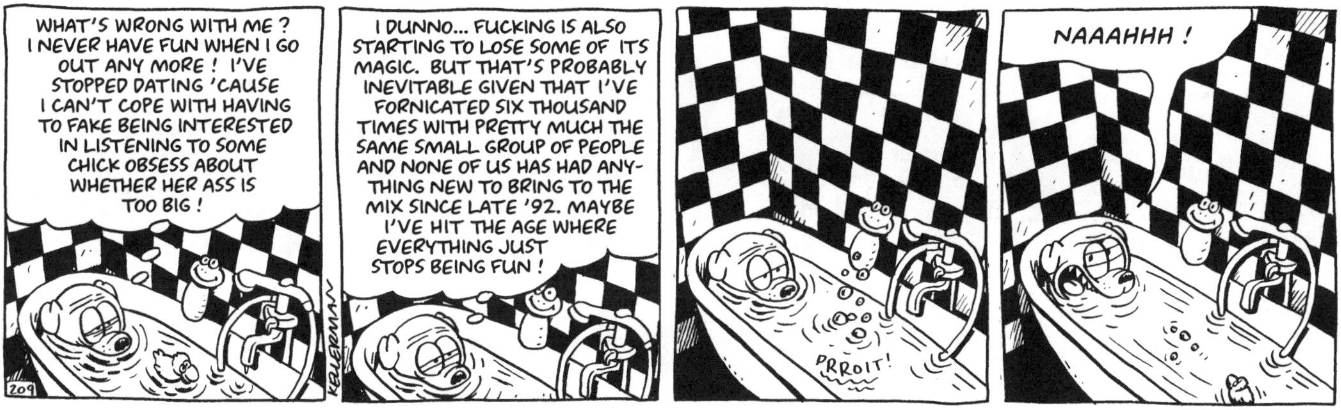
WHAT'S WRONG WITH ME ? I NEVER HAVE FUN WHEN I GO OUT ANY MORE ! I'VE STOPPED DATING 'CAUSE I CAN'T COPE WITH HAVING TO FAKE BEING INTERESTED IN LISTENING TO SOME CHICK OBSESS ABOUT WHETHER HER ASS IS TOO BIG !
I DUNNO... FUCKING IS ALSO STARTING TO LOSE SOME OF ITS MAGIC. BUT THAT'S PROBABLY INEVITABLE GIVEN THAT I'VE FORNICATED SIX THOUSAND TIMES WITH PRETTY MUCH THE SAME SMALL GROUP OF PEOPLE AND NONE OF US HAS HAD ANY-THING NEW TO BRING TO THE MIX SINCE LATE '92. MAYBE I'VE HIT THE AGE WHERE EVERYTHING JUST STOPS BEING FUN !
PRROIT!
NAAAHHH !

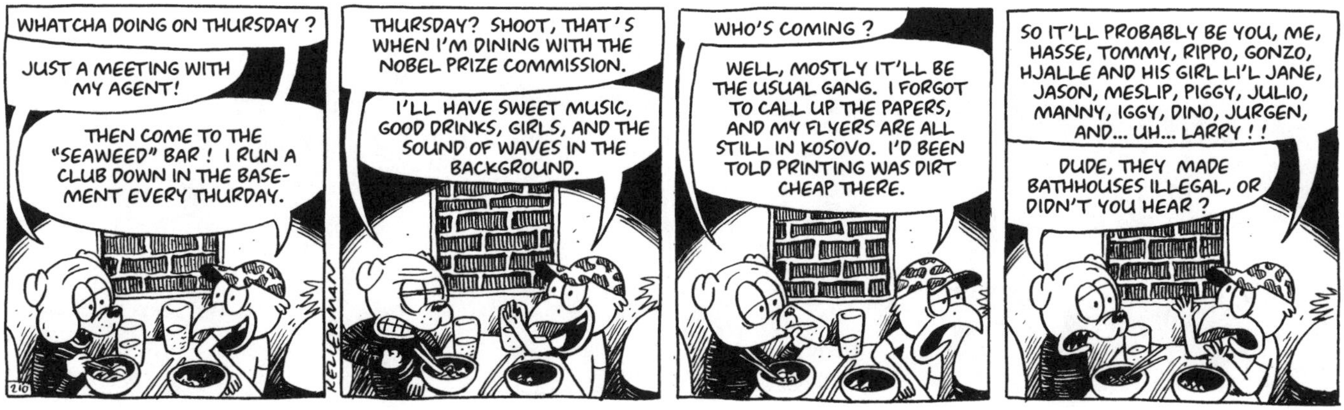
WHATCHA DOING ON THURSDAY ?
JUST A MEETING WITH MY AGENT!
THEN COME TO THE "SEAWEED" BAR ! I RUN A CLUB DOWN IN THE BASE-MENT EVERY THURDAY.
THURSDAY? SHOOT, THAT'S WHEN I'M DINING WITH THE NOBEL PRIZE COMMISSION.
I'LL HAVE SWEET MUSIC, GOOD DRINKS, GIRLS, AND THE SOUND OF WAVES IN THE BACKGROUND.
WHO'S COMING ?
WELL, MOSTLY IT'LL BE THE USUAL GANG. I FORGOT TO CALL UP THE PAPERS, AND MY FLYERS ARE ALL STILL IN KOSOVO. I'D BEEN TOLD PRINTING WAS DIRT CHEAP THERE.
SO IT'LL PROBABLY BE YOU, ME, HASSE, TOMMY, RIPPO, GONZO, HJALLE AND HIS GIRL LI'L JANE, JASON, MESLIP, PIGGY, JULIO, MANNY, IGGY, DINO, JURGEN, AND... UH... LARRY ! !
DUDE, THEY MADE BATHHOUSES ILLEGAL, OR DIDN'T YOU HEAR ?

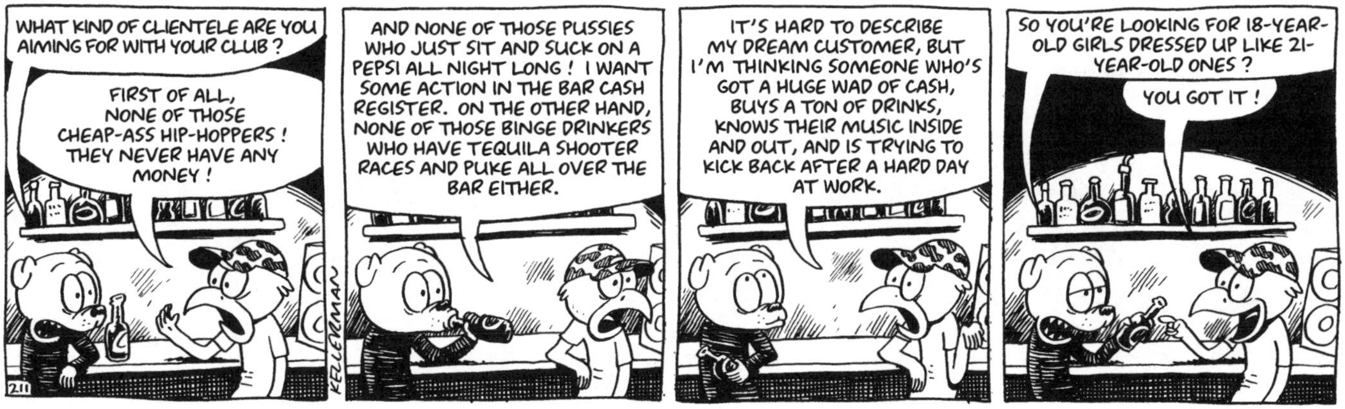
WHAT KIND OF CLIENTELE ARE YOU AIMING FOR WITH YOUR CLUB ?
FIRST OF ALL, NONE OF THOSE CHEAP-ASS HIP-HOPPERS ! THEY NEVER HAVE ANY MONEY !
AND NONE OF THOSE PUSSIES WHO JUST SIT AND SUCK ON A PEPSI ALL NIGHT LONG ! I WANT SOME ACTION IN THE BAR CASH REGISTER. ON THE OTHER HAND, NONE OF THOSE BINGE DRINKERS WHO HAVE TEQUILA SHOOTER RACES AND PUKE ALL OVER THE BAR EITHER.
IT'S HARD TO DESCRIBE MY DREAM CUSTOMER, BUT I'M THINKING SOMEONE WHO'S GOT A HUGE WAD OF CASH, BUYS A TON OF DRINKS, KNOWS THEIR MUSIC INSIDE AND OUT, AND IS TRYING TO KICK BACK AFTER A HARD DAY AT WORK.
SO YOU'RE LOOKING FOR 18-YEAR-OLD GIRLS DRESSED UP LIKE 21-YEAR-OLD ONES ?
YOU GOT IT !

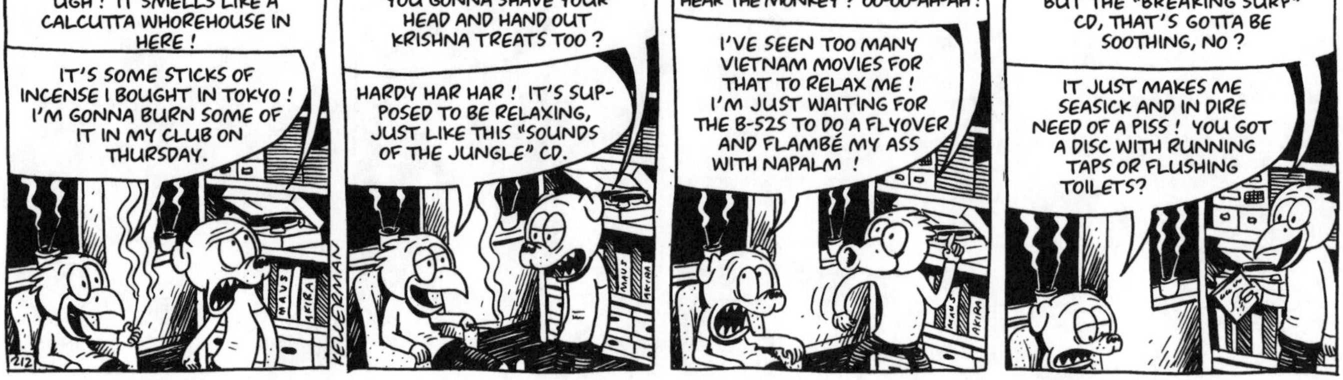
212
UGH ! IT SMELLS LIKE A CALCUTTA WHOREHOUSE IN HERE !
IT'S SOME STICKS OF INCENSE I BOUGHT IN TOKYO ! I'M GONNA BURN SOME OF IT IN MY CLUB ON THURSDAY.
KELLERMAN
YOU GONNA SHAVE YOUR HEAD AND HAND OUT KRISHNA TREATS TOO ?
HARDY HAR HAR ! IT'S SUPPOSED TO BE RELAXING, JUST LIKE THIS "SOUNDS OF THE JUNGLE" CD.
HEAR THE MONKEY ? OO-OO-AH-AH !
I'VE SEEN TOO MANY VIETNAM MOVIES FOR THAT TO RELAX ME ! I'M JUST WAITING FOR THE B-52S TO DO A FLYOVER AND FLAMBÉ MY ASS WITH NAPALM !
BUT THE "BREAKING SURF" CD, THAT'S GOTTA BE SOOTHING, NO ?
IT JUST MAKES ME SEASICK AND IN DIRE NEED OF A PISS ! YOU GOT A DISC WITH RUNNING TAPS OR FLUSHING TOILETS?

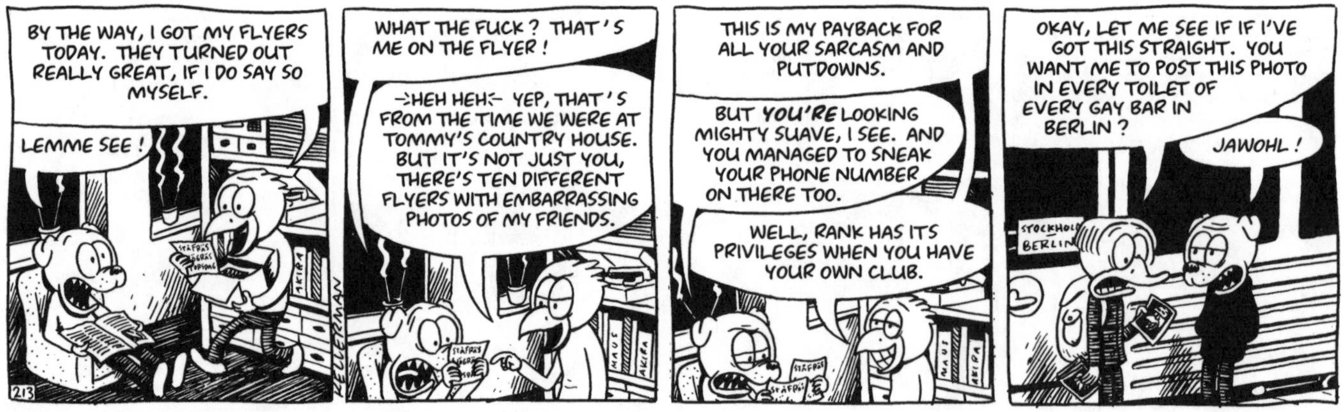
213
BY THE WAY, I GOT MY FLYERS TODAY. THEY TURNED OUT REALLY GREAT, IF I DO SAY SO MYSELF.
LEMME SEE !
KELLERMAN
WHAT THE FUCK ? THAT'S ME ON THE FLYER !
HEH HEH YEP, THAT'S FROM THE TIME WE WERE AT TOMMY'S COUNTRY HOUSE. BUT IT'S NOT JUST YOU, THERE'S TEN DIFFERENT FLYERS WITH EMBARRASSING PHOTOS OF MY FRIENDS.
THIS IS MY PAYBACK FOR ALL YOUR SARCASM AND PUTDOWNS.
BUT YOU'RE LOOKING MIGHTY SUAVE, I SEE. AND YOU MANAGED TO SNEAK YOUR PHONE NUMBER ON THERE TOO.
WELL, RANK HAS ITS PRIVILEGES WHEN YOU HAVE YOUR OWN CLUB.
OKAY, LET ME SEE IF IF I'VE GOT THIS STRAIGHT. YOU WANT ME TO POST THIS PHOTO IN EVERY TOILET OF EVERY GAY BAR IN BERLIN ?
JAWOHL !

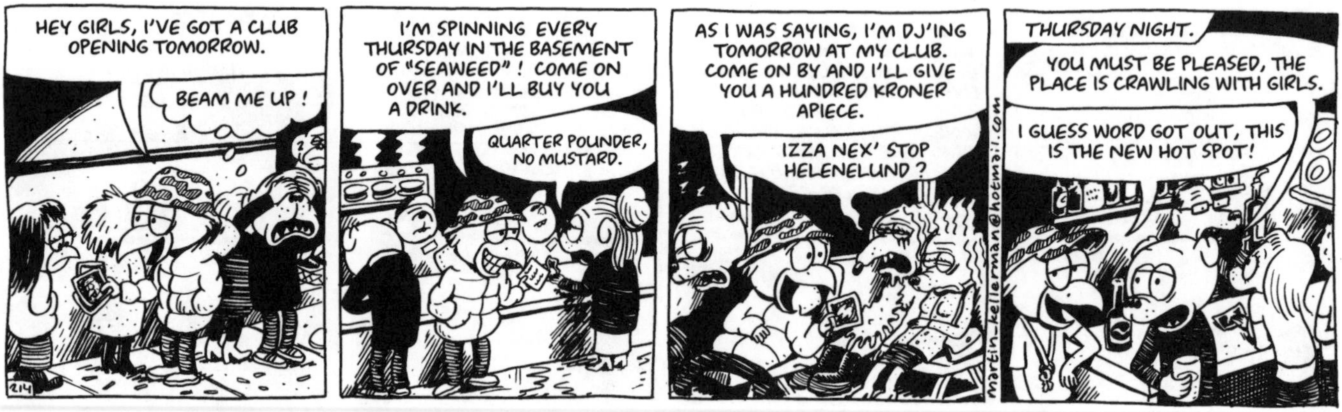
214
HEY GIRLS, I'VE GOT A CLUB OPENING TOMORROW.
BEAM ME UP !
I'M SPINNING EVERY THURSDAY IN THE BASEMENT OF "SEAWEED" ! COME ON OVER AND I'LL BUY YOU A DRINK.
QUARTER POUNDER, NO MUSTARD.
AS I WAS SAYING, I'M DJ'ING TOMORROW AT MY CLUB. COME ON BY AND I'LL GIVE YOU A HUNDRED KRONER APIECE.
IZZA NEX' STOP HELENELUND ?
martin_kellerman@hotmail.com
THURSDAY NIGHT.
YOU MUST BE PLEASED, THE PLACE IS CRAWLING WITH GIRLS.
I GUESS WORD GOT OUT, THIS IS THE NEW HOT SPOT!

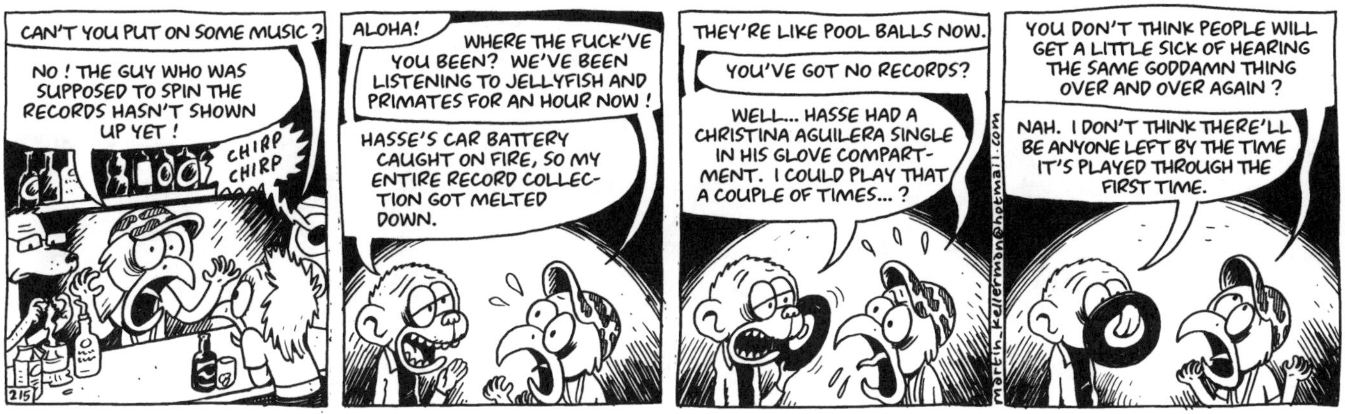
CAN'T YOU PUT ON SOME MUSIC ?
NO ! THE GUY WHO WAS SUPPOSED TO SPIN THE RECORDS HASN'T SHOWN UP YET !
CHIRP CHIRP
215
ALOHA!
WHERE THE FUCK'VE YOU BEEN? WE'VE BEEN LISTENING TO JELLYFISH AND PRIMATES FOR AN HOUR NOW !
HASSE'S CAR BATTERY CAUGHT ON FIRE, SO MY ENTIRE RECORD COLLECTION GOT MELTED DOWN.
THEY'RE LIKE POOL BALLS NOW.
YOU'VE GOT NO RECORDS?
WELL... HASSE HAD A CHRISTINA AGUILERA SINGLE IN HIS GLOVE COMPARTMENT. I COULD PLAY THAT A COUPLE OF TIMES... ?
martin_kellerman@hotmail.com
YOU DON'T THINK PEOPLE WILL GET A LITTLE SICK OF HEARING THE SAME GODDAMN THING OVER AND OVER AGAIN ?
NAH. I DON'T THINK THERE'LL BE ANYONE LEFT BY THE TIME IT'S PLAYED THROUGH THE FIRST TIME.

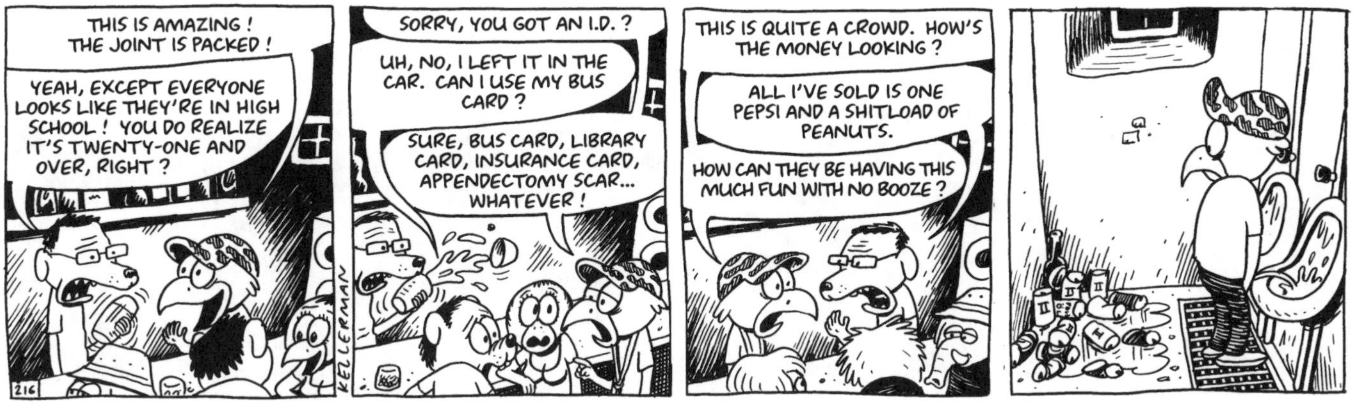
THIS IS AMAZING ! THE JOINT IS PACKED !
YEAH, EXCEPT EVERYONE LOOKS LIKE THEY'RE IN HIGH SCHOOL ! YOU DO REALIZE IT'S TWENTY-ONE AND OVER, RIGHT ?
216
KELLERMAN
SORRY, YOU GOT AN I.D. ?
UH, NO, I LEFT IT IN THE CAR. CAN I USE MY BUS CARD ?
SURE, BUS CARD, LIBRARY CARD, INSURANCE CARD, APPENDECTOMY SCAR... WHATEVER !
THIS IS QUITE A CROWD. HOW'S THE MONEY LOOKING ?
ALL I'VE SOLD IS ONE PEPSI AND A SHITLOAD OF PEANUTS.
HOW CAN THEY BE HAVING THIS MUCH FUN WITH NO BOOZE ?

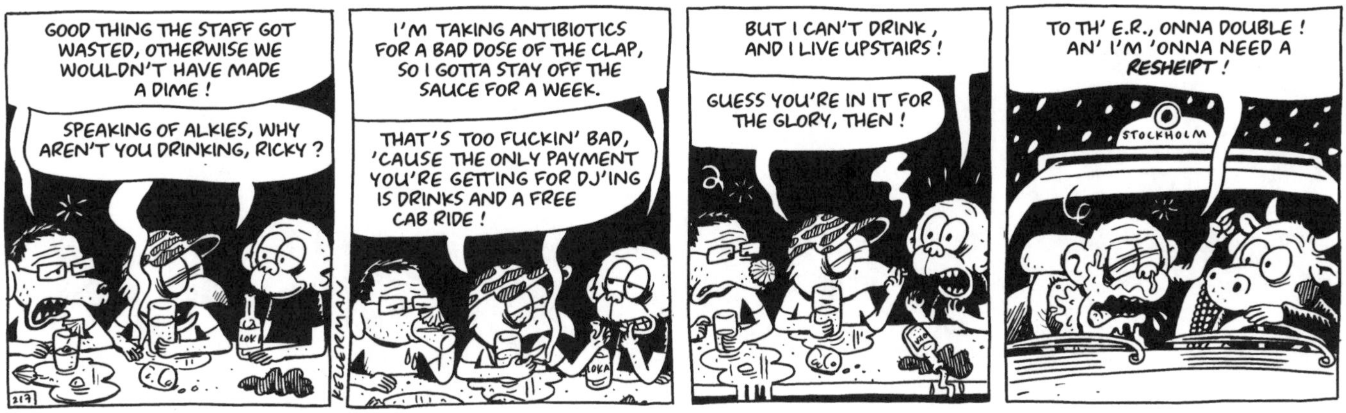
GOOD THING THE STAFF GOT WASTED, OTHERWISE WE WOULDN'T HAVE MADE A DIME !
SPEAKING OF ALKIES, WHY AREN'T YOU DRINKING, RICKY ?
217
KELLERMAN
I'M TAKING ANTIBIOTICS FOR A BAD DOSE OF THE CLAP, SO I GOTTA STAY OFF THE SAUCE FOR A WEEK.
THAT'S TOO FUCKIN' BAD, 'CAUSE THE ONLY PAYMENT YOU'RE GETTING FOR DJ'ING IS DRINKS AND A FREE CAB RIDE !
BUT I CAN'T DRINK , AND I LIVE UPSTAIRS !
GUESS YOU'RE IN IT FOR THE GLORY, THEN !
TO TH' E.R., ONNA DOUBLE ! AN' I'M 'ONNA NEED A ***RESHEIPT*** !
STOCKHOLM

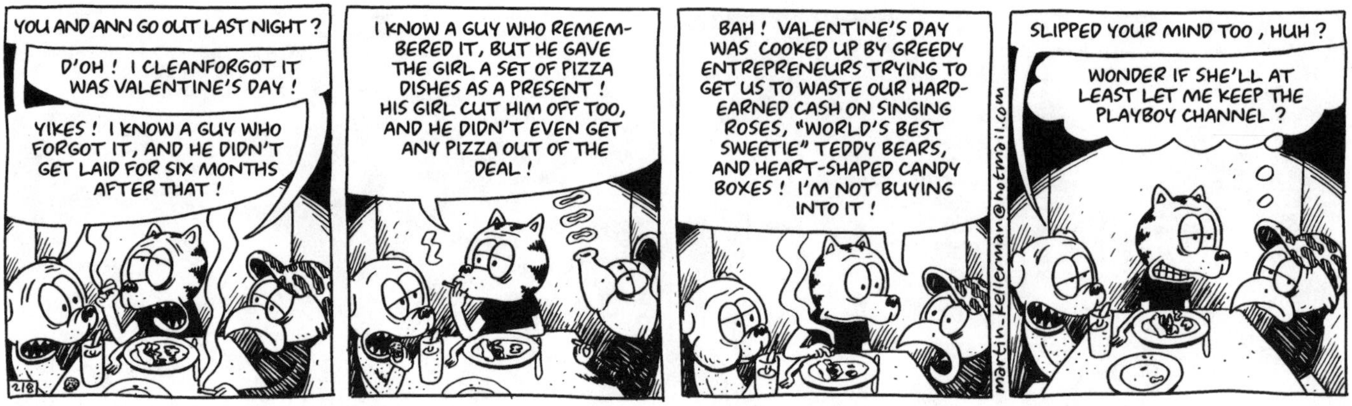
YOU AND ANN GO OUT LAST NIGHT ?
D'OH ! I CLEANFORGOT IT WAS VALENTINE'S DAY !
YIKES ! I KNOW A GUY WHO FORGOT IT, AND HE DIDN'T GET LAID FOR SIX MONTHS AFTER THAT !
218
I KNOW A GUY WHO REMEMBERED IT, BUT HE GAVE THE GIRL A SET OF PIZZA DISHES AS A PRESENT ! HIS GIRL CUT HIM OFF TOO, AND HE DIDN'T EVEN GET ANY PIZZA OUT OF THE DEAL !
BAH ! VALENTINE'S DAY WAS COOKED UP BY GREEDY ENTREPRENEURS TRYING TO GET US TO WASTE OUR HARD-EARNED CASH ON SINGING ROSES, "WORLD'S BEST SWEETIE" TEDDY BEARS, AND HEART-SHAPED CANDY BOXES ! I'M NOT BUYING INTO IT !
martin_kellerman@hotmail.com
SLIPPED YOUR MIND TOO , HUH ?
WONDER IF SHE'LL AT LEAST LET ME KEEP THE PLAYBOY CHANNEL ?

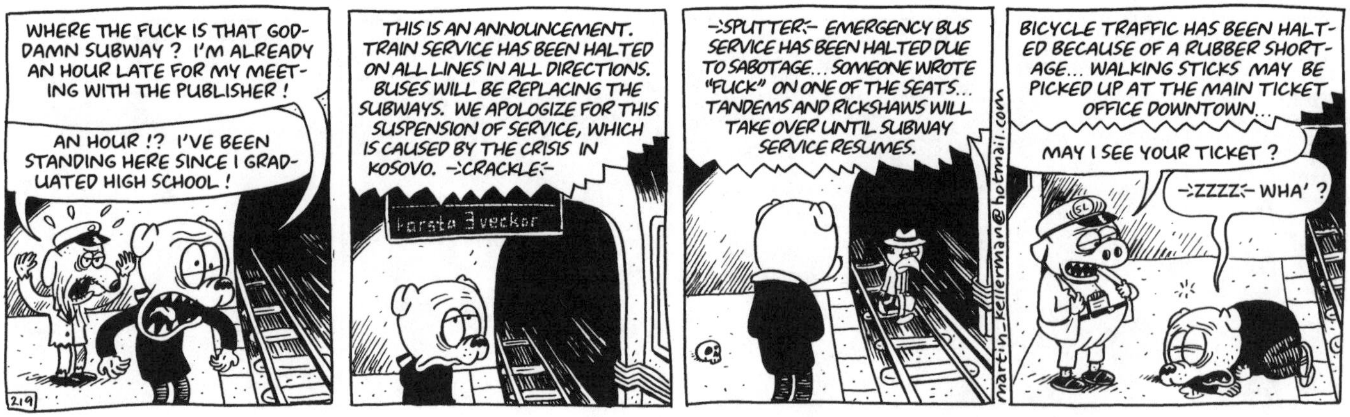
WHERE THE FUCK IS THAT GODDAMN SUBWAY ? I'M ALREADY AN HOUR LATE FOR MY MEETING WITH THE PUBLISHER !
AN HOUR !? I'VE BEEN STANDING HERE SINCE I GRADUATED HIGH SCHOOL !
219
THIS IS AN ANNOUNCEMENT. TRAIN SERVICE HAS BEEN HALTED ON ALL LINES IN ALL DIRECTIONS. BUSES WILL BE REPLACING THE SUBWAYS. WE APOLOGIZE FOR THIS SUSPENSION OF SERVICE, WHICH IS CAUSED BY THE CRISIS IN KOSOVO. -CRACKLE-
Första 3veckor
-SPUTTER- EMERGENCY BUS SERVICE HAS BEEN HALTED DUE TO SABOTAGE... SOMEONE WROTE "FUCK" ON ONE OF THE SEATS... TANDEMS AND RICKSHAWS WILL TAKE OVER UNTIL SUBWAY SERVICE RESUMES.
martin_kellerman@hotmail.com
BICYCLE TRAFFIC HAS BEEN HALTED BECAUSE OF A RUBBER SHORTAGE... WALKING STICKS MAY BE PICKED UP AT THE MAIN TICKET OFFICE DOWNTOWN...
MAY I SEE YOUR TICKET ?
-ZZZZ- WHA' ?

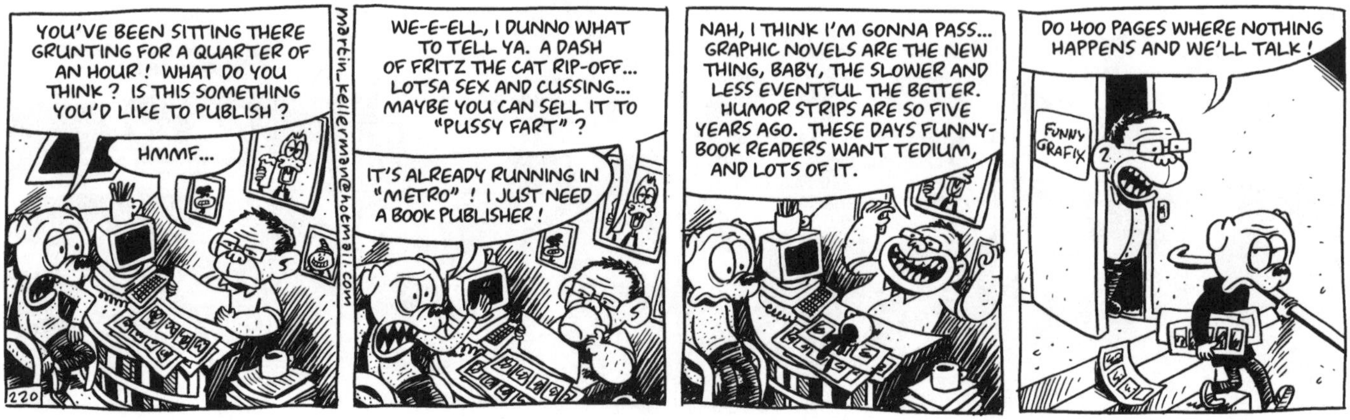
YOU'VE BEEN SITTING THERE GRUNTING FOR A QUARTER OF AN HOUR ! WHAT DO YOU THINK ? IS THIS SOMETHING YOU'D LIKE TO PUBLISH ?
HMMF...
220
martin_kellerman@hotmail.com
WE-E-ELL, I DUNNO WHAT TO TELL YA. A DASH OF FRITZ THE CAT RIP-OFF... LOTSA SEX AND CUSSING... MAYBE YOU CAN SELL IT TO "PUSSY FART" ?
IT'S ALREADY RUNNING IN "METRO" ! I JUST NEED A BOOK PUBLISHER !
NAH, I THINK I'M GONNA PASS... GRAPHIC NOVELS ARE THE NEW THING, BABY, THE SLOWER AND LESS EVENTFUL THE BETTER. HUMOR STRIPS ARE SO FIVE YEARS AGO. THESE DAYS FUNNYBOOK READERS WANT TEDIUM, AND LOTS OF IT.
DO 400 PAGES WHERE NOTHING HAPPENS AND WE'LL TALK !
FUNNY GRAFIX

DIFFIDENT LIAISONS

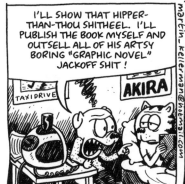

I'LL SHOW THAT HIPPER-THAN-THOU SHITHEEL. I'LL PUBLISH THE BOOK MYSELF AND OUTSELL ALL OF HIS ARTSY BORING "GRAPHIC NOVEL" JACKOFF SHIT !
TAXIDRIVE
AKIRA
martin_kellerman@hotmail.com
221
THIS IS HOW IT'S DONE, MAN ! YOU GOTTA DO IT ALL YOURSELF, JUST LIKE THE BEASTIE BOYS ! THEY STARTED OFF AS A PUNK BAND, AND NOW THEY'VE GOT THEIR OWN RECORD COMPANY, THEIR OWN CLOTHING LINE AND WHO KNOWS WHAT ELSE !
ACTUALLY, THEY WERE ALREADY LIVING ON PARK AVENUE WHEN THEY WERE PUNKS !
OH JESUS, TOMMY ! I GOT AN E-MAIL FROM A GROUPIE !
XIDRIVER
AKIRA
I STARTED RUNNING MY E-MAIL ADDRESS IN THE STRIPS, AND THIS GIRL WANTS TO MEET ME! FINALLY, SOME ROCK 'N' ROLL !
UH-HUH... SO, YOU GONNA START SMASHING YOUR PEN TO PIECES EVERY TIME YOU FINISH A STRIP ?
XIDRIVER

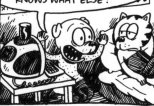

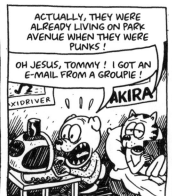

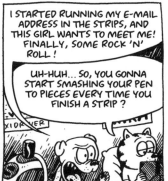

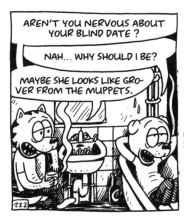

AREN'T YOU NERVOUS ABOUT YOUR BLIND DATE ?
NAH... WHY SHOULD I BE?
MAYBE SHE LOOKS LIKE GROVER FROM THE MUPPETS.
222
FUCK YOU ! YOU'RE JUST JEALOUS THAT I'VE GOT A GROUPIE !
GROUPIE ! IT'S PROBABLY SOME COMPUTER GEEK WITH A SWEATY UPPER LIP WHO THINKS YOU'RE A CHICK!
AH, BUT SEE, I HAVE A PLAN B! D'YA EVER CATCH THAT MOVIE "UNMADE BEDS" ? IT'S ABOUT SINGLES IN NEW YORK, AND ONE OF THEM ALWAYS BRINGS HIS PAGER, SO HE CAN ASK A BARTENDER TO CALL HIM IF THE GIRL TURNS OUT TO BE A TOTAL HOG.
martin_kellerman@hotmail.com
THEN HE SAYS A STUDENT'S THREATENING TO KILL A TEACHER AT THE SCHOOL WHERE HE WORKS AND HE HAS TO LEAVE ! CLEVER, HUH ?
YOU GOT A PLAN C ?
THROW THE PAGER IN HER FACE, RUN FOR THE EXIT !

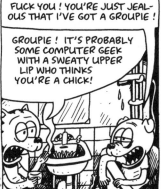

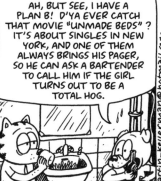

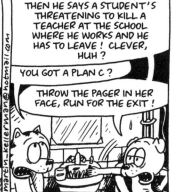

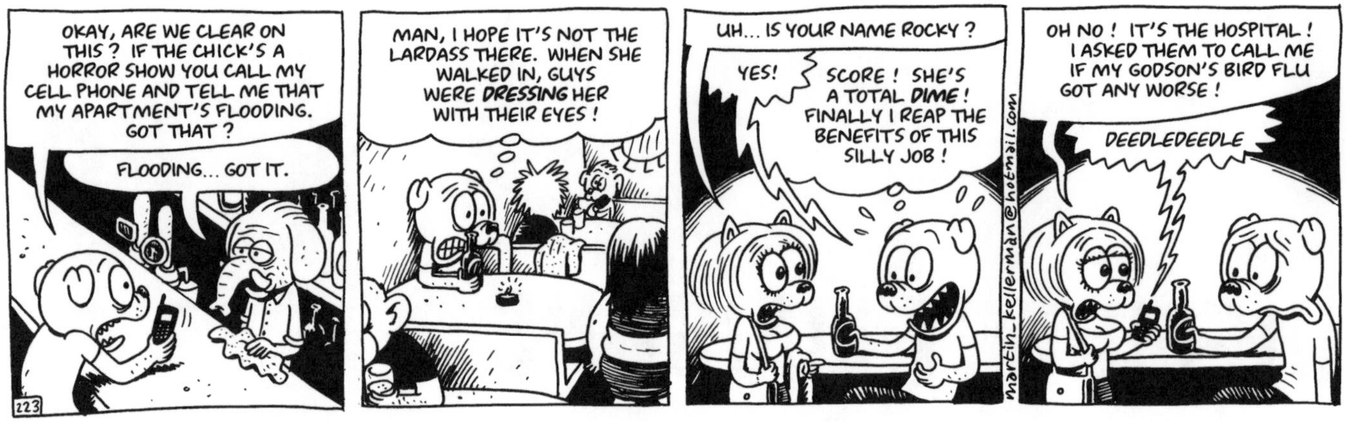
223
OKAY, ARE WE CLEAR ON THIS ? IF THE CHICK'S A HORROR SHOW YOU CALL MY CELL PHONE AND TELL ME THAT MY APARTMENT'S FLOODING. GOT THAT ?
FLOODING... GOT IT.
MAN, I HOPE IT'S NOT THE LARDASS THERE. WHEN SHE WALKED IN, GUYS WERE DRESSING HER WITH THEIR EYES !
UH... IS YOUR NAME ROCKY ?
YES!
SCORE ! SHE'S A TOTAL DIME ! FINALLY I REAP THE BENEFITS OF THIS SILLY JOB !
martin_kellerman@hotmail.com
OH NO ! IT'S THE HOSPITAL ! I ASKED THEM TO CALL ME IF MY GODSON'S BIRD FLU GOT ANY WORSE !
DEEDLEDEEDLE

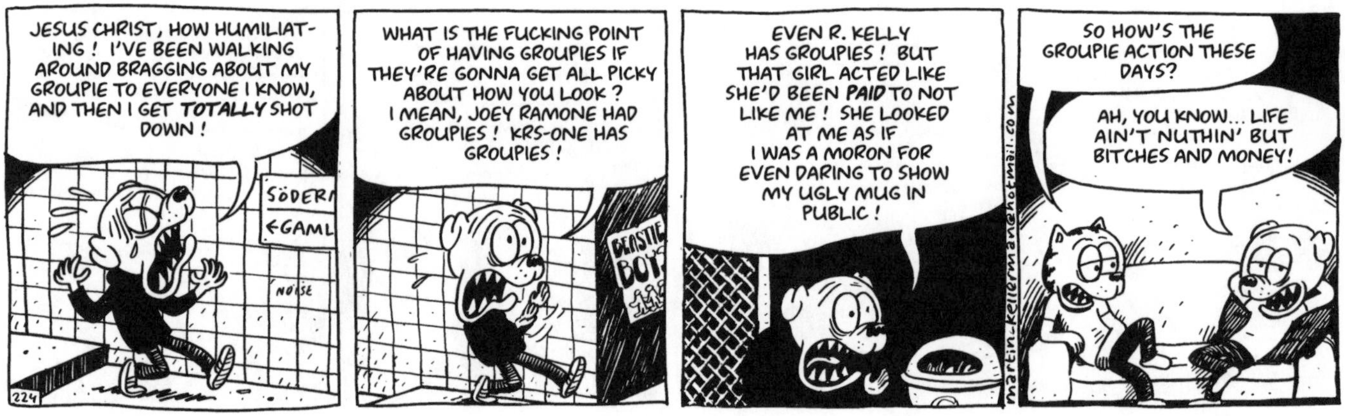
224
JESUS CHRIST, HOW HUMILIAT-ING ! I'VE BEEN WALKING AROUND BRAGGING ABOUT MY GROUPIE TO EVERYONE I KNOW, AND THEN I GET TOTALLY SHOT DOWN !
NOISE
WHAT IS THE FUCKING POINT OF HAVING GROUPIES IF THEY'RE GONNA GET ALL PICKY ABOUT HOW YOU LOOK ? I MEAN, JOEY RAMONE HAD GROUPIES ! KRS-ONE HAS GROUPIES !
EVEN R. KELLY HAS GROUPIES ! BUT THAT GIRL ACTED LIKE SHE'D BEEN PAID TO NOT LIKE ME ! SHE LOOKED AT ME AS IF I WAS A MORON FOR EVEN DARING TO SHOW MY UGLY MUG IN PUBLIC !
martin_kellerman@hotmail.com
SO HOW'S THE GROUPIE ACTION THESE DAYS?
AH, YOU KNOW... LIFE AIN'T NUTHIN' BUT BITCHES AND MONEY!

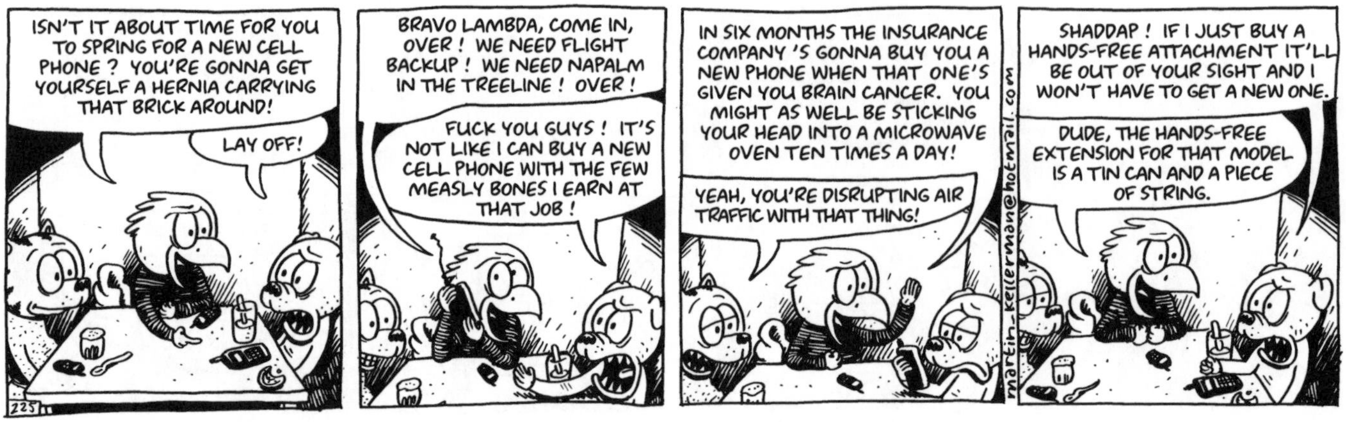
225
ISN'T IT ABOUT TIME FOR YOU TO SPRING FOR A NEW CELL PHONE ? YOU'RE GONNA GET YOURSELF A HERNIA CARRYING THAT BRICK AROUND!
LAY OFF!
BRAVO LAMBDA, COME IN, OVER ! WE NEED FLIGHT BACKUP ! WE NEED NAPALM IN THE TREELINE ! OVER !
FUCK YOU GUYS ! IT'S NOT LIKE I CAN BUY A NEW CELL PHONE WITH THE FEW MEASLY BONES I EARN AT THAT JOB !
IN SIX MONTHS THE INSURANCE COMPANY 'S GONNA BUY YOU A NEW PHONE WHEN THAT ONE'S GIVEN YOU BRAIN CANCER. YOU MIGHT AS WELL BE STICKING YOUR HEAD INTO A MICROWAVE OVEN TEN TIMES A DAY!
YEAH, YOU'RE DISRUPTING AIR TRAFFIC WITH THAT THING!
martin_kellerman@hotmail.com
SHADDAP ! IF I JUST BUY A HANDS-FREE ATTACHMENT IT'LL BE OUT OF YOUR SIGHT AND I WON'T HAVE TO GET A NEW ONE.
DUDE, THE HANDS-FREE EXTENSION FOR THAT MODEL IS A TIN CAN AND A PIECE OF STRING.

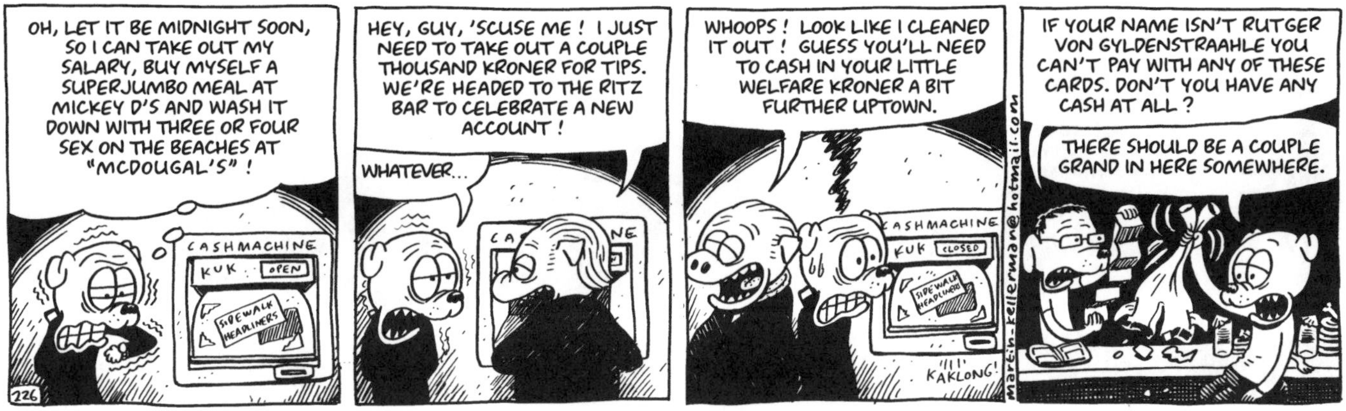
OH, LET IT BE MIDNIGHT SOON, SO I CAN TAKE OUT MY SALARY, BUY MYSELF A SUPERJUMBO MEAL AT MICKEY D'S AND WASH IT DOWN WITH THREE OR FOUR SEX ON THE BEACHES AT "MCDOUGAL'S" !
CASHMACHINE
KUK
OPEN
SIDEWALK HEADLINERS
226
HEY, GUY, 'SCUSE ME ! I JUST NEED TO TAKE OUT A COUPLE THOUSAND KRONER FOR TIPS. WE'RE HEADED TO THE RITZ BAR TO CELEBRATE A NEW ACCOUNT !
WHATEVER...
WHOOPS ! LOOK LIKE I CLEANED IT OUT ! GUESS YOU'LL NEED TO CASH IN YOUR LITTLE WELFARE KRONER A BIT FURTHER UPTOWN.
CASHMACHINE
KUK
CLOSED
SIDEWALK HEADLINERS
KAKLONG!
martin-kellerman@hotmail.com
IF YOUR NAME ISN'T RUTGER VON GYLDENSTRAAHLE YOU CAN'T PAY WITH ANY OF THESE CARDS. DON'T YOU HAVE ANY CASH AT ALL ?
THERE SHOULD BE A COUPLE GRAND IN HERE SOMEWHERE.

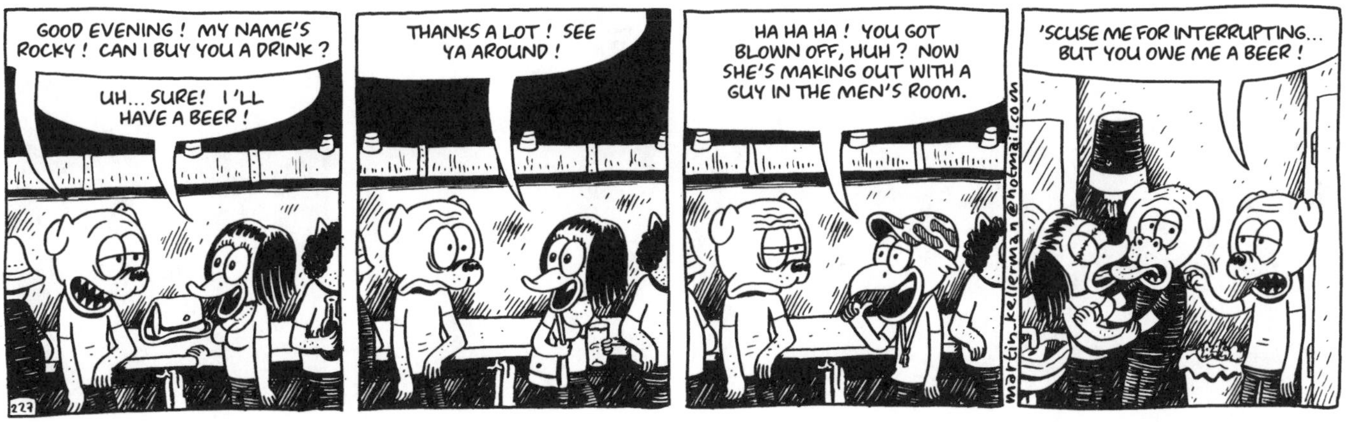
GOOD EVENING ! MY NAME'S ROCKY ! CAN I BUY YOU A DRINK ?
UH... SURE! I'LL HAVE A BEER !
227
THANKS A LOT ! SEE YA AROUND !
HA HA HA ! YOU GOT BLOWN OFF, HUH ? NOW SHE'S MAKING OUT WITH A GUY IN THE MEN'S ROOM.
martin-kellerman@hotmail.com
'SCUSE ME FOR INTERRUPTING... BUT YOU OWE ME A BEER !

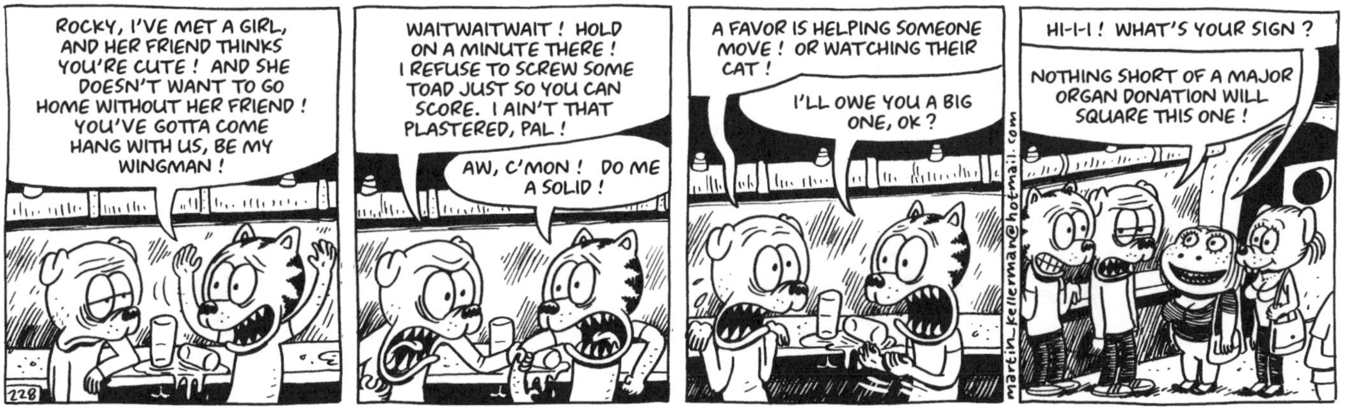
ROCKY, I'VE MET A GIRL, AND HER FRIEND THINKS YOU'RE CUTE ! AND SHE DOESN'T WANT TO GO HOME WITHOUT HER FRIEND ! YOU'VE GOTTA COME HANG WITH US, BE MY WINGMAN !
228
WAITWAITWAIT ! HOLD ON A MINUTE THERE ! I REFUSE TO SCREW SOME TOAD JUST SO YOU CAN SCORE. I AIN'T THAT PLASTERED, PAL !
AW, C'MON ! DO ME A SOLID !
A FAVOR IS HELPING SOMEONE MOVE ! OR WATCHING THEIR CAT !
I'LL OWE YOU A BIG ONE, OK ?
martin-kellerman@hotmail.com
HI-I-I ! WHAT'S YOUR SIGN ?
NOTHING SHORT OF A MAJOR ORGAN DONATION WILL SQUARE THIS ONE !

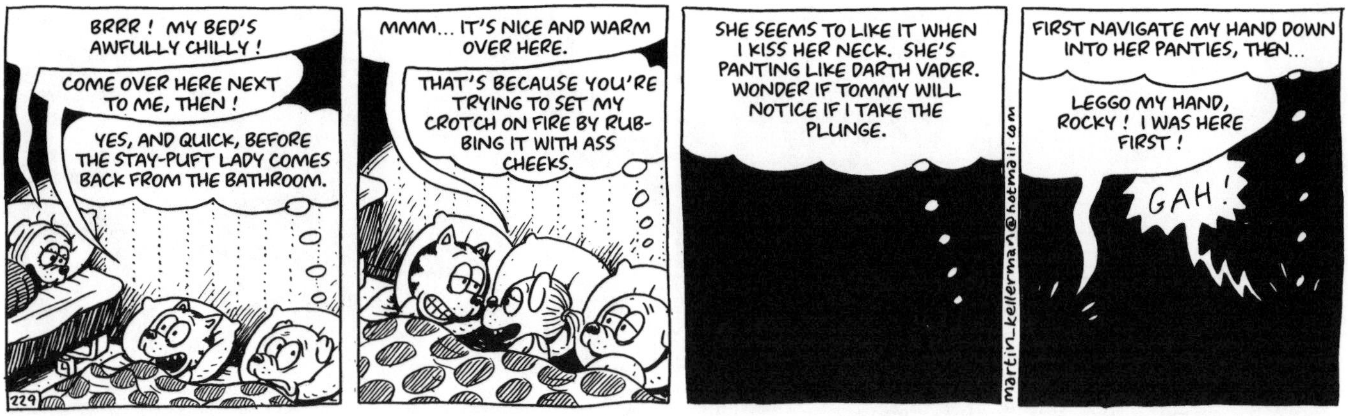
229
BRRR ! MY BED'S AWFULLY CHILLY !
COME OVER HERE NEXT TO ME, THEN !
YES, AND QUICK, BEFORE THE STAY-PUFT LADY COMES BACK FROM THE BATHROOM.
MMM... IT'S NICE AND WARM OVER HERE.
THAT'S BECAUSE YOU'RE TRYING TO SET MY CROTCH ON FIRE BY RUBBING IT WITH ASS CHEEKS.
SHE SEEMS TO LIKE IT WHEN I KISS HER NECK. SHE'S PANTING LIKE DARTH VADER. WONDER IF TOMMY WILL NOTICE IF I TAKE THE PLUNGE.
martin_kellerman@hotmail.com
FIRST NAVIGATE MY HAND DOWN INTO HER PANTIES, THEN...
LEGGO MY HAND, ROCKY ! I WAS HERE FIRST !
GAH !

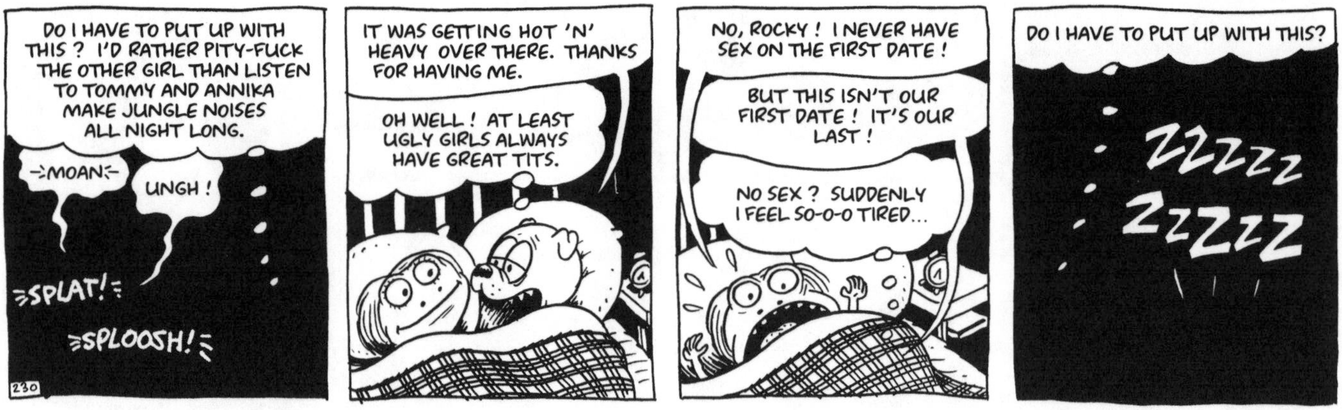
230
DO I HAVE TO PUT UP WITH THIS ? I'D RATHER PITY-FUCK THE OTHER GIRL THAN LISTEN TO TOMMY AND ANNIKA MAKE JUNGLE NOISES ALL NIGHT LONG.
MOAN
UNGH !
SPLAT!
SPLOOSH!
IT WAS GETTING HOT 'N' HEAVY OVER THERE. THANKS FOR HAVING ME.
OH WELL ! AT LEAST UGLY GIRLS ALWAYS HAVE GREAT TITS.
NO, ROCKY ! I NEVER HAVE SEX ON THE FIRST DATE !
BUT THIS ISN'T OUR FIRST DATE ! IT'S OUR LAST !
NO SEX ? SUDDENLY I FEEL SO-O-O TIRED...
DO I HAVE TO PUT UP WITH THIS?
ZZZZZ
ZZZZZ

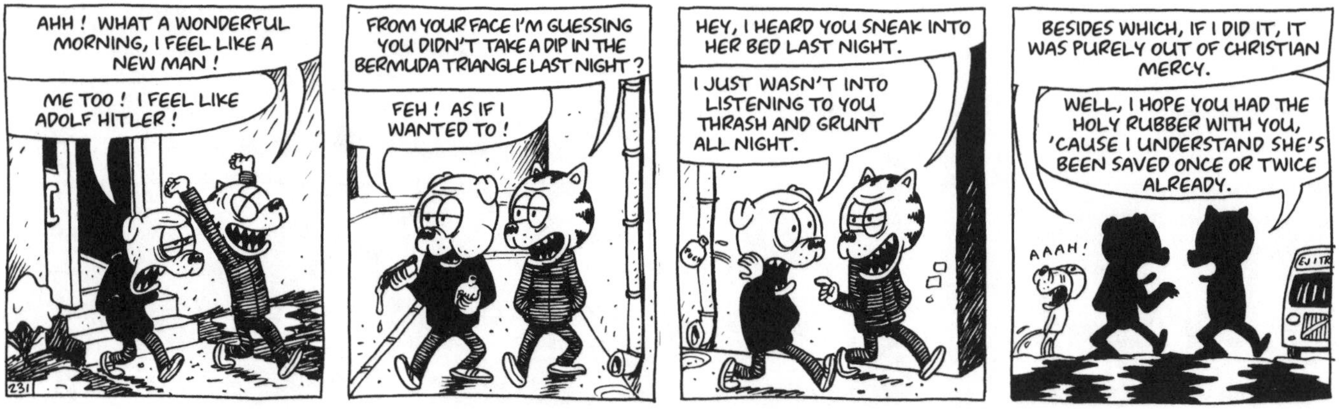
231
AHH ! WHAT A WONDERFUL MORNING, I FEEL LIKE A NEW MAN !
ME TOO ! I FEEL LIKE ADOLF HITLER !
FROM YOUR FACE I'M GUESSING YOU DIDN'T TAKE A DIP IN THE BERMUDA TRIANGLE LAST NIGHT ?
FEH ! AS IF I WANTED TO !
HEY, I HEARD YOU SNEAK INTO HER BED LAST NIGHT.
I JUST WASN'T INTO LISTENING TO YOU THRASH AND GRUNT ALL NIGHT.
BESIDES WHICH, IF I DID IT, IT WAS PURELY OUT OF CHRISTIAN MERCY.
WELL, I HOPE YOU HAD THE HOLY RUBBER WITH YOU, 'CAUSE I UNDERSTAND SHE'S BEEN SAVED ONCE OR TWICE ALREADY.
AAAH !

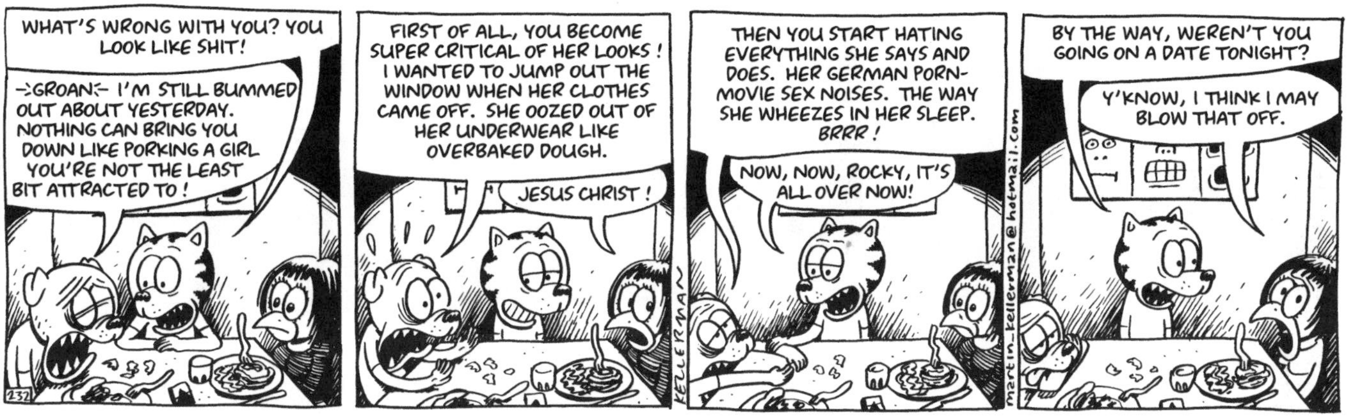
WHAT'S WRONG WITH YOU? YOU LOOK LIKE SHIT!
-:GROAN:- I'M STILL BUMMED OUT ABOUT YESTERDAY. NOTHING CAN BRING YOU DOWN LIKE PORKING A GIRL YOU'RE NOT THE LEAST BIT ATTRACTED TO!
232
FIRST OF ALL, YOU BECOME SUPER CRITICAL OF HER LOOKS! I WANTED TO JUMP OUT THE WINDOW WHEN HER CLOTHES CAME OFF. SHE OOZED OUT OF HER UNDERWEAR LIKE OVERBAKED DOUGH.
JESUS CHRIST!
KELLERMAN
THEN YOU START HATING EVERYTHING SHE SAYS AND DOES. HER GERMAN PORN-MOVIE SEX NOISES. THE WAY SHE WHEEZES IN HER SLEEP. BRRR!
NOW, NOW, ROCKY, IT'S ALL OVER NOW!
martin_kellerman@hotmail.com
BY THE WAY, WEREN'T YOU GOING ON A DATE TONIGHT?
Y'KNOW, I THINK I MAY BLOW THAT OFF.

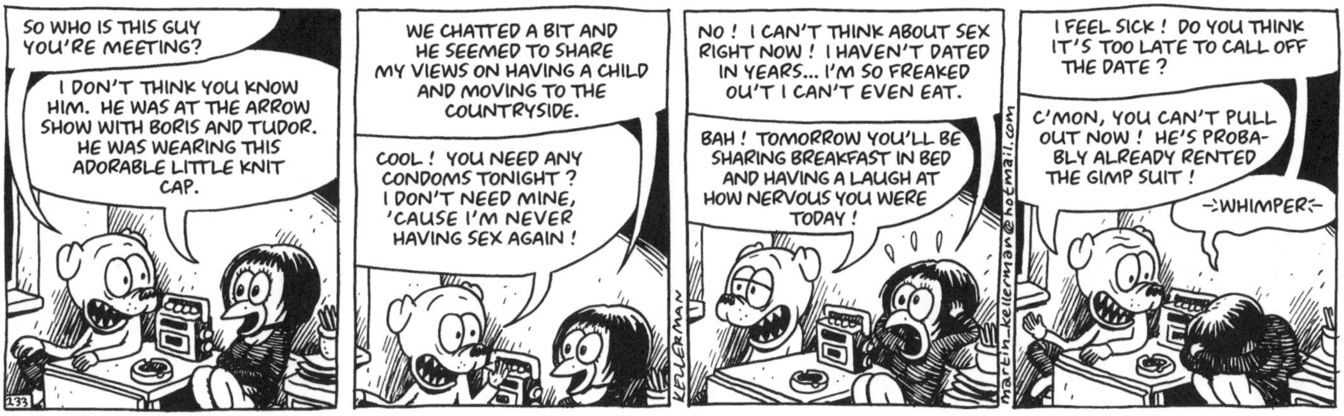
SO WHO IS THIS GUY YOU'RE MEETING?
I DON'T THINK YOU KNOW HIM. HE WAS AT THE ARROW SHOW WITH BORIS AND TUDOR. HE WAS WEARING THIS ADORABLE LITTLE KNIT CAP.
233
WE CHATTED A BIT AND HE SEEMED TO SHARE MY VIEWS ON HAVING A CHILD AND MOVING TO THE COUNTRYSIDE.
COOL! YOU NEED ANY CONDOMS TONIGHT? I DON'T NEED MINE, 'CAUSE I'M NEVER HAVING SEX AGAIN!
KELLERMAN
NO! I CAN'T THINK ABOUT SEX RIGHT NOW! I HAVEN'T DATED IN YEARS... I'M SO FREAKED OUT I CAN'T EVEN EAT.
BAH! TOMORROW YOU'LL BE SHARING BREAKFAST IN BED AND HAVING A LAUGH AT HOW NERVOUS YOU WERE TODAY!
martin_kellerman@hotmail.com
I FEEL SICK! DO YOU THINK IT'S TOO LATE TO CALL OFF THE DATE?
C'MON, YOU CAN'T PULL OUT NOW! HE'S PROBABLY ALREADY RENTED THE GIMP SUIT!
-:WHIMPER:-

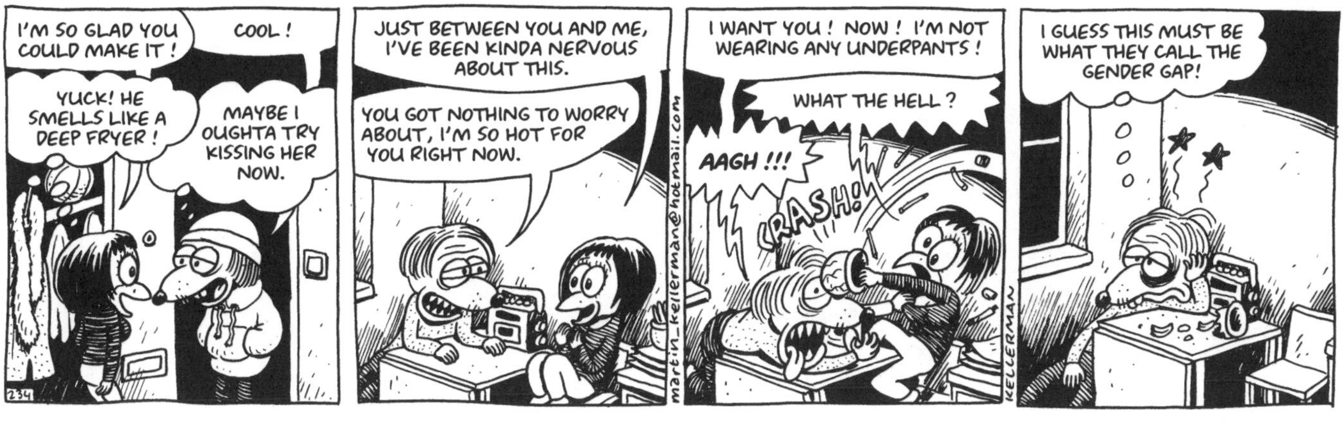
I'M SO GLAD YOU COULD MAKE IT!
COOL!
YUCK! HE SMELLS LIKE A DEEP FRYER!
MAYBE I OUGHTA TRY KISSING HER NOW.
234
JUST BETWEEN YOU AND ME, I'VE BEEN KINDA NERVOUS ABOUT THIS.
YOU GOT NOTHING TO WORRY ABOUT, I'M SO HOT FOR YOU RIGHT NOW.
martin_kellerman@hotmail.com
I WANT YOU! NOW! I'M NOT WEARING ANY UNDERPANTS!
WHAT THE HELL?
AAGH!!!
CRASH!
KELLERMAN
I GUESS THIS MUST BE WHAT THEY CALL THE GENDER GAP!

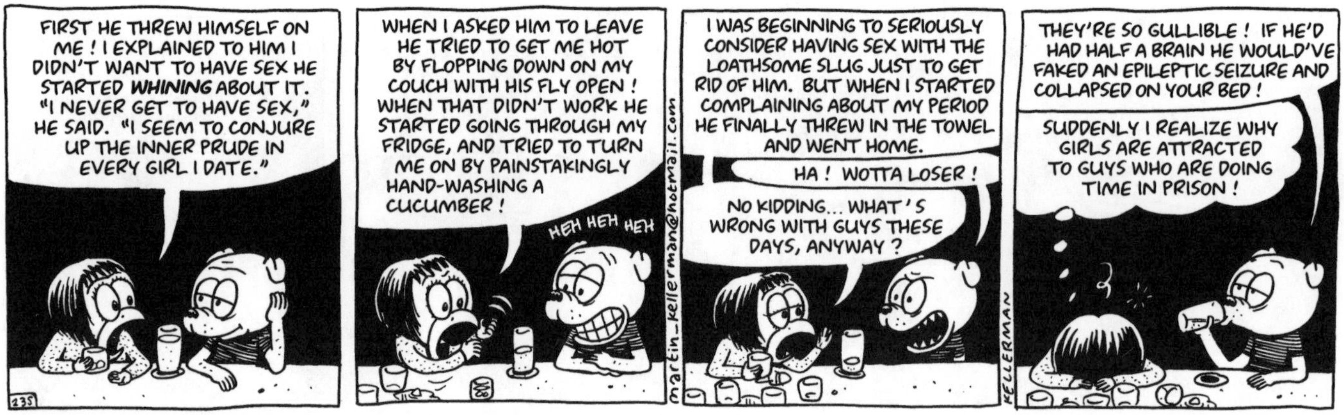
235
FIRST HE THREW HIMSELF ON ME ! I EXPLAINED TO HIM I DIDN'T WANT TO HAVE SEX HE STARTED **WHINING** ABOUT IT. "I NEVER GET TO HAVE SEX," HE SAID. "I SEEM TO CONJURE UP THE INNER PRUDE IN EVERY GIRL I DATE."
WHEN I ASKED HIM TO LEAVE HE TRIED TO GET ME HOT BY FLOPPING DOWN ON MY COUCH WITH HIS FLY OPEN ! WHEN THAT DIDN'T WORK HE STARTED GOING THROUGH MY FRIDGE, AND TRIED TO TURN ME ON BY PAINSTAKINGLY HAND-WASHING A CUCUMBER !
HEH HEH HEH
martin_kellerman@hotmail.com
I WAS BEGINNING TO SERIOUSLY CONSIDER HAVING SEX WITH THE LOATHSOME SLUG JUST TO GET RID OF HIM. BUT WHEN I STARTED COMPLAINING ABOUT MY PERIOD HE FINALLY THREW IN THE TOWEL AND WENT HOME.
HA ! WOTTA LOSER !
NO KIDDING... WHAT'S WRONG WITH GUYS THESE DAYS, ANYWAY ?
KELLERMAN
THEY'RE SO GULLIBLE ! IF HE'D HAD HALF A BRAIN HE WOULD'VE FAKED AN EPILEPTIC SEIZURE AND COLLAPSED ON YOUR BED !
SUDDENLY I REALIZE WHY GIRLS ARE ATTRACTED TO GUYS WHO ARE DOING TIME IN PRISON !

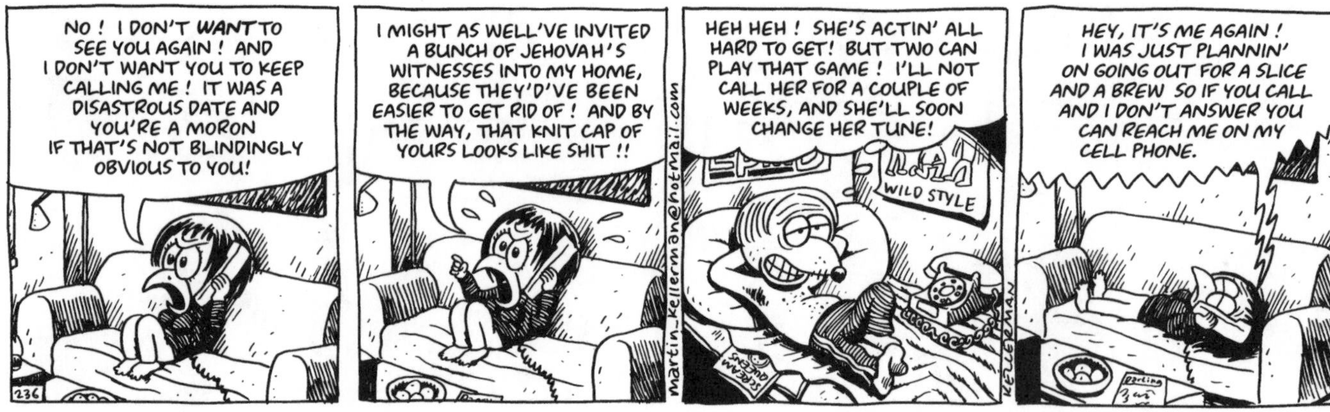
236
NO ! I DON'T **WANT** TO SEE YOU AGAIN ! AND I DON'T WANT YOU TO KEEP CALLING ME ! IT WAS A DISASTROUS DATE AND YOU'RE A MORON IF THAT'S NOT BLINDINGLY OBVIOUS TO YOU!
I MIGHT AS WELL'VE INVITED A BUNCH OF JEHOVAH'S WITNESSES INTO MY HOME, BECAUSE THEY'D'VE BEEN EASIER TO GET RID OF ! AND BY THE WAY, THAT KNIT CAP OF YOURS LOOKS LIKE SHIT !!
martin_kellerman@hotmail.com
HEH HEH ! SHE'S ACTIN' ALL HARD TO GET! BUT TWO CAN PLAY THAT GAME ! I'LL NOT CALL HER FOR A COUPLE OF WEEKS, AND SHE'LL SOON CHANGE HER TUNE!
WILD STYLE
SCREAM QUEENS
KELLERMAN
HEY, IT'S ME AGAIN ! I WAS JUST PLANNIN' ON GOING OUT FOR A SLICE AND A BREW SO IF YOU CALL AND I DON'T ANSWER YOU CAN REACH ME ON MY CELL PHONE.

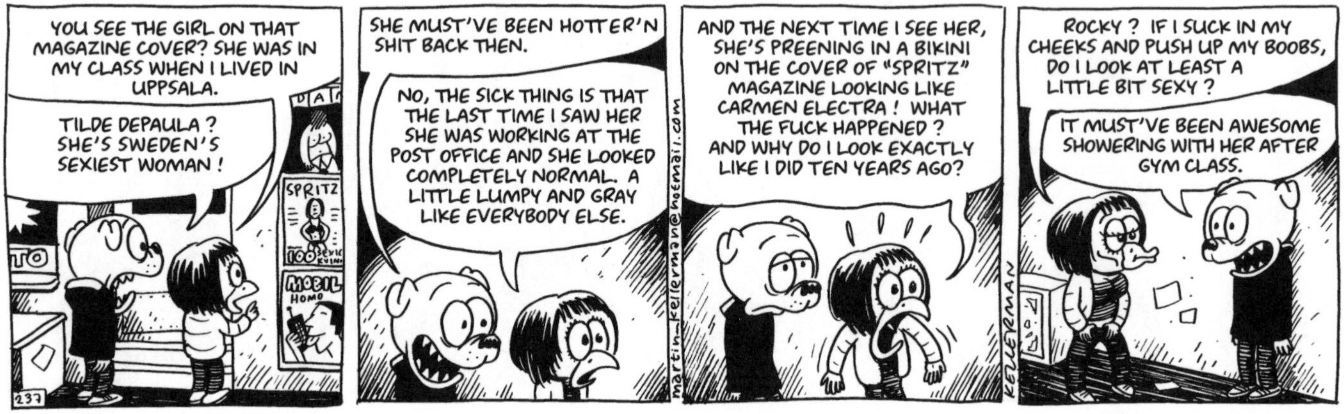
237
YOU SEE THE GIRL ON THAT MAGAZINE COVER? SHE WAS IN MY CLASS WHEN I LIVED IN UPPSALA.
TILDE DEPAULA ? SHE'S SWEDEN'S SEXIEST WOMAN !
SPRITZ
MOBIL
HOMO
SHE MUST'VE BEEN HOTTER'N SHIT BACK THEN.
NO, THE SICK THING IS THAT THE LAST TIME I SAW HER SHE WAS WORKING AT THE POST OFFICE AND SHE LOOKED COMPLETELY NORMAL. A LITTLE LUMPY AND GRAY LIKE EVERYBODY ELSE.
martin_kellerman@hotmail.com
AND THE NEXT TIME I SEE HER, SHE'S PREENING IN A BIKINI ON THE COVER OF "SPRITZ" MAGAZINE LOOKING LIKE CARMEN ELECTRA ! WHAT THE FUCK HAPPENED ? AND WHY DO I LOOK EXACTLY LIKE I DID TEN YEARS AGO?
KELLERMAN
ROCKY ? IF I SUCK IN MY CHEEKS AND PUSH UP MY BOOBS, DO I LOOK AT LEAST A LITTLE BIT SEXY ?
IT MUST'VE BEEN AWESOME SHOWERING WITH HER AFTER GYM CLASS.

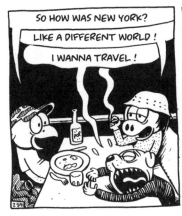

SO HOW WAS NEW YORK?
LIKE A DIFFERENT WORLD !
I WANNA TRAVEL !
POP
239
YEAH, YOU REALLY OUGHT TO ! STUFF'S HAPPENING ALL THE TIME... NEW NIGHT CLUBS, TRENDY NEW SHOPS, NEW PEOPLE. EVERYTHING BACK HERE IS THE SAME OL', SAME OL'.
KELLERMAN
WHEN YOU COME HOME EVERYTHING IS JUST THE WAY YOU LEFT IT. SAME CLUBS, SAME SHOPS, SAME FRIENDS SITTING AROUND TALKING ABOUT THE SAME SHIT.
martin_kellerman@hotmail.com
BUT YOU'VE MOVED ON, RIGHT ? YOU'RE ON ANOTHER LEVEL ?
YES... I REALIZE I'M NOT THE SAME PERSON I WAS WHEN I LEFT...
...LAST THURSDAY!

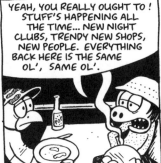

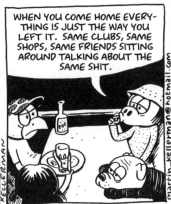

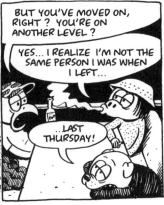

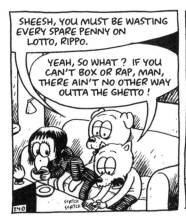

SHEESH, YOU MUST BE WASTING EVERY SPARE PENNY ON LOTTO, RIPPO.
YEAH, SO WHAT ? IF YOU CAN'T BOX OR RAP, MAN, THERE AIN'T NO OTHER WAY OUTTA THE GHETTO !
SCRTCH SCRTCH
240
IF I WIN FIFTY MILLION KRONER, I'M QUITTING MY JOB, MOVING TO THAILAND AND SPENDING THE REST OF MY LIFE IN A HAMMOCK WITH A SUPERMODEL AND A PLAYSTATION.
KELLERMAN
BUT MONEY DOESN'T BRING HAPPINESS, RIPPO ! EVERYONE YOU KNOW TURNS INTO A TWO-FACED MONSTER ! I KNOW A GUY WHO WON THE LOTTERY, AND THE NEXT DAY FIVE OF HIS EX-GIRLFRIENDS CALLED HIM !
martin_kellerman@hotmail.com
SCRTCH SCRTCH

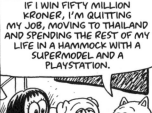

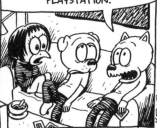

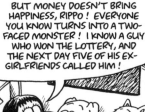

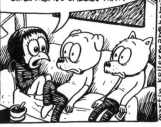

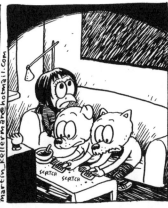

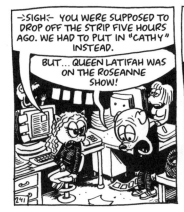

-SIGH- YOU WERE SUPPOSED TO DROP OFF THE STRIP FIVE HOURS AGO. WE HAD TO PUT IN "CATHY" INSTEAD.
BUT... QUEEN LATIFAH WAS ON THE ROSEANNE SHOW!
241
OH, THIS GIRL FROM A COLLEGE NEWSPAPER CALLED AND WANTED TO INTERVIEW YOU. I GAVE HER YOUR NUMBER.
HUH. OKAY, I GUESS...
WHAT? WAS I NOT SUPPOSED TO DO THAT ?
martin_kellerman@hotmail.com
WELL, IT GETS TO BE A HASSLE WHEN REPORTERS ARE CALLING ALL THE TIME WHEN I'M TRYING TO GET SOME WORK DONE. I'D JUST LIKE TO KEEP MY PRIVATE LIFE OUT OF THE LIMELIGHT.
KELLERMAN
AH YES, WELL, IN SOME SENSE I DO THINK THAT IT'S MY DUTY TO, TO, TO, TO DEPICT MY GENERATION AND, AND, AND, AND...

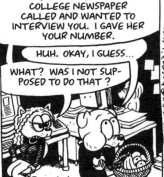

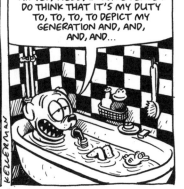

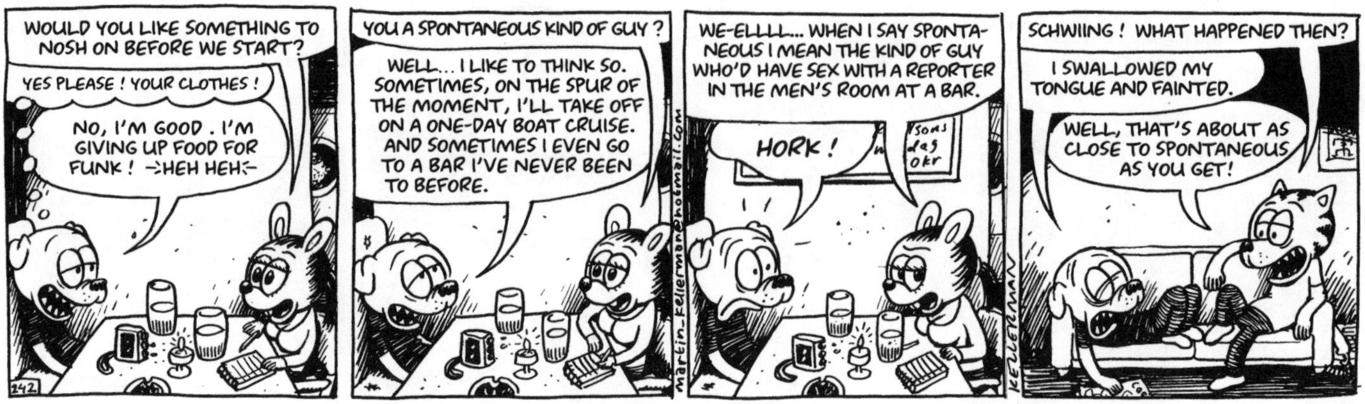
WOULD YOU LIKE SOMETHING TO NOSH ON BEFORE WE START?
YES PLEASE ! YOUR CLOTHES !
NO, I'M GOOD . I'M GIVING UP FOOD FOR FUNK ! HEH HEH
YOU A SPONTANEOUS KIND OF GUY ?
WELL... I LIKE TO THINK SO. SOMETIMES, ON THE SPUR OF THE MOMENT, I'LL TAKE OFF ON A ONE-DAY BOAT CRUISE. AND SOMETIMES I EVEN GO TO A BAR I'VE NEVER BEEN TO BEFORE.
martin_kellerman@hotmail.com
WE-ELLLL... WHEN I SAY SPONTANEOUS I MEAN THE KIND OF GUY WHO'D HAVE SEX WITH A REPORTER IN THE MEN'S ROOM AT A BAR.
HORK !
KELLERMAN
SCHWIING ! WHAT HAPPENED THEN?
I SWALLOWED MY TONGUE AND FAINTED.
WELL, THAT'S ABOUT AS CLOSE TO SPONTANEOUS AS YOU GET!
242

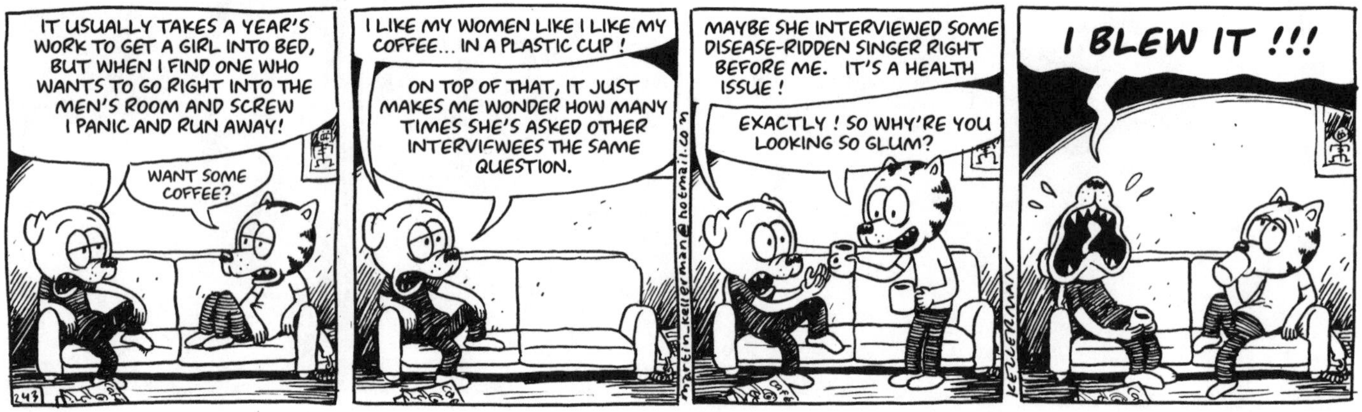
IT USUALLY TAKES A YEAR'S WORK TO GET A GIRL INTO BED, BUT WHEN I FIND ONE WHO WANTS TO GO RIGHT INTO THE MEN'S ROOM AND SCREW I PANIC AND RUN AWAY!
WANT SOME COFFEE?
I LIKE MY WOMEN LIKE I LIKE MY COFFEE... IN A PLASTIC CUP !
ON TOP OF THAT, IT JUST MAKES ME WONDER HOW MANY TIMES SHE'S ASKED OTHER INTERVIEWEES THE SAME QUESTION.
martin_kellerman@hotmail.com
MAYBE SHE INTERVIEWED SOME DISEASE-RIDDEN SINGER RIGHT BEFORE ME. IT'S A HEALTH ISSUE !
EXACTLY ! SO WHY'RE YOU LOOKING SO GLUM?
KELLERMAN
I BLEW IT !!!
243

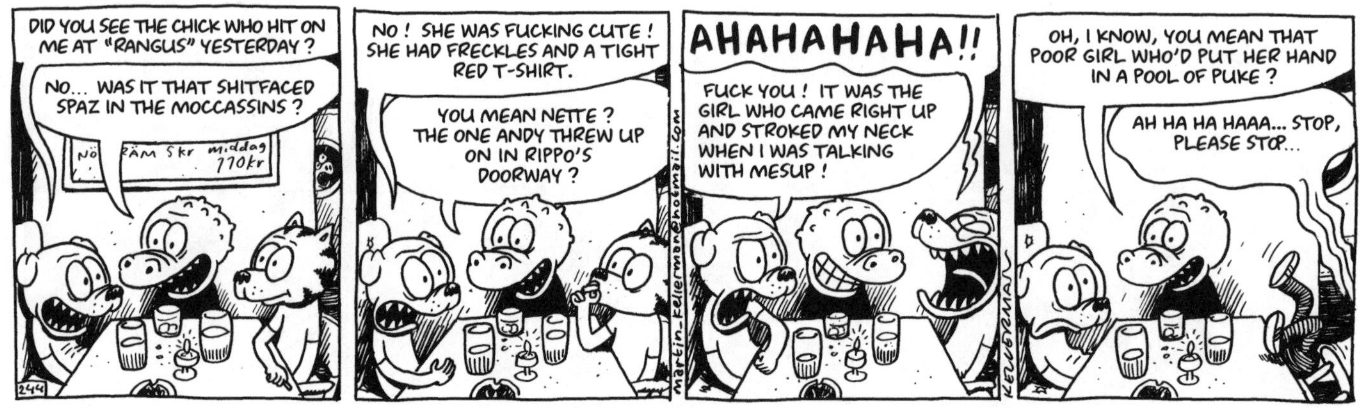
DID YOU SEE THE CHICK WHO HIT ON ME AT "RANGUS" YESTERDAY ?
NO... WAS IT THAT SHITFACED SPAZ IN THE MOCCASSINS ?
NO ! SHE WAS FUCKING CUTE ! SHE HAD FRECKLES AND A TIGHT RED T-SHIRT.
YOU MEAN NETTE ? THE ONE ANDY THREW UP ON IN RIPPO'S DOORWAY ?
martin_kellerman@hotmail.com
AHAHAHAHA!!
FUCK YOU ! IT WAS THE GIRL WHO CAME RIGHT UP AND STROKED MY NECK WHEN I WAS TALKING WITH MESUP !
KELLERMAN
OH, I KNOW, YOU MEAN THAT POOR GIRL WHO'D PUT HER HAND IN A POOL OF PUKE ?
AH HA HA HAAA... STOP, PLEASE STOP...
244

MANNY'S HOUSEWARMING

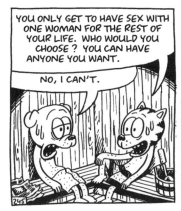

YOU ONLY GET TO HAVE SEX WITH ONE WOMAN FOR THE REST OF YOUR LIFE. WHO WOULD YOU CHOOSE? YOU CAN HAVE ANYONE YOU WANT.
NO, I CAN'T.
YES, YOU CAN, BECAUSE THE PROPHET MUHAMMAD IS REINCARNATED IN MY BODY AND I FULFILL ANY WISH YOU HAVE?
AHH... OK... UH, MAYBE THE CHICK FROM A-TEENS?
YOU CAN'T JUST SETTLE FOR THE CHICK FROM A-TEENS WHEN I'M GIVING YOU **ANYTHING AT ALL**. CAN'T YOU PICK TYRA BANKS OR SOMETHING?
LET'S MOVE ON, THIS IS BULLSHIT! A GIRL LIKE TYRA BANKS WOULDN'T SPIT ON ME IF I WAS ON FIRE.
KELLERMAN
WHY THE LOW SELF-ESTEEM? THE WORLD IS FULL OF BEAUTIFUL WOMEN WHO'D BE HAPPY TO SPIT ON YOU!
SLIPPIN'...

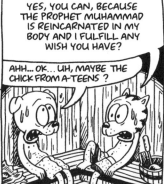

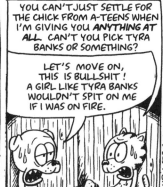

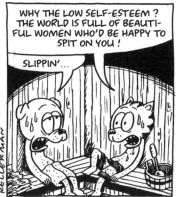

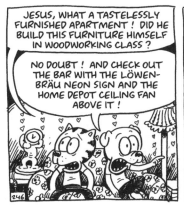

JESUS, WHAT A TASTELESSLY FURNISHED APARTMENT! DID HE BUILD THIS FURNITURE HIMSELF IN WOODWORKING CLASS?
NO DOUBT! AND CHECK OUT THE BAR WITH THE LÖWENBRÄU NEON SIGN AND THE HOME DEPOT CEILING FAN ABOVE IT!
ACTUALLY, I'M IMMUNE TO BAD DECOR. I'VE RENTED FURNISHED APARTMENTS HUNDREDS OF TIMES, SO I'VE SEEN IT ALL! THIS ONE TIME I LIVED IN AN APARTMENT DECKED OUT FLOOR TO CEILING WITH "GARFIELD" MERCHANDISE. I'D WAKE UP SCREAMING EVERY SINGLE NIGHT!
THE PORNO DIGS WEREN'T TOO SHABBY EITHER. WITH THE MIRRORS ON THE CEILING AND RED LIGHT BULBS EVERYWHERE.
OR THE ONE WITH THE HAMSTERS I LET OUT OF THE CAGE SO ALL MY CLOTHES GOT EATEN.
martin_kellerman@hotmail.com
IF I EVER GET RUN OVER BY A TRUCK AND MY LIFE FLASHES BEFORE MY EYES IT'LL LOOK LIKE THE SAMPLE REEL OF AN INSANE SET DESIGNER!

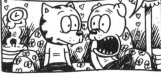

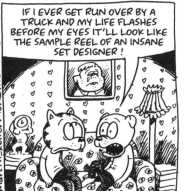

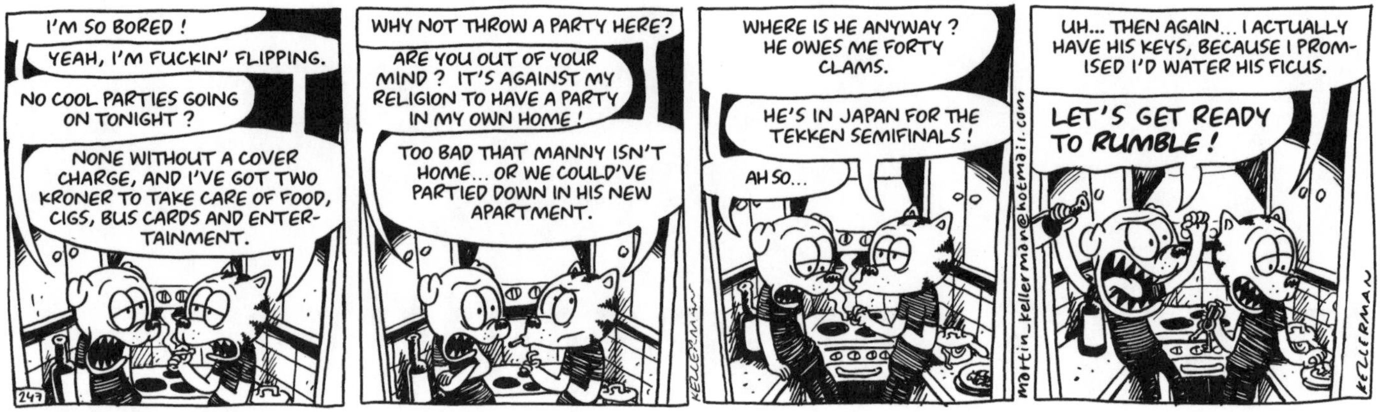
I'M SO BORED !
YEAH, I'M FUCKIN' FLIPPING.
NO COOL PARTIES GOING ON TONIGHT ?
NONE WITHOUT A COVER CHARGE, AND I'VE GOT TWO KRONER TO TAKE CARE OF FOOD, CIGS, BUS CARDS AND ENTERTAINMENT.
247
WHY NOT THROW A PARTY HERE?
ARE YOU OUT OF YOUR MIND ? IT'S AGAINST MY RELIGION TO HAVE A PARTY IN MY OWN HOME !
TOO BAD THAT MANNY ISN'T HOME... OR WE COULD'VE PARTIED DOWN IN HIS NEW APARTMENT.
KELLERMAN
WHERE IS HE ANYWAY ? HE OWES ME FORTY CLAMS.
HE'S IN JAPAN FOR THE TEKKEN SEMIFINALS !
AH SO...
martin_kellerman@hotmail.com
UH... THEN AGAIN... I ACTUALLY HAVE HIS KEYS, BECAUSE I PROMISED I'D WATER HIS FICUS.
LET'S GET READY TO **RUMBLE** !
KELLERMAN

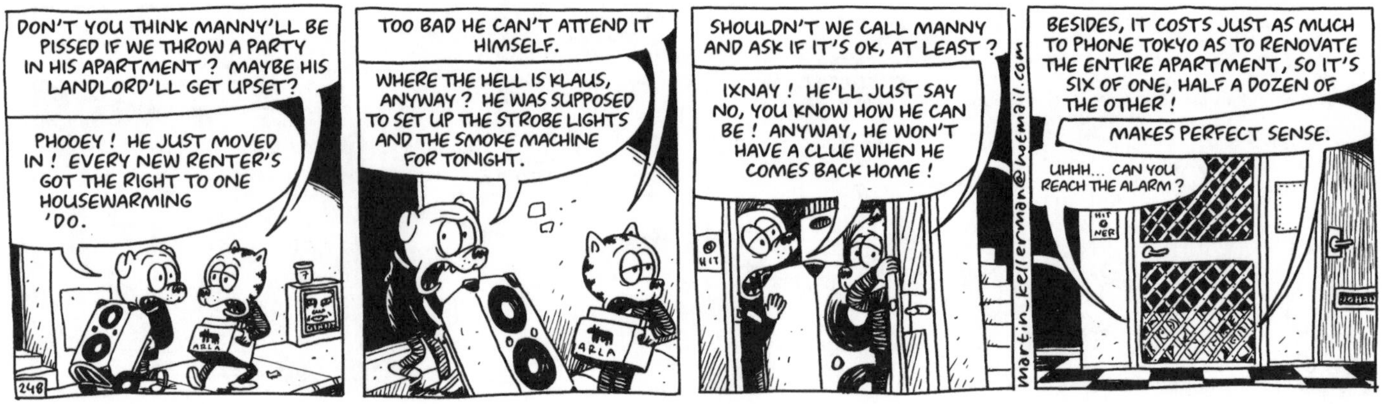
DON'T YOU THINK MANNY'LL BE PISSED IF WE THROW A PARTY IN HIS APARTMENT ? MAYBE HIS LANDLORD'LL GET UPSET?
PHOOEY ! HE JUST MOVED IN ! EVERY NEW RENTER'S GOT THE RIGHT TO ONE HOUSEWARMING 'DO.
ARLA
248
TOO BAD HE CAN'T ATTEND IT HIMSELF.
WHERE THE HELL IS KLAUS, ANYWAY ? HE WAS SUPPOSED TO SET UP THE STROBE LIGHTS AND THE SMOKE MACHINE FOR TONIGHT.
ARLA
SHOULDN'T WE CALL MANNY AND ASK IF IT'S OK, AT LEAST ?
IXNAY ! HE'LL JUST SAY NO, YOU KNOW HOW HE CAN BE ! ANYWAY, HE WON'T HAVE A CLUE WHEN HE COMES BACK HOME !
HIT
martin_kellerman@hotmail.com
BESIDES, IT COSTS JUST AS MUCH TO PHONE TOKYO AS TO RENOVATE THE ENTIRE APARTMENT, SO IT'S SIX OF ONE, HALF A DOZEN OF THE OTHER !
MAKES PERFECT SENSE.
UHHH... CAN YOU REACH THE ALARM ?
HIT NER
JOHAN

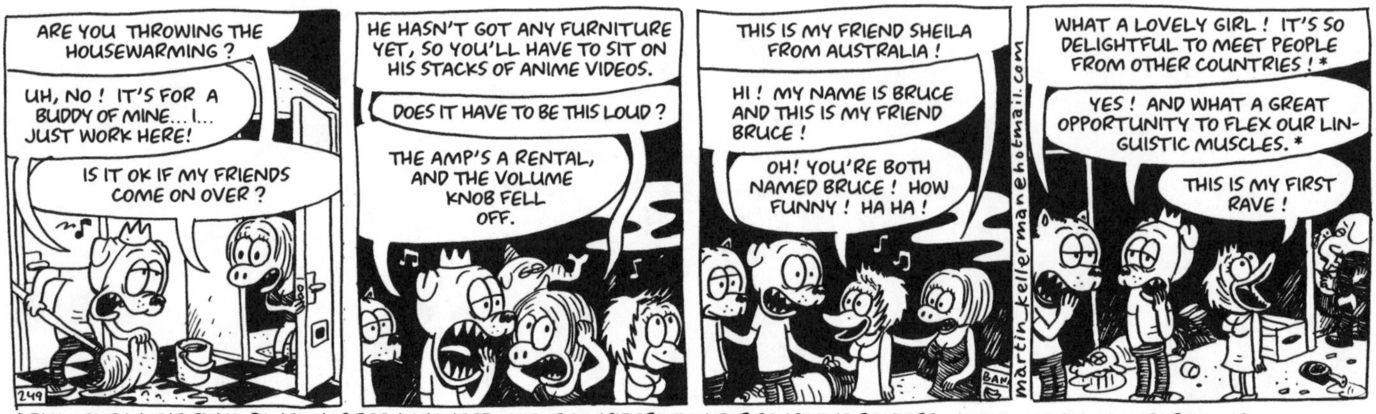
ARE YOU THROWING THE HOUSEWARMING ?
UH, NO ! IT'S FOR A BUDDY OF MINE... I... JUST WORK HERE!
IS IT OK IF MY FRIENDS COME ON OVER ?
249
HE HASN'T GOT ANY FURNITURE YET, SO YOU'LL HAVE TO SIT ON HIS STACKS OF ANIME VIDEOS.
DOES IT HAVE TO BE THIS LOUD ?
THE AMP'S A RENTAL, AND THE VOLUME KNOB FELL OFF.
THIS IS MY FRIEND SHEILA FROM AUSTRALIA !
HI ! MY NAME IS BRUCE AND THIS IS MY FRIEND BRUCE !
OH! YOU'RE BOTH NAMED BRUCE ! HOW FUNNY ! HA HA !
martin_kellerman@hotmail.com
WHAT A LOVELY GIRL ! IT'S SO DELIGHTFUL TO MEET PEOPLE FROM OTHER COUNTRIES ! *
YES ! AND WHAT A GREAT OPPORTUNITY TO FLEX OUR LINGUISTIC MUSCLES. *
THIS IS MY FIRST RAVE !

* DIALOGUE IN THE FINAL PANEL HAS BEEN CHANGED OUT OF CONSIDERATION FOR SENSITIVE READERS, NOT TO MENTION AUSTRALIANS.

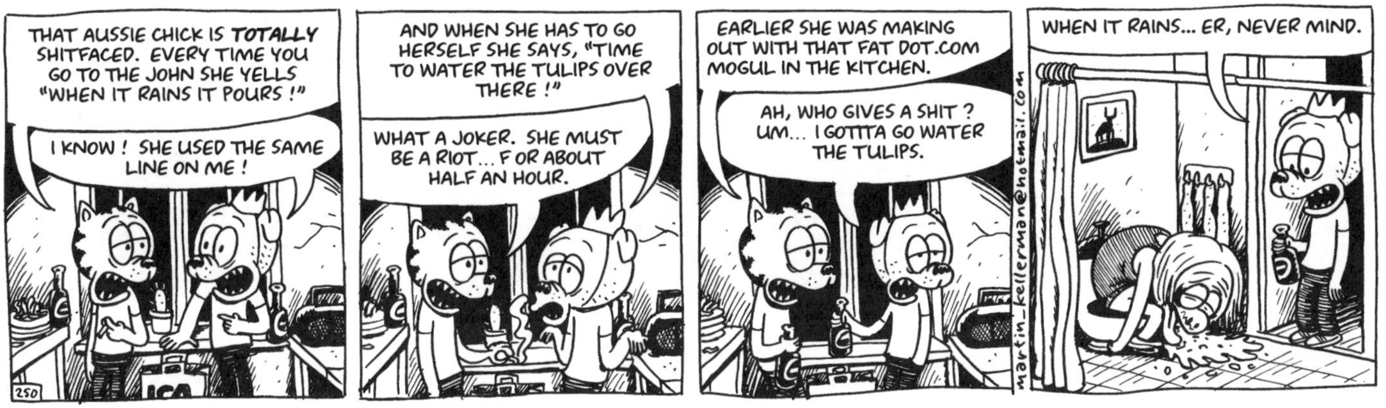
THAT AUSSIE CHICK IS TOTALLY SHITFACED. EVERY TIME YOU GO TO THE JOHN SHE YELLS "WHEN IT RAINS IT POURS!"
I KNOW! SHE USED THE SAME LINE ON ME!
250
ICA
AND WHEN SHE HAS TO GO HERSELF SHE SAYS, "TIME TO WATER THE TULIPS OVER THERE!"
WHAT A JOKER. SHE MUST BE A RIOT... FOR ABOUT HALF AN HOUR.
EARLIER SHE WAS MAKING OUT WITH THAT FAT DOT.COM MOGUL IN THE KITCHEN.
AH, WHO GIVES A SHIT? UM... I GOTTA GO WATER THE TULIPS.
martin_kellerman@hotmail.com
WHEN IT RAINS... ER, NEVER MIND.

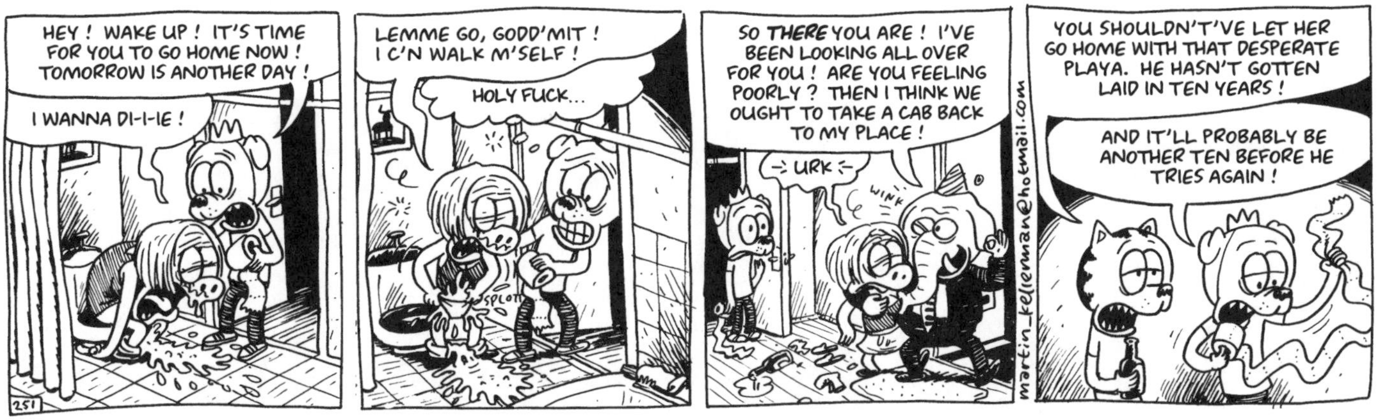
HEY! WAKE UP! IT'S TIME FOR YOU TO GO HOME NOW! TOMORROW IS ANOTHER DAY!
I WANNA DI-I-IE!
251
LEMME GO, GODD'MIT! I C'N WALK M'SELF!
HOLY FUCK...
SPLOT
SO THERE YOU ARE! I'VE BEEN LOOKING ALL OVER FOR YOU! ARE YOU FEELING POORLY? THEN I THINK WE OUGHT TO TAKE A CAB BACK TO MY PLACE!
URK
WINK
martin_kellerman@hotmail.com
YOU SHOULDN'T'VE LET HER GO HOME WITH THAT DESPERATE PLAYA. HE HASN'T GOTTEN LAID IN TEN YEARS!
AND IT'LL PROBABLY BE ANOTHER TEN BEFORE HE TRIES AGAIN!

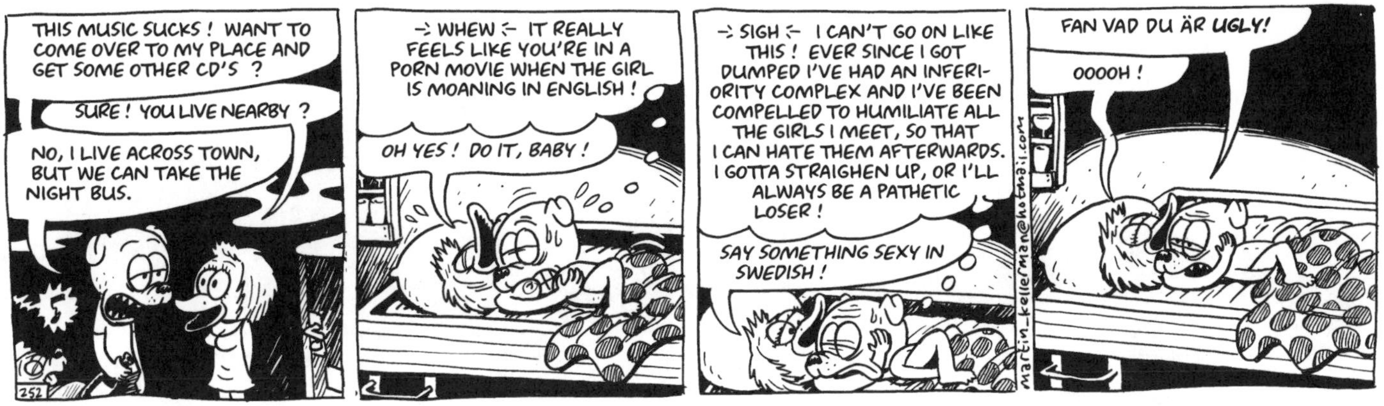
THIS MUSIC SUCKS! WANT TO COME OVER TO MY PLACE AND GET SOME OTHER CD'S?
SURE! YOU LIVE NEARBY?
NO, I LIVE ACROSS TOWN, BUT WE CAN TAKE THE NIGHT BUS.
252
WHEW IT REALLY FEELS LIKE YOU'RE IN A PORN MOVIE WHEN THE GIRL IS MOANING IN ENGLISH!
OH YES! DO IT, BABY!
SIGH I CAN'T GO ON LIKE THIS! EVER SINCE I GOT DUMPED I'VE HAD AN INFERIORITY COMPLEX AND I'VE BEEN COMPELLED TO HUMILIATE ALL THE GIRLS I MEET, SO THAT I CAN HATE THEM AFTERWARDS. I GOTTA STRAIGHEN UP, OR I'LL ALWAYS BE A PATHETIC LOSER!
SAY SOMETHING SEXY IN SWEDISH!
martin_kellerman@hotmail.com
FAN VAD DU ÄR UGLY!
OOOOH!

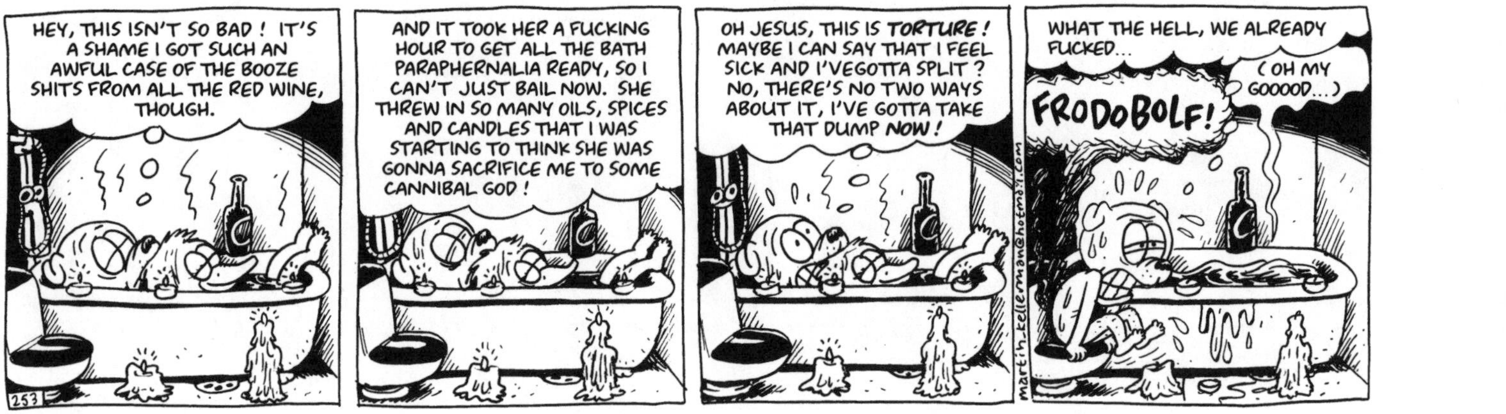
253
HEY, THIS ISN'T SO BAD ! IT'S A SHAME I GOT SUCH AN AWFUL CASE OF THE BOOZE SHITS FROM ALL THE RED WINE, THOUGH.
AND IT TOOK HER A FUCKING HOUR TO GET ALL THE BATH PARAPHERNALIA READY, SO I CAN'T JUST BAIL NOW. SHE THREW IN SO MANY OILS, SPICES AND CANDLES THAT I WAS STARTING TO THINK SHE WAS GONNA SACRIFICE ME TO SOME CANNIBAL GOD !
OH JESUS, THIS IS **TORTURE** ! MAYBE I CAN SAY THAT I FEEL SICK AND I'VEGOTTA SPLIT ? NO, THERE'S NO TWO WAYS ABOUT IT, I'VE GOTTA TAKE THAT DUMP **NOW** !
martin_kellerman@hotmail.com
WHAT THE HELL, WE ALREADY FUCKED...
FRODOBOLF!
(OH MY GOOOOD...)

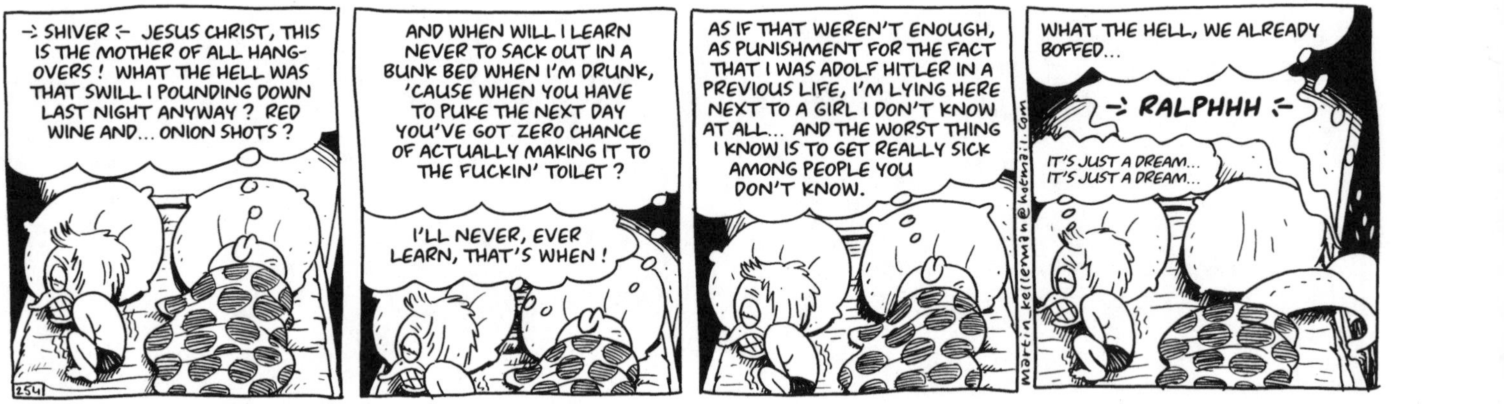
254
⇀ SHIVER ↼ JESUS CHRIST, THIS IS THE MOTHER OF ALL HANG-OVERS ! WHAT THE HELL WAS THAT SWILL I POUNDING DOWN LAST NIGHT ANYWAY ? RED WINE AND... ONION SHOTS ?
AND WHEN WILL I LEARN NEVER TO SACK OUT IN A BUNK BED WHEN I'M DRUNK, 'CAUSE WHEN YOU HAVE TO PUKE THE NEXT DAY YOU'VE GOT ZERO CHANCE OF ACTUALLY MAKING IT TO THE FUCKIN' TOILET ?
I'LL NEVER, EVER LEARN, THAT'S WHEN !
AS IF THAT WEREN'T ENOUGH, AS PUNISHMENT FOR THE FACT THAT I WAS ADOLF HITLER IN A PREVIOUS LIFE, I'M LYING HERE NEXT TO A GIRL I DON'T KNOW AT ALL... AND THE WORST THING I KNOW IS TO GET REALLY SICK AMONG PEOPLE YOU DON'T KNOW.
martin_kellerman@hotmail.com
WHAT THE HELL, WE ALREADY BOFFED...
⇀ RALPHHH ↼
IT'S JUST A DREAM... IT'S JUST A DREAM...

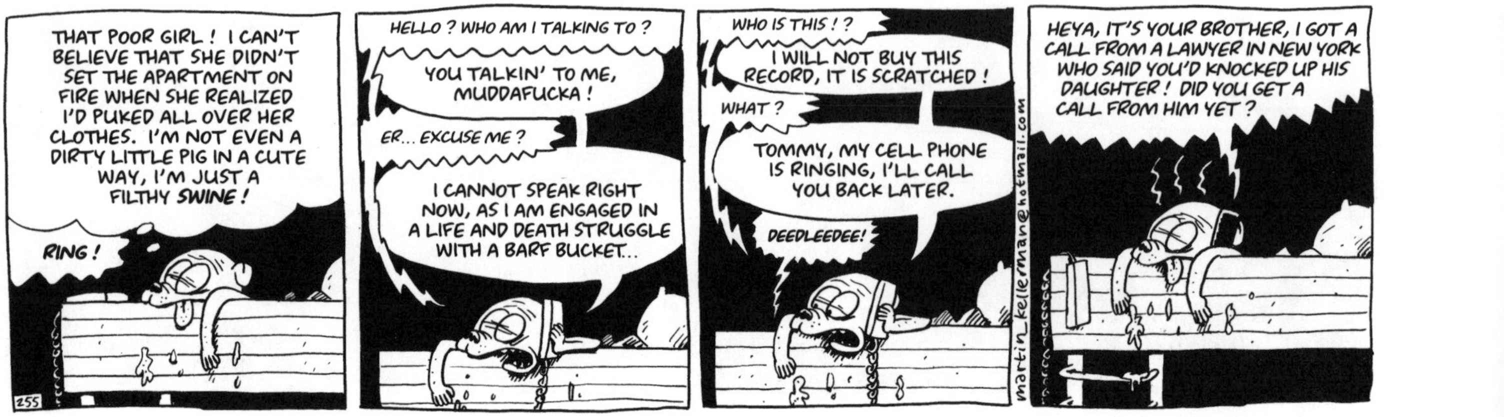
255
THAT POOR GIRL ! I CAN'T BELIEVE THAT SHE DIDN'T SET THE APARTMENT ON FIRE WHEN SHE REALIZED I'D PUKED ALL OVER HER CLOTHES. I'M NOT EVEN A DIRTY LITTLE PIG IN A CUTE WAY, I'M JUST A FILTHY **SWINE** !
RING !
HELLO ? WHO AM I TALKING TO ?
YOU TALKIN' TO ME, MUDDAFUCKA !
ER... EXCUSE ME ?
I CANNOT SPEAK RIGHT NOW, AS I AM ENGAGED IN A LIFE AND DEATH STRUGGLE WITH A BARF BUCKET...
WHO IS THIS ! ?
I WILL NOT BUY THIS RECORD, IT IS SCRATCHED !
WHAT ?
TOMMY, MY CELL PHONE IS RINGING, I'LL CALL YOU BACK LATER.
DEEDLEEDEE!
martin_kellerman@hotmail.com
HEYA, IT'S YOUR BROTHER, I GOT A CALL FROM A LAWYER IN NEW YORK WHO SAID YOU'D KNOCKED UP HIS DAUGHTER ! DID YOU GET A CALL FROM HIM YET ?

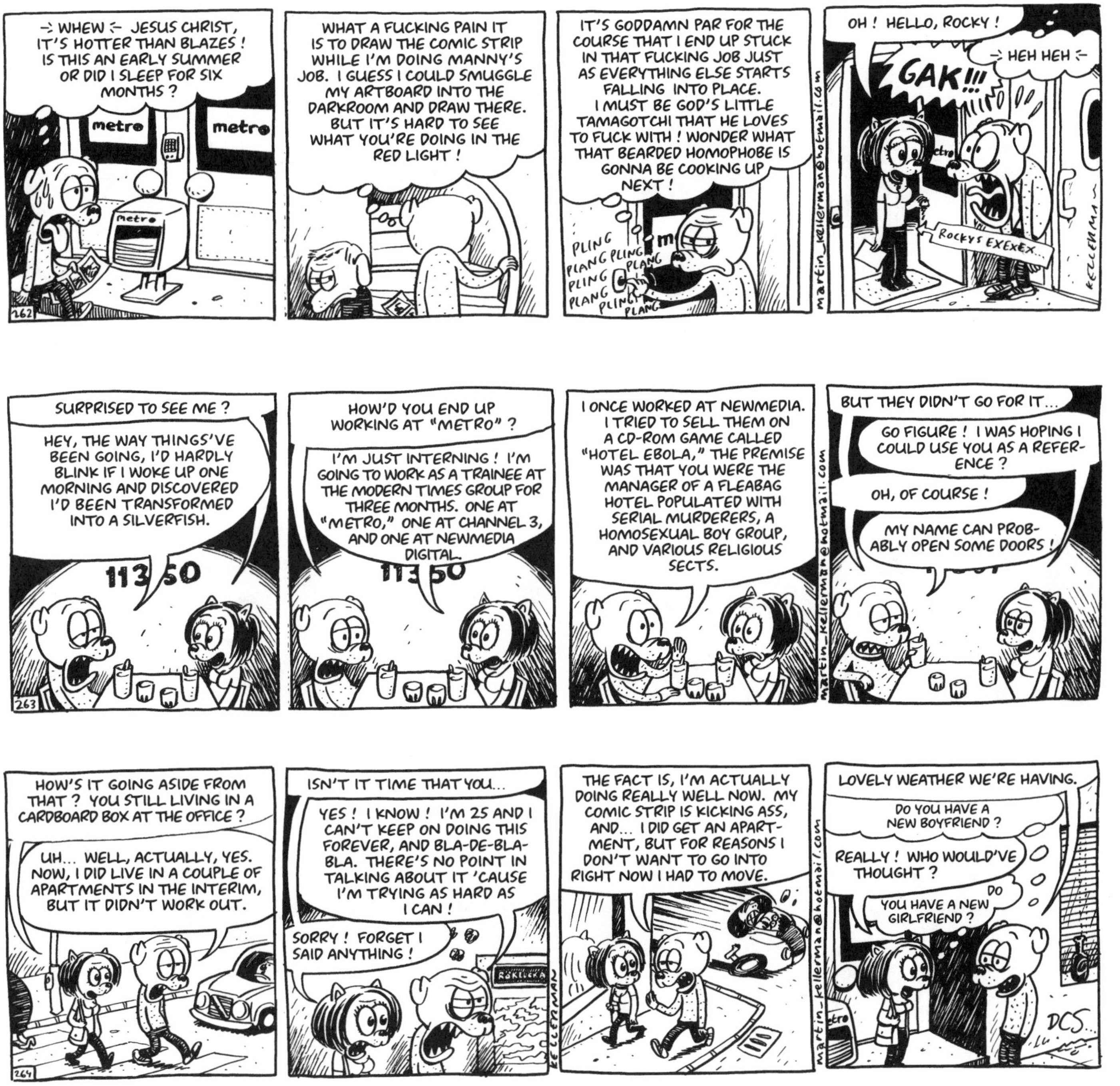

262
–: WHEW :– JESUS CHRIST, IT'S HOTTER THAN BLAZES! IS THIS AN EARLY SUMMER OR DID I SLEEP FOR SIX MONTHS?
metro
metro
metro
WHAT A FUCKING PAIN IT IS TO DRAW THE COMIC STRIP WHILE I'M DOING MANNY'S JOB. I GUESS I COULD SMUGGLE MY ARTBOARD INTO THE DARKROOM AND DRAW THERE. BUT IT'S HARD TO SEE WHAT YOU'RE DOING IN THE RED LIGHT!
IT'S GODDAMN PAR FOR THE COURSE THAT I END UP STUCK IN THAT FUCKING JOB JUST AS EVERYTHING ELSE STARTS FALLING INTO PLACE. I MUST BE GOD'S LITTLE TAMAGOTCHI THAT HE LOVES TO FUCK WITH! WONDER WHAT THAT BEARDED HOMOPHOBE IS GONNA BE COOKING UP NEXT!
PLING PLANG PLING PLANG PLING PLANG PLING PLANG
martin_kellerman@hotmail.com
OH! HELLO, ROCKY!
GAK!!!
–: HEH HEH :–
ROCKYS EXEXEX...
KELLERMAN
263
SURPRISED TO SEE ME?
HEY, THE WAY THINGS'VE BEEN GOING, I'D HARDLY BLINK IF I WOKE UP ONE MORNING AND DISCOVERED I'D BEEN TRANSFORMED INTO A SILVERFISH.
HOW'D YOU END UP WORKING AT "METRO"?
I'M JUST INTERNING! I'M GOING TO WORK AS A TRAINEE AT THE MODERN TIMES GROUP FOR THREE MONTHS. ONE AT "METRO," ONE AT CHANNEL 3, AND ONE AT NEWMEDIA DIGITAL.
I ONCE WORKED AT NEWMEDIA. I TRIED TO SELL THEM ON A CD-ROM GAME CALLED "HOTEL EBOLA," THE PREMISE WAS THAT YOU WERE THE MANAGER OF A FLEABAG HOTEL POPULATED WITH SERIAL MURDERERS, A HOMOSEXUAL BOY GROUP, AND VARIOUS RELIGIOUS SECTS.
martin_kellerman@hotmail.com
BUT THEY DIDN'T GO FOR IT...
GO FIGURE! I WAS HOPING I COULD USE YOU AS A REFERENCE?
OH, OF COURSE!
MY NAME CAN PROBABLY OPEN SOME DOORS!
264
HOW'S IT GOING ASIDE FROM THAT? YOU STILL LIVING IN A CARDBOARD BOX AT THE OFFICE?
UH... WELL, ACTUALLY, YES. NOW, I DID LIVE IN A COUPLE OF APARTMENTS IN THE INTERIM, BUT IT DIDN'T WORK OUT.
ISN'T IT TIME THAT YOU...
YES! I KNOW! I'M 25 AND I CAN'T KEEP ON DOING THIS FOREVER, AND BLA-DE-BLA-BLA. THERE'S NO POINT IN TALKING ABOUT IT 'CAUSE I'M TRYING AS HARD AS I CAN!
SORRY! FORGET I SAID ANYTHING!
KELLERMAN
THE FACT IS, I'M ACTUALLY DOING REALLY WELL NOW. MY COMIC STRIP IS KICKING ASS, AND... I DID GET AN APARTMENT, BUT FOR REASONS I DON'T WANT TO GO INTO RIGHT NOW I HAD TO MOVE.
martin_kellerman@hotmail.com
LOVELY WEATHER WE'RE HAVING.
DO YOU HAVE A NEW BOYFRIEND?
REALLY! WHO WOULD'VE THOUGHT?
DO YOU HAVE A NEW GIRLFRIEND?
DCS...

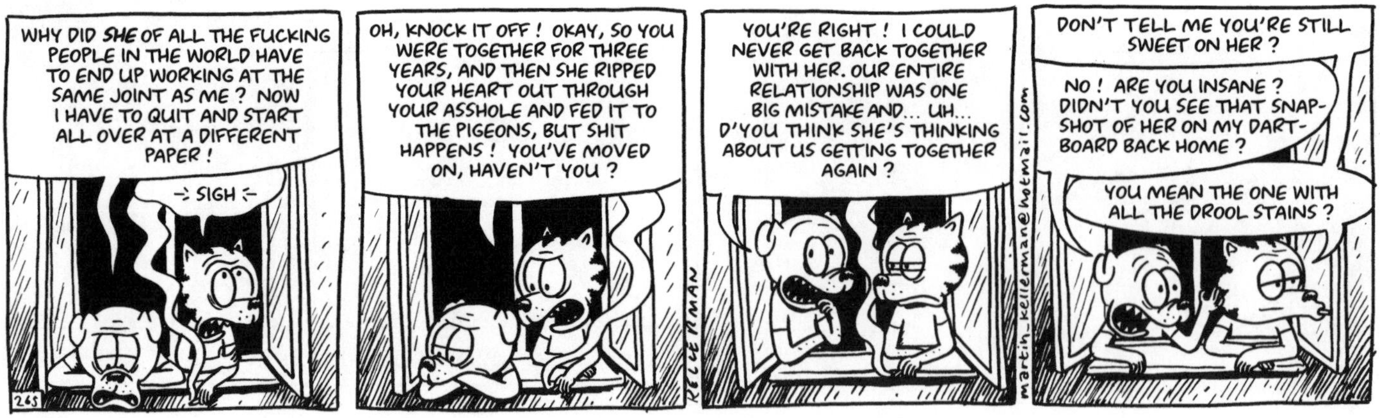
265
WHY DID *SHE* OF ALL THE FUCKING PEOPLE IN THE WORLD HAVE TO END UP WORKING AT THE SAME JOINT AS ME? NOW I HAVE TO QUIT AND START ALL OVER AT A DIFFERENT PAPER!
SIGH
OH, KNOCK IT OFF! OKAY, SO YOU WERE TOGETHER FOR THREE YEARS, AND THEN SHE RIPPED YOUR HEART OUT THROUGH YOUR ASSHOLE AND FED IT TO THE PIGEONS, BUT SHIT HAPPENS! YOU'VE MOVED ON, HAVEN'T YOU?
KELLERMAN
YOU'RE RIGHT! I COULD NEVER GET BACK TOGETHER WITH HER. OUR ENTIRE RELATIONSHIP WAS ONE BIG MISTAKE AND... UH... D'YOU THINK SHE'S THINKING ABOUT US GETTING TOGETHER AGAIN?
martin_kellerman@hotmail.com
DON'T TELL ME YOU'RE STILL SWEET ON HER?
NO! ARE YOU INSANE? DIDN'T YOU SEE THAT SNAPSHOT OF HER ON MY DARTBOARD BACK HOME?
YOU MEAN THE ONE WITH ALL THE DROOL STAINS?

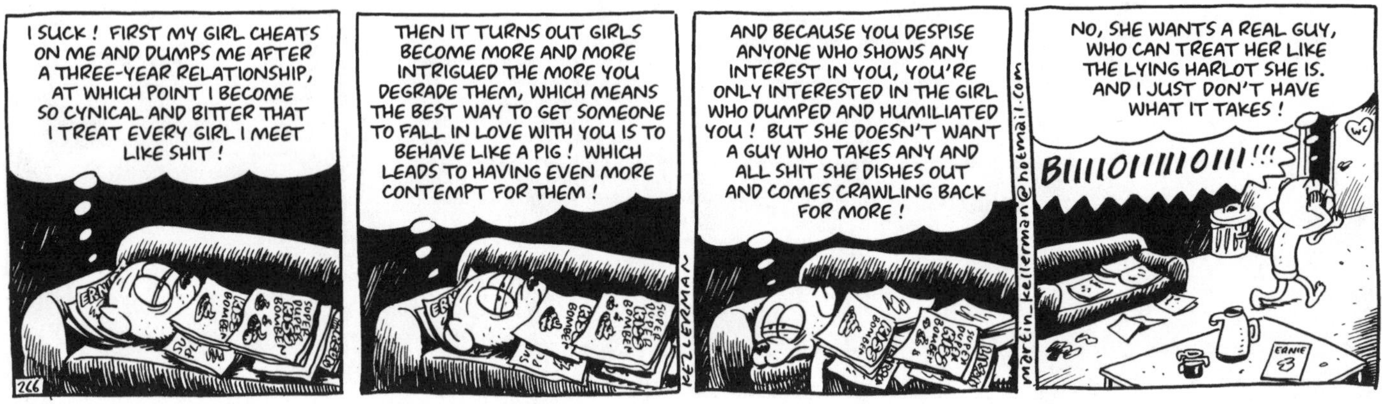
266
I SUCK! FIRST MY GIRL CHEATS ON ME AND DUMPS ME AFTER A THREE-YEAR RELATIONSHIP, AT WHICH POINT I BECOME SO CYNICAL AND BITTER THAT I TREAT EVERY GIRL I MEET LIKE SHIT!
THEN IT TURNS OUT GIRLS BECOME MORE AND MORE INTRIGUED THE MORE YOU DEGRADE THEM, WHICH MEANS THE BEST WAY TO GET SOMEONE TO FALL IN LOVE WITH YOU IS TO BEHAVE LIKE A PIG! WHICH LEADS TO HAVING EVEN MORE CONTEMPT FOR THEM!
KELLERMAN
AND BECAUSE YOU DESPISE ANYONE WHO SHOWS ANY INTEREST IN YOU, YOU'RE ONLY INTERESTED IN THE GIRL WHO DUMPED AND HUMILIATED YOU! BUT SHE DOESN'T WANT A GUY WHO TAKES ANY AND ALL SHIT SHE DISHES OUT AND COMES CRAWLING BACK FOR MORE!
martin_kellerman@hotmail.com
NO, SHE WANTS A REAL GUY, WHO CAN TREAT HER LIKE THE LYING HARLOT SHE IS. AND I JUST DON'T HAVE WHAT IT TAKES!
BIIIIOIIIIIOIII!!!
WC
ERNIE

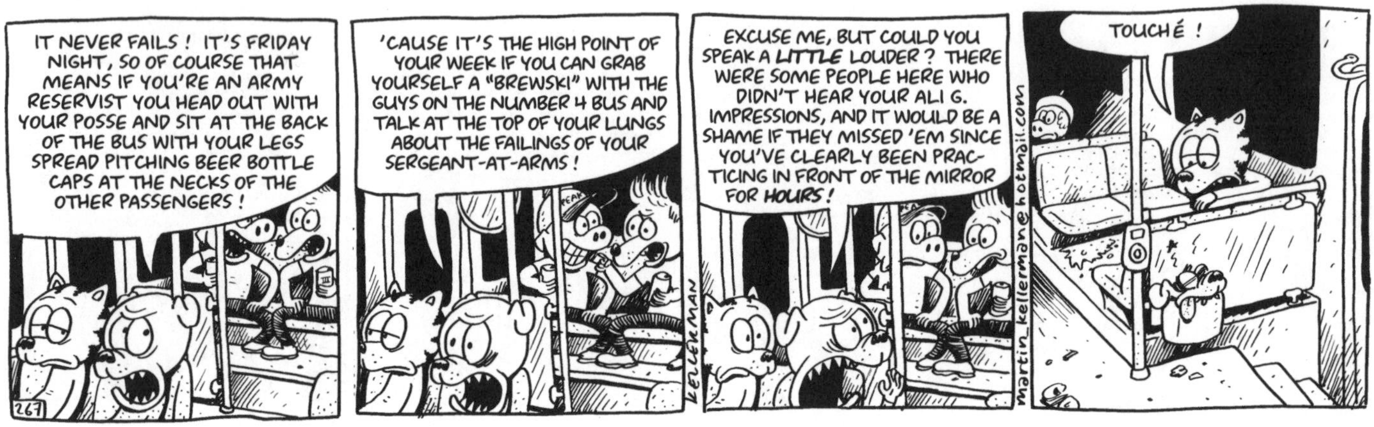
267
IT NEVER FAILS! IT'S FRIDAY NIGHT, SO OF COURSE THAT MEANS IF YOU'RE AN ARMY RESERVIST YOU HEAD OUT WITH YOUR POSSE AND SIT AT THE BACK OF THE BUS WITH YOUR LEGS SPREAD PITCHING BEER BOTTLE CAPS AT THE NECKS OF THE OTHER PASSENGERS!
'CAUSE IT'S THE HIGH POINT OF YOUR WEEK IF YOU CAN GRAB YOURSELF A "BREWSKI" WITH THE GUYS ON THE NUMBER 4 BUS AND TALK AT THE TOP OF YOUR LUNGS ABOUT THE FAILINGS OF YOUR SERGEANT-AT-ARMS!
KELLERMAN
EXCUSE ME, BUT COULD YOU SPEAK A *LITTLE* LOUDER? THERE WERE SOME PEOPLE HERE WHO DIDN'T HEAR YOUR ALI G. IMPRESSIONS, AND IT WOULD BE A SHAME IF THEY MISSED 'EM SINCE YOU'VE CLEARLY BEEN PRACTICING IN FRONT OF THE MIRROR FOR *HOURS*!
martin_kellerman@hotmail.com
TOUCHÉ!

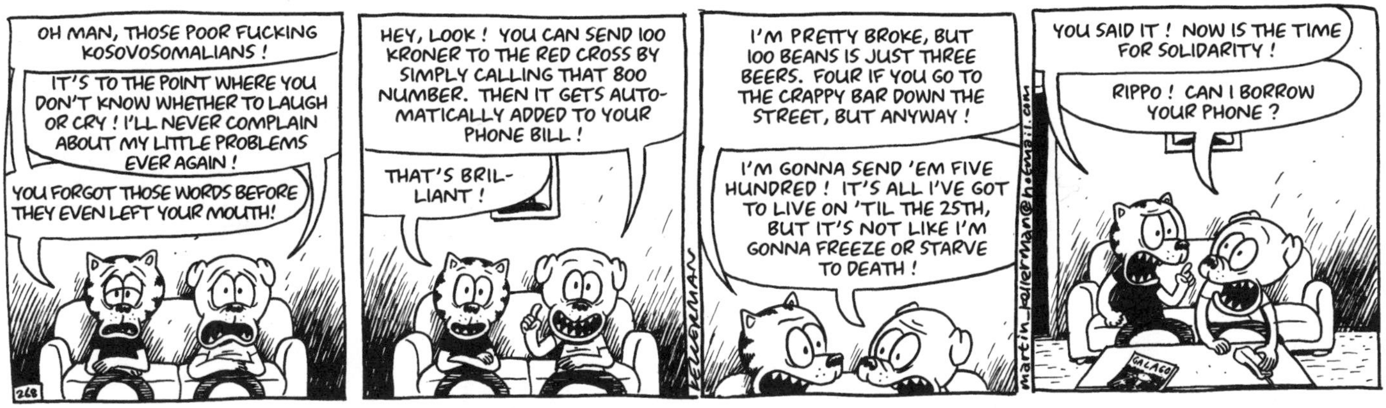
268
OH MAN, THOSE POOR FUCKING KOSOVOSOMALIANS !
IT'S TO THE POINT WHERE YOU DON'T KNOW WHETHER TO LAUGH OR CRY ! I'LL NEVER COMPLAIN ABOUT MY LITTLE PROBLEMS EVER AGAIN !
YOU FORGOT THOSE WORDS BEFORE THEY EVEN LEFT YOUR MOUTH!
HEY, LOOK ! YOU CAN SEND 100 KRONER TO THE RED CROSS BY SIMPLY CALLING THAT 800 NUMBER. THEN IT GETS AUTOMATICALLY ADDED TO YOUR PHONE BILL !
THAT'S BRILLIANT !
KELLERMAN
I'M PRETTY BROKE, BUT 100 BEANS IS JUST THREE BEERS. FOUR IF YOU GO TO THE CRAPPY BAR DOWN THE STREET, BUT ANYWAY !
I'M GONNA SEND 'EM FIVE HUNDRED ! IT'S ALL I'VE GOT TO LIVE ON 'TIL THE 25TH, BUT IT'S NOT LIKE I'M GONNA FREEZE OR STARVE TO DEATH !
martin_kellerman@hotmail.com
YOU SAID IT ! NOW IS THE TIME FOR SOLIDARITY !
RIPPO ! CAN I BORROW YOUR PHONE ?
GALAGO

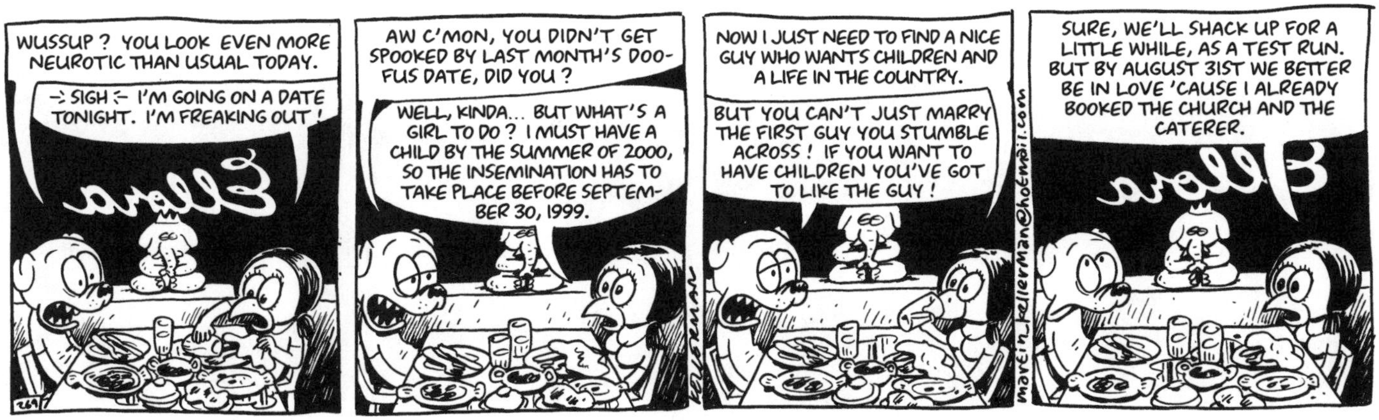
269
WUSSUP ? YOU LOOK EVEN MORE NEUROTIC THAN USUAL TODAY.
⇢ SIGH ⇠ I'M GOING ON A DATE TONIGHT. I'M FREAKING OUT !
Ellora
AW C'MON, YOU DIDN'T GET SPOOKED BY LAST MONTH'S DOOFUS DATE, DID YOU ?
WELL, KINDA... BUT WHAT'S A GIRL TO DO ? I MUST HAVE A CHILD BY THE SUMMER OF 2000, SO THE INSEMINATION HAS TO TAKE PLACE BEFORE SEPTEMBER 30, 1999.
KELLERMAN
NOW I JUST NEED TO FIND A NICE GUY WHO WANTS CHILDREN AND A LIFE IN THE COUNTRY.
BUT YOU CAN'T JUST MARRY THE FIRST GUY YOU STUMBLE ACROSS ! IF YOU WANT TO HAVE CHILDREN YOU'VE GOT TO LIKE THE GUY !
martin_kellerman@hotmail.com
SURE, WE'LL SHACK UP FOR A LITTLE WHILE, AS A TEST RUN. BUT BY AUGUST 31ST WE BETTER BE IN LOVE 'CAUSE I ALREADY BOOKED THE CHURCH AND THE CATERER.
Ellora

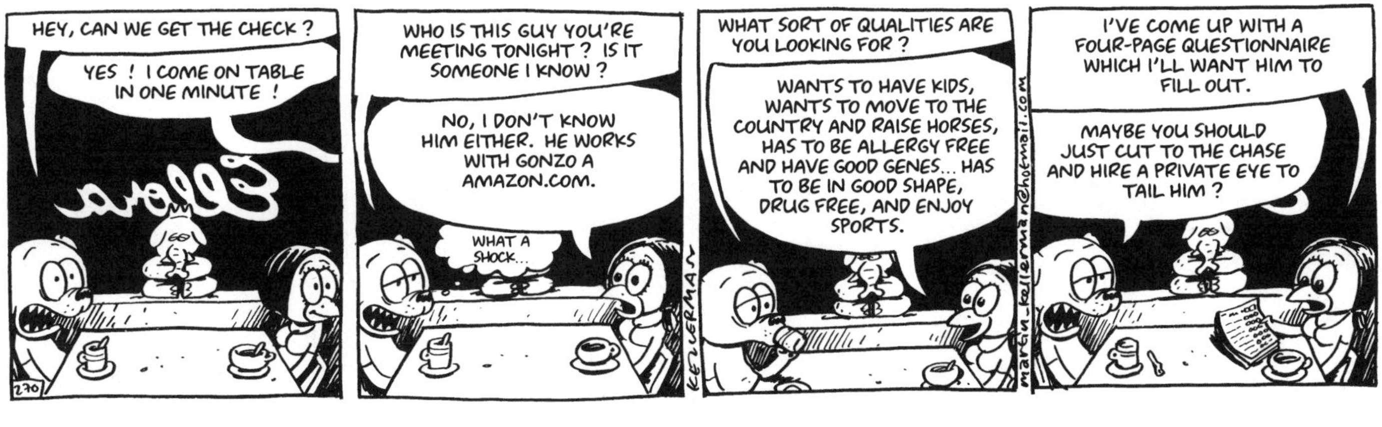
270
HEY, CAN WE GET THE CHECK ?
YES ! I COME ON TABLE IN ONE MINUTE !
Ellora
WHO IS THIS GUY YOU'RE MEETING TONIGHT ? IS IT SOMEONE I KNOW ?
NO, I DON'T KNOW HIM EITHER. HE WORKS WITH GONZO A AMAZON.COM.
WHAT A SHOCK...
KELLERMAN
WHAT SORT OF QUALITIES ARE YOU LOOKING FOR ?
WANTS TO HAVE KIDS, WANTS TO MOVE TO THE COUNTRY AND RAISE HORSES, HAS TO BE ALLERGY FREE AND HAVE GOOD GENES... HAS TO BE IN GOOD SHAPE, DRUG FREE, AND ENJOY SPORTS.
martin_kellerman@hotmail.com
I'VE COME UP WITH A FOUR-PAGE QUESTIONNAIRE WHICH I'LL WANT HIM TO FILL OUT.
MAYBE YOU SHOULD JUST CUT TO THE CHASE AND HIRE A PRIVATE EYE TO TAIL HIM ?

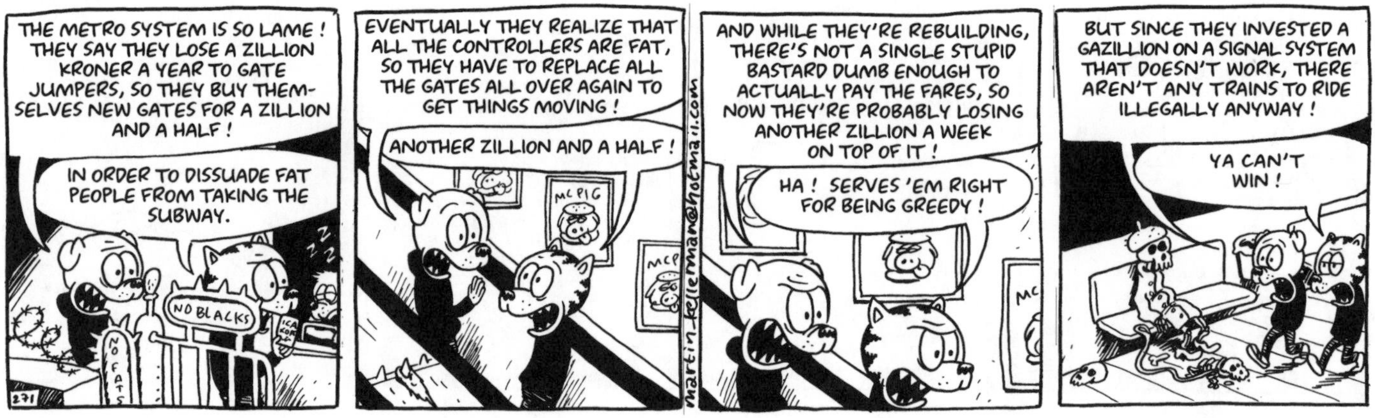
271
THE METRO SYSTEM IS SO LAME ! THEY SAY THEY LOSE A ZILLION KRONER A YEAR TO GATE JUMPERS, SO THEY BUY THEMSELVES NEW GATES FOR A ZILLION AND A HALF !
IN ORDER TO DISSUADE FAT PEOPLE FROM TAKING THE SUBWAY.
NO BLACKS
NO FATS
EVENTUALLY THEY REALIZE THAT ALL THE CONTROLLERS ARE FAT, SO THEY HAVE TO REPLACE ALL THE GATES ALL OVER AGAIN TO GET THINGS MOVING !
ANOTHER ZILLION AND A HALF !
MC PIG
martin_kellerman@hotmail.com
AND WHILE THEY'RE REBUILDING, THERE'S NOT A SINGLE STUPID BASTARD DUMB ENOUGH TO ACTUALLY PAY THE FARES, SO NOW THEY'RE PROBABLY LOSING ANOTHER ZILLION A WEEK ON TOP OF IT !
HA ! SERVES 'EM RIGHT FOR BEING GREEDY !
BUT SINCE THEY INVESTED A GAZILLION ON A SIGNAL SYSTEM THAT DOESN'T WORK, THERE AREN'T ANY TRAINS TO RIDE ILLEGALLY ANYWAY !
YA CAN'T WIN !

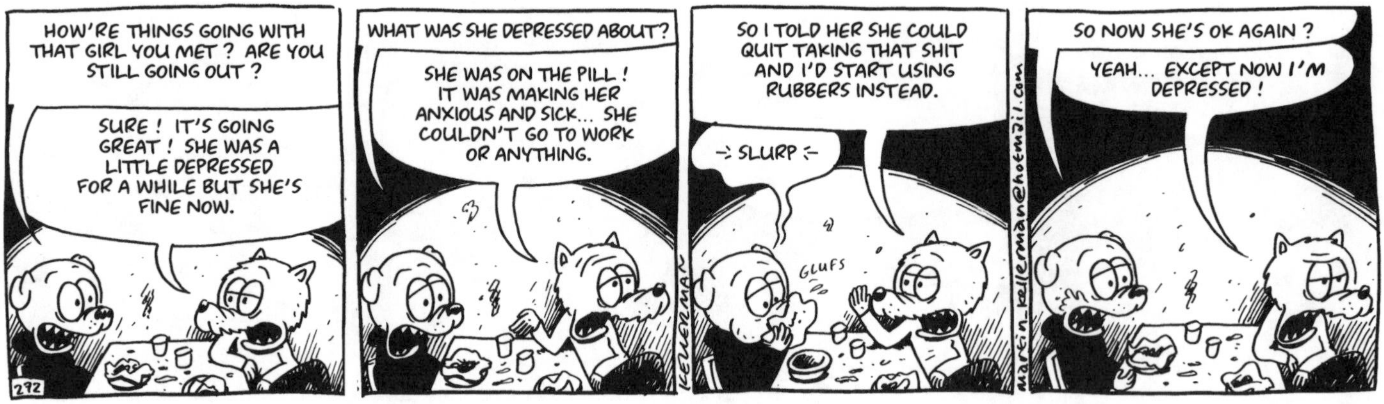
272
HOW'RE THINGS GOING WITH THAT GIRL YOU MET ? ARE YOU STILL GOING OUT ?
SURE ! IT'S GOING GREAT ! SHE WAS A LITTLE DEPRESSED FOR A WHILE BUT SHE'S FINE NOW.
WHAT WAS SHE DEPRESSED ABOUT ?
SHE WAS ON THE PILL ! IT WAS MAKING HER ANXIOUS AND SICK... SHE COULDN'T GO TO WORK OR ANYTHING.
KELLERMAN
SO I TOLD HER SHE COULD QUIT TAKING THAT SHIT AND I'D START USING RUBBERS INSTEAD.
SLURP
GLUFS
martin_kellerman@hotmail.com
SO NOW SHE'S OK AGAIN ?
YEAH... EXCEPT NOW I'M DEPRESSED !

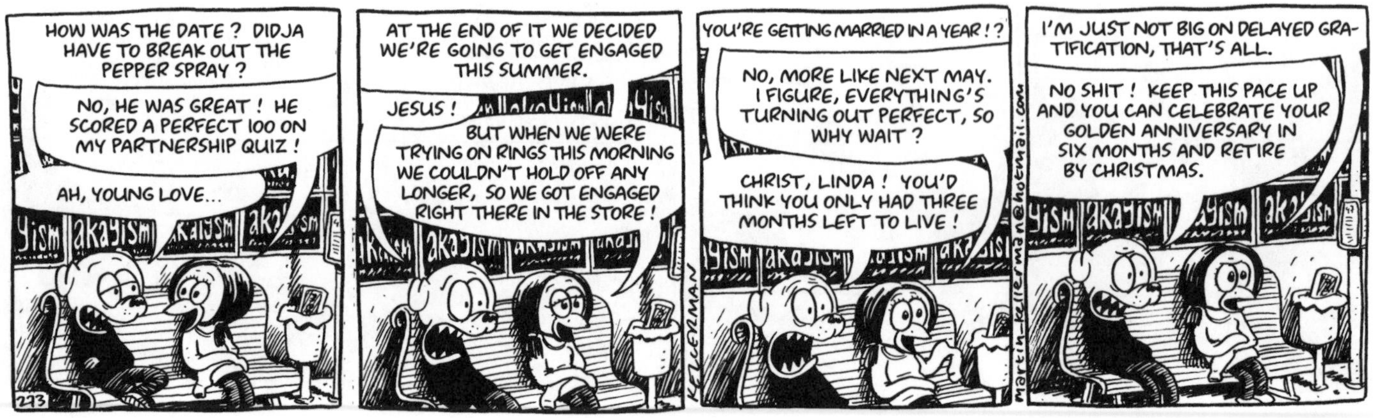
273
HOW WAS THE DATE ? DIDJA HAVE TO BREAK OUT THE PEPPER SPRAY ?
NO, HE WAS GREAT ! HE SCORED A PERFECT 100 ON MY PARTNERSHIP QUIZ !
AH, YOUNG LOVE...
AT THE END OF IT WE DECIDED WE'RE GOING TO GET ENGAGED THIS SUMMER.
JESUS !
BUT WHEN WE WERE TRYING ON RINGS THIS MORNING WE COULDN'T HOLD OFF ANY LONGER, SO WE GOT ENGAGED RIGHT THERE IN THE STORE !
KELLERMAN
YOU'RE GETTING MARRIED IN A YEAR ! ?
NO, MORE LIKE NEXT MAY. I FIGURE, EVERYTHING'S TURNING OUT PERFECT, SO WHY WAIT ?
CHRIST, LINDA ! YOU'D THINK YOU ONLY HAD THREE MONTHS LEFT TO LIVE !
martin_kellerman@hotmail.com
I'M JUST NOT BIG ON DELAYED GRATIFICATION, THAT'S ALL.
NO SHIT ! KEEP THIS PACE UP AND YOU CAN CELEBRATE YOUR GOLDEN ANNIVERSARY IN SIX MONTHS AND RETIRE BY CHRISTMAS.
akayism

DOWN AND OUT WITH TINKY

BLEAGHH ! THESE SPARE RIBS ARE SUPER SALTY ! DID THEY FIND THIS MEAT WHEN THEY RAISED THE FUCKING TITANIC ?
I'LL GET THE WAITRESS.
ROADKILL
SALT MENY
274
NO ! I HAD TO WAIT AN HOUR TO GET THIS CRAP ! I'VE GOTTA CHOKE DOWN EVERY BITE, EVEN IF MY ARTERIES TURN INTO PRETZEL STICKS !
DON'T DO IT ! YOU'LL END UP ABSORBING PUDDLES THROUGH THE SOLES OF YOUR FEET AS YOU WALK DOWN THE STREET !
ROADKILL
KELLERMAN
EXCUSE ME, WHAT DID YOU ORDER ?
I DON'T RECALL. PROBABLY SOMETHING FROM LAST SEASON'S MENU !
WE'RE A LITTLE SHORT-STAFFED IN THE KITCHEN.
martin_kellerman@hotmail.com
BUT HERE'S SOME MORE RADISHES WHILE YOU WAIT... AND I'LL TAKE HALF OFF OF YOUR BILL !
SWEET ! THEN ONLY ONE OF US'LL BE SKIPPING OUT ON THE CHECK !

KOM TILL HANINGE
277
HEY, DIDJA KNOW THE PURPLE TELETUBBY IS A FAG ?
YES, I KNOW. I'VE HEARD IT A MILLION TIMES ! IT WAS THE ONLY COSTUME LEFT !
martin_kellerman@hotmail.com
AND GET YOUR MOM TO TEACH YOU A LITTLE TOLERANCE, YOU PINT-SIZED BIGOT !
KOM TILL HANINGE
KELLERMAN
LALALAAA♪

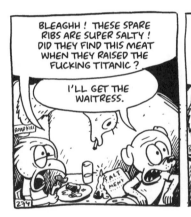

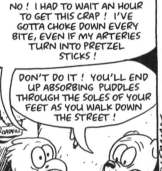

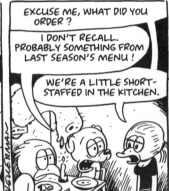

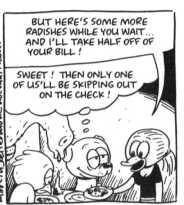

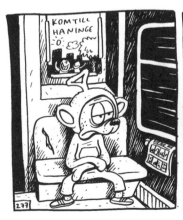

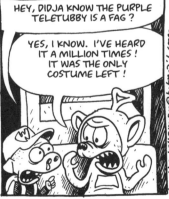

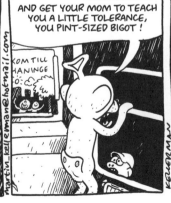

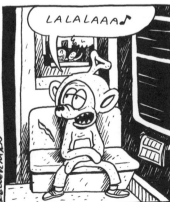

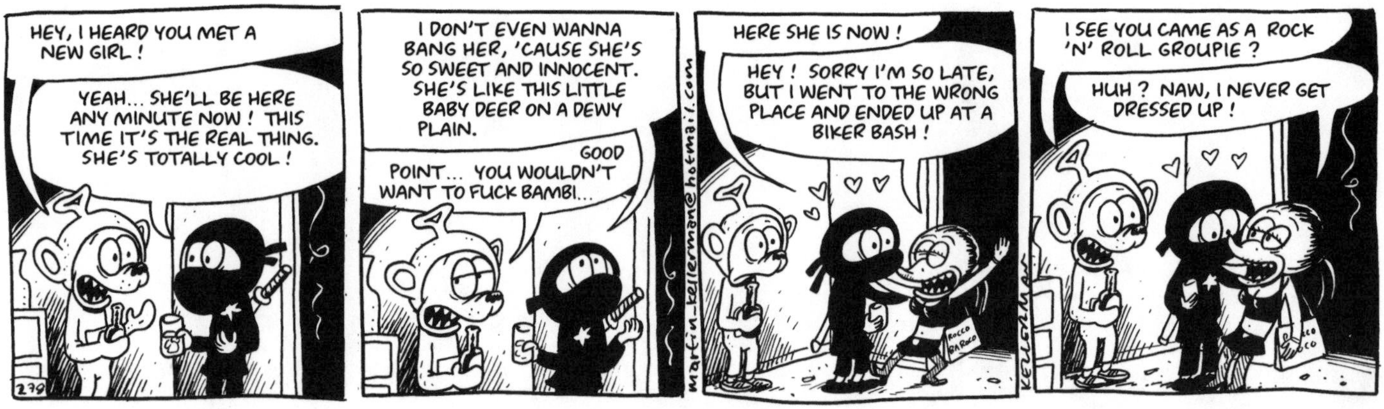
HEY, I HEARD YOU MET A NEW GIRL!
YEAH... SHE'LL BE HERE ANY MINUTE NOW! THIS TIME IT'S THE REAL THING. SHE'S TOTALLY COOL!
278
I DON'T EVEN WANNA BANG HER, 'CAUSE SHE'S SO SWEET AND INNOCENT. SHE'S LIKE THIS LITTLE BABY DEER ON A DEWY PLAIN.
GOOD POINT... YOU WOULDN'T WANT TO FUCK BAMBI...
martin_kellerman@hotmail.com
HERE SHE IS NOW!
HEY! SORRY I'M SO LATE, BUT I WENT TO THE WRONG PLACE AND ENDED UP AT A BIKER BASH!
ROCCO BAROCO
KELLERMAN
I SEE YOU CAME AS A ROCK 'N' ROLL GROUPIE?
HUH? NAW, I NEVER GET DRESSED UP!

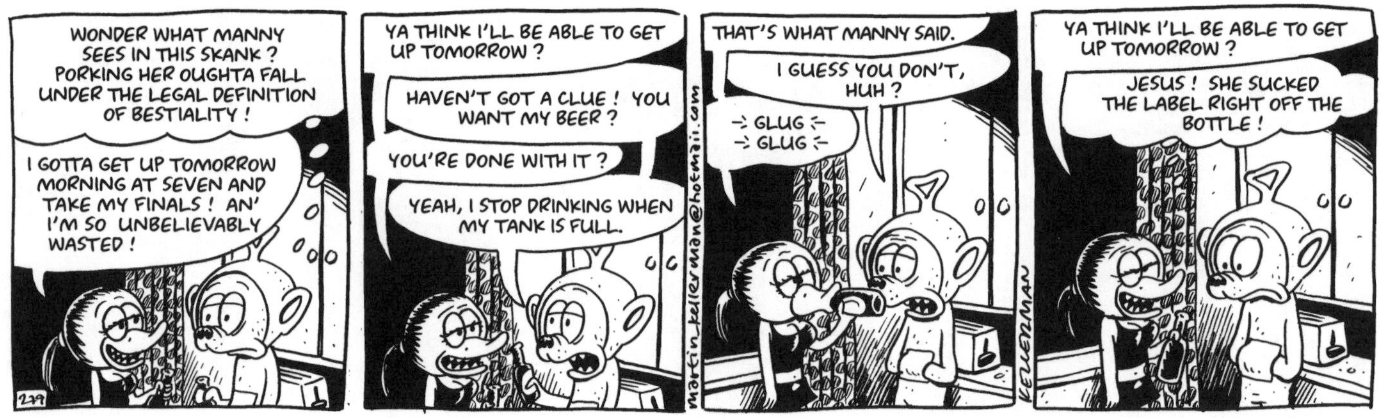
WONDER WHAT MANNY SEES IN THIS SKANK? PORKING HER OUGHTA FALL UNDER THE LEGAL DEFINITION OF BESTIALITY!
I GOTTA GET UP TOMORROW MORNING AT SEVEN AND TAKE MY FINALS! AN' I'M SO UNBELIEVABLY WASTED!
279
YA THINK I'LL BE ABLE TO GET UP TOMORROW?
HAVEN'T GOT A CLUE! YOU WANT MY BEER?
YOU'RE DONE WITH IT?
YEAH, I STOP DRINKING WHEN MY TANK IS FULL.
martin_kellerman@hotmail.com
THAT'S WHAT MANNY SAID.
I GUESS YOU DON'T, HUH?
GLUG
GLUG
KELLERMAN
YA THINK I'LL BE ABLE TO GET UP TOMORROW?
JESUS! SHE SUCKED THE LABEL RIGHT OFF THE BOTTLE!

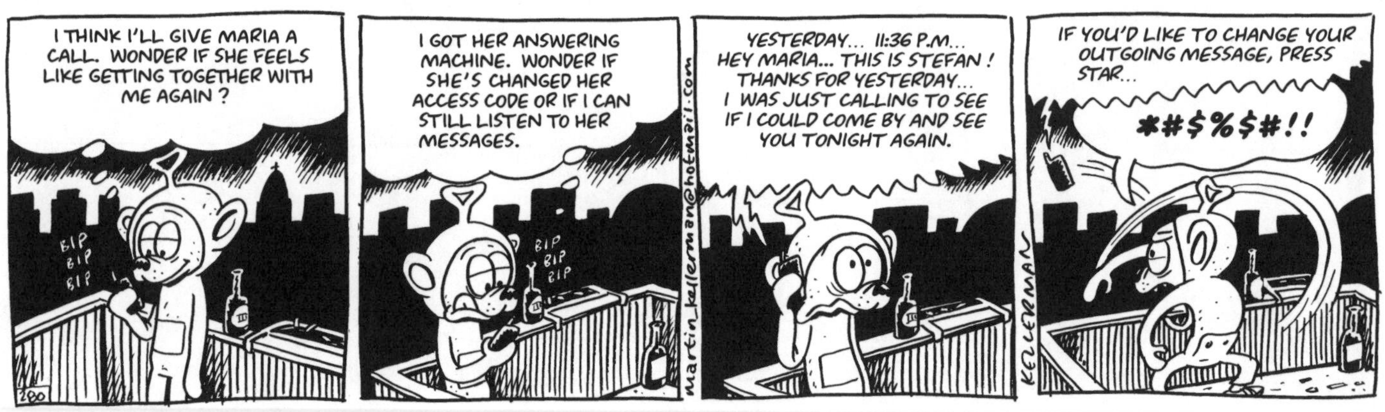
I THINK I'LL GIVE MARIA A CALL. WONDER IF SHE FEELS LIKE GETTING TOGETHER WITH ME AGAIN?
BIP
BIP
BIP
280
I GOT HER ANSWERING MACHINE. WONDER IF SHE'S CHANGED HER ACCESS CODE OR IF I CAN STILL LISTEN TO HER MESSAGES.
BIP
BIP
BIP
martin_kellerman@hotmail.com
YESTERDAY... 11:36 P.M... HEY MARIA... THIS IS STEFAN! THANKS FOR YESTERDAY... I WAS JUST CALLING TO SEE IF I COULD COME BY AND SEE YOU TONIGHT AGAIN.
KELLERMAN
IF YOU'D LIKE TO CHANGE YOUR OUTGOING MESSAGE, PRESS STAR...
*#$%$#!!

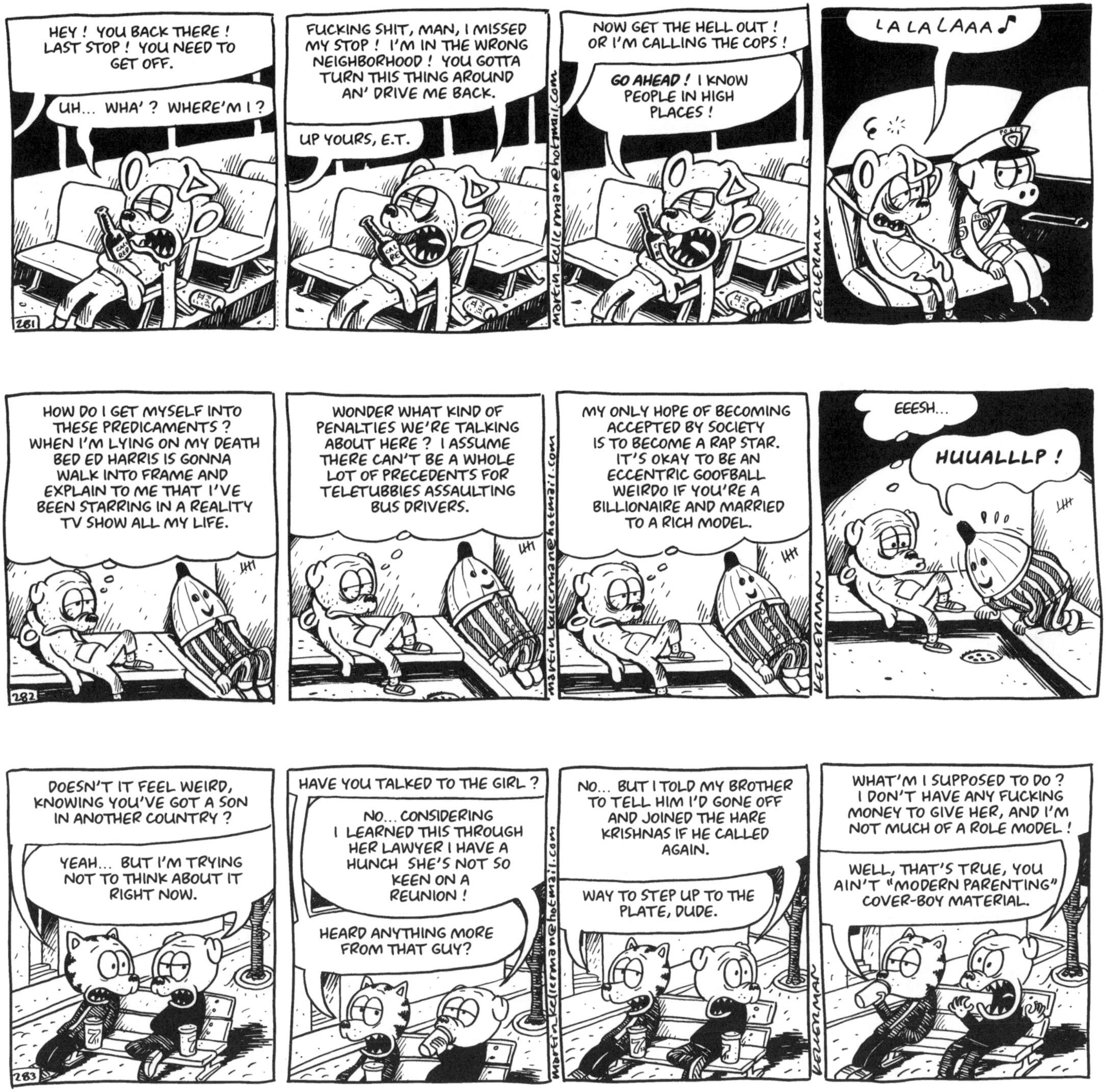
281
HEY ! YOU BACK THERE ! LAST STOP ! YOU NEED TO GET OFF.
UH... WHA' ? WHERE'M I ?
FUCKING SHIT, MAN, I MISSED MY STOP ! I'M IN THE WRONG NEIGHBORHOOD ! YOU GOTTA TURN THIS THING AROUND AN' DRIVE ME BACK.
UP YOURS, E.T.
martin_kellerman@hotmail.com
NOW GET THE HELL OUT ! OR I'M CALLING THE COPS !
GO AHEAD ! I KNOW PEOPLE IN HIGH PLACES !
KELLERMAN
LA LA LAAA
282
HOW DO I GET MYSELF INTO THESE PREDICAMENTS ? WHEN I'M LYING ON MY DEATH BED ED HARRIS IS GONNA WALK INTO FRAME AND EXPLAIN TO ME THAT I'VE BEEN STARRING IN A REALITY TV SHOW ALL MY LIFE.
WONDER WHAT KIND OF PENALTIES WE'RE TALKING ABOUT HERE ? I ASSUME THERE CAN'T BE A WHOLE LOT OF PRECEDENTS FOR TELETUBBIES ASSAULTING BUS DRIVERS.
martin_kellerman@hotmail.com
MY ONLY HOPE OF BECOMING ACCEPTED BY SOCIETY IS TO BECOME A RAP STAR. IT'S OKAY TO BE AN ECCENTRIC GOOFBALL WEIRDO IF YOU'RE A BILLIONAIRE AND MARRIED TO A RICH MODEL.
KELLERMAN
EEESH...
HUUALLLP !
283
DOESN'T IT FEEL WEIRD, KNOWING YOU'VE GOT A SON IN ANOTHER COUNTRY ?
YEAH... BUT I'M TRYING NOT TO THINK ABOUT IT RIGHT NOW.
HAVE YOU TALKED TO THE GIRL ?
NO... CONSIDERING I LEARNED THIS THROUGH HER LAWYER I HAVE A HUNCH SHE'S NOT SO KEEN ON A REUNION !
HEARD ANYTHING MORE FROM THAT GUY?
martin_kellerman@hotmail.com
NO... BUT I TOLD MY BROTHER TO TELL HIM I'D GONE OFF AND JOINED THE HARE KRISHNAS IF HE CALLED AGAIN.
WAY TO STEP UP TO THE PLATE, DUDE.
KELLERMAN
WHAT'M I SUPPOSED TO DO ? I DON'T HAVE ANY FUCKING MONEY TO GIVE HER, AND I'M NOT MUCH OF A ROLE MODEL !
WELL, THAT'S TRUE, YOU AIN'T "MODERN PARENTING" COVER-BOY MATERIAL.

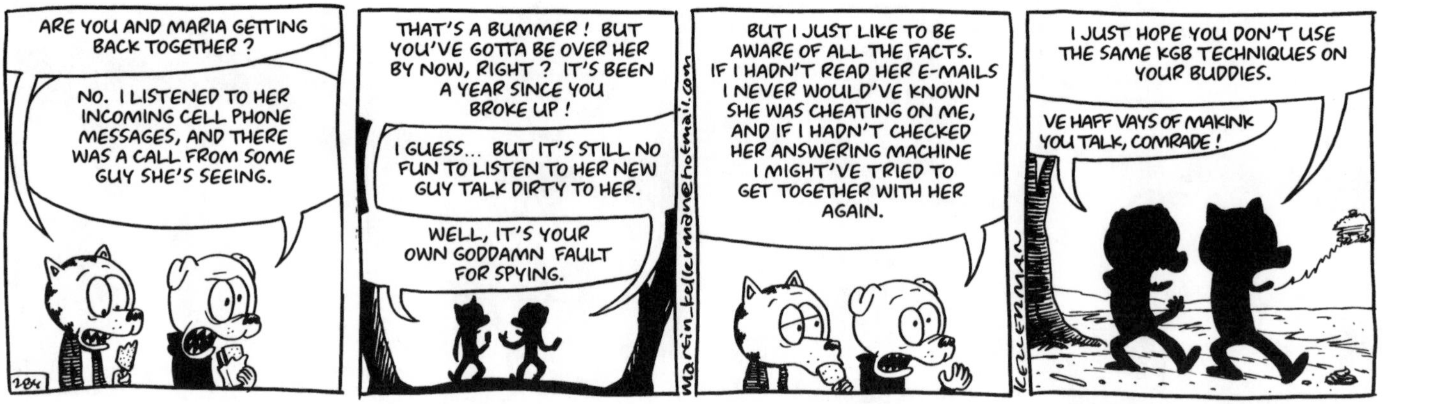
ARE YOU AND MARIA GETTING BACK TOGETHER ?
NO. I LISTENED TO HER INCOMING CELL PHONE MESSAGES, AND THERE WAS A CALL FROM SOME GUY SHE'S SEEING.
284
THAT'S A BUMMER ! BUT YOU'VE GOTTA BE OVER HER BY NOW, RIGHT ? IT'S BEEN A YEAR SINCE YOU BROKE UP !
I GUESS... BUT IT'S STILL NO FUN TO LISTEN TO HER NEW GUY TALK DIRTY TO HER.
WELL, IT'S YOUR OWN GODDAMN FAULT FOR SPYING.
martin_kellerman@hotmail.com
BUT I JUST LIKE TO BE AWARE OF ALL THE FACTS. IF I HADN'T READ HER E-MAILS I NEVER WOULD'VE KNOWN SHE WAS CHEATING ON ME, AND IF I HADN'T CHECKED HER ANSWERING MACHINE I MIGHT'VE TRIED TO GET TOGETHER WITH HER AGAIN.
KELLERMAN
I JUST HOPE YOU DON'T USE THE SAME KGB TECHNIQUES ON YOUR BUDDIES.
VE HAFF VAYS OF MAKINK YOU TALK, COMRADE !

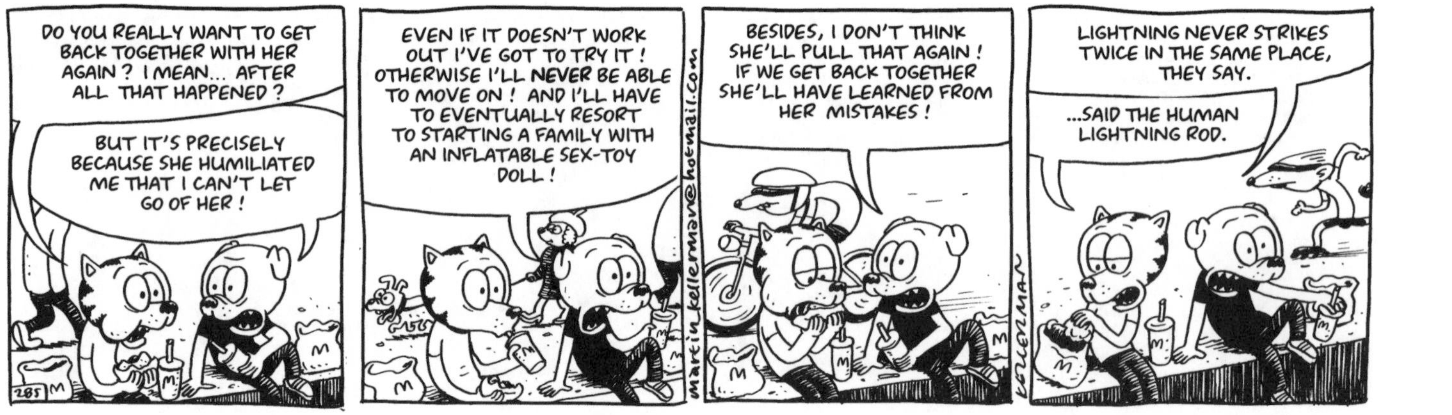
DO YOU REALLY WANT TO GET BACK TOGETHER WITH HER AGAIN ? I MEAN... AFTER ALL THAT HAPPENED ?
BUT IT'S PRECISELY BECAUSE SHE HUMILIATED ME THAT I CAN'T LET GO OF HER !
285
EVEN IF IT DOESN'T WORK OUT I'VE GOT TO TRY IT ! OTHERWISE I'LL NEVER BE ABLE TO MOVE ON ! AND I'LL HAVE TO EVENTUALLY RESORT TO STARTING A FAMILY WITH AN INFLATABLE SEX-TOY DOLL !
martin_kellerman@hotmail.com
BESIDES, I DON'T THINK SHE'LL PULL THAT AGAIN ! IF WE GET BACK TOGETHER SHE'LL HAVE LEARNED FROM HER MISTAKES !
KELLERMAN
LIGHTNING NEVER STRIKES TWICE IN THE SAME PLACE, THEY SAY.
...SAID THE HUMAN LIGHTNING ROD.

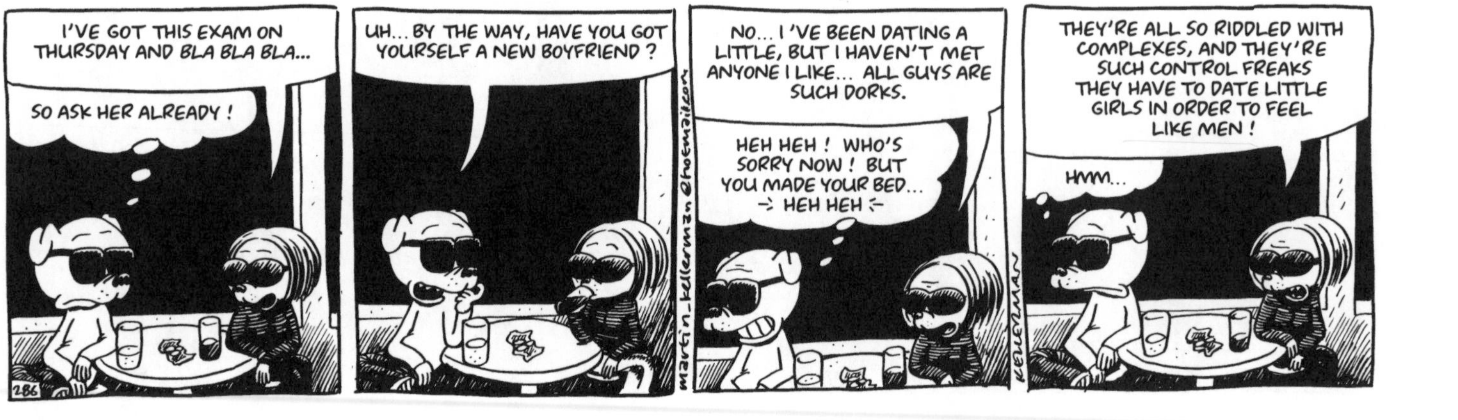
I'VE GOT THIS EXAM ON THURSDAY AND BLA BLA BLA...
SO ASK HER ALREADY !
286
UH... BY THE WAY, HAVE YOU GOT YOURSELF A NEW BOYFRIEND ?
martin_kellerman@hotmail.com
NO... I'VE BEEN DATING A LITTLE, BUT I HAVEN'T MET ANYONE I LIKE... ALL GUYS ARE SUCH DORKS.
HEH HEH ! WHO'S SORRY NOW ! BUT YOU MADE YOUR BED... HEH HEH
KELLERMAN
THEY'RE ALL SO RIDDLED WITH COMPLEXES, AND THEY'RE SUCH CONTROL FREAKS THEY HAVE TO DATE LITTLE GIRLS IN ORDER TO FEEL LIKE MEN !
HMM...

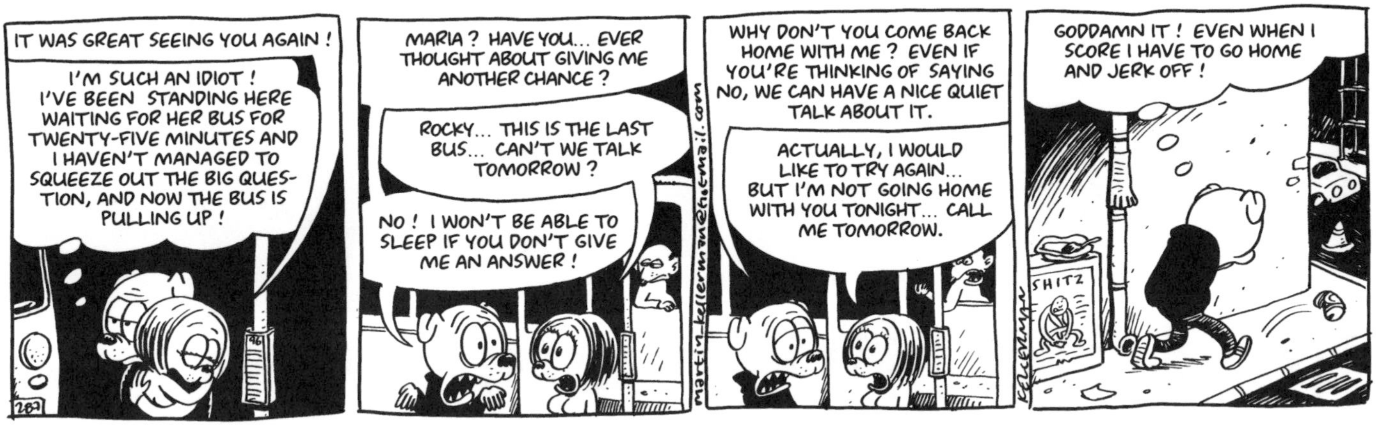
IT WAS GREAT SEEING YOU AGAIN !
I'M SUCH AN IDIOT ! I'VE BEEN STANDING HERE WAITING FOR HER BUS FOR TWENTY-FIVE MINUTES AND I HAVEN'T MANAGED TO SQUEEZE OUT THE BIG QUESTION, AND NOW THE BUS IS PULLING UP !
287
MARIA ? HAVE YOU... EVER THOUGHT ABOUT GIVING ME ANOTHER CHANCE ?
ROCKY... THIS IS THE LAST BUS... CAN'T WE TALK TOMORROW ?
NO ! I WON'T BE ABLE TO SLEEP IF YOU DON'T GIVE ME AN ANSWER !
martin_kellerman@hotmail.com
WHY DON'T YOU COME BACK HOME WITH ME ? EVEN IF YOU'RE THINKING OF SAYING NO, WE CAN HAVE A NICE QUIET TALK ABOUT IT.
ACTUALLY, I WOULD LIKE TO TRY AGAIN... BUT I'M NOT GOING HOME WITH YOU TONIGHT... CALL ME TOMORROW.
KELLERMAN
GODDAMN IT ! EVEN WHEN I SCORE I HAVE TO GO HOME AND JERK OFF !
SHITZ

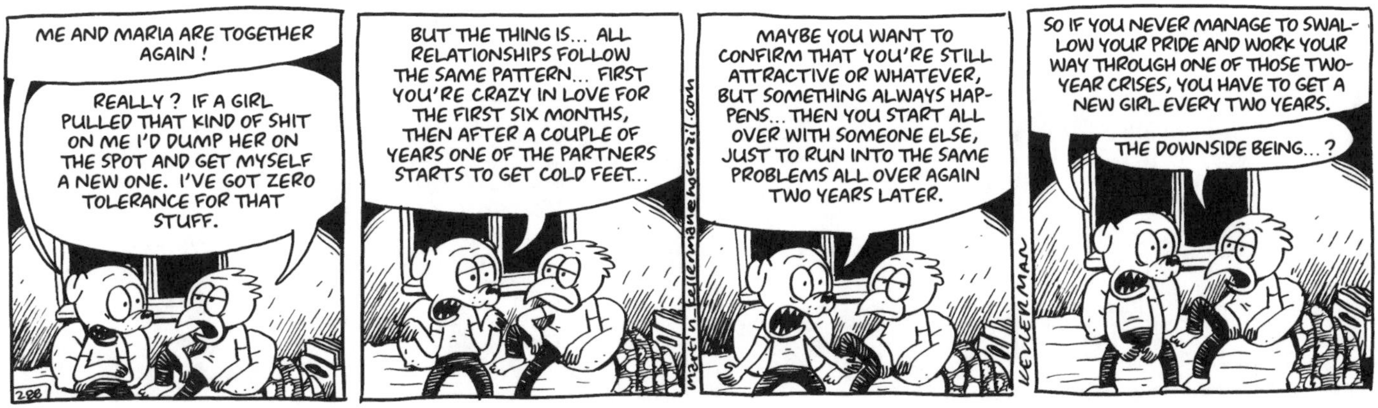
ME AND MARIA ARE TOGETHER AGAIN !
REALLY ? IF A GIRL PULLED THAT KIND OF SHIT ON ME I'D DUMP HER ON THE SPOT AND GET MYSELF A NEW ONE. I'VE GOT ZERO TOLERANCE FOR THAT STUFF.
288
BUT THE THING IS... ALL RELATIONSHIPS FOLLOW THE SAME PATTERN... FIRST YOU'RE CRAZY IN LOVE FOR THE FIRST SIX MONTHS, THEN AFTER A COUPLE OF YEARS ONE OF THE PARTNERS STARTS TO GET COLD FEET...
martin_kellerman@hotmail.com
MAYBE YOU WANT TO CONFIRM THAT YOU'RE STILL ATTRACTIVE OR WHATEVER, BUT SOMETHING ALWAYS HAPPENS... THEN YOU START ALL OVER WITH SOMEONE ELSE, JUST TO RUN INTO THE SAME PROBLEMS ALL OVER AGAIN TWO YEARS LATER.
KELLERMAN
SO IF YOU NEVER MANAGE TO SWALLOW YOUR PRIDE AND WORK YOUR WAY THROUGH ONE OF THOSE TWO-YEAR CRISES, YOU HAVE TO GET A NEW GIRL EVERY TWO YEARS.
THE DOWNSIDE BEING... ?

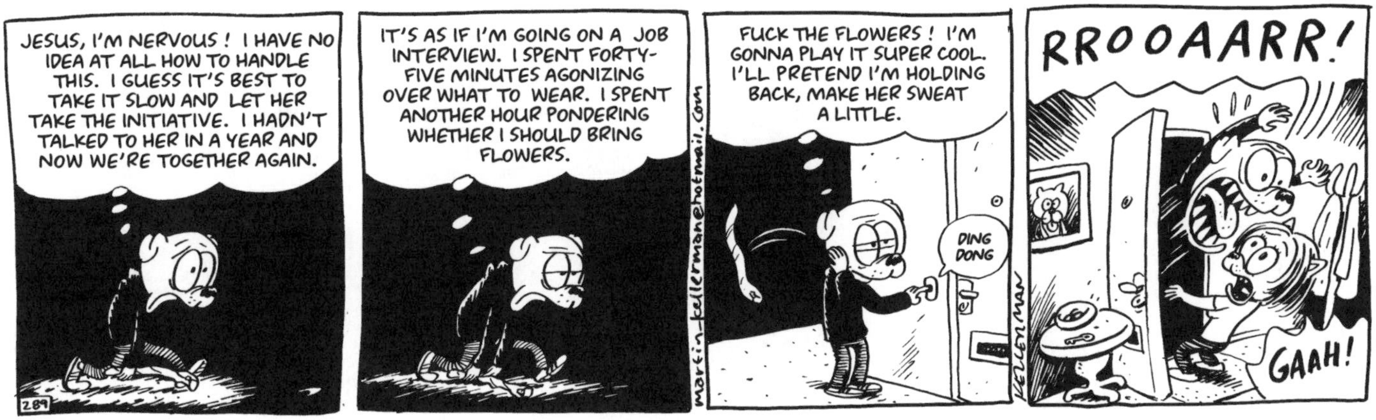
JESUS, I'M NERVOUS ! I HAVE NO IDEA AT ALL HOW TO HANDLE THIS. I GUESS IT'S BEST TO TAKE IT SLOW AND LET HER TAKE THE INITIATIVE. I HADN'T TALKED TO HER IN A YEAR AND NOW WE'RE TOGETHER AGAIN.
289
IT'S AS IF I'M GOING ON A JOB INTERVIEW. I SPENT FORTY-FIVE MINUTES AGONIZING OVER WHAT TO WEAR. I SPENT ANOTHER HOUR PONDERING WHETHER I SHOULD BRING FLOWERS.
martin_kellerman@hotmail.com
FUCK THE FLOWERS ! I'M GONNA PLAY IT SUPER COOL. I'LL PRETEND I'M HOLDING BACK, MAKE HER SWEAT A LITTLE.
DING DONG
KELLERMAN
RROOAARR!
GAAH!

RELATIONSHIPS REDUX

NO, WAIT, ROCKY, CAN'T WE SLOW THINGS DOWN A LITTLE ?
WHAT ? WHY ?
I STILL FEEL ICKY ABOUT EVERYTHING THAT HAPPENED. CAN'T WE JUST TAKE IT ONE STEP AT A TIME ?
WELL, WHAT'S WRONG WITH *THIS* STEP ?
CAN'T WE JUST HAVE A NICE TIME TOGETHER ? SEX ISN'T THE MOST IMPORTANT THING, IS IT ?
WHAT IS THIS, SOME SORT OF ENDURANCE TEST ?
PLEASE DON'T BE MAD ! NOW IT'S ALL TURNING UGLY !
NO, I'M SORRY ! OF COURSE WE CAN WAIT, FOR CHRISSAKE ! STOP CRYING NOW ! I'LL GO HOME !
SURE ! I CAN WAIT ANOTHER YEAR ! DON'T EVEN THINK ABOUT ME !
-:- SNIFF -:-
290
martin_kellerman@hotmail.com
KELLERMAN

SO, ARE YOU MOVING BACK IN WITH MARIA NOW ?
WELL, IT'S GONNA BE A LITTLE BIT TIGHT IN HER STUDIO APARTMENT, BUT IT'LL BE FINE.
EVERYTHING COOL BETWEEN YOU ? SHE KNOWS YOU'VE GOT A KID ?
UH, NO... THAT'S A CONVERSATION I'M SAVING FOR A LATER DAY.
FIRST I HAVE TO ENJOY THIS NORMAL LIFE FOR A LITTLE WHILE. IT'S THE LITTLE THINGS THAT ARE AWESOME ! LIKE GETTING SEX WITHOUT HAVING TO DEBASE YOURSELF, OR NOT HAVING TO DO YOUR LAUNDRY IN THE OFFICE BATHROOM SINK...
SO IS THIS THE REAL THING ?
YOU BET ! LAST NIGHT I RAN ACROSS A PIER IN SLOW MOTION... SEAGULLS FLYING EVERYWHERE ! SPONTANEOUSLY DANCING WITH OLD LADIES !
JUST A CRAZY FOOL IN LOVE !
291
martin_kellerman@hotmail.com
KELLERMAN

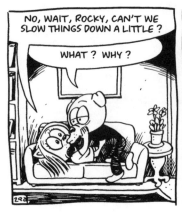

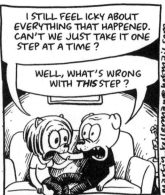

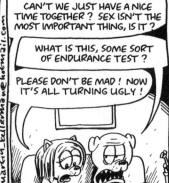

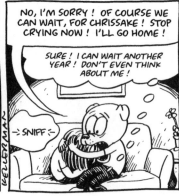

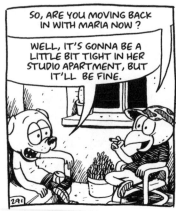

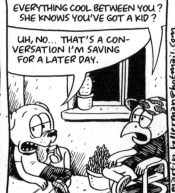

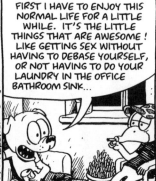

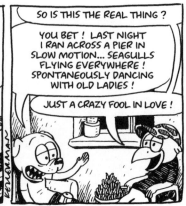

SO WHAT EXACTLY IS THIS PARTY FOR?

STEFAN'S MOVING TO TOKYO, SO THIS IS HIS GOODBYE PARTY.

¡GIGANTE!

292.

WHAT'RE YOUR PLANS?

OH, YOU KNOW... TEND SOME BAR, MAYBE DO A LITTLE MODELING. THEY'RE CRAZY ABOUT WESTERNERS OVER THERE.

GOT YOUR PLANE TICKET?

I'M TAKING CARE OF THAT TOMORROW. I'VE SOLD ALL OF MY RECORDS, GIVEN UP MY APARTMENT, AND TOLD MY BOSS HE CAN TAKE HIS JOB AND SHOVE IT!

¡GIGANTE!

martin_kellerman@hotmail.com

THAT'S WHY I'M THROWING THIS PARTY... I NEED TO SCRAPE TOGETHER 7000 KRONER BY TOMORROW!

YOU'RE CHARGING 100 BONES FOR A BEER?

¡GIGANTE!

KELLERMAN

FUCKIN' A, GUYS, I'M GONNA MISS YOU ALL SO-O-O MUCH!

I WAS JUST THINKING TO MYSELF THAT WE OUGHTA BLOW THIS JOINT BEFORE HE STARTS BLUBBERING, BUT, OH WELL...

¡GIGANTE!

293.

WE'LL PROBABLY NEVER SEE EACH OTHER AGAIN, SO GOOD LUCK WITH EVERYTHING! PROMISE YOU'LL COME SEE ME!

YOU BET! AT "SEA-WEED," IN A WEEK OR TWO!

¡GIGANTE!

I'LL BE STAYING IN TOKYO FOR THREE MONTHS UNTIL MY VISA EXPIRES, THEN I'LL HEAD OVER TO THAILAND AND LIVE OFF WHAT-EVER NATURE HAS TO OFFER.

WHAT, DUTY-FREE GUMMI BEARS?

¡GIGANTE!

martin_kellerman@hotmail.com

I DON'T THINK YOU GIVE STEFAN ENOUGH CREDIT! ONCE HE'S GOT HIS MIND SET ON SOMETHING HE ALWAYS FOLLOWS THROUGH!

YOU MEAN LIKE ORDERING A BEER EVEN THOUGH HE'S TOO PLASTERED TO SPEAK?

¡GIGANTE!

KELLERMAN

HEYA STEFAN. HAVEN'T YOU LEFT YET?

WELL, NO... I'M LEAVING TOMORROW. I'M DOING MY LAST PRE-TRAVEL CLEANING!

IS THAT YOUR LUGGAGE?

RECYCLING

PLASTIC BAGS HERE

294.

NO... I DON'T HAVE A WHOLE LOT, BUT I'M GONNA BRING SOME SWEDISH FOLK RECORDS AND RE-SELL 'EM OVER THERE. THEY PAY TOP DOLLAR FOR THAT SHIT IN JAPAN.

THIS GUY IS TOO FUCKING MUCH!

RECYCLING

PLASTIC BAGS HER

THIS CITY IS DEAD TO ME NOW! YOU OUGHTA BLOW THIS BURG TOO, MAN!

ISN'T IT KINDA STUPID TO BLOW OFF YOUR JOB, YOUR APARTMENT AND YOUR GIRL TO GO OVERSEAS? TALK ABOUT BURNING ALL YOUR BRIDGES!

BY THE WAY! MY EX-LANDLORD'S WONDERING IF I KNOW ANYONE WHO'S LOOKING FOR AN APARTMENT!

GUY, I THINK IT'S TOTALLY AWESOME THAT YOU'RE TAKING OFF JUST LIKE THAT!

RECYCLING

martin_kellerman@hotmail.com

101

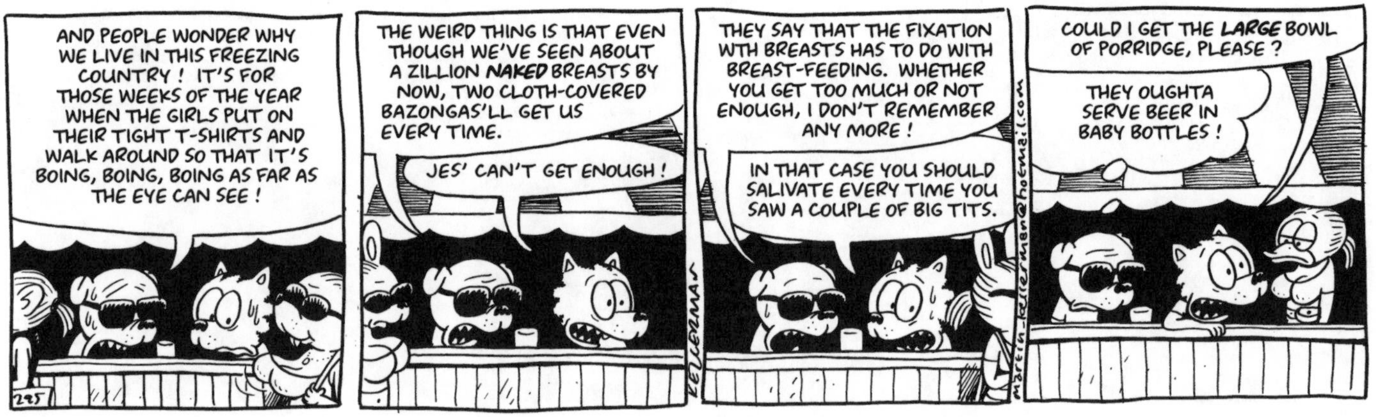
AND PEOPLE WONDER WHY WE LIVE IN THIS FREEZING COUNTRY ! IT'S FOR THOSE WEEKS OF THE YEAR WHEN THE GIRLS PUT ON THEIR TIGHT T-SHIRTS AND WALK AROUND SO THAT IT'S BOING, BOING, BOING AS FAR AS THE EYE CAN SEE !
295
THE WEIRD THING IS THAT EVEN THOUGH WE'VE SEEN ABOUT A ZILLION **NAKED** BREASTS BY NOW, TWO CLOTH-COVERED BAZONGAS'LL GET US EVERY TIME.
JES' CAN'T GET ENOUGH !
KELLERMAN
THEY SAY THAT THE FIXATION WTH BREASTS HAS TO DO WITH BREAST-FEEDING. WHETHER YOU GET TOO MUCH OR NOT ENOUGH, I DON'T REMEMBER ANY MORE !
IN THAT CASE YOU SHOULD SALIVATE EVERY TIME YOU SAW A COUPLE OF BIG TITS.
martin_kellerman@hotmail.com
COULD I GET THE **LARGE** BOWL OF PORRIDGE, PLEASE ?
THEY OUGHTA SERVE BEER IN BABY BOTTLES !

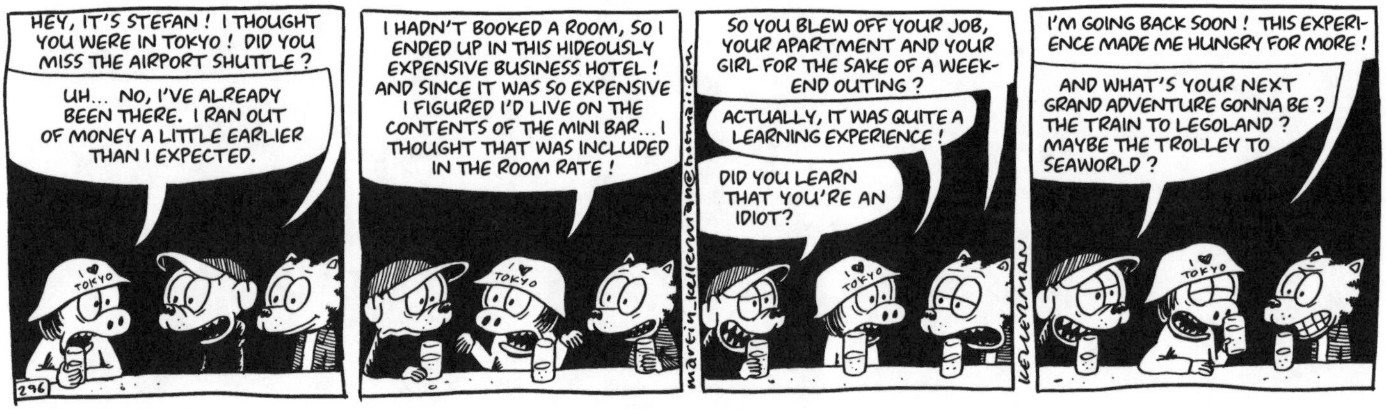
HEY, IT'S STEFAN ! I THOUGHT YOU WERE IN TOKYO ! DID YOU MISS THE AIRPORT SHUTTLE ?
UH... NO, I'VE ALREADY BEEN THERE. I RAN OUT OF MONEY A LITTLE EARLIER THAN I EXPECTED.
I ♥ TOKYO
296
I HADN'T BOOKED A ROOM, SO I ENDED UP IN THIS HIDEOUSLY EXPENSIVE BUSINESS HOTEL ! AND SINCE IT WAS SO EXPENSIVE I FIGURED I'D LIVE ON THE CONTENTS OF THE MINI BAR... I THOUGHT THAT WAS INCLUDED IN THE ROOM RATE !
martin_kellerman@hotmail.com
SO YOU BLEW OFF YOUR JOB, YOUR APARTMENT AND YOUR GIRL FOR THE SAKE OF A WEEK-END OUTING ?
ACTUALLY, IT WAS QUITE A LEARNING EXPERIENCE !
DID YOU LEARN THAT YOU'RE AN IDIOT?
KELLERMAN
I'M GOING BACK SOON ! THIS EXPERI-ENCE MADE ME HUNGRY FOR MORE !
AND WHAT'S YOUR NEXT GRAND ADVENTURE GONNA BE ? THE TRAIN TO LEGOLAND ? MAYBE THE TROLLEY TO SEAWORLD ?

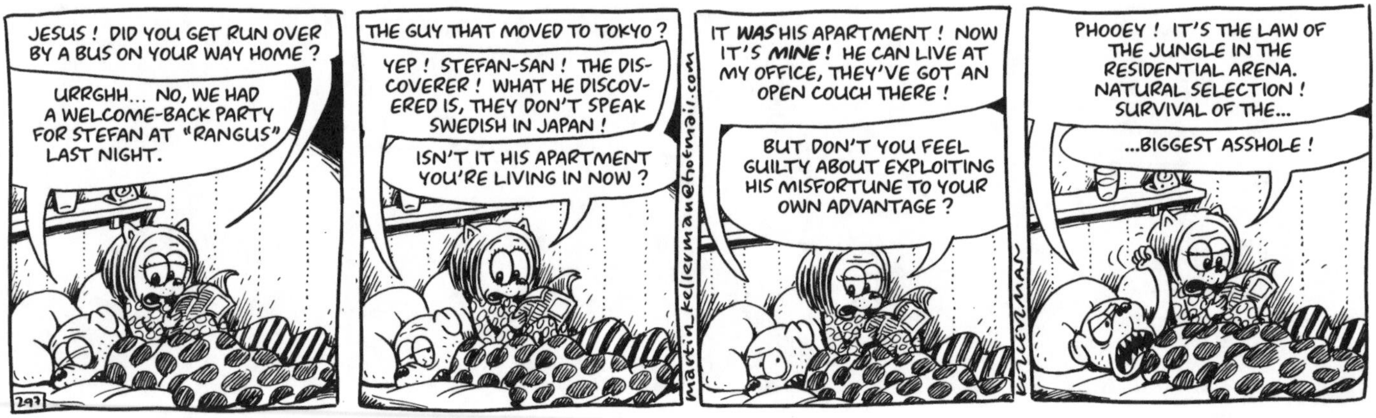
JESUS ! DID YOU GET RUN OVER BY A BUS ON YOUR WAY HOME ?
URRGHH... NO, WE HAD A WELCOME-BACK PARTY FOR STEFAN AT "RANGUS" LAST NIGHT.
297
THE GUY THAT MOVED TO TOKYO ?
YEP ! STEFAN-SAN ! THE DIS-COVERER ! WHAT HE DISCOV-ERED IS, THEY DON'T SPEAK SWEDISH IN JAPAN !
ISN'T IT HIS APARTMENT YOU'RE LIVING IN NOW ?
martin_kellerman@hotmail.com
IT **WAS** HIS APARTMENT ! NOW IT'S **MINE** ! HE CAN LIVE AT MY OFFICE, THEY'VE GOT AN OPEN COUCH THERE !
BUT DON'T YOU FEEL GUILTY ABOUT EXPLOITING HIS MISFORTUNE TO YOUR OWN ADVANTAGE ?
KELLERMAN
PHOOEY ! IT'S THE LAW OF THE JUNGLE IN THE RESIDENTIAL ARENA. NATURAL SELECTION ! SURVIVAL OF THE...
...BIGGEST ASSHOLE !

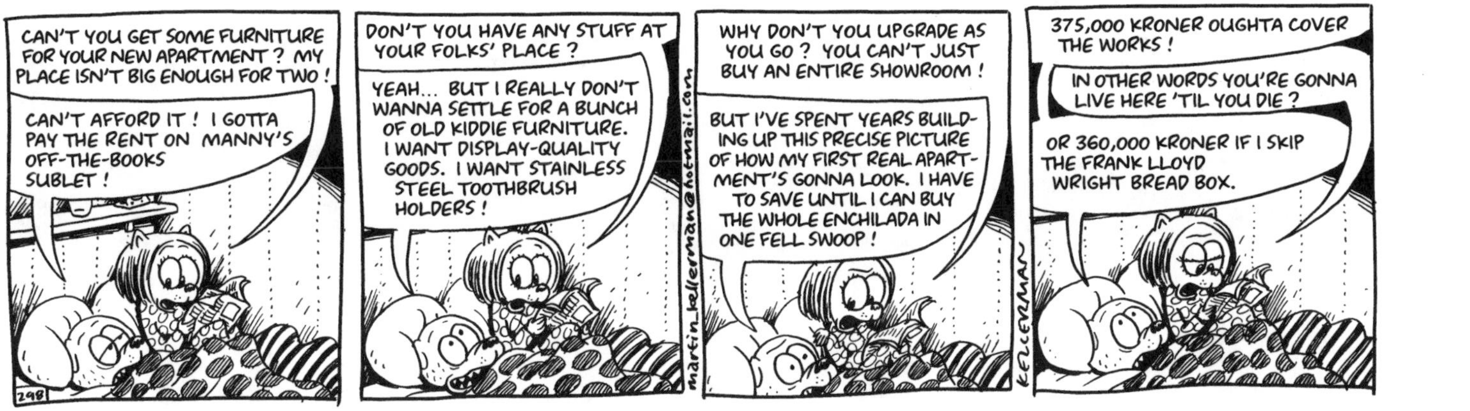
CAN'T YOU GET SOME FURNITURE FOR YOUR NEW APARTMENT ? MY PLACE ISN'T BIG ENOUGH FOR TWO !
CAN'T AFFORD IT ! I GOTTA PAY THE RENT ON MANNY'S OFF-THE-BOOKS SUBLET !
298
DON'T YOU HAVE ANY STUFF AT YOUR FOLKS' PLACE ?
YEAH... BUT I REALLY DON'T WANNA SETTLE FOR A BUNCH OF OLD KIDDIE FURNITURE. I WANT DISPLAY-QUALITY GOODS. I WANT STAINLESS STEEL TOOTHBRUSH HOLDERS !
martin_kellerman@hotmail.com
WHY DON'T YOU UPGRADE AS YOU GO ? YOU CAN'T JUST BUY AN ENTIRE SHOWROOM !
BUT I'VE SPENT YEARS BUILDING UP THIS PRECISE PICTURE OF HOW MY FIRST REAL APARTMENT'S GONNA LOOK. I HAVE TO SAVE UNTIL I CAN BUY THE WHOLE ENCHILADA IN ONE FELL SWOOP !
KELLERMAN
375,000 KRONER OUGHTA COVER THE WORKS !
IN OTHER WORDS YOU'RE GONNA LIVE HERE 'TIL YOU DIE ?
OR 360,000 KRONER IF I SKIP THE FRANK LLOYD WRIGHT BREAD BOX.

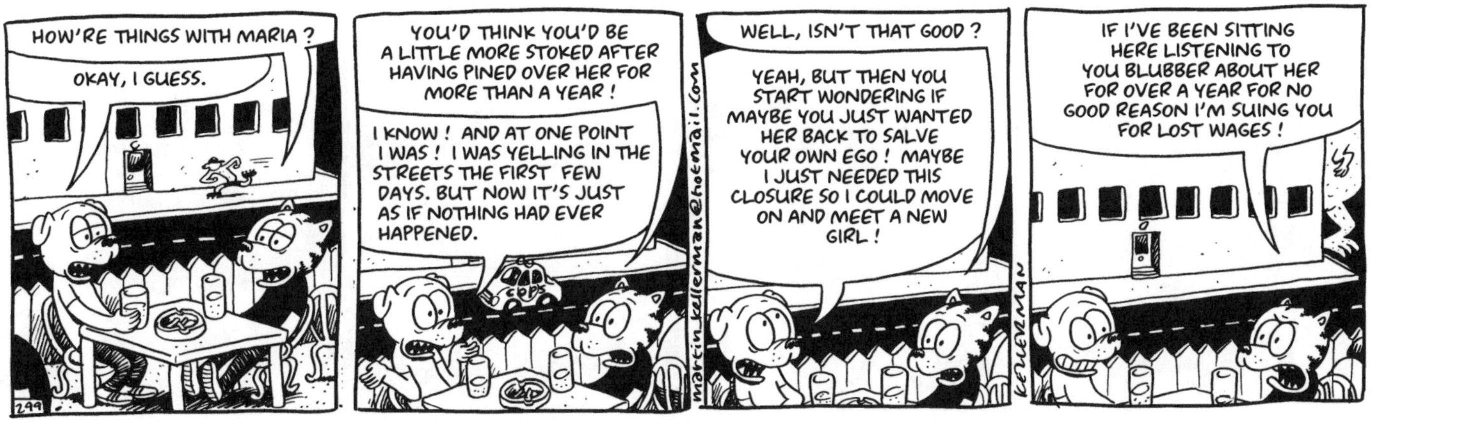
HOW'RE THINGS WITH MARIA ?
OKAY, I GUESS.
299
YOU'D THINK YOU'D BE A LITTLE MORE STOKED AFTER HAVING PINED OVER HER FOR MORE THAN A YEAR !
I KNOW ! AND AT ONE POINT I WAS ! I WAS YELLING IN THE STREETS THE FIRST FEW DAYS. BUT NOW IT'S JUST AS IF NOTHING HAD EVER HAPPENED.
martin_kellerman@hotmail.com
WELL, ISN'T THAT GOOD ?
YEAH, BUT THEN YOU START WONDERING IF MAYBE YOU JUST WANTED HER BACK TO SALVE YOUR OWN EGO ! MAYBE I JUST NEEDED THIS CLOSURE SO I COULD MOVE ON AND MEET A NEW GIRL !
KELLERMAN
IF I'VE BEEN SITTING HERE LISTENING TO YOU BLUBBER ABOUT HER FOR OVER A YEAR FOR NO GOOD REASON I'M SUING YOU FOR LOST WAGES !

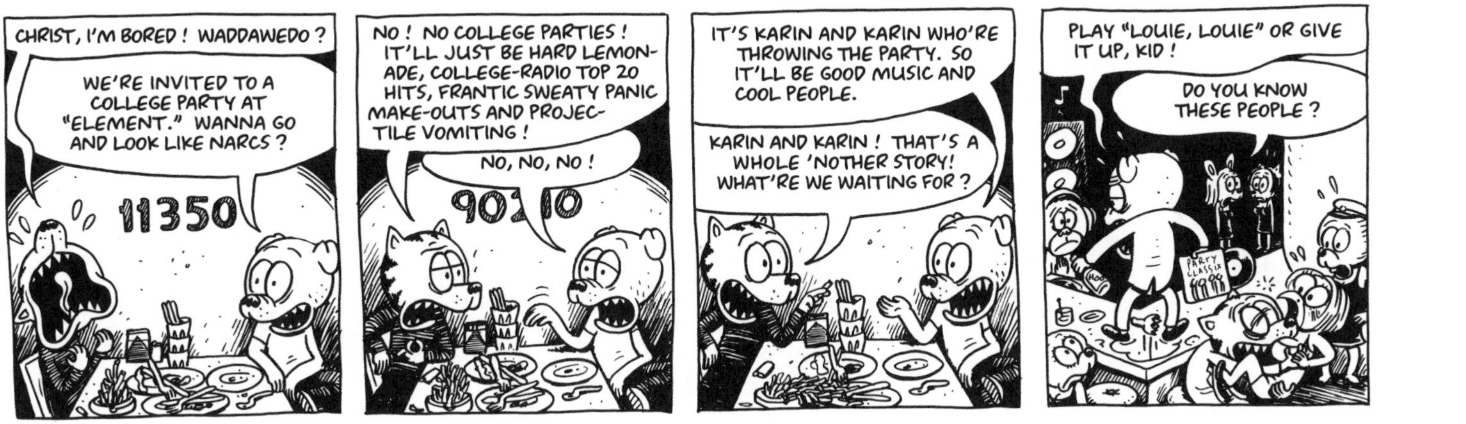
CHRIST, I'M BORED ! WADDAWEDO ?
WE'RE INVITED TO A COLLEGE PARTY AT "ELEMENT." WANNA GO AND LOOK LIKE NARCS ?
11350
NO ! NO COLLEGE PARTIES ! IT'LL JUST BE HARD LEMONADE, COLLEGE-RADIO TOP 20 HITS, FRANTIC SWEATY PANIC MAKE-OUTS AND PROJECTILE VOMITING !
NO, NO, NO !
IT'S KARIN AND KARIN WHO'RE THROWING THE PARTY. SO IT'LL BE GOOD MUSIC AND COOL PEOPLE.
KARIN AND KARIN ! THAT'S A WHOLE 'NOTHER STORY! WHAT'RE WE WAITING FOR ?
PLAY "LOUIE, LOUIE" OR GIVE IT UP, KID !
DO YOU KNOW THESE PEOPLE ?
PARTY CLASSIX

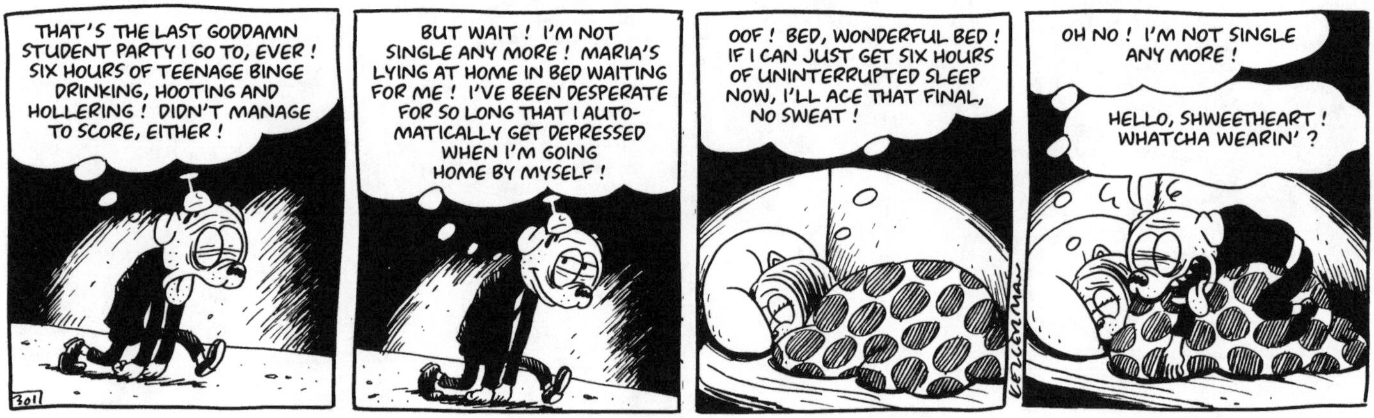
THAT'S THE LAST GODDAMN STUDENT PARTY I GO TO, EVER! SIX HOURS OF TEENAGE BINGE DRINKING, HOOTING AND HOLLERING! DIDN'T MANAGE TO SCORE, EITHER!
301
BUT WAIT! I'M NOT SINGLE ANY MORE! MARIA'S LYING AT HOME IN BED WAITING FOR ME! I'VE BEEN DESPERATE FOR SO LONG THAT I AUTOMATICALLY GET DEPRESSED WHEN I'M GOING HOME BY MYSELF!
OOF! BED, WONDERFUL BED! IF I CAN JUST GET SIX HOURS OF UNINTERRUPTED SLEEP NOW, I'LL ACE THAT FINAL, NO SWEAT!
KELLERMAN
OH NO! I'M NOT SINGLE ANY MORE!
HELLO, SHWEETHEART! WHATCHA WEARIN'?

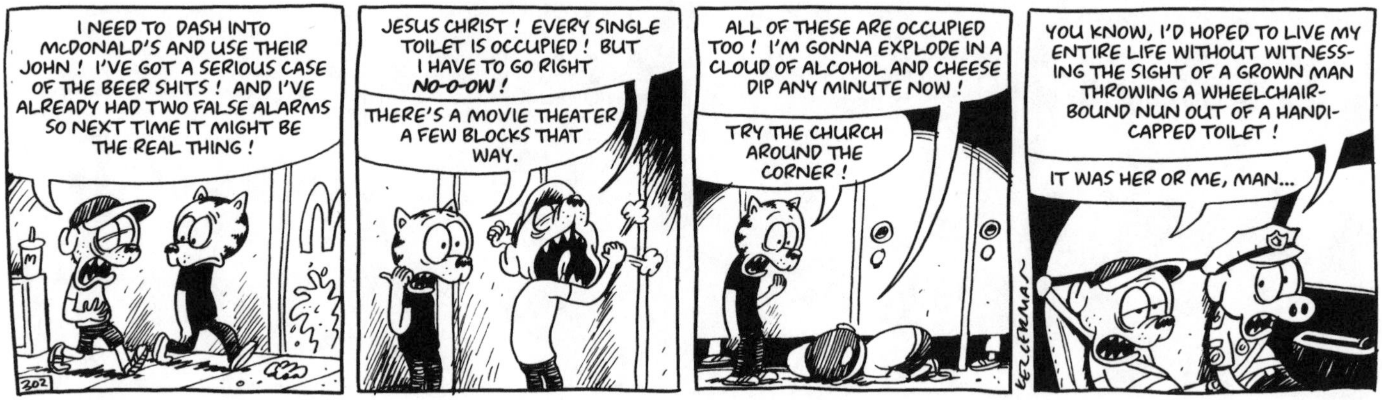
I NEED TO DASH INTO McDONALD'S AND USE THEIR JOHN! I'VE GOT A SERIOUS CASE OF THE BEER SHITS! AND I'VE ALREADY HAD TWO FALSE ALARMS SO NEXT TIME IT MIGHT BE THE REAL THING!
302
JESUS CHRIST! EVERY SINGLE TOILET IS OCCUPIED! BUT I HAVE TO GO RIGHT **NO-O-OW!**
THERE'S A MOVIE THEATER A FEW BLOCKS THAT WAY.
ALL OF THESE ARE OCCUPIED TOO! I'M GONNA EXPLODE IN A CLOUD OF ALCOHOL AND CHEESE DIP ANY MINUTE NOW!
TRY THE CHURCH AROUND THE CORNER!
KELLERMAN
YOU KNOW, I'D HOPED TO LIVE MY ENTIRE LIFE WITHOUT WITNESSING THE SIGHT OF A GROWN MAN THROWING A WHEELCHAIR-BOUND NUN OUT OF A HANDICAPPED TOILET!
IT WAS HER OR ME, MAN...

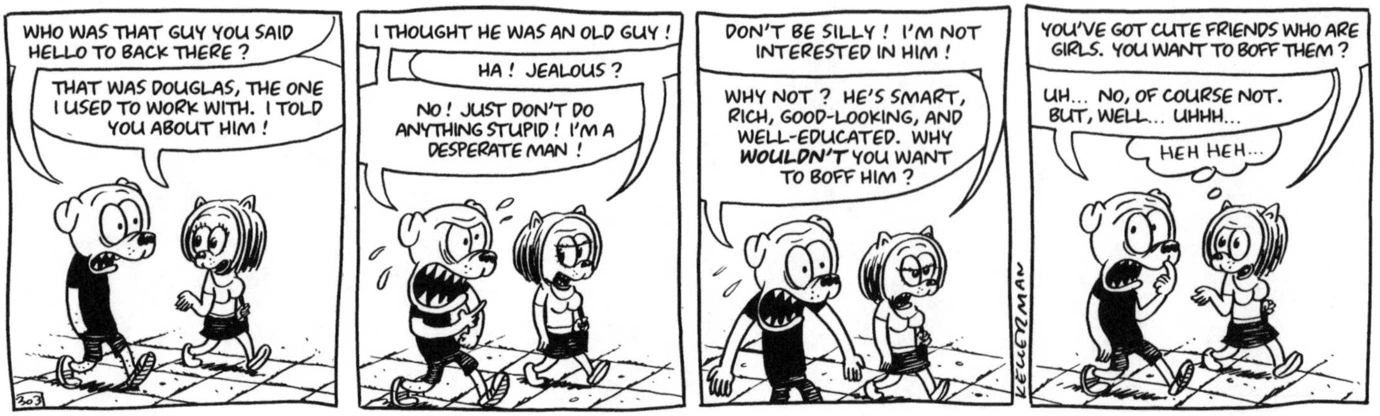
WHO WAS THAT GUY YOU SAID HELLO TO BACK THERE?
THAT WAS DOUGLAS, THE ONE I USED TO WORK WITH. I TOLD YOU ABOUT HIM!
303
I THOUGHT HE WAS AN OLD GUY!
HA! JEALOUS?
NO! JUST DON'T DO ANYTHING STUPID! I'M A DESPERATE MAN!
DON'T BE SILLY! I'M NOT INTERESTED IN HIM!
WHY NOT? HE'S SMART, RICH, GOOD-LOOKING, AND WELL-EDUCATED. WHY **WOULDN'T** YOU WANT TO BOFF HIM?
KELLERMAN
YOU'VE GOT CUTE FRIENDS WHO ARE GIRLS. YOU WANT TO BOFF THEM?
UH... NO, OF COURSE NOT. BUT, WELL... UHHH...
HEH HEH...

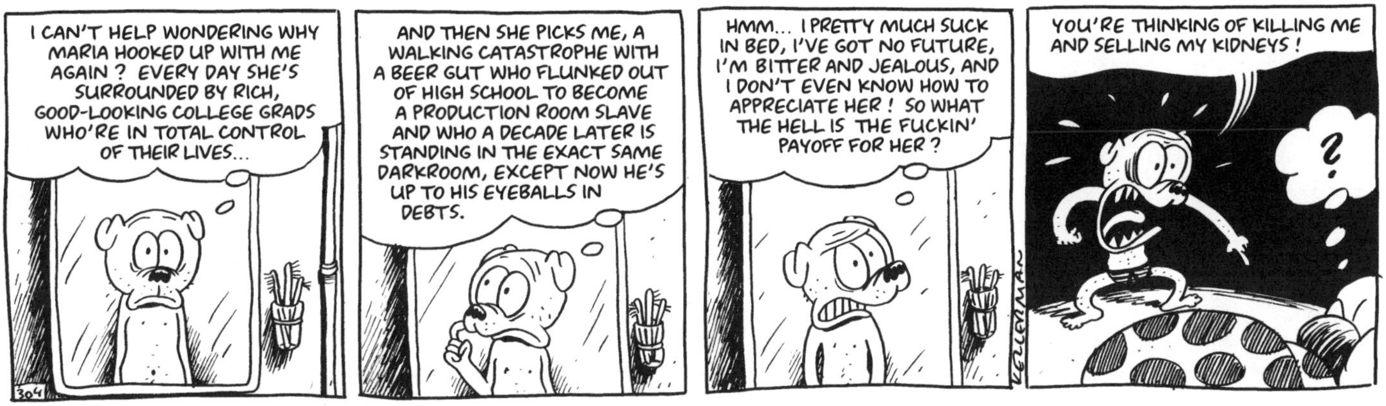
I CAN'T HELP WONDERING WHY MARIA HOOKED UP WITH ME AGAIN ? EVERY DAY SHE'S SURROUNDED BY RICH, GOOD-LOOKING COLLEGE GRADS WHO'RE IN TOTAL CONTROL OF THEIR LIVES...
AND THEN SHE PICKS ME, A WALKING CATASTROPHE WITH A BEER GUT WHO FLUNKED OUT OF HIGH SCHOOL TO BECOME A PRODUCTION ROOM SLAVE AND WHO A DECADE LATER IS STANDING IN THE EXACT SAME DARKROOM, EXCEPT NOW HE'S UP TO HIS EYEBALLS IN DEBTS.
HMM... I PRETTY MUCH SUCK IN BED, I'VE GOT NO FUTURE, I'M BITTER AND JEALOUS, AND I DON'T EVEN KNOW HOW TO APPRECIATE HER ! SO WHAT THE HELL IS THE FUCKIN' PAYOFF FOR HER ?
YOU'RE THINKING OF KILLING ME AND SELLING MY KIDNEYS !
?

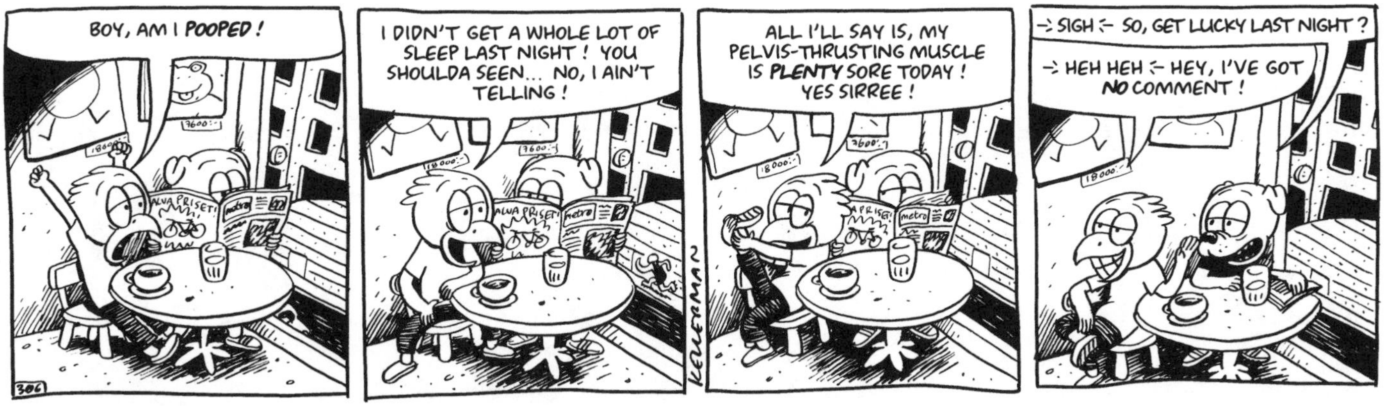
BOY, AM I **POOPED** !
I DIDN'T GET A WHOLE LOT OF SLEEP LAST NIGHT ! YOU SHOULDA SEEN... NO, I AIN'T TELLING !
ALL I'LL SAY IS, MY PELVIS-THRUSTING MUSCLE IS **PLENTY** SORE TODAY ! YES SIRREE !
→ SIGH ← SO, GET LUCKY LAST NIGHT ?
→ HEH HEH ← HEY, I'VE GOT **NO** COMMENT !

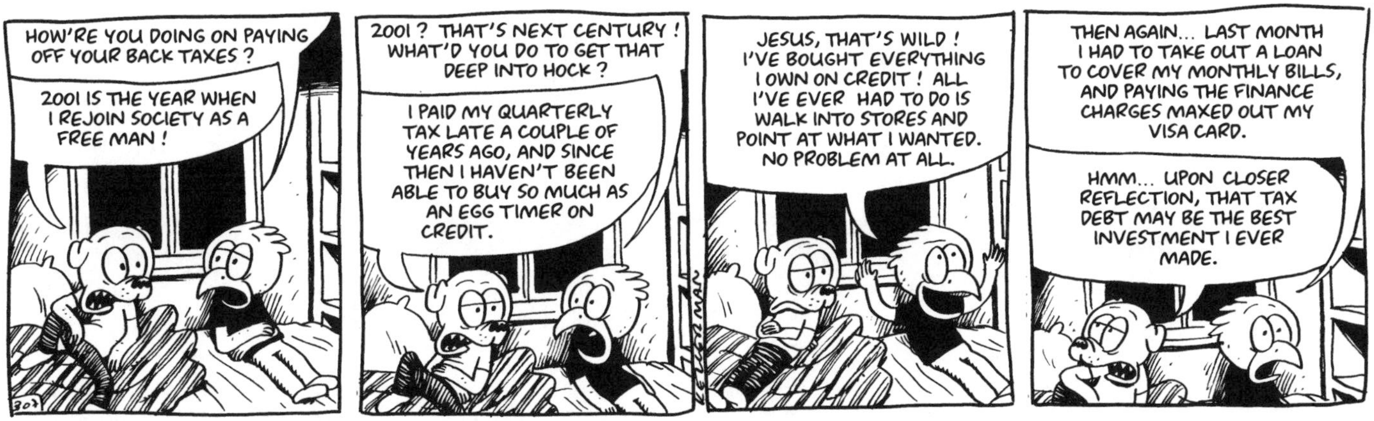
HOW'RE YOU DOING ON PAYING OFF YOUR BACK TAXES ?
2001 IS THE YEAR WHEN I REJOIN SOCIETY AS A FREE MAN !
2001 ? THAT'S NEXT CENTURY ! WHAT'D YOU DO TO GET THAT DEEP INTO HOCK ?
I PAID MY QUARTERLY TAX LATE A COUPLE OF YEARS AGO, AND SINCE THEN I HAVEN'T BEEN ABLE TO BUY SO MUCH AS AN EGG TIMER ON CREDIT.
JESUS, THAT'S WILD ! I'VE BOUGHT EVERYTHING I OWN ON CREDIT ! ALL I'VE EVER HAD TO DO IS WALK INTO STORES AND POINT AT WHAT I WANTED. NO PROBLEM AT ALL.
THEN AGAIN... LAST MONTH I HAD TO TAKE OUT A LOAN TO COVER MY MONTHLY BILLS, AND PAYING THE FINANCE CHARGES MAXED OUT MY VISA CARD.
HMM... UPON CLOSER REFLECTION, THAT TAX DEBT MAY BE THE BEST INVESTMENT I EVER MADE.

SEPARATION ANXIETY

ROCKY ! I GOT A JOB IN NEW YORK !
REALLY ! THAT'S GREAT ! WHEN'RE YOU LEAVING ?
308
NEXT WEEK, AND I'LL BE GONE FOR THREE MONTHS.
THIS IS AWESOME. IF I GET ON THE STICK I CAN THEORETICALLY BANG NINETY GIRLS WHILE SHE'S GONE! HOO-HAH !
KELLERMAN
YOU CAN'T PASS UP AN OPPORTUNITY LIKE THAT ! HOW'D YOU SCORE THAT GIG ?
DOUGLAS GOT A JOB THERE AND RECOMMENDED ME. HE'S A REAL SWEETHEART !
WHAT ? SO I'M SUPPOSED TO SIT ALL ALONE AT HOME CRYING MY ASS OFF WHILE YOU'RE ON A SEX TRIP WITH THAT YUPPIE MOTHER-FUCKER ? NICE PLAN, BITCH !

I'M NOT GIVING YOU AN ULTIMATUM OR ANYTHING, BUT IF YOU GO TO NEW YORK WITH THAT YUPPIE BASTARD THEN I DON'T WANNA BE WITH YOU ANY MORE ! I HAVE NO INTENTION OF SITTING AROUND WORRYING FOR THREE MONTHS !
309
SO YOU'RE NOT GIVING ME AN ULTIMATUM, BUT IF I GO TO NEW YORK YOU'RE BREAKING UP WITH BE, IS THAT WHAT YOU'RE SAYING ? I THINK IT'S REALLY PATHETIC THAT YOU DON'T TRUST ME !
NO FURTHER COMMENT.
KELLERMAN
YOU'VE GOT TO BE GROWN-UP ABOUT THIS, ROCKY ! THIS IS SOMETHING I NEED TO DO, AND IT'S ONLY A MATTER OF THREE MONTHS !
I'M HOLDING MY BREATH 'TIL YOU CHANGE YOUR MIND !
I ONCE READ IN "DEAR ABBY" THAT SOME COUPLES ONLY NEED TO LOOK AT ONE ANOTHER TO SEE WHAT'S GOING THROUGH THEIR PARTNER'S MIND !

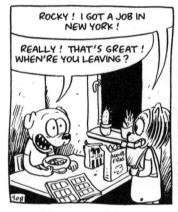

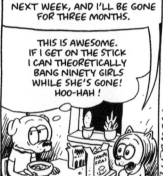

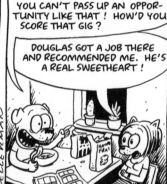

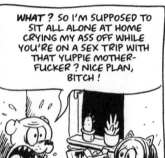

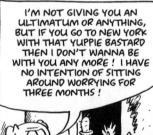

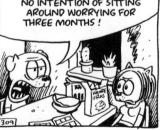

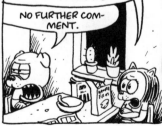

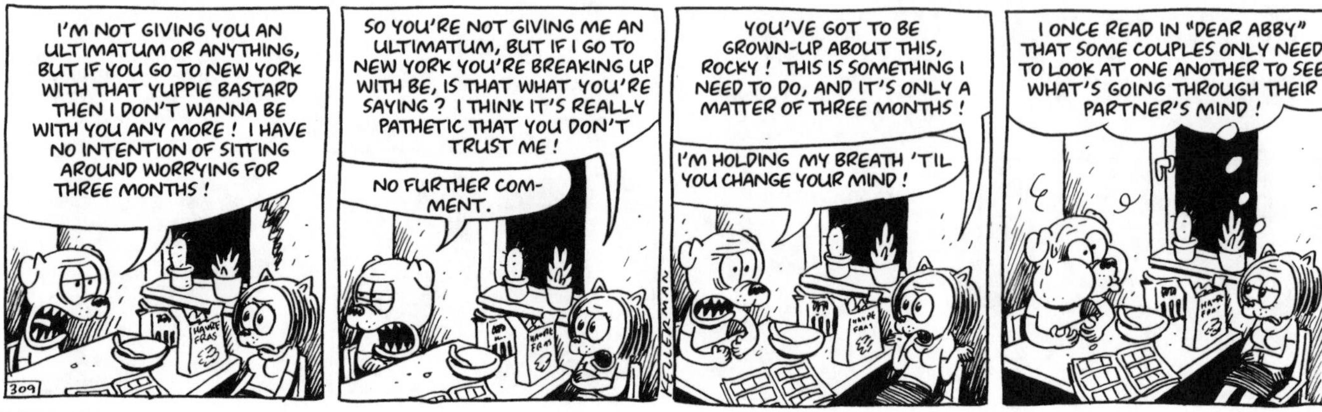

Panel 1: I HAVE SOME GOOD NEWS FOR YOU, ROCKY! I MANAGED TO GET THE APARTMENT BACK, SO YOU DON'T HAVE TO WORK HERE ANY MORE! HERE'S YOUR SALARY FOR THE LAST COUPLE OF MONTHS!

WHA...?

Panel 2: THANK YOU, GOD, FOR GIVING ME A SECOND CHANCE THIS ONE TIME! NOW I CAN FINALLY GET MY OWN APARTMENT! OR TAKE THAT TRIP AROUND THE GLOBE!

Panel 3: I'VE GOTTA TELL YOU, MAN, THIS MEANS THE WORLD TO ME! THIS MONEY HAS GIVEN ME A NEW LEASE ON LIFE! I'LL NEVER, EVER FORGET THIS!

Panel 4: I'LL HAVE FIFTY THOUSAND KRONER'S WORTH OF LICORICE SHOTS, PLEASE!

Panel 5: ARE YOU SURE YOU KNOW WHAT YOU'RE DOING?

HEY, YOU'RE TALKING TO AN EX-BOY SCOUT!

Panel 6: FIRST YOU SURROUND THE PAPER WITH SMALL TWIGS, THEN BUILD IT UP WITH BIGGER BRANCHES MIXED UP WITH BARK.

CHECK OUT MACGYVER!

Panel 7: THEN YOU POUR ON AN ENTIRE CANNISTER OF GAS AND NUKE THE SHIT OUT OF IT!

FWOOM!

Panel 8: WHAT THE FUCK, GONZO? THIS ISN'T "THE FLINTSTONES"! WE'RE GRILLING HOT DOGS, NOT BRONTOSAURUSBURGERS!

OUT OF WOOD! NEED MORE!

Panel 9: CAN'T WE LEAVE SOON? IT'S GETTING A LITTLE CHILLY!

YEAH, MY ARMS LOOK LIKE TWO RAW CHICKEN WINGS.

Panel 10: HOW'S IT FEEL TO KNOW MARIA'S GONNA BE MOVING?

IT SUCKS! IT'S A PERFECT SET-UP FOR HER UP TO FALL IN LOVE WITH SOME YUPPIE DOUCHEBAG!

Panel 11: YEAH, CHICKS ALWAYS FALL IN LOVE WHEN THEY'RE ON THE ROAD! THEY TRAVEL TO CUBA, NEW YORK, L.A. OR LONDON AND COME BACK ENGAGED AND PRATTLING ON ABOUT HOW STOCKHOLM JUST ISN'T BIG ENOUGH FOR THEM!

Panel 12: MAYBE I OUGHTA FOLLOW HER TO NEW YORK...

I KNOW WHAT YOU'RE THINKING AND AS YOUR LAWYER I ADVISE AGAINST IT.

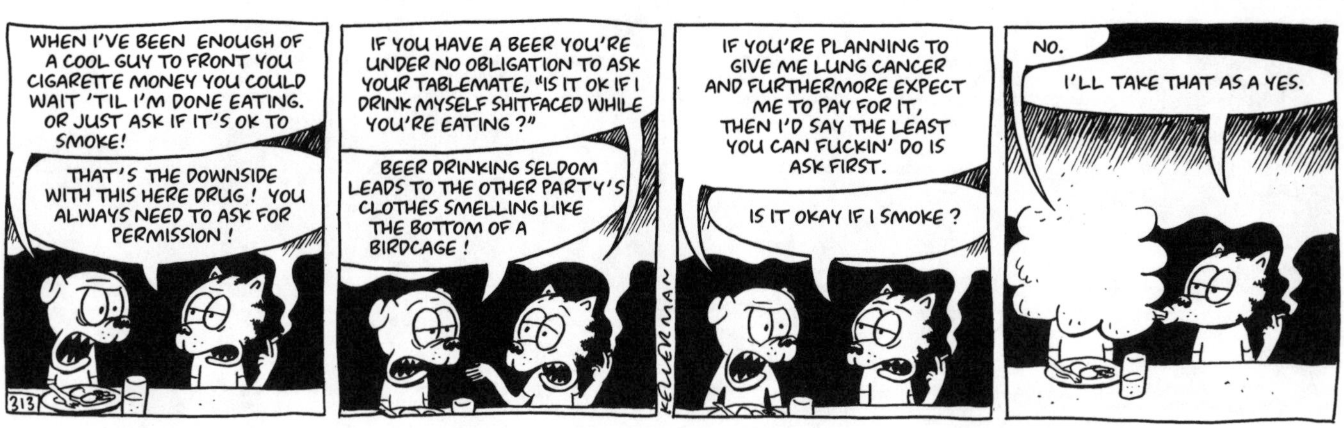
WHEN I'VE BEEN ENOUGH OF A COOL GUY TO FRONT YOU CIGARETTE MONEY YOU COULD WAIT 'TIL I'M DONE EATING. OR JUST ASK IF IT'S OK TO SMOKE!
THAT'S THE DOWNSIDE WITH THIS HERE DRUG ! YOU ALWAYS NEED TO ASK FOR PERMISSION !
IF YOU HAVE A BEER YOU'RE UNDER NO OBLIGATION TO ASK YOUR TABLEMATE, "IS IT OK IF I DRINK MYSELF SHITFACED WHILE YOU'RE EATING ?"
BEER DRINKING SELDOM LEADS TO THE OTHER PARTY'S CLOTHES SMELLING LIKE THE BOTTOM OF A BIRDCAGE !
IF YOU'RE PLANNING TO GIVE ME LUNG CANCER AND FURTHERMORE EXPECT ME TO PAY FOR IT, THEN I'D SAY THE LEAST YOU CAN FUCKIN' DO IS ASK FIRST.
IS IT OKAY IF I SMOKE ?
NO.
I'LL TAKE THAT AS A YES.

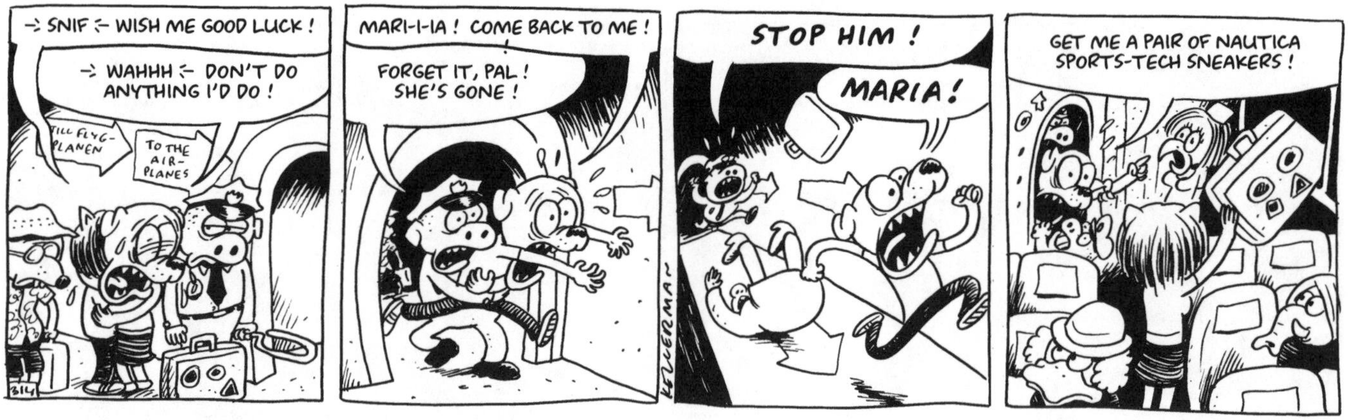
⇾ SNIF ⇽ WISH ME GOOD LUCK !
⇾ WAHHH ⇽ DON'T DO ANYTHING I'D DO !
TILL FLYG-PLANEN
TO THE AIR-PLANES
MARI-I-IA ! COME BACK TO ME !
FORGET IT, PAL ! SHE'S GONE !
STOP HIM !
MARIA !
GET ME A PAIR OF NAUTICA SPORTS-TECH SNEAKERS !

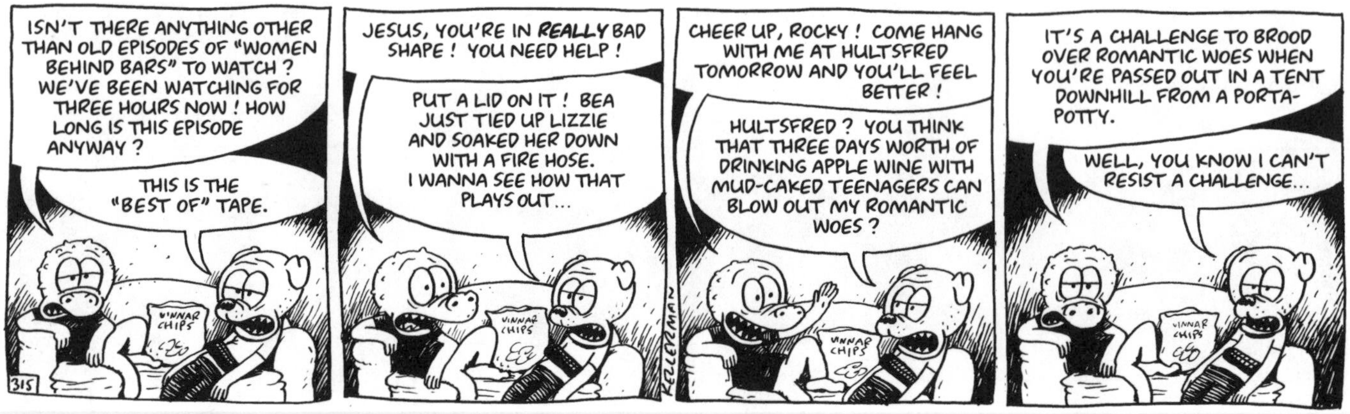
ISN'T THERE ANYTHING OTHER THAN OLD EPISODES OF "WOMEN BEHIND BARS" TO WATCH ? WE'VE BEEN WATCHING FOR THREE HOURS NOW ! HOW LONG IS THIS EPISODE ANYWAY ?
THIS IS THE "BEST OF" TAPE.
VINNAR CHIPS
JESUS, YOU'RE IN REALLY BAD SHAPE ! YOU NEED HELP !
PUT A LID ON IT ! BEA JUST TIED UP LIZZIE AND SOAKED HER DOWN WITH A FIRE HOSE. I WANNA SEE HOW THAT PLAYS OUT...
CHEER UP, ROCKY ! COME HANG WITH ME AT HULTSFRED TOMORROW AND YOU'LL FEEL BETTER !
HULTSFRED ? YOU THINK THAT THREE DAYS WORTH OF DRINKING APPLE WINE WITH MUD-CAKED TEENAGERS CAN BLOW OUT MY ROMANTIC WOES ?
IT'S A CHALLENGE TO BROOD OVER ROMANTIC WOES WHEN YOU'RE PASSED OUT IN A TENT DOWNHILL FROM A PORTA-POTTY.
WELL, YOU KNOW I CAN'T RESIST A CHALLENGE...

FESTIVAL EXPRESS

AHH ! GREAT TO ESCAPE THE BIG CITY'S TUMULT FOR A DAY !
BREATHE IN THE BOUQUET OF LILACS IN FLOWER !
FUCK ! THERE'S MORTEN ! HE WAS THE ONE WHO STOLE EMILY !
NO ! DIDN'T YOU HEAR ? SHE DUMPED HIS ASS ! SHE'S GOING OUT WITH HIS KID BROTHER NOW !
HA ! SERVES THE SON OF A BITCH RIGHT ! IF HE THINKS I'M GONNA FORGIVE HIM HE'S GOT ANOTHER THINK COMING ! ROCKY NEVER FORGETS A BETRAYAL !
ALL GIRLSH'RE **WHORESH** !
YOU SHAID A MOUFFUL, OL' BUDDY !

WHO'S THAT PLAYING NOW ?
UH... I THINK THOSE GUYS... YOU KNOW... THE ONES WITH THE VIDEO...
SHIT ! THEY REALLY SUCK ! AREN'T THERE **ANY** GOOD BANDS THIS YEAR ?
YEAH... THAT GUY... WA'SISNAME.... REGGAE... LIPTON SOMETHING...
YEAH, HE'S COOL, WHEN'S HE ON ?
I THINK YESTERDAY.
I WAS GONNA RAP WITH THE SWEDISH HIFI INSTITUTE.
HUH... YOU WERE SUPPOSED TO GO ON THREE HOURS AGO.
SHIT... BUT KOOL KEITH IS ON NOW, HE'S THE KING !
YEAH, LET'S CHECK HIM OUT !
THEN AGAIN, THEY'LL PROB'LY SHOW IT ON TV.

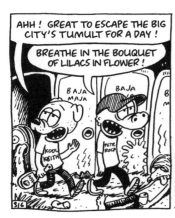

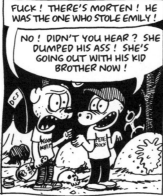

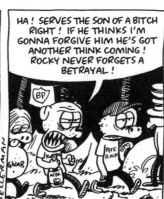

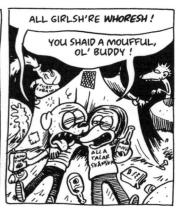

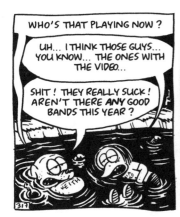

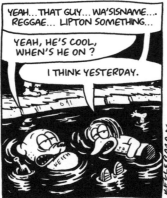

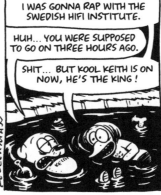

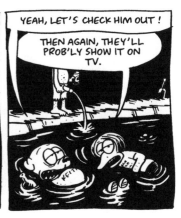

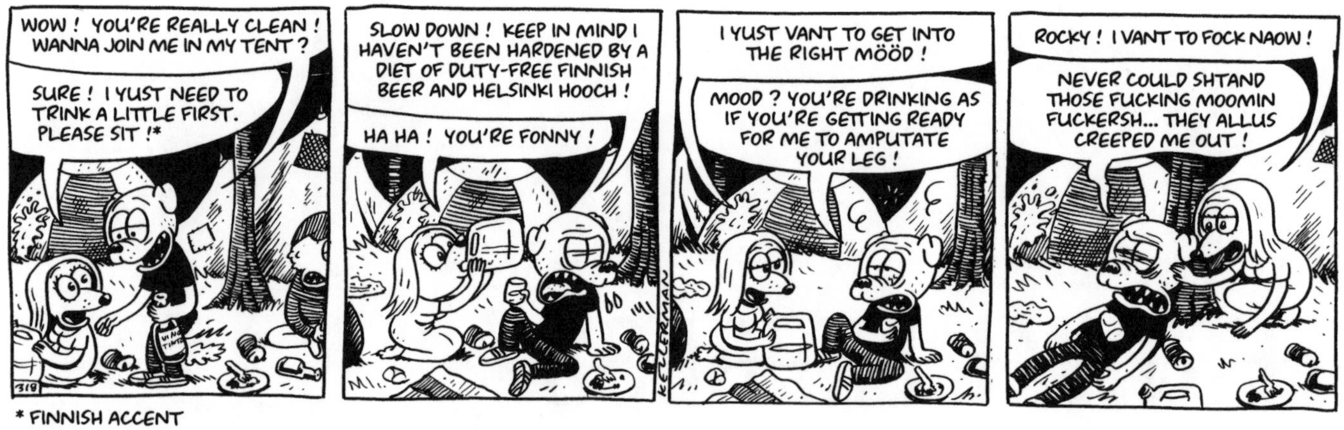
WOW ! YOU'RE REALLY CLEAN ! WANNA JOIN ME IN MY TENT ?
SURE ! I YUST NEED TO TRINK A LITTLE FIRST. PLEASE SIT !*
SLOW DOWN ! KEEP IN MIND I HAVEN'T BEEN HARDENED BY A DIET OF DUTY-FREE FINNISH BEER AND HELSINKI HOOCH !
HA HA ! YOU'RE FONNY !
I YUST VANT TO GET INTO THE RIGHT MÖÖD !
MOOD ? YOU'RE DRINKING AS IF YOU'RE GETTING READY FOR ME TO AMPUTATE YOUR LEG !
ROCKY ! I VANT TO FOCK NAOW !
NEVER COULD SHTAND THOSE FUCKING MOOMIN FUCKERSH... THEY ALLUS CREEPED ME OUT !

* FINNISH ACCENT

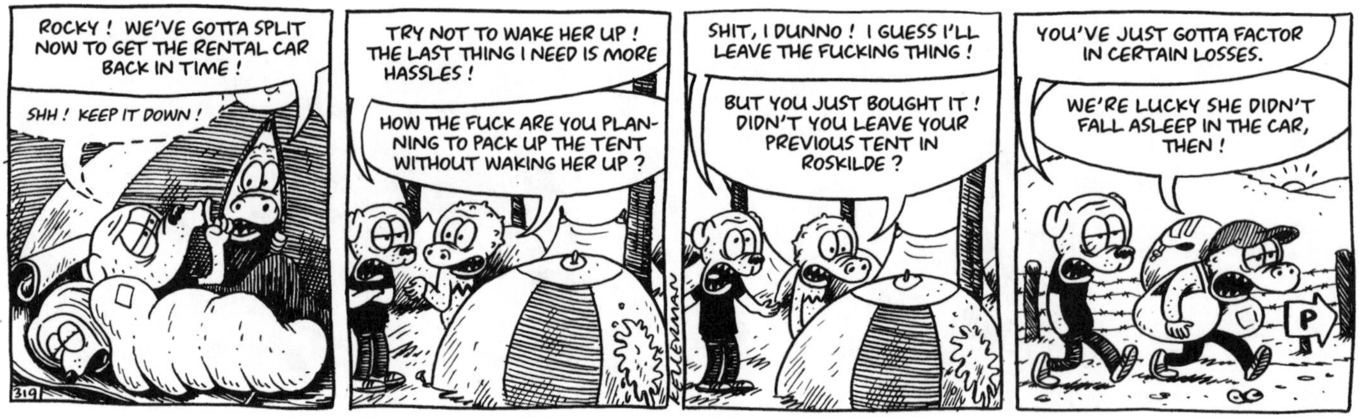
ROCKY ! WE'VE GOTTA SPLIT NOW TO GET THE RENTAL CAR BACK IN TIME !
SHH ! KEEP IT DOWN !
TRY NOT TO WAKE HER UP ! THE LAST THING I NEED IS MORE HASSLES !
HOW THE FUCK ARE YOU PLANNING TO PACK UP THE TENT WITHOUT WAKING HER UP ?
SHIT, I DUNNO ! I GUESS I'LL LEAVE THE FUCKING THING !
BUT YOU JUST BOUGHT IT ! DIDN'T YOU LEAVE YOUR PREVIOUS TENT IN ROSKILDE ?
YOU'VE JUST GOTTA FACTOR IN CERTAIN LOSSES.
WE'RE LUCKY SHE DIDN'T FALL ASLEEP IN THE CAR, THEN !
P

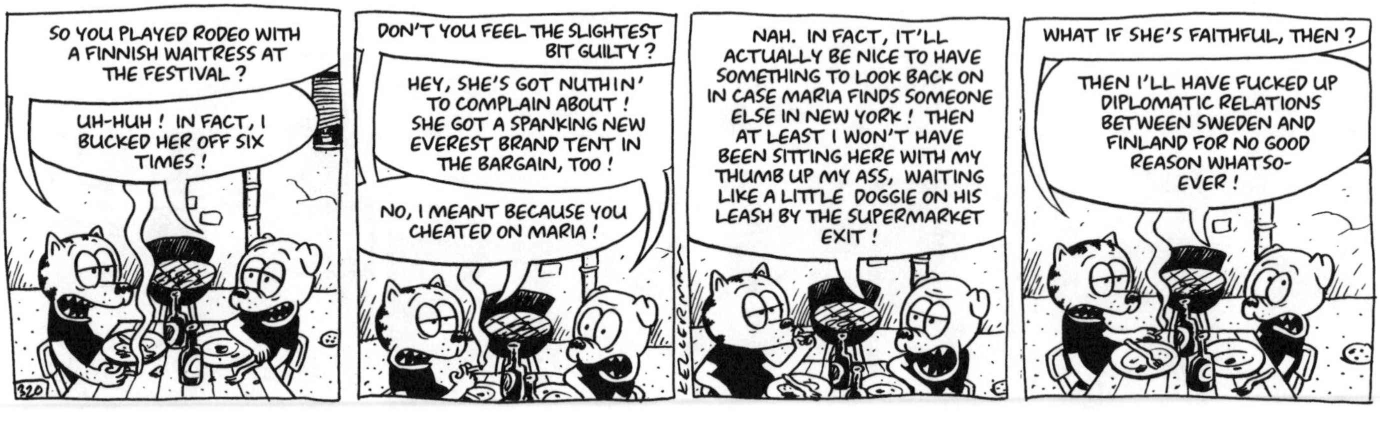
SO YOU PLAYED RODEO WITH A FINNISH WAITRESS AT THE FESTIVAL ?
UH-HUH ! IN FACT, I BUCKED HER OFF SIX TIMES !
DON'T YOU FEEL THE SLIGHTEST BIT GUILTY ?
HEY, SHE'S GOT NUTHIN' TO COMPLAIN ABOUT ! SHE GOT A SPANKING NEW EVEREST BRAND TENT IN THE BARGAIN, TOO !
NO, I MEANT BECAUSE YOU CHEATED ON MARIA !
NAH. IN FACT, IT'LL ACTUALLY BE NICE TO HAVE SOMETHING TO LOOK BACK ON IN CASE MARIA FINDS SOMEONE ELSE IN NEW YORK ! THEN AT LEAST I WON'T HAVE BEEN SITTING HERE WITH MY THUMB UP MY ASS, WAITING LIKE A LITTLE DOGGIE ON HIS LEASH BY THE SUPERMARKET EXIT !
WHAT IF SHE'S FAITHFUL, THEN ?
THEN I'LL HAVE FUCKED UP DIPLOMATIC RELATIONS BETWEEN SWEDEN AND FINLAND FOR NO GOOD REASON WHATSOEVER !

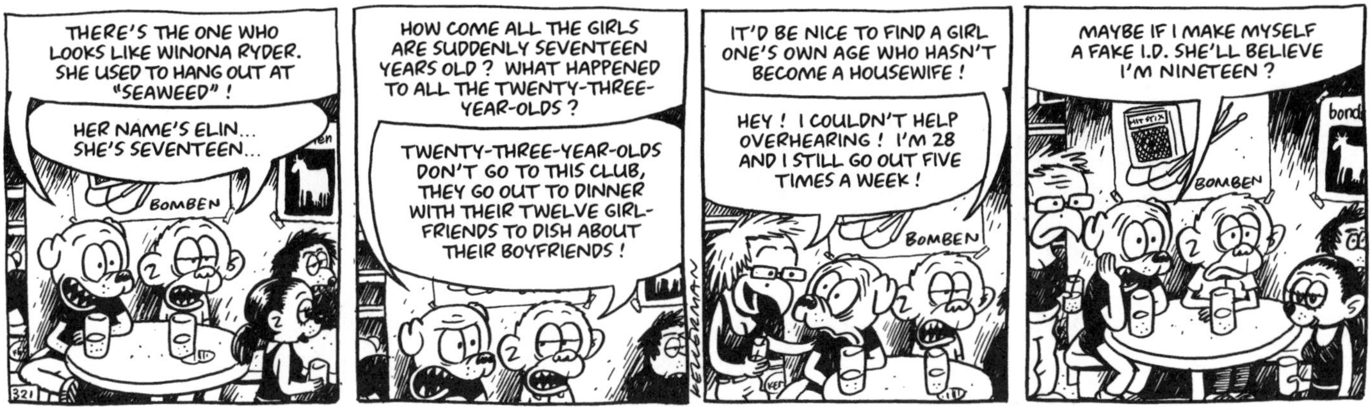
321
THERE'S THE ONE WHO LOOKS LIKE WINONA RYDER. SHE USED TO HANG OUT AT "SEAWEED"!
HER NAME'S ELIN... SHE'S SEVENTEEN...
BOMBEN
HOW COME ALL THE GIRLS ARE SUDDENLY SEVENTEEN YEARS OLD? WHAT HAPPENED TO ALL THE TWENTY-THREE-YEAR-OLDS?
TWENTY-THREE-YEAR-OLDS DON'T GO TO THIS CLUB, THEY GO OUT TO DINNER WITH THEIR TWELVE GIRLFRIENDS TO DISH ABOUT THEIR BOYFRIENDS!
KELLERMAN
IT'D BE NICE TO FIND A GIRL ONE'S OWN AGE WHO HASN'T BECOME A HOUSEWIFE!
HEY! I COULDN'T HELP OVERHEARING! I'M 28 AND I STILL GO OUT FIVE TIMES A WEEK!
BOMBEN
MAYBE IF I MAKE MYSELF A FAKE I.D. SHE'LL BELIEVE I'M NINETEEN?
BOMBEN

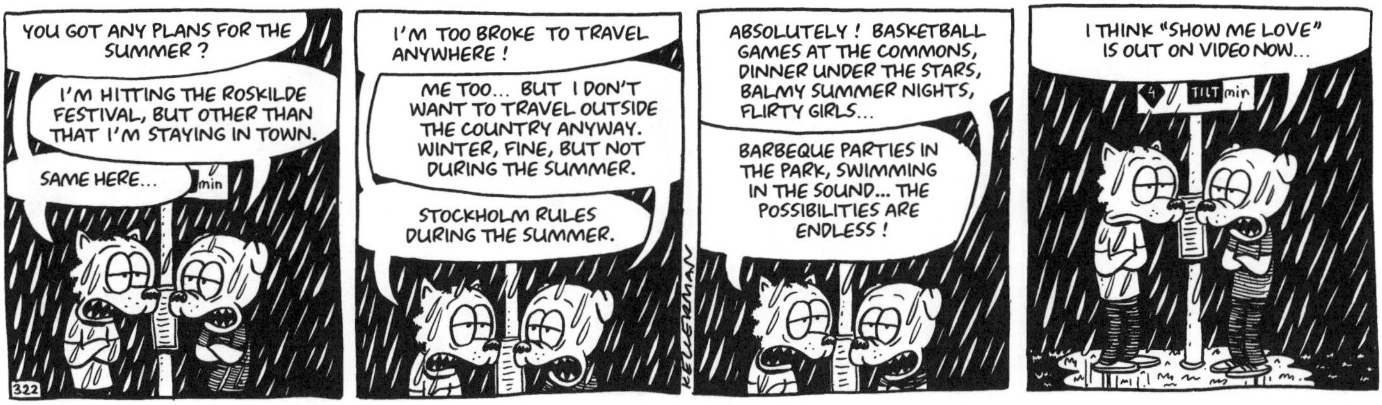
322
YOU GOT ANY PLANS FOR THE SUMMER?
I'M HITTING THE ROSKILDE FESTIVAL, BUT OTHER THAN THAT I'M STAYING IN TOWN.
SAME HERE...
I'M TOO BROKE TO TRAVEL ANYWHERE!
ME TOO... BUT I DON'T WANT TO TRAVEL OUTSIDE THE COUNTRY ANYWAY. WINTER, FINE, BUT NOT DURING THE SUMMER.
STOCKHOLM RULES DURING THE SUMMER.
KELLERMAN
ABSOLUTELY! BASKETBALL GAMES AT THE COMMONS, DINNER UNDER THE STARS, BALMY SUMMER NIGHTS, FLIRTY GIRLS...
BARBEQUE PARTIES IN THE PARK, SWIMMING IN THE SOUND... THE POSSIBILITIES ARE ENDLESS!
I THINK "SHOW ME LOVE" IS OUT ON VIDEO NOW...
TILT min

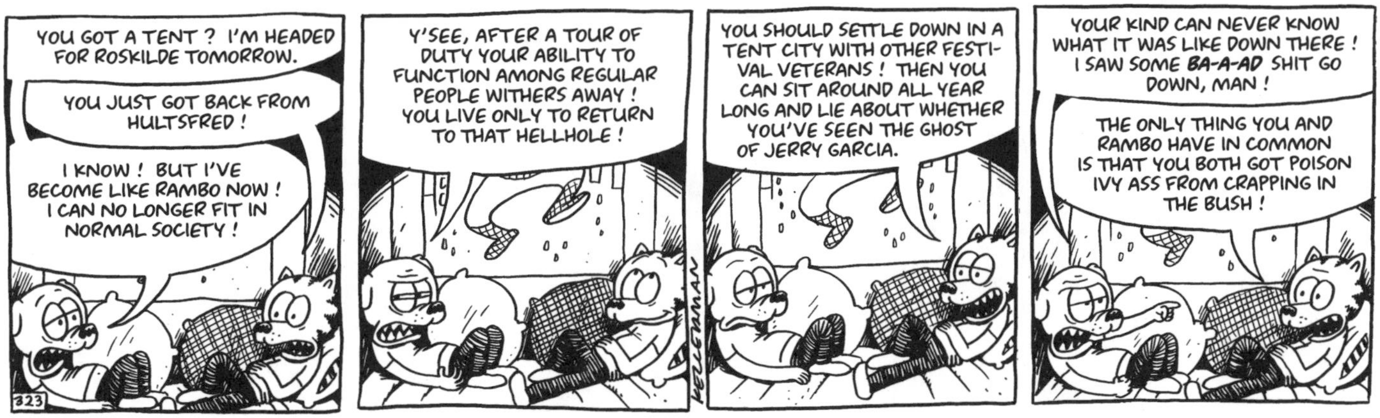
323
YOU GOT A TENT? I'M HEADED FOR ROSKILDE TOMORROW.
YOU JUST GOT BACK FROM HULTSFRED!
I KNOW! BUT I'VE BECOME LIKE RAMBO NOW! I CAN NO LONGER FIT IN NORMAL SOCIETY!
Y'SEE, AFTER A TOUR OF DUTY YOUR ABILITY TO FUNCTION AMONG REGULAR PEOPLE WITHERS AWAY! YOU LIVE ONLY TO RETURN TO THAT HELLHOLE!
KELLERMAN
YOU SHOULD SETTLE DOWN IN A TENT CITY WITH OTHER FESTIVAL VETERANS! THEN YOU CAN SIT AROUND ALL YEAR LONG AND LIE ABOUT WHETHER YOU'VE SEEN THE GHOST OF JERRY GARCIA.
YOUR KIND CAN NEVER KNOW WHAT IT WAS LIKE DOWN THERE! I SAW SOME BA-A-AD SHIT GO DOWN, MAN!
THE ONLY THING YOU AND RAMBO HAVE IN COMMON IS THAT YOU BOTH GOT POISON IVY ASS FROM CRAPPING IN THE BUSH!

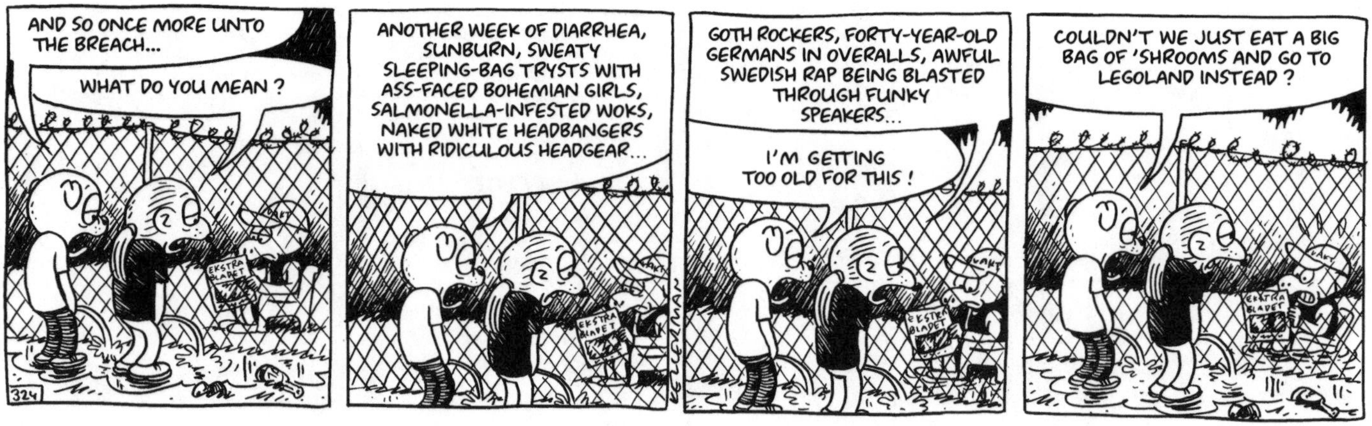
AND SO ONCE MORE UNTO THE BREACH...
WHAT DO YOU MEAN ?
ANOTHER WEEK OF DIARRHEA, SUNBURN, SWEATY SLEEPING-BAG TRYSTS WITH ASS-FACED BOHEMIAN GIRLS, SALMONELLA-INFESTED WOKS, NAKED WHITE HEADBANGERS WITH RIDICULOUS HEADGEAR...
GOTH ROCKERS, FORTY-YEAR-OLD GERMANS IN OVERALLS, AWFUL SWEDISH RAP BEING BLASTED THROUGH FUNKY SPEAKERS...
I'M GETTING TOO OLD FOR THIS !
COULDN'T WE JUST EAT A BIG BAG OF 'SHROOMS AND GO TO LEGOLAND INSTEAD ?

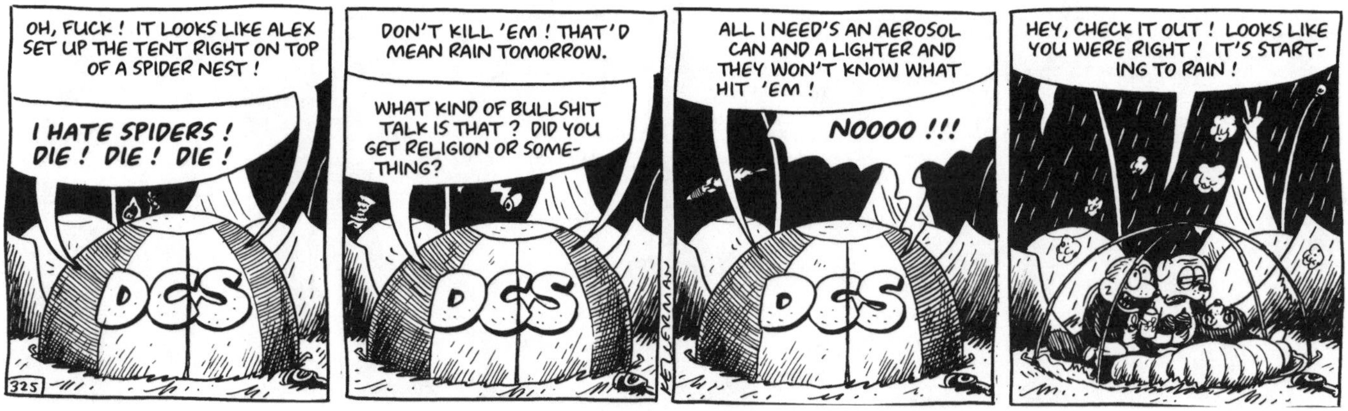
OH, FUCK ! IT LOOKS LIKE ALEX SET UP THE TENT RIGHT ON TOP OF A SPIDER NEST !
I HATE SPIDERS ! DIE ! DIE ! DIE !
DON'T KILL 'EM ! THAT'D MEAN RAIN TOMORROW.
WHAT KIND OF BULLSHIT TALK IS THAT ? DID YOU GET RELIGION OR SOMETHING?
ALL I NEED'S AN AEROSOL CAN AND A LIGHTER AND THEY WON'T KNOW WHAT HIT 'EM !
NOOOO !!!
HEY, CHECK IT OUT ! LOOKS LIKE YOU WERE RIGHT ! IT'S STARTING TO RAIN !

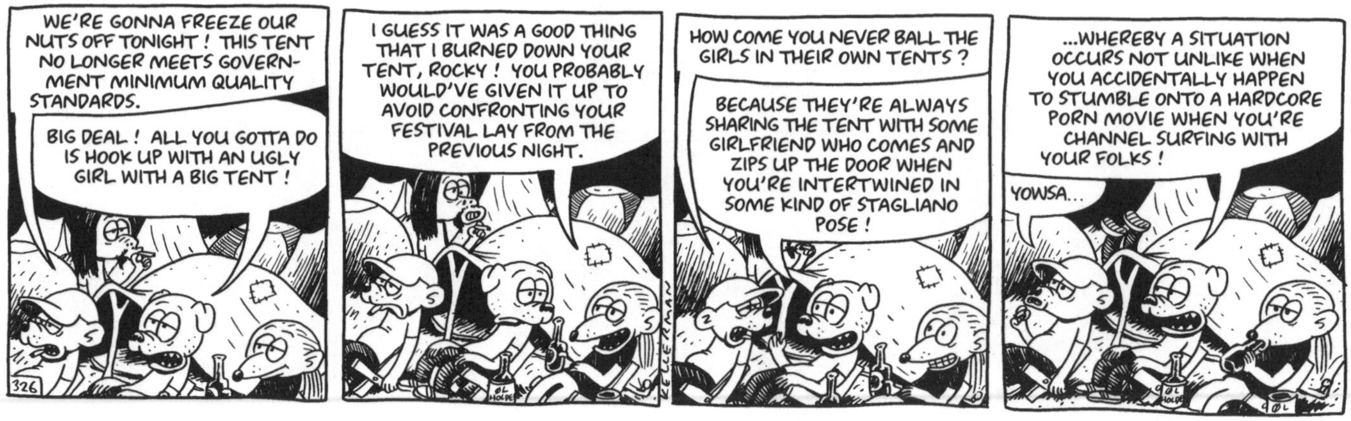
WE'RE GONNA FREEZE OUR NUTS OFF TONIGHT ! THIS TENT NO LONGER MEETS GOVERNMENT MINIMUM QUALITY STANDARDS.
BIG DEAL ! ALL YOU GOTTA DO IS HOOK UP WITH AN UGLY GIRL WITH A BIG TENT !
I GUESS IT WAS A GOOD THING THAT I BURNED DOWN YOUR TENT, ROCKY ! YOU PROBABLY WOULD'VE GIVEN IT UP TO AVOID CONFRONTING YOUR FESTIVAL LAY FROM THE PREVIOUS NIGHT.
HOW COME YOU NEVER BALL THE GIRLS IN THEIR OWN TENTS ?
BECAUSE THEY'RE ALWAYS SHARING THE TENT WITH SOME GIRLFRIEND WHO COMES AND ZIPS UP THE DOOR WHEN YOU'RE INTERTWINED IN SOME KIND OF STAGLIANO POSE !
...WHEREBY A SITUATION OCCURS NOT UNLIKE WHEN YOU ACCIDENTALLY HAPPEN TO STUMBLE ONTO A HARDCORE PORN MOVIE WHEN YOU'RE CHANNEL SURFING WITH YOUR FOLKS !
YOWSA...

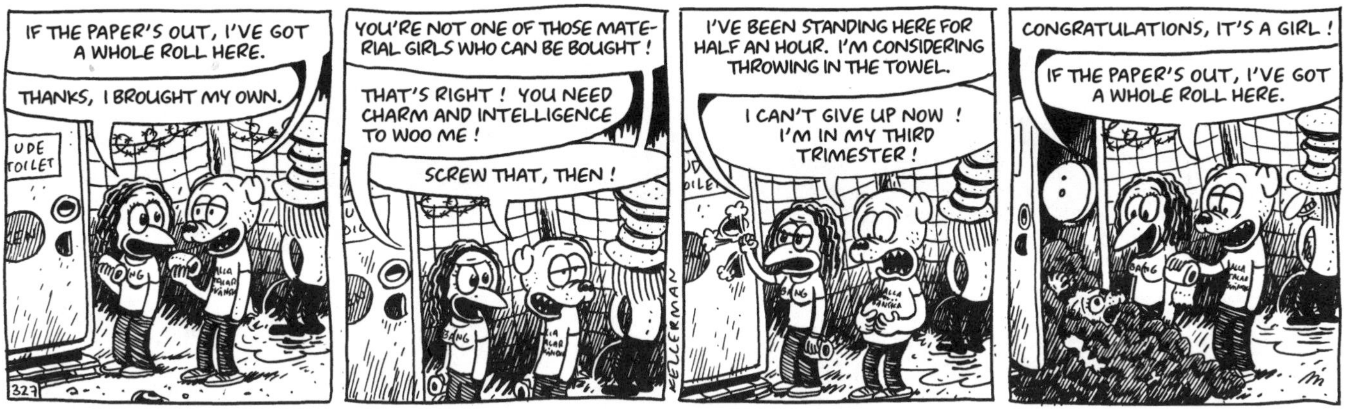
IF THE PAPER'S OUT, I'VE GOT A WHOLE ROLL HERE.
THANKS, I BROUGHT MY OWN.
UDE TOILET
327
YOU'RE NOT ONE OF THOSE MATERIAL GIRLS WHO CAN BE BOUGHT !
THAT'S RIGHT ! YOU NEED CHARM AND INTELLIGENCE TO WOO ME !
SCREW THAT, THEN !
KELLERMAN
I'VE BEEN STANDING HERE FOR HALF AN HOUR. I'M CONSIDERING THROWING IN THE TOWEL.
I CAN'T GIVE UP NOW ! I'M IN MY THIRD TRIMESTER !
CONGRATULATIONS, IT'S A GIRL !
IF THE PAPER'S OUT, I'VE GOT A WHOLE ROLL HERE.

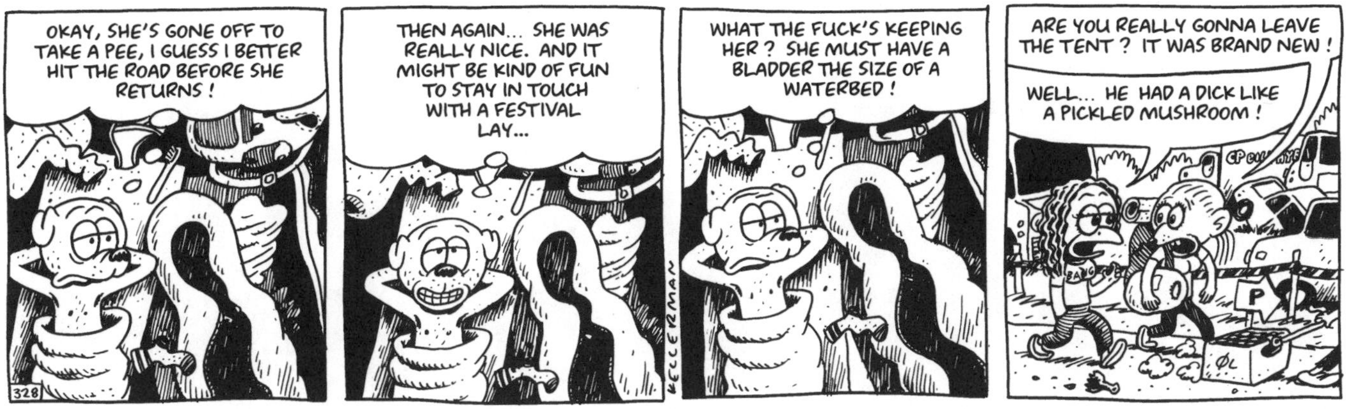
OKAY, SHE'S GONE OFF TO TAKE A PEE, I GUESS I BETTER HIT THE ROAD BEFORE SHE RETURNS !
328
THEN AGAIN... SHE WAS REALLY NICE. AND IT MIGHT BE KIND OF FUN TO STAY IN TOUCH WITH A FESTIVAL LAY...
KELLERMAN
WHAT THE FUCK'S KEEPING HER ? SHE MUST HAVE A BLADDER THE SIZE OF A WATERBED !
ARE YOU REALLY GONNA LEAVE THE TENT ? IT WAS BRAND NEW !
WELL... HE HAD A DICK LIKE A PICKLED MUSHROOM !
P
ØL

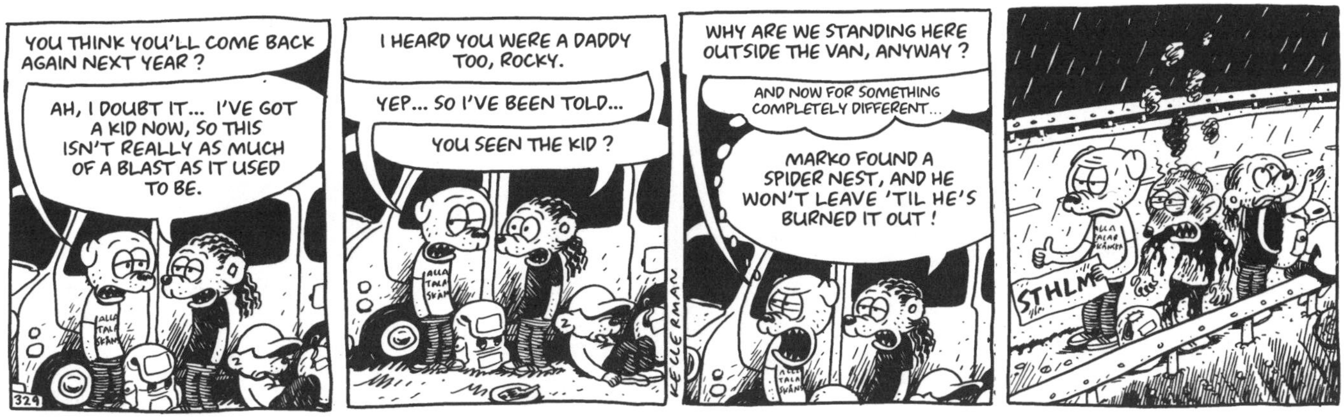
YOU THINK YOU'LL COME BACK AGAIN NEXT YEAR ?
AH, I DOUBT IT... I'VE GOT A KID NOW, SO THIS ISN'T REALLY AS MUCH OF A BLAST AS IT USED TO BE.
329
I HEARD YOU WERE A DADDY TOO, ROCKY.
YEP... SO I'VE BEEN TOLD...
YOU SEEN THE KID ?
KELLERMAN
WHY ARE WE STANDING HERE OUTSIDE THE VAN, ANYWAY ?
AND NOW FOR SOMETHING COMPLETELY DIFFERENT...
MARKO FOUND A SPIDER NEST, AND HE WON'T LEAVE 'TIL HE'S BURNED IT OUT !
STHLM

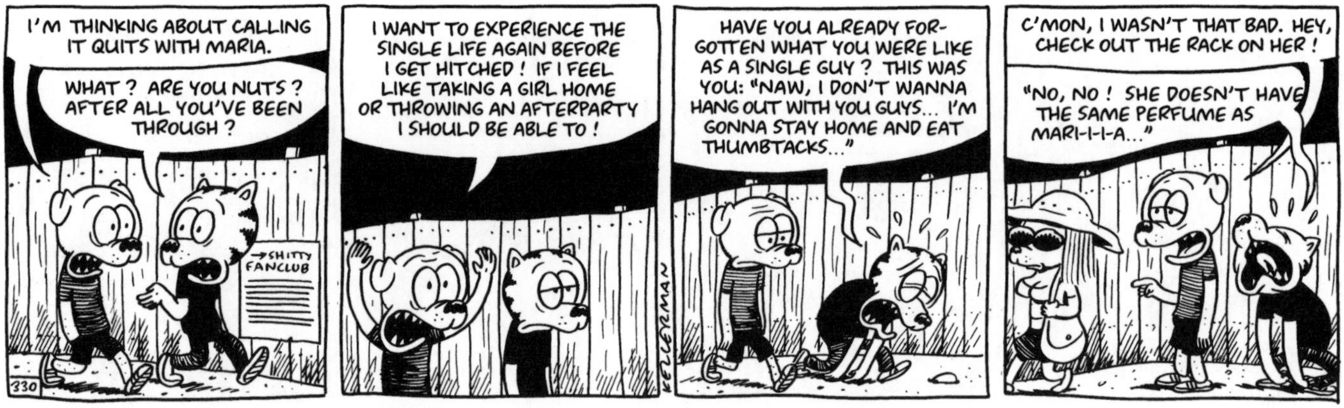
I'M THINKING ABOUT CALLING IT QUITS WITH MARIA.
WHAT ? ARE YOU NUTS ? AFTER ALL YOU'VE BEEN THROUGH ?
→SHITTY FANCLUB
330
I WANT TO EXPERIENCE THE SINGLE LIFE AGAIN BEFORE I GET HITCHED ! IF I FEEL LIKE TAKING A GIRL HOME OR THROWING AN AFTERPARTY I SHOULD BE ABLE TO !
KELLERMAN
HAVE YOU ALREADY FORGOTTEN WHAT YOU WERE LIKE AS A SINGLE GUY ? THIS WAS YOU: "NAW, I DON'T WANNA HANG OUT WITH YOU GUYS... I'M GONNA STAY HOME AND EAT THUMBTACKS..."
C'MON, I WASN'T THAT BAD. HEY, CHECK OUT THE RACK ON HER !
"NO, NO ! SHE DOESN'T HAVE THE SAME PERFUME AS MARI-I-I-A..."

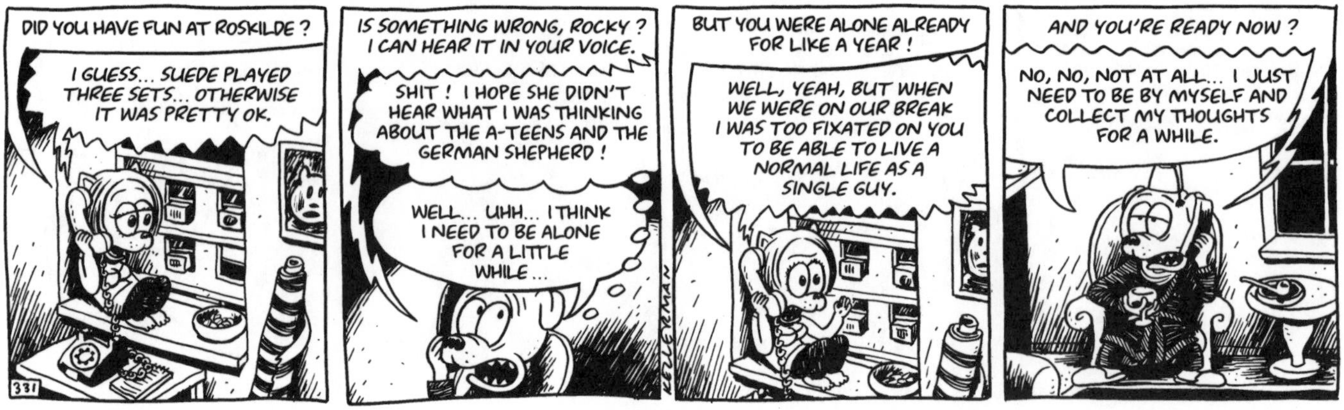
DID YOU HAVE FUN AT ROSKILDE ?
I GUESS... SUEDE PLAYED THREE SETS... OTHERWISE IT WAS PRETTY OK.
331
IS SOMETHING WRONG, ROCKY ? I CAN HEAR IT IN YOUR VOICE.
SHIT ! I HOPE SHE DIDN'T HEAR WHAT I WAS THINKING ABOUT THE A-TEENS AND THE GERMAN SHEPHERD !
WELL... UHH... I THINK I NEED TO BE ALONE FOR A LITTLE WHILE...
KELLERMAN
BUT YOU WERE ALONE ALREADY FOR LIKE A YEAR !
WELL, YEAH, BUT WHEN WE WERE ON OUR BREAK I WAS TOO FIXATED ON YOU TO BE ABLE TO LIVE A NORMAL LIFE AS A SINGLE GUY.
AND YOU'RE READY NOW ?
NO, NO, NOT AT ALL... I JUST NEED TO BE BY MYSELF AND COLLECT MY THOUGHTS FOR A WHILE.

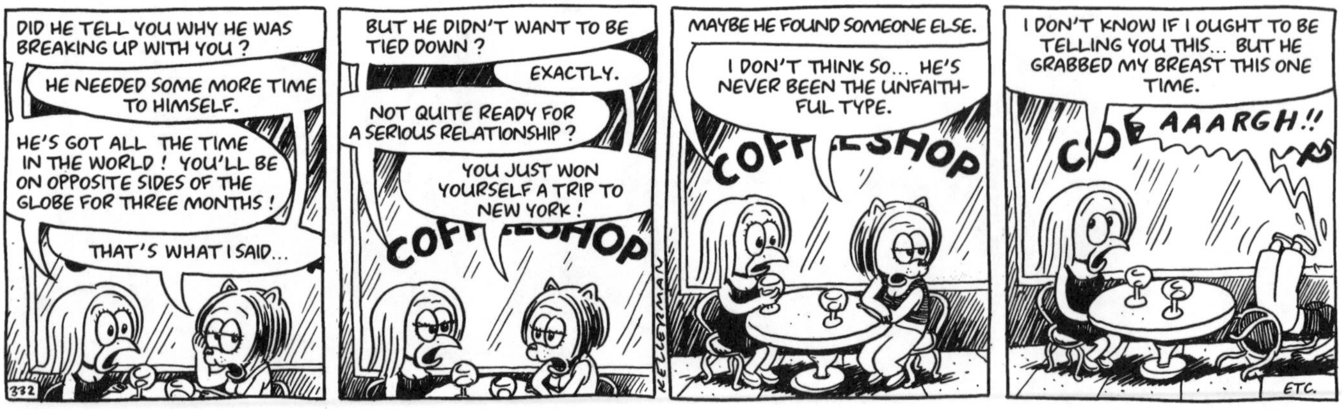
DID HE TELL YOU WHY HE WAS BREAKING UP WITH YOU ?
HE NEEDED SOME MORE TIME TO HIMSELF.
HE'S GOT ALL THE TIME IN THE WORLD ! YOU'LL BE ON OPPOSITE SIDES OF THE GLOBE FOR THREE MONTHS !
THAT'S WHAT I SAID...
332
BUT HE DIDN'T WANT TO BE TIED DOWN ?
EXACTLY.
NOT QUITE READY FOR A SERIOUS RELATIONSHIP ?
YOU JUST WON YOURSELF A TRIP TO NEW YORK !
KELLERMAN
MAYBE HE FOUND SOMEONE ELSE.
I DON'T THINK SO... HE'S NEVER BEEN THE UNFAITHFUL TYPE.
I DON'T KNOW IF I OUGHT TO BE TELLING YOU THIS... BUT HE GRABBED MY BREAST THIS ONE TIME.
AAARGH!!
ETC.

SAY SOMETHING SEXY IN SWEDISH !

A NOTE FROM THE AMERICAN PUBLISHER

The original *Rocky* strip bristles with contemporary pop-culture and local references, many of them very specific to Sweden. We have tried to maintain this European flavor, while tweaking, dodging and weaving as necessary in order to insure that certain punch lines or sequences are not indecipherable to English-speaking audiences – substituting as necessary American (or at least more widely known European) references.

We should note, however, that thanks to the bullying hegemony of American culture, many of the references (Tarantino, *Seinfeld*, *The Godfather*, *Rambo*, hip-hop...) are actually in the original *Rocky* strip to begin with – as is the characters' Monty Python obsession.

When Swedish text (signs, newspapers, etc.) is simply background material, it has been left alone, but when it actually serves a narrative purpose, it has been translated. Although perhaps a little startling at first, this should be no more disorienting than American World War II movies in which the Germans speak English amongst themselves (albeit with German accents, which if you think about it is even more bewildering), pausing to scream in German at their hapless American captives.

A few strips (such as an in-depth discussion of Swedish rap stars) were excised from the book as being too hopelessly Swede-centric.

All of this mucking about has been done with Martin Kellerman's tacit or explicit approval. (He even re-wrote some of the jokes himself for us.) However, we must emphasize that all the funny strips are funny thanks to Martin, and all the ones you don't find funny, it's almost certainly because we fucked them up, and we apologize in advance. Albeit only back here, in tiny type, in the section you're reading after you bought the book.